HISPANIC

DATE DUE

DEMCO, INC. 38-2971

Hispanic Spaces, Latino Places

Community and Cultural Diversity in Contemporary America

Daniel D. Arreola, editor

 UNIVERSITY OF TEXAS PRESS AUSTIN

Requests for permission to reproduce material from
this work should be sent to Permissions, University of
Texas Press, P.O. Box 7819, Austin, TX 78713-7819.

♾ The paper used in this book meets the minimum
requirements of ANSI/NISO Z39.48-1992 (R1997)
(Permanence of Paper).

Library of Congress Cataloging-in-Publication Data

Hispanic spaces, Latino places : community
and cultural diversity in contemporary America /
Daniel D. Arreola, editor.— 1st ed.
    p.   cm.
  Includes bibliographical references and index.
  ISBN 0-292-70267-1 (cl. : alk. paper) —
  ISBN 0-292-70562-X (pbk. : alk. paper)
  1. Hispanic Americans—Social conditions—Case
studies. 2. Human geography—United States—Case
studies. I. Arreola, Daniel D. (Daniel David)
  E184.S75H5843 2004
  304.2′089′68073—dc22

                     2004007746

CONTENTS

ACKNOWLEDGMENTS

Hispanic Spaces, Latino Places was inspired by a series of special-paper sessions presented to the March 2002 Annual Meeting of the Association of American Geographers in Los Angeles. The editor of this volume organized and asked participants to contribute to the project. Authors were selected for their expertise in Hispanic/Latino subgroups in their respective locales. The chapters thus represent both original and authoritative writings.

The editor thanks all contributors who responded to the original request to participate. Their cooperation throughout the project has made the transition from professional presentations to print smooth.

At Arizona State University, senior research associate and staff cartographer Barbara Trapido-Lurie graciously acted as graphics editor for the volume, drafted and redrafted many maps and graphs, and provided sage advice on conversions of print, slide, and digital images to acceptable formats. On behalf of all contributors, I thank Barbara for her tremendous assistance in this critical role.

Kate Berry expresses thanks to the University of Nevada, Reno for an International Activities Grant that helped support the project that resulted in Chapter 11. She is thankful as well to Marcel Fernando Schraer and others at the Hispanic Chamber of Commerce of Northern Nevada, without whom the project never would have happened. "Muchas gracias" are extended to Brian Bonnefant of the University of Nevada Small Business Development Center for his assistance with maps. Thanks go as well to Marina Flood and Vanessa Burch for their tremendous efforts on this project, and to the students who contributed to the study as part of their course work in ethnic geography and Latin American geography classes at the University of Nevada, Reno.

Brian Godfrey gratefully acknowledges a grant from the Vassar Committee on Research to support fieldwork that was critical to Chapter 4. He thanks his former research assistant, Thomas Conoscenti (Vassar College class of 2002), for preparation of the San Francisco maps. He also benefited from the generous assistance of James Chappell, Carlos Romero, Gladys Sandlin, Nickolas Pagoulatos, Sarah Shaker, Toby Levine, Richard Juhl, and Eileen Donahue in San Francisco.

Terry Haverluk thanks his lovely daughters, Claire Elise and Elena Marie, for their pleasant distractions during the writing of Chapter 14.

William Kandel and Emilio Parrado thank Michael Ollinger and James MacDonald, both of the Economic Research Service, U.S. Department of Agriculture, for their helpful comments on Chapter 13.

Inés Miyares thanks all Hunter College students, who, over a decade, have introduced her to the changing ethnic dynamics and neighborhoods of New York City. Their initial observations were inspiration for her study in Chapter 7.

Jeffrey Smith thanks Chris Wilson and Arthur Olivas for sharing their time and wisdom, and the employees at Fort Union and the University of New Mexico Library for their assistance in the preparation of Chapter 2. He also acknowledges the residents of New Mexico who provided much-appreciated time and information, and his wife, Kim, for her unending support.

Michael Yoder and Renée LaPerrière de Gutiérrez thank Francisco Barrientos for his cartographic expertise, and Joe Moreno Jr., Special Collections librarian, Luciano Guajardo Historical Collection, Laredo Public Library, for assistance in researching Chapter 3.

Finally, the editor thanks William Bishel, sponsoring editor at the University of Texas Press, for his support of the project, the staff at the Press for its speedy and efficient handling of the manuscript during review and production, and Kathy Bork, who edited the manuscript.

Hispanic Spaces, Latino Places

INTRODUCTION

Daniel D. Arreola

Hispanic Spaces, Latino Places explores the regional cultural geography of Americans of Hispanic/Latino ancestry as defined by the U.S. Census. In its broadest scope, the book is a scholarly assessment of ethnic-group diversity examined across geographic scales from nation to region to place. The organization and themes of *Hispanic Spaces, Latino Places* are innovative in three ways.

First, Hispanic/Latino Americans represent the fourth-largest concentration of Spanish-heritage people in the world, after Mexicans, Colombians, and Spaniards. A popular yet erroneous conception holds that Hispanic/Latino Americans are a homogeneous group. The members of this large population—reported in 2003 to be some thirty-nine million, 13 percent of the U.S. population—tend to identify themselves by national ancestry, although the labels "Hispanic" and "Latino" remain current in government circles and in the media. In fact, Hispanic/Latino Americans are not one group, but many. They are not simply Hispanics or Latinos, as these panethnic names suggest, but Mexicans, Dominicans, Puerto Ricans, Salvadorans, Guatemalans, Cubans, Ecuadorians, Bolivians, Hispanos (Spanish Americans), and others. In this book, diversity will be fundamental to the exploration of Hispanic/Latino Americans.

Further, some continue to imagine that Hispanic/Latino Americans are found only in the Southwest or in New York or Miami. While regional concentrations exist, Hispanic/Latino Americans are now spread across the nation. *Hispanic Spaces, Latino Places* breaks ground in its treatment of regional populations by evaluating the plurality of Hispanics/Latinos across America, their different geographies and social adjustments to diverse places from small and medium-sized towns to metropolitan areas. No other single book treats Hispanic/Latino Americans in this way.

A second significant contribution of this volume is the diversity of so-cial and cultural themes investigated from a geographic perspective. Much writing about Hispanic/Latino Americans tends to concentrate on issues of immigration, migration, and economic and political roles. Sociologists and anthropologists investigate the structural integration of this popula-tion with the larger population (Flores and Benmayor 1997; Moore and Pinderhughes 1993; Romero, Hondagneu-Sotelo, Ortiz 1997). Historians and others conduct research about Hispanic/Latino Americans across mul-tidisciplinary boundaries, to examine a plethora of societal themes (Suárez-Orozco and Páez 2002). Nevertheless, the questions explored and investi-gations performed by these social scientists and humanists rarely concern geographical aspects, regional diversity, or adaptations to place among the populations. *Hispanic Spaces, Latino Places* addresses themes of spatial dis-tribution and cultural identity specific to each subgroup and relevant to the places Hispanic/Latino Americans have created. Issues of contested space, social networks, and landscape imprint reveal identity and explore how spaces have become places charged with meaning for specific His-panic/Latino subgroups. These themes are examined across social contexts in which some Hispanics/Latinos are only just beginning to create a place identity as new immigrants and others in which Hispanics/Latinos have deeply etched landscapes, which communicate long attachment to places.

Also innovative is this volume's application of time and population proportion to the discussion of Hispanic/Latino community types. Sub-group diversity is complicated by temporal variability, where some His-panic/Latino Americans are new residents and others have been in this country for centuries. In some places, they dominate the total population, and in others they are a minority. Thus, understanding the geographical impact of Hispanic/Latino Americans requires sensitivity to time of settle-ment and the percentage of the ethnic population in a place. *Hispanic Spaces, Latino Places* introduces communities studied by type: continuous, discontinuous, and new (Haverluk 1998). A continuous community is one founded by Hispanics/Latinos and one where they always have been a ma-jority. A discontinuous community is one where Hispanic/Latino Ameri-cans founded or dominated the community at one time, but ceded domi-nance to non-Hispanics/Latinos at another time. Finally, a new community is one where Hispanics/Latinos are chiefly new immigrants, and where they have gained importance in a place in which they have not previously been present.

Combined, these original perspectives on Hispanic/Latino Americans —regional diversity, cultural geographic identity, and community type—

will ground and inform the discussion about this major ethnic population, one that is transforming America.

GEOGRAPHICAL PERSPECTIVES ON AMERICAN ETHNIC SPACE AND PLACE

Geographical writings about ethnic Americans, especially Hispanic/Latino Americans, are recent compared with such writings in fields like history, sociology, and the arts (see Kanellos 1993; Thernstrom 1980). David Ward's (1971) *Cities and Immigrants* was perhaps the first geographical analysis of urban ethnic America and was almost exclusively an investigation of change among European ethnic groups in nineteenth-century eastern and midwestern cities. Wilbur Zelinsky ([1973] 1992) devoted some discussion to territorial patterns when he mapped ethnic groups in his slim but provocative book, *The Cultural Geography of the United States*. However, it was not until 1985 that geographers banded together to produce an ethnic geography reader, *Ethnicity in Contemporary America*, that investigated selected groups (McKee [1985] 2000), including discussions of Mexican, Puerto Rican, and Cuban subgroups. This was followed by a seminal work, *We the People: An Atlas of America's Ethnic Diversity* (Allen and Turner 1988), that showcased ethnic population distributions on detailed county-level maps based on the 1980 Census and accompanied by substantial supporting text.

Anthologies that have followed, especially studies of material culture among selected groups, are thematically linked to ethnic geography (Noble 1992) and through their examination of the concept of homelands in the United States (Nostrand and Estaville 2001). *Geographical Identities of Ethnic America: Race, Space, and Place* (Berry and Henderson 2002) is the most recent anthology of this type and contributes especially by its inclusion of diverse Native American, Asian, and lesser-known European populations.

Some geographical writings (see selected references in Zelinsky 1992) are monographs written about specific ethnic populations, but only five have investigated Hispanic/Latino American subgroups geographically. Boswell and Curtis (1984) pioneered the geographical study of Cuban Americans in Florida; Carlson (1990), Nostrand (1992), and Usner (1995) have researched the Spanish Americans or Hispanos of New Mexico; and Arreola (2002) has studied the Tejanos, or Texas Mexicans. Significantly, others have written about Hispanic/Latino American subgroups in book-length investigations of ethnic populations in San Francisco (Godfrey 1988) and Los Angeles (Allen and Turner 1997). While some theses and dissertations in geography have explored Hispanics/Latinos, few such studies have been published (Broadbent 1972; Ropka 1975; Zecchi 2002).

Notwithstanding the limited number of book-length geographical writings about Hispanic/Latino Americans, geographers have contributed importantly to our base knowledge about this ethnic population through other investigations and writings. Some early papers about Hispanics/Latinos published in professional journals assessed Mexicans in Detroit (Humphrey 1943), Mexicans in the Southwest (Broadbent 1941), and the distribution of Puerto Ricans in Manhattan (Novak 1956). Chiefly, however, such research has been more recent and focused on Mexican and, to a lesser extent, Cuban, Puerto Rican, and other subgroup populations. These contributions may be grouped under geographical perspectives of space and place.

Spatial-perspective research is concerned especially with the study of these population distributions, movements, and regional patterns. This research is typically executed at a regional-to-national analytical scale and often, although not exclusively, relies on large data sets and statistics to render spatial relationships. In other instances, spatial perspective is achieved by the reconstruction of historical geographic patterns and situations to understand the spatial expression of a particular subgroup population at some point in time or over time.

Place-perspective studies, on the other hand, tend to be field-based investigations, and the analytical scale is typically local. Data are observed and accumulated on the ground through an ethnographic perspective that sees landscape, as opposed to regional patterns, as the geographical means for differentiating a subgroup population. Landscape study in the field is then corroborated by historical and archival documents.

Table I.1 reveals the range by category and subgroup of spatial-perspective research about Hispanic/Latino Americans chiefly from the 1970s through 2002. During the 1970s, geographers began to publish writings about the regional character of Puerto Rican and Mexican populations in the United States and about Mexican American migration. Regional geography and migration continue to account for the bulk of geographical writings about Hispanic/Latino Americans. Most researchers have investigated the regional character of Hispanic/Latino subgroup populations, especially Mexicans and Hispanos, who have the longest tenure of occupation, and, to a lesser extent, Puerto Ricans and Cubans, who are more recent arrivals. Geographers have also studied migration, primarily of Mexicans in the United States, because they are the largest single Hispanic/Latino subgroup and, arguably, the most mobile, especially those who are

TABLE I.1 — SPATIAL-PERSPECTIVE RESEARCH ON HISPANICS/LATINOS

RESEARCH CATEGORY	HISPANIC/LATINO SUBGROUP				
	MEXICAN	HISPANO	PUERTO RICAN	CUBAN	OTHER
TRANSNATIONALISM	Mountz/ Wright 1996				Bailey et al. 2002
LABOR, ASSIMILATION, CLASS, HOUSING	McGlade 2002 Dagodag 1974 Carlson 1973				Johnson-Webb 2002 Clark 2001 Cravey 1997
MIGRATION	Foulkes/ Newbold 2000 Harner 1995 McHugh 1989 Gutiérrez 1984 Jones 1984, 1982 Scheck 1971		Foulkes/ Newbold 2000 Bailey/Ellis 1993	Skop/ Menjívar 2001 Foulkes/ Newbold 2000	Jokisch-Pribilsky 2002
IMMIGRANT SETTLEMENT, SOCIAL CONDITIONS	Harner 2000 Valdez/Jones 1984 Dagodag 1984, 1975			McHugh/ Miyares/ Skop 1997 Boswell/ Díaz/Pérez 1982	Skop/ Menjívar 2001 Johnson/ Johnson-Webb/Farrell 1999 Miyares/ Gowen 1998 Carlson 1982
REGIONAL CHARACTER	Arreola 2002, 2001, 2000, 1993a, 1993c Haverluk 1998, 1994, 1997 Johnson-Webb/ Johnson 1996 Arreola/ Haverluk 1996 Jones 1994 Jordan 1982 Boswell/ Jones 1980 Boswell 1979 Nostrand 1975, 1970	Nostrand 2001, 1993, 1992, 1987, 1980, 1970 Usner 1995 Carlson 1990	Boswell/ Cruz-Báez 2000 Boswell 1976 Novak 1956	Boswell 2000, 1993 Boswell/ Curtis 1984	

Source: See References.

TABLE I.2—PLACE-PERSPECTIVE RESEARCH ON HISPANICS/LATINOS

RESEARCH CATEGORY	HISPANIC/LATINO SUBGROUP				
	MEXICAN	HISPANO	PUERTO RICAN	CUBAN	OTHER
SHOPPING STREETS	Méndez/ Miyares 1997				Roseman/ Vigil 1993
MURALS	Arreola 1984 Ford/Griffin 1981				
HOUSESCAPES	Manger 2000 Arreola 1988, 1981		Kent/Gandia-Ojeda 1999	Curtis 1980	
IDENTITY	Zecchi 2002 Tovares 2001 Arreola 1995, 1987 Godfrey 1985	Smith 2002, 2000	Zecchi 2002		Zecchi 2002
BUILT ENVIRONMENT, MATERIAL CULTURE, PLAZAS	Veregge 1993 Arreola 1993b, 1992 Herzog 1986 Nostrand 1982	Smith et al. 2001 Smith 1999, 1998 Gritzner 1990, 1974			

Source: See References.

immigrants. Others have researched immigrant settlement and social conditions among Mexican ancestry populations and other Hispanic/Latino populations. Finally, researchers have considered labor; assimilation, class, and housing; and transnationalism of Hispanic/Latino Americans, but exclusively among those subgroups who still emigrate from Latin America. Puerto Ricans, because they are U.S. citizens, do not immigrate, but migrate, and Cubans, who have chiefly been political refugees, are not particularly well studied by geographers in these categories.

Table I.2 illustrates the types of place-perspective research geographers have conducted about Hispanic/Latino Americans. The 1980s saw the emergence of cultural landscape studies as another research theme for geographers writing about Hispanic/Latino Americans. These studies examine the relationship between specific Hispanic/Latino subgroups and their ways of shaping distinctive places through cultural traditions and adaptive strategies. Field studies document Cuban yard shrines (Curtis 1980) and Puerto Rican yards (Kent and Gandia-Ojeda 1999). Others examine Mexican housescapes (Arreola 1981, 1988; Manger 2000), murals (Arreola 1984; Ford and Griffin 1981), and public spaces (Arreola 1992, 1993b; Tovares 2001). Still other landscape studies concern place identity (Arreola 1987,

1995; Godfrey 1985; Smith 2000, 2002; Zecchi 2002), built environments (Herzog 1986; Veregge 1993), and material culture (Gritzner 1974, 1990; Smith et al. 2001). Researchers more recently have observed Latino shopping streets (Méndez and Miyares 1997; Roseman and Vigil 1993), and Spanish American village anatomy and landscape change (Nostrand 1982; Smith 1998, 1999). Overwhelmingly, these place-based geographical writings explore Mexican and Hispano subgroups, with only a handful of investigations about other subgroup populations.

Both space and place perspectives are beginning to influence nongeographers. There is an emerging consciousness among social historians, architects, and others who see space (Davis 2000) and especially place (Hayden 1995; Leclerc, Dear, Dishman 2000; Leclerc, Villa, Dear 1999; Villa 2000) as appropriate filters through which to discern the diversity of Hispanic/Latino cultures in the United States. *Hispanic Spaces, Latino Places* elaborates these themes—space and place—to expose the variety of Hispanic/Latino geography across America.

ORGANIZATION AND THEMATIC STRUCTURE

Chapter 1 describes the national regional context of Hispanic/Latino Americans, especially who, how many, and where. The book is then organized into three parts to include contributions about continuous, discontinuous, and new Hispanic/Latino communities.

Part I deals with continuous communities, that is, places where Hispanics/Latinos have always been the dominant population group. Jeffrey S. Smith, in Chapter 2, relates the story of the plaza in Las Vegas, New Mexico. Hispanos in Las Vegas, as is typical of traditional Spanish American communities, have created an extraordinary attachment to public space. Unlike in other New Mexican towns that have transformed their plazas into places that appeal to tourists, in Las Vegas, the plaza continues to function as a social gathering place and has evolved to accommodate chiefly community-based activities.

In Chapter 3, Michael D. Yoder and Renée LaPerrière de Gutiérrez assess the social geography of neighborhoods in a majority Hispanic city, Laredo, Texas. Holding ethnicity as a near constant because Laredo's population is 94 percent Mexican ancestry, these authors compare barrios and suburbs to discern both distinctiveness and diversity in residential landscapes that result from social and economic class differences as much as from ethnic tradition.

In Part I, then, we see how the long occupation of the Southwest borderland by Hispanic Americans persists into the contemporary era. Traditions of place attachment, like the Las Vegas *resolana,* or sheltered spot on the plaza, and social celebrations like the *carnes asadas,* or backyard cookouts, of rancho days that survive in Laredo's new subdivisions testify to the continuous cultural practices of early Hispanic settlers in these places.

Part II examines discontinuous communities, that is, communities where Hispanic/Latino Americans were once the dominant population but where chiefly non-Hispanic Anglo Americans later came to control social space. In Chapters 4 and 5, Brian J. Godfrey and Lawrence A. Herzog, respectively, explain how Hispanic/Latino barrio spaces have been contested, transformed, and reinvigorated by community action. Godfrey shows how San Francisco's Mission District, a Spanish colonial quarter, was invaded by Anglo Americans in the nineteenth century, only to be recaptured and converted into a traditional Latino American barrio in the twentieth century by Mexican and Central American immigrants. Today, the Mission District is again threatened, this time by a gentrification process that brings young urban professionals to a neighborhood perceived as affordable and bohemian in one of the nation's most expensive real estate markets.

Herzog explores San Diego and San Ysidro, California's, yin and yang process of "barrioization," or old order, segregated, defensible city space shaped by Mexican Americans and "barriology," or new order, assertive urban space where Mexican Americans display ethnic pride and heritage as positive values that transform urban space. Through the examples of urban "ecologies," we see how communities in this border environment where Mexico and America meet borrow from and adopt place-making strategies that mirror a transnational and globalizing experience.

Finally, James R. Curtis dissects Southeast Los Angeles, a traditional non-Hispanic, Anglo American industrial district that has been radically transformed by Hispanic/Latino Americans. In 1960, chiefly white working-class communities like Huntington Park and South Gate were only fractionally Hispanic, but today they are greater than 90 percent Latino. Curtis explains how a process of deindustrialization prompted white flight from these neighborhoods, and how the southward expansion of the greater East Los Angeles barrio combined with recent waves of chiefly Mexican and Central American immigrants to turn solid blue-collar communities into substantial Latino working-class barrios. Curtis then offers a geographic typology of barrio formation that generalizes the process and its forms for Southern California Hispanic/Latino communities.

The changing geography of Hispanic/Latino Americans is reflected in their presence now in every state of the union and in almost every county of the United States. America's Hispanic legacy, once associated almost exclusively with the borderland Southwest, has become a Latino diaspora, spreading to every corner of the country. Accordingly, Part III of this book investigates the plurality of spaces and places that are new communities for Hispanic/Latino Americans. Eight chapters examine this diversity.

Inés M. Miyares (Chapter 7) and Marie Price and Courtney Whitworth (Chapter 8) explore the changing Hispanic character of New York and metropolitan Washington, respectively. Miyares challenges the assumption held by some that New York's Hispanic/Latino identity is chiefly Puerto Rican. In 2000, New York City had the largest number of Hispanics/Latinos of all major U.S. cities, but the greatest percentage of that population was not Puerto Rican; it was "Other Hispanic." This suggests the incredible plurality of the ethnic population that has evolved in the city. Miyares reviews the Hispanic/Latino geography of New York City, then explores so-called ethnic main streets as indicators of Hispanic/Latino diversity in the city's boroughs. These banner streets are both landscape expressions of economic vitality among Hispanic/Latino subgroups and symbolic streetscapes of ethnic national identity.

Price and Whitworth use soccer leagues in metropolitan Washington as a means to investigate Hispanic/Latino communities in the nation's capital. Unlike in many Hispanic/Latino communities, however, most Hispanics/Latinos here are not organized into barrios or even specific neighborhoods. Rather, Latinos in the capital are diffuse geographically, occupying varied residential neighborhoods and typically in low concentrations. Price and Whitworth argue that Hispanic soccer leagues create real, if ephemeral, places, so-called third spaces, that are different from home and work. Close examination of the Bolivian community in the capital illustrates how a transnational community survives, creates space, yet remains tied to its home village through the highly important recreational and symbolic role of soccer.

Albert Benedict and Robert B. Kent (Chapter 9), and Stephen L. Driever (Chapter 10) explore the influence of Hispanics/Latinos in two important heartland cities—Cleveland and Kansas City. Benedict and Kent perform a detailed analysis of the cultural landscape of Cleveland's Near Westside, a predominantly Puerto Rican community. Using semifixed landscape features as diagnostics, these authors survey markers like Spanish-language signage, symbolic displays like national flags and other political proclamations, and religious statuary to determine the landscape imprint of Puerto Rican as opposed to other Hispanic influences in the Near Westside community. While Puerto Rican place making is found to be evident, the low frequency of indicators may suggest that Puerto Rican dominance here is accepted by members of the Hispanic subgroup and, therefore, it becomes unnecessary to claim space through a dense pattern of ethnic markers.

Driever explains how several generations of Hispanic Americans, chiefly Mexicans, have created a polynucleated settlement arrangement in Kansas City, with old and new barrios in different parts of a metropolitan area that stretches across the Kansas and Missouri state boundary. The first barrios were situated near meatpacking plants and railroad yards that employed Mexican immigrants. Today, however, newer barrios are emerging in the urban periphery, where immigrants find employment in service sector economies, and where vibrant, mostly segregated neighborhoods and commercial districts locate proximate to and sometimes within upper-middle-class suburbs. Anticipating fragmentation and division among the many barrios, Hispanic community activists have championed critical metropolitan area–wide organizations, including media outlets, to cement Hispanic solidarity in this urban area.

Kate A. Berry (Chapter 11)and Alex Oberle (Chapter 12) study the emerging Hispanic commercial landscapes of northern Nevada, and Phoenix, Arizona, respectively. In cities and suburbs in the West, where Hispanic/Latino Americans are an increasing percentage of the metropolitan population, Hispanic business ownership is increasing, and certain businesses have become landscape indicators of a Latino community. Berry documents how neighborhood commercial shopping streets in Reno emerge to service Hispanic/Latino residents. While the Hispanic/Latino population of Reno has more than doubled, to 17 percent of the total population since 1990, Berry finds that a true ethnic-enclave economy does not develop where Hispanic businesses concentrate. Rather, these spaces become multifunctional, appealing to and servicing both Hispanic and non-Hispanic residents.

Oberle maps the distributions of key business types in Phoenix to differentiate between those that cater to immigrant Hispanics and those that are chiefly patronized by earlier generations of Mexican Americans. Oberle's analysis illustrates that Hispanic business types exist along a continuum that allows the size and age of the Hispanic community to be predicted by the character of business types—smaller and emerging versus larger and established. Berry's and Oberle's studies are important models for the continued exploration of Hispanic/Latino America because they create templates that can be tested in other fields to confirm familiar patterns or discover important variations.

Finally, Chapters 13 and 14 assess one of the newest Hispanic/Latino regions—the South—and a new Hispanic community in the High Plains of Texas that may be our first example of a new community that has emerged as a dominant Hispanic place, although it was founded by non-Hispanics. William Kandel and Emilio A. Parrado provide a cogent analysis of the explosion of Hispanic/Latino populations in the nonmetropolitan South, an area that includes a handful of states where Hispanic populations have tripled in the last decade. Their correlation of Hispanic population with particular areas demonstrates how the region's poultry industry has acted like a magnet pulling Hispanic labor to rural communities. Kandel and Parrado investigate Accomack County in Virginia and Duplin County in North Carolina to ground their chapter. They illustrate especially the social and economic conditions of these communities and how Hispanics fare among other populations when they enter as laborers at different phases of incorporation into communities. Their study thereby expands our understanding of the relationship between industrial development and international migration and of the differential impact on native residents in rural communities.

Hereford, Texas, is more than a thousand miles from the rural communities of the American South, yet its story may shed the greatest light on the process Terrence Haverluk calls "Hispanization." Hereford was founded by Anglo Americans in the late nineteenth century, but starting in the 1950s and the 1960s, it became increasingly Mexican, with most residents tracing their roots to communities in South Texas. Haverluk shows how Hereford's Mexican Americans have evolved from migrant laborers over several generations to working professionals who are increasingly better educated, who own land, who are politically integrated, in short, who are middle-class citizens. Hereford's Hispanics were 61 percent of the city's population in 2000, and they are projected to be 90 percent in 2030. In Hereford and other Texas High Plains towns, suggests Haverluk, we may be witnessing a fundamentally new process of Hispanic place making, in which former Anglo-dominant towns transform entirely into Latino places, hybridizing with non-Hispanic populations. Haverluk calls these types of places "*nuevo*" [new] communities, a metaphor that accentuates their Hispanic merging with non-Hispanic society.

TERMINOLOGY

Throughout *Hispanic Spaces, Latino Places,* authors use the terms "Hispanic" and "Latino" interchangeably when referring to the larger group of the ethnic population. Specific nationality group names are used to refer to individual subgroups, for example, Puerto Rican, Salvadoran, or Bolivian. Mexican ancestry terminology is differentiated by the use of self-referents like "Mexican American" or "Chicano/Chicana," which suggest generational differences within the subgroup. The census term "Other Hispanic" is an undifferentiated category that includes many subgroup respondents (see Chapter 1).

Similarly, other ethnic and racial terms, like "black" and "African American" or "white" and "Anglo American," are used interchangeably. While there is not always consensus on the appropriateness of these terms, they nevertheless reflect the general range of descriptive names typically applied to these populations.

Finally, in March 2003, the U.S. Immigration and Naturalization Service (INS), an important institution and agency in the story of Hispanic/Latino Americans, was reorganized to become part of the Bureau of Citizenship and Immigration Services (BCIS). Because contributors completed research for their respective chapters before this change, INS is referenced in several places, rather than BCIS.

1 | HISPANIC AMERICAN LEGACY, LATINO AMERICAN DIASPORA

Daniel D. Arreola

The ancestors of Hispanic/Latino Americans were present in the territory of the United States before it was a nation-state. That legacy extends from the sixteenth century in parts of present-day New Mexico and Florida and from the seventeenth and eighteenth centuries in parts of Arizona, Texas, and California. Yet, we read in our popular media about the explosion of Hispanic/Latino populations across the United States, and we are thus tempted to conclude that this ethnic dispersion is a recent diaspora.

In truth, Hispanic/Latino Americans are one of the oldest and one of the newest groups of American immigrants. They are also enormously diverse, consisting of not one group, but many subgroups. In 1948, writer Carey McWilliams made this prescient observation in his then path-breaking work, *North from Mexico* (McWilliams 1968: 7): "There can be no doubt that the Spanish-speaking constitute a clearly delineated ethnic group. But one must also recognize that there is no more heterogeneous ethnic group in the United States than the Spanish-speaking." Further, as Ilan Stavans cautions (2001: 19), "To begin, it is utterly impossible to examine Latinos without regard to the geography they come from."

In this chapter I introduce the general framework of Hispanic/Latino cultural geography based chiefly on U.S. Census information, and with references to selected writings about these peoples and their places. The chapter pivots on three questions: Who are Hispanic/Latino Americans? How many Hispanic/Latino Americans are there? Where are Hispanic/Latino Americans located? In conclusion, I review some of the debates about the present political and geographical significance of this ethnic population.

WHO ARE HISPANIC/LATINO AMERICANS?

About a decade ago, a headline in the *New York Times* proclaimed the following: "What's the Problem with 'Hispanic'? Just Ask a 'Latino'" (González 1992). More recently, in his book *Hispanic Nation*, Geoffrey Fox (1997: 179) notes that, aside from their Spanish-language heritage, the only other thing held in common by these people is the fact that they are "lumped" together as Hispanics. Issues of nomenclature and acceptability have long shrouded what we call people of Hispanic or Latino ancestry. Distinctions are further complicated by official designations versus popular sentiment.

Sociologist Suzanne Oboler (1997) suggests that the definition and uses of the term "Hispanic" in the United States are not to be found in its Spanish colonial heritage or even in the Latin American context. Rather, "Hispanic" as a label is rooted in the political and daily life of this nation, in its past ideological self-image as an immigrant place, and in its present ethnic mosaic. To wit, the U.S. Census has used a number of labels to designate people of Hispanic heritage at different times over the past seven decades. While the 2000 Census uses both "Hispanic" and "Latino" as general referents, people of Spanish/Hispanic/Latino origin could identify specifically as Mexican, Puerto Rican, Cuban, or Other Spanish/Hispanic/Latino. Respondents who marked the last category (Other) in 2000 could further indicate a specific subgroup, such as Salvadoran or Dominican. "Latino" was first used in 2000, because in 1990 and 1980, respondents were designated as only of "Spanish/Hispanic origin or descent" and allowed to select among Mexican, Puerto Rican, Cuban, or Other Spanish/Hispanic. In 1970, respondent options were "origin or descendent Mexican, Puerto Rican, Cuban, Central or South American," or "Other Spanish." During the 1960 and 1950 Censuses, these data were collected for "persons of Spanish surname," but only in five southwestern states (Arizona, California, Colorado, New Mexico, and Texas). The 1940 Census identified those who reported Spanish as their "mother tongue," whereas "Mexican" was included as an optional race response in 1930 (Bean and Tienda 1987; Guzmán 2001).

Nevertheless, there is still considerable discussion about the use of labels like "Hispanic" and "Latino." The *New York Times* reported in 1992 that the King of Spain was asked what name he used for those people in the United States who were related to him by language. "Hispanic," he said with regal certainty. Ricardo Gutiérrez, a salesman from East Los Angeles, responded, with equal certainty, "Latino" when asked the same question (Shorris 1992a).

An independent survey that measured the frequency of use of the terms "Hispanic" and "Latino" corroborated this variability (Skop 1997). Emily Skop compiled data from newspaper indices for the following dailies: the *Los Angeles Times*, the *New York Times*, the *Washington Post*, the *Chicago Tribune*, the *Boston Globe*, the *Houston Post*, the *Denver Post*, the *San Francisco Chronicle*, and the *Atlanta Constitution*. Between 1989 and 1990, "Hispanic" was used 1,606 times in these newspapers, with the greatest frequency in the *Los Angeles Times* (341), the *Denver Post* (221), and the *New York Times* (217); combined, these papers accounted for nearly half of the references. The word "Latino," by comparison, occurred 357 times from 1989 to 1990 in the same sources, and 261 of those references were in the *Los Angeles Times*, accounting for some 73 percent of all references for "Latino." Overall, these data suggest newspapers' overwhelming preference at the time for "Hispanic," while "Latino" was clearly an emerging term of preference in Southern California almost exclusively. Richard Rodríguez (2002: 110), who frequently appears in the pages of the *Los Angeles Times*, notes that "the newspaper's computer becomes sensitive, not to say jumpy, as regards correct political usage. Every Hispanic the computer busts is digitally repatriated to Latino."

In 1999, however, the cover story of the July 12 issue of *Newsweek* was titled "Latino America" (Larmer 1999). Further, in December 2000 the specialty magazine *Hispanic* published the results of a poll conducted by Hispanic Trends, Inc., about preferences for use of "Hispanic" and "Latino" (Granados 2000). Some twelve hundred Hispanic/Latino registered voters were polled; 65 percent preferred "Hispanic," and 30 percent chose to identify themselves as "Latino." The poll had a margin of error of plus or minus 3 percent. The results showed that 67 percent of those surveyed in Texas preferred "Hispanic," as did 52 percent of respondents in California and New York.

What most of us know and what the results from the 1992 Latino National Political Survey demonstrate is a preference for place of origin or national identity in what we call ourselves. Face-to-face interviews of 2,817 people were conducted in 1989 and 1990. Some 57 percent to 86 percent of Mexicans and Puerto Ricans—whether born in Mexico or born in the United States, whether born on the island or on the mainland—preferred to call themselves Mexican or Puerto Rican rather than panethnic names like Hispanic and Latino. Only Cubans showed a marked difference in response to the same question. Where 83 percent of those born in Cuba preferred to call themselves "Cuban," the percentage among those born in the United States who favored "Cuban" versus those who favored "American" was almost equal (41 percent and 39 percent, respectively) (de la Garza et al. 1992; González 1992).

Notwithstanding these differences in self-identification, Hispanic/ Latino Americans are not one people, but many. When sixteenth-century Europeans from Spain came to politically dominate the Latin American realm, Euro–Native American blending created a mestizo race that includes most, but not all, Latin Americans today. A common Hispanic heritage, roots in varied homelands of Latin America and the Caribbean, differences in historical experience in the United States, and distinctive strains of subgroup identity combine to make Hispanics/Latinos a plural population diverse in several important cultural ways.

Language, for example, is sometimes argued as the glue that holds Hispanic/Latino populations together and that gives them a common bond and unifies them as an ethnic people. Putting aside for the moment that not all Hispanic/Latino Americans speak Spanish and that ability and or desire can vary among subgroups and by generations, the fact remains that varieties of spoken Spanish are now recognized by sociolinguists (Silva-Corvalán 1994; Zentella 2002). These varieties are derived from language drift, evolution in varied environments, and distinctiveness resulting from specific cultural settings. Caribbean Spanish, for example, is known for the practice of swallowing final consonants, thereby creating the impression of a faster spoken Spanish. Puerto Rican Spanish pronounces the trilled *rr* like the English *h,* so that a name like Ramón sounds like *jamón* (ham). It also pronounces some *r*'s like an *l,* so that *trabajar* (to work) becomes "*trabajal*" or *carta* (letter) becomes "*calta.*" Yet another speech variant is the doubling of consonants, so that *algo* (something) can be said as "*aggo*" or *puerta* (door) can become "*puetta.*" Further, Caribbean Spanish vocabularies can be quite different from those of Mexican or Central American Spanish. Some examples include *guagua* rather than *autobús* (bus), *goma* instead of *llanta* (tire), or *ají* as opposed to *chile* (hot pepper). Beans known as *frijoles* in Mexico and Central America are *habichuelas* in the Caribbean, oranges are *chinas* rather than *naranjas,* and bananas are *plátanos* or *guineos* (Lipski 1993).

Beyond the growth of spoken Spanish-language usage, there is considerable variability by generation and income level among Hispanics and Latinos who consume Spanish media. While Spanish radio programming is the fastest growth sector in the American ethnic media, it chiefly attracts lower-income and older Hispanics and Latinos (Carlson 1997). Marketers are sensitive to language segments, and they have created a scale based on usage and proficiency: Spanish Dominant, Spanish Preferred, True Bilin-

1.1. The number of Hispanic/Latino nationalities in Miami is captured by the variety of Spanish-language newspapers from Latin America. *Photograph by D. Arreola, 1985.*

guals, English Preferred, and English Dominant (Valdés and Seoane 1997). A geographical study of Spanish-language newspapers in the United States reveals that the places where Spanish newspapers were published between 1900 and 1929 varied significantly from where such newspapers were published between 1960 and 1992 (Kent and Huntz 1996). Early in the twentieth century, the greatest number of Spanish-language newspapers were published in San Antonio, Santa Fe, Los Angeles, and El Paso, because these places were major centers for the Mexican immigrants who were drawn to the greater Southwest. Between 1960 and 1992, however, the cities that counted the greatest numbers of Spanish-language newspapers were Los Angeles, Chicago, New York, and Miami, municipalities pulsing with large numbers of recent Hispanic/Latino immigrants (Fig. 1.1).

Finally, Hispanic/Latino Americans are a relatively youthful population compared with all Americans. In 2000, 35 percent of Hispanics/Latinos were younger than eighteen, whereas only 26 percent of all Americans were under eighteen. The median age of Hispanics/Latinos was twenty-six, while that for all Americans was thirty-five. Although Hispanics/Latinos are clearly a younger population than the entire population of the United States, there is considerable variability in age profiles within subgroups. In 2000, Mexican median age was twenty-four years; Puerto Rican, twenty-seven; Central American, twenty-nine; Dominican, twenty-nine; South American, thirty-three; Spaniard, thirty-six; and Cuban, forty-one (Guzmán 2001). This variation is evident as well when subgroup populations are totaled and compared.

HOW MANY HISPANIC/LATINO AMERICANS ARE THERE?

Hispanic/Latino Americans are one of the fastest-growing population groups in the United States. In 1960, they totaled 6.9 million, just 3.9 percent of the U.S. population. By 1970, Hispanics counted 9.1 million, some 4.5 percent of all Americans. In 1980, Hispanics had grown to 14.6 million, then 6.4 percent of the total population of the United States (Bean and Tienda 1987: Table 3.1). Hispanic/Latino Americans numbered 22.3 million in 1990, 9.0 percent of all Americans, and in 2000, the number had grown to 35.3 million, 12.5 percent of the U.S. population (Fig. 1.2). In 2003, the U.S. Bureau of the Census declared Hispanics/Latinos the largest minority group, estimating their numbers at 38.8 million ("Hispanics Now Largest Minority Group" 2003). By 2010, Hispanic/Latino Americans may well be counted the largest minority in the United States.

Yet, as suggested earlier, Hispanic/Latino Americans are many, not one. A number of subgroups characterize this population, mirroring the varied and historical experiences and interactions of Latin America with North, or Anglo, America. In 2000, the Mexican subgroup included almost six of every ten Hispanic/Latino Americans. No other single subgroup comes close to this number among Hispanic/Latino Americans. The Puerto Rican and Central and South American subgroups are the second and third largest, respectively, at circa four million and three million each. Cubans and Dominicans each account for fewer than two million (Fig. 1.2).

Mexico, ancestral home to the largest subgroup of Hispanic/Latino Americans, is the only Latin American country that borders the United States. Much of the western United States before 1848 was part of the Republic of Mexico. Proximity, a two thousand–mile-long boundary, and demand, especially for labor that could easily migrate from Mexico to the United States, created bonds and cycles of interaction between the nations. This has produced a large resident subgroup of Mexicans in the United States (Mexican Americans and Chicanos/Chicanas), as well as nearly continuous shuttling of thousands of migrants (Mexican nationals) from across Mexico who seek economic opportunity in the United States (Arreola 2000).

Puerto Ricans are unique among Hispanic/Latino Americans because

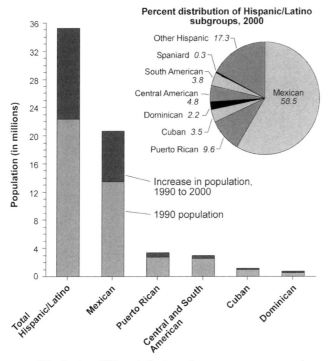

1.2.   Distribution of Hispanic/Latino subgroups, 1990–2000, and percentage distribution, 2000. *Source: U.S. Bureau of the Census 1990, 2000.*

they are the only major subgroup in the population who are American citizens on the mainland United States as well as on their island homeland of Puerto Rico. Puerto Ricans thus have freedom to move back and forth between the island and the mainland without immigration restriction (Fitzpatrick 1987). Unlike most Hispanic/Latino populations rooted in mainland Latin America, but like other Hispanic/Latino migrants from the Caribbean, Puerto Ricans are of significantly mixed black and white racial ancestry (Boswell and Cruz-Báez 2000).

Cubans, compared with Mexicans and Puerto Ricans, are a more recent Hispanic/Latino subgroup in the United States, having come in large numbers only since 1958, and chiefly as political refugees from Castro's Cuba (Boswell and Curtis 1984). Cubans are distinguishable in several ways from other Hispanics/Latinos. They are an older subgroup, in part resulting from selective migration and low fertility rates. Cubans have also been more successful in occupational achievement, employment levels, and income than most other Hispanic/Latino subgroups (Boswell 2000).

Dominicans are the newest Caribbean Hispanic/Latino subgroup in the United States (Hendricks 1974). The numbers of this subgroup were small before 1990, but they have exploded as a regional population since the 1980s (Grasmuck and Pessar 1991). Dominicans will likely surpass the Cuban subgroup in 2010. Dominicans are a transnational community because they maintain strong connections to their island homeland, returning often from the United States, chiefly New York (Dwyer 1991; Georges 1990; Hernández and Torres-Saillant 1996). Most recently, members of this subgroup have been called "los Dominicanyorks" and are now said to be a "binational society" (Guarnizo 1997). Perhaps Dominican visibility has been greatest as the result of their success in America's national pastime. In the early 1990s, Dominicans represented the largest group of Latin Americans in professional baseball (Oleksak and Oleksak 1991). The 1997 World Champion Florida Marlins included more than a dozen Hispanic/Latino Americans, and more than half of these players were Dominican. In 2002, Dominicans were 8 percent of all professional baseball players ("Strike Would Hit Dominican Economy Hard" 2002).

Hispanics from Central and South America have become some of America's most recent Latino immigrants. In 1990, there were 2.6 million Hispanics/Latinos in the United States from these regions of Latin America; in 2000, there were three million (Fig. 1.2). Table 1.1 reveals that this large grouping, in fact, comprises Hispanics/Latinos from many nations. Salvadorans and Guatemalans are the largest Central American subgroups, while Colombians and Ecuadorians are the largest subgroups from South America. Salvadorans and Guatemalans have immigrated principally since the 1980s, fleeing civil conflict in their homelands and seeking economic opportunity in the United States. Most are foreign born, from humble origins, with little education, chiefly employed in low-wage service and manufacturing jobs, and largely undocumented (Bachelis 1990; Hart 1997; López, Popkin, and Telles 1996). In fact, the undocumented status of so many Salvadorans and Guatemalans may suggest that the census totals for 2000 were a significant undercount (" 'Other Spanish' Led to Census Missteps" 2002). Colombians and Ecuadorians, like their Central American brethren, are largely foreign born, have chiefly immigrated in large numbers since the 1980s, include undocumented immigrants, and, in the case of Colombians, have sought refuge from political violence in their homeland. Unlike Salvadorans and Guatemalans, however, many Colombians and some Ecuadorians are often middle class and well educated and possess greater employment skills. However, some professionals in these subgroups have experienced downward economic and social mobility as a result of migration to the United States (Cullison 1991; Haslip-Viera and Baver 1996; "Coming from the Americas" 2002).

TABLE 1.1—CENTRAL AND SOUTH AMERICAN SUBGROUP POPULATIONS, 2000

SUBGROUP	POPULATION	% OF U.S. HISPANIC/ LATINO POPULATION
CENTRAL AMERICAN	1,686,937	4.8
SALVADORAN	655,165	1.9
GUATEMALAN	372,487	1.1
HONDURAN	217,569	0.6
NICARAGUAN	177,684	0.5
PANAMANIAN	91,723	0.3
COSTA RICAN	68,588	0.2
OTHER	103,721	0.3
SOUTH AMERICAN	1,353,562	3.8
COLOMBIAN	470,684	1.3
ECUADORIAN	260,559	0.7
PERUVIAN	233,926	0.7
ARGENTINEAN	100,864	0.3
VENEZUELAN	91,507	0.2
CHILEAN	68,849	0.2
BOLIVIAN	42,068	0.1
URUGUAYAN	18,804	0.1
PARAGUAYAN	8,769	0.1
OTHER	57,532	0.2

Source: U.S. Bureau of the Census 2000.

Beyond Mexican, Puerto Rican, Cuban, Dominican, Central American, and South American, there are small numbers of Spaniards in the United States, and a very large undistinguishable grouping labeled "Other Hispanic," some 17 percent of all Hispanic/Latino Americans, and who numbered 6.1 million in 2000 (Fig. 1.2). The "Other Hispanic" grouping has baffled census investigators and demographers, because most respondents in this category in the census have simply checked or written in "Hispanic" without further designation of nationality or Hispanic ancestry (Guzmán 2001: Table 1). Some researchers believe that the large numbers of "Other Hispanic" counted in 2000 mirror changes in the way questions were asked on census forms (Suro 2002). In 1990 and again in 2000, "Other Hispanic" respondents were counted mostly in states that had large Hispanic/Latino populations, such as California, Texas, New York, Florida, and New Jersey. Other researchers believe that those marking "Other Hispanic" in these states represent members of Hispanic/Latino subgroups (Mexican,

Puerto Rican, etc.) who choose to designate themselves "Hispanic" because they prefer a panethnic identity rather than a subgroup identity.

In New Mexico, however, some 428,000 respondents to the 2000 Census marked "Other Hispanic." That number represents more than half of all Hispanic/Latino Americans counted in the state in 2000, more even than those who declared themselves "Mexican" (Guzmán 2001: Table 2). This fact supports the assertion by some that the so-called Spanish Americans, also known as Hispanos, are a distinctive subgroup of Hispanic/ Latino Americans whose cultural ancestry derives from the earliest Spanish colonial settlement of New Mexico (Carlson 1990; Nostrand 1992). Hispanos do not consider themselves Mexican and thus mark "Other Hispanic" because no census category exists for Spanish American.

The Hispanic/Latino population is growing much faster than the rest of the U.S. population. Assuming moderate levels of fertility and immigration, it is estimated that by 2020, Hispanics/Latinos will number fifty-two million, representing 24 percent of the U.S. population (del Pinal and Singer 1997). By 2050, Hispanic/Latino Americans could total ninety-seven million, a veritable Hispanic nation within a nation (Fox 1997). Yet, Hispanic/Latino American geography is diverse, a spatial mosaic exhibiting high and low population concentrations and composed of regional strongholds and city-state–like nodes, of settlement archipelagos and extensive urban social areas, of compact inner-city and even diffuse suburban barrios.

WHERE ARE HISPANIC/LATINO AMERICANS LOCATED?

Seven states—California, Texas, New York, Florida, Illinois, Arizona, and New Jersey—contained one million or more Hispanic/Latino Americans in 2000. These states counted some 27 million of the 35 million members of this population group in the United States, 77 percent of all Hispanic/Latino Americans (Guzmán 2001: Table 2). Half of all Hispanic/ Latino Americans live in two states: California (10.9 million) and Texas (6.6 million).

In nineteen states, Hispanic/Latino Americans were the largest minority group in the state in 2000 (Fig. 1.3). Most of these states were in the western United States, but four were New England states. New Mexico was the most Hispanic/Latino in 2000: 42.0 percent of the state's population was from this ethnic group. Both California and Texas had greater than 30.0 percent Hispanic/Latino population, and Arizona had more than 25.0 percent. Five additional states—Florida, Colorado, Nevada, New York, and

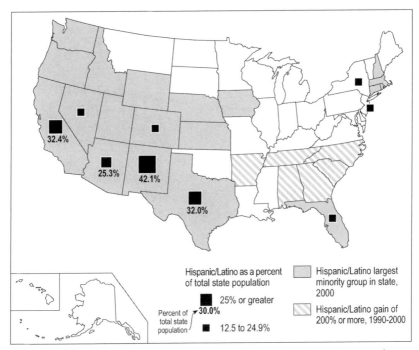

1.3.   Hispanic/Latino percentage of total state population, 2000. *Source: Brewer and Suchan 2001: 17, 86, 87.*

New Jersey—counted greater than the national percentage of 12.5 percent Hispanic/Latino, but less than 25 percent.

Six states in the South—North Carolina, South Carolina, Georgia, Alabama, Tennessee, and Arkansas—experienced Hispanic/Latino population gains of 200 percent or more in the 1990s (Fig. 1.3). Excluding the peripheral southern states of Florida and Virginia, the number of Hispanics/Latinos in the South more than tripled, from 402,000 to 1.3 million, between 1990 and 2000.

Shifting scale from states to counties illuminates another geography of Hispanic/Latino Americans. While some states, like New York and Illinois, have large absolute numbers of the ethnic group, Hispanic/Latino Americans in those states are a small percentage of individual county populations. Figure 1.4 shows, for example, that Hispanic/Latino Americans in New York and Illinois did not anywhere exceed 50 percent of a county's population. Along the East Coast, only Dade County (greater Miami), in southern Florida, counted more than 50 percent Hispanics/Latinos. Moving west on the national map, not until one reaches the northeastern edge

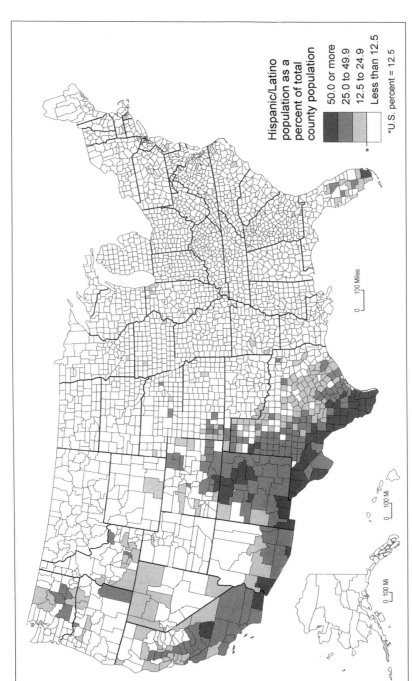

Hispanic/Latino population as a percent of total county population

50.0 or more
25.0 to 49.9
12.5 to 24.9
Less than 12.5

*U.S. percent = 12.5

0   100 Miles

0   100 Mi

0   100 Mi

1.4.   Percentage Hispanic/Latino population, by county, 2000. *Source: Guzmán 2001: Fig. 3.*

of South Texas are there counties that are predominantly Hispanic/Latino. This emphasizes the substantial vacuum of Hispanic/Latino concentration at the county level across the middle of America. In fact, only Nebraska, South Dakota, North Dakota, and Montana had counties in 1990 without a single Hispanic/Latino resident (Roseman 2002: Map 1.3).

Hispanic/Latino population concentration is most pronounced along the southwestern borderland, where the Mexican subgroup is dominant. A rimland of counties in South and West Texas that are overwhelmingly Mexican is the most intensive and extensive Hispanic/Latino zone (Arreola 1995). Outlier clusters of counties that also have high (greater than 50 percent) concentrations of the ethnic group are notable in southwestern New Mexico, southwestern Arizona and southeastern California, the western Panhandle of Texas, and single counties in South-Central Arizona and California (Fig. 1.4). The large cluster of counties in North-Central New Mexico and southern Colorado is chiefly the remnant of the once-extensive highland Hispano homeland (Nostrand 2001).

In borderland states, there is a substantial domain of counties more than 25 percent but less than 50 percent Hispanic/Latino. These extend from coastal, Trans-Pecos, and Panhandle Texas across parts of western Oklahoma and Kansas, touching parts of southern Colorado, most of New Mexico, scattered counties of southern Arizona, most of Southern California, and pieces of central and coastal California, especially the San Joaquin Valley (Fig. 1.4). This area was early identified as the Hispanic-American borderland, "a culture region because of the intensity of a distinctive subculture, the longtime existence of Hispanic settlements, a rich Hispanic legacy, and the presence of Anglo-Americans who have been 'Hispanicized' (Nostrand 1970: 638)."

Pieces of central Washington, eastern Oregon, Idaho, and Colorado, too, have scattered counties where Hispanics/Latinos make up a significant, if relatively smaller, concentration (Fig. 1.4). On the margins of these areas, there are other and greater numbers of counties where Hispanic/Latino Americans are recent arrivals, especially in the Yakima River, Columbia River, and Snake River stretches of Washington and Oregon, the South Platte River area of Colorado, and northern Nevada. These concentrations have been documented as "new" communities where recent Hispanic/Latino immigrants have settled among Anglos in small towns that are still tied to rural economies (Haverluk 1998; McGlade 2002).

A breakdown of Hispanic/Latino Americans by major subgroup populations creates yet another picture of this ethnic mosaic. Figure 1.5 emphasizes how Mexicans are not only the most numerous of Hispanic/Latino

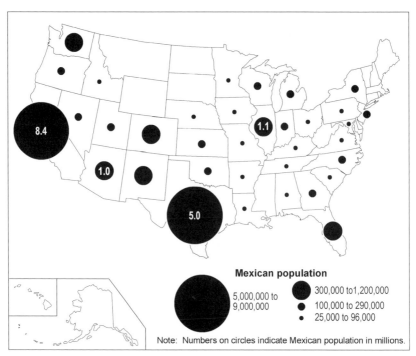

1.5.   Mexican population greater than 25,000, by state, 2000. *Source: Guzmán 2001:*
Table 2.

Americans, but also the most geographically distributed. In each of thirty-
five states, there are at least twenty-five thousand Mexicans, and four of
those states have at least one million. The borderland focus is explained by
the legacy of Spanish and Mexican entrenchment there, but the range of the
distribution is attributable in part to the long history of Mexican migrant
labor, both inside of and, especially, outside of borderland states (Cardoso
1980; Grebler, Moore, Guzmán 1970; Reisler 1976). Mexicans were drawn
to mining districts, railroad centers, farming regions, and industrial nodes.
Today, immigrant labor continues to be a major component of urban service economies, and Mexicans labor in many sectors of regional economies
across the country. A comparison of the distribution shown in Figure 1.5
with Mexican population distributions from 1980 and 1990 shows that
Mexicans are now extended to parts of the South, the Middle Atlantic,
and New England where they were not concentrated earlier (Allen and
Turner 1988: Mexican Origin map: 154; Arreola and Haverluk 1996: Maps
1 and 2).

    Puerto Ricans and Cubans are unevenly distributed compared with

Mexicans. Figure 1.6a illustrates the pronounced geographic skew to the East Coast and upper Midwest for Puerto Ricans. New York and neighboring New Jersey combined account for almost half the population of the subgroup, and Florida alone is a significant concentration. Secondary distributions are found in Massachusetts, Connecticut, Pennsylvania, and Illinois. Only California in the West maintains a large number of Puerto Ricans, who are otherwise a minor population in the middle of the country. The geography for this subgroup has not changed significantly from that mapped in 1980 and 1990 (Allen and Turner 1988: Puerto Rican Origin map: 154; Boswell and Cruz-Báez 2000: Fig. 6.5). Further, secondary migration appears to account for the greater part of the Puerto Rican relocation from New York to other regions (Allen and Turner 1988: U.S.-born Puerto Rican Origin Population map: 158).

Cubans are even more geographically concentrated than are Puerto Ricans. Figure 1.6b shows that more than two-thirds of all Cubans in the United States reside in Florida. New Jersey, California, and New York are secondary centers of this subgroup population, and only five other states have concentrations greater than ten thousand. Cuban ethnic geography has been equated to an "archipelago" consisting of small islands, because the distribution of population is diffuse beyond Florida, the "big island" (McHugh, Miyares, Skop 1997: Fig. 1). Further, the 2000 national map for Cubans did not change fundamentally from distributions plotted in 1980 and 1990 (Allen and Turner 1988: Cuban Origin map: 162; McHugh, Miyares, Skop 1997: Fig. 2).

Salvadorans and Guatemalans are the leading Central American subgroups in the United States (see Table 1.1). Although Salvadorans are almost two times as numerous as Guatemalans, their respective geographies are amazingly similar (Figs. 1.7a, 1.7b). California ranks first as the destination of choice for each subgroup, with approximately 40 percent of both Salvadorans and Guatemalans resident in the Golden State. A West Coast proximity of origin and destination may contribute to this skewed distribution, but one cannot discount the perceived economic opportunities of California, one of the world's major regional economies, as well as any preexisting channels for overland migration through Mexico (Jones 1989; Menjívar 2000). Texas and New York are secondary centers of Salvadoran immigrants, whereas New York and Florida serve as secondary destinations for Guatemalans. While the Lone Star State is linked to conduits of overland migration via Mexico, Houston and Miami are each closer by air to both El Salvador and Guatemala than the Central American countries are to California. Massachusetts, New Jersey (Bailey et al. 2002), and Virginia are ter-

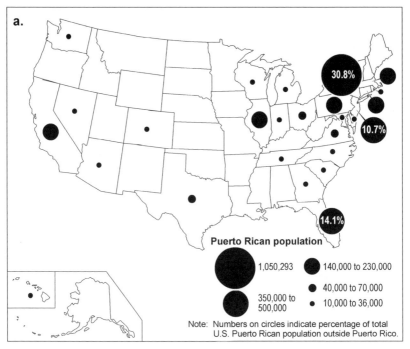

a.

30.8%

10.7%

14.1%

Puerto Rican population

1,050,293   140,000 to 230,000

                 40,000 to 70,000

350,000 to   10,000 to 36,000
500,000

Note: Numbers on circles indicate percentage of total
U.S. Puerto Rican population outside Puerto Rico.

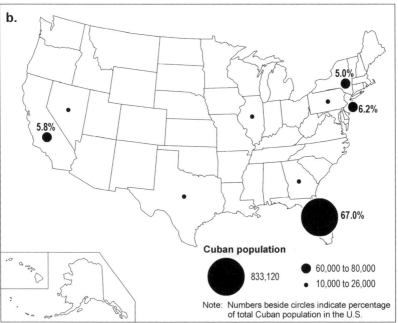

b.

5.0%

6.2%

5.8%

67.0%

Cuban population

833,120   60,000 to 80,000

                 10,000 to 26,000

Note: Numbers beside circles indicate percentage
of total Cuban population in the U.S.

1.6a.   Puerto Rican population as percentage of total, by states with more than 10,000
population, 2000.

1.6b.   Cuban population as percentage of total, by states with more than 10,000
population, 2000. *Source: U.S. Bureau of the Census 2000.*

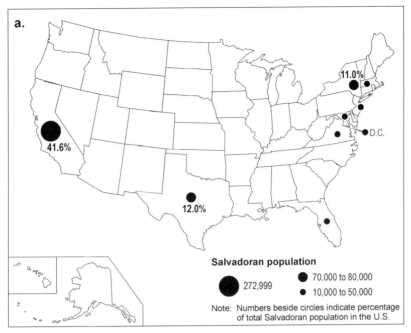

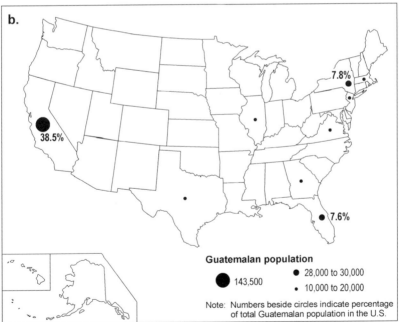

1.7a.   Salvadoran population as percentage of total, by states with more than 10,000 population, 2000.

1.7b.   Guatemalan population as percentage of total, by states with more than 10,000 population, 2000. *Source: U.S. Bureau of the Census 2000.*

tiary destinations for both subgroups, while Maryland and the District of Columbia are separate, significant locations of Salvadorans. Other Central American subgroups like Nicaraguans and Hondurans are concentrated, albeit in small numbers, in Florida (Miami) and Louisiana (New Orleans), respectively (Hamilton and Chinchilla 1991; Portes and Stepick 1993).

Colombians and Ecuadorians are the major South American subgroups in the United States, although Peruvians rank a very close third (see Table 1.1). More than half of all Colombians in the United States are concentrated in Florida and New York. These concentrations appear to represent Colombians from different parts of the homeland. The oldest migrant channel is chiefly from Bogotá and first came to New York after World War I. However, the largest migrations have occurred since 1960, especially since 1970, and the population of this subgroup has nearly doubled every decade since 1960 (Haslip-Viera and Baver 1996: Table 3). Colombians who migrated to New York City found residence in the Jackson Heights area of Queens and began to call their neighborhood "Chaperino" after a middle-class suburb of Bogotá. The migrant stream that settled Florida, however, is said to be mostly *costeños*, from the coastal regions of Colombia and chiefly of mixed African, Native American, and Spanish ancestry (Gann and Duignan 1986: 121–122) (Fig. 1.8a).

Ecuadorian emigration is a relatively recent phenomenon, stimulated in part by changes in agrarian structure in the homeland. Most emigrants come from the provinces of Cañar and Azuay in South-Central Ecuador, and their primary destination has been New York City, via stopovers in Central America and overland through Mexico (Jokisch 1997; Jokisch and Pribilsky 2002). Because Ecuadorians are chiefly illegal immigrants, the total given in the 2000 census (Table 1.1) may be a serious undercount and populations may be several times higher, possibly making Ecuadorians the largest South American subgroup, exceeding even Colombians. Like Colombians, however, Ecuadorians in the United States are highly concentrated, with approximately two-thirds in New York—especially Queens—and New Jersey, and smaller numbers in Florida, Illinois, and California (Fig. 1.8b).

Notwithstanding the geographical dispersion of Hispanic/Latino Americans, the ethnic group is more urban than the national population as a whole. In 2000, nine of every ten members of the group lived in metropolitan areas, whereas only seven of every ten non-Hispanic whites lived in metropolitan regions. Further, nearly half of all Hispanic/Latino Americans lived in the central city of a metropolitan area, whereas the percentage in similar areas for non-Hispanic whites was about 20 (Therrien and

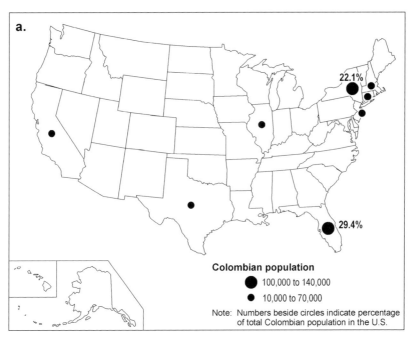

a.

22.1%

29.4%

Colombian population

● 100,000 to 140,000

● 10,000 to 70,000

Note: Numbers beside circles indicate percentage
of total Colombian population in the U.S.

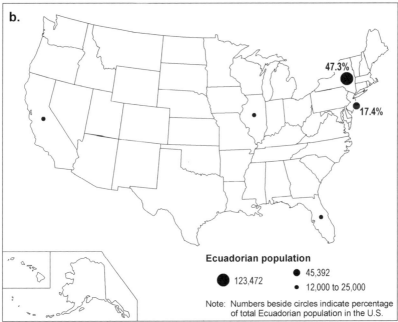

b.

47.3%

17.4%

Ecuadorian population

● 123,472   ● 45,392

                    • 12,000 to 25,000

Note: Numbers beside circles indicate percentage
of total Ecuadorian population in the U.S.

1.8a.   Colombian population as percentage of total, by states with more than 10,000
population, 2000.

1.8b.   Ecuadorian population as percentage of total, by states with more than 10,000
population, 2000. *Source: U.S. Bureau of the Census 2000.*

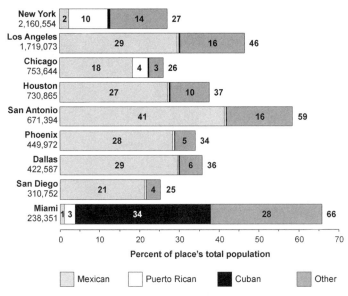

Notes: Number below city is total number of Hispanics/Latinos in the city in 2000.
Unlabelled bar segments represent populations less than 1% of place's total population.

1.9.   Cities with more than one million population, at least 200,000
Hispanic/Latino residents, and more than 25 percent Hispanic/Latino
population, 2000. *Source: U.S. Bureau of the Census 2000.*

Ramírez 2001). Nevertheless, Hispanic/Latino Americans are now predominantly a suburban population in the one hundred largest metropolitan
areas, having grown 71 percent in these districts in the 1990s (Suro and
Singer 2002).

Figure 1.9 illustrates cities with more than one million population, more
than two hundred thousand Hispanic/Latino residents, and more than 25
percent Hispanic/Latino in 2000. New York and Los Angeles have the
greatest numbers of the ethnic group, but only Miami and San Antonio
are places that are predominantly Hispanic/Latino. Los Angeles (see Allen
and Turner 1997: Figs. 4.2–4.9; Allen and Turner 2002: Figs. 5.2–5.4) is
nearly half Hispanic/Latino, and cities like Houston, Dallas, and Phoenix
are now more than one-third Hispanic/Latino. In seven of these nine cities,
Mexicans are the leading Hispanic/Latino subgroup, and only in Miami
is another subgroup, Cuban, a plurality. Even New York City, which contains the greatest number of Hispanics/Latinos, is now a mixed population where "Other Hispanic" is the leading category, exceeding even Puerto
Ricans. In fact, in all remaining cities, with the exception of New York
and Chicago, "Other Hispanic" is the second-ranking category. Central

and South Americans in Los Angeles, New York, Miami, Houston, and Washington, and Dominicans in New York and Miami are now part of the ethnic mix in major cities with Hispanic/Latino populations (Arreola 1997; Boswell and Skop 1995; Davis 2000; Hamilton and Chinchilla 2001; Haslip-Viera and Baver 1996; Miyares and Gowen 1998; Moore and Pinderhughes 1993; Padilla 1987; Portes and Stepick 1993; Waldinger and Bozorgmehr 1996).

IS THIS A NATION?

In the introduction to his considerable tome, *Latinos: A Biography of the People,* Earl Shorris (1992b: 12) writes, "Although the name of this book is *Latinos,* the theory of it is that there are no Latinos, only diverse peoples struggling to remain who they are while becoming someone else." In his own struggles with the word "Hispanic," Richard Rodríguez (2002: 117) writes, "You won't find Hispanics in Latin America . . . not in the quickening cities, not in the emasculated villages. You need to come to the United States to meet Hispanics . . . What Hispanic immigrants learn within the United States is to view themselves in a new way, as belonging to Latin America entire—precisely at the moment they no longer do."

These antipodes of inclusion and exclusion—are Hispanic/Latino Americans Latin Americans, or some new nation within the United States—are stimulating volatile debates in scholarly as well as popular literature. To a large extent, these debates center on the idea of cultural confrontation and identity. Cultural critic Ilan Stavans (2001) explores this notion in the context of his stimulating book *The Hispanic Condition,* where he also asks questions about the ways in which cultures behave among themselves and toward others.

Among Hispanic/Latino Americans, perhaps the most intense exploration of the issue of exclusion has been trained on Mexican Americans. Historians especially have deliberated on Anglo attitudes toward Mexicans in Texas (De León 1983), in California (Monroy 1990), and in Los Angeles (Acuña 1996). In his 1999 book, *¡Pobre Raza!,* Arturo Rosales explores how elite Mexican immigrants in the early twentieth century formed a "México Lindo" (beautiful Mexico) nationalism to confront discrimination and violence against Mexicans in the United States.

Borrowing anthropologist Renato Rosaldo's term "cultural citizenship," some social scientists have refashioned his concept to mean "a range of social practices which, taken together, claim and establish a distinct social space for Latinos in this country" (Flores and Benmayor 1997: 1). Arguably, the most advanced discussion about the idea of a Hispanic/Latino consciousness is sociologist Geoffrey Fox's *Hispanic Nation*. Fox (1997: 4) starts with anthropologist Benedict Anderson's concept of nation as "an imagined political community" where members have very little in common beyond language and a few traditions, yet where they may feel affiliated with one another and with some larger collective entity. The media have largely carried the nationalist banner for Hispanics/Latinos. Fox examines how and why this component of society, especially, has worked to forge a national agenda. Improvements in communications technologies are spreading notions of imagined community. Nationally broadcast Spanish-language television, for example, creates a united Hispanic/Latino audience, where the same events in the same homogenized Spanish accent get communicated. A large part of these media, not surprisingly, is tied to marketing geared toward Hispanic/Latino Americans. Other segments of society, like political organizations, are much more fragmented by alliances that hold tightly to subgroup identity. And, geographically, most Hispanic/Latino Americans do not lay claim to a united territory. "It may therefore be objected," says Fox (1997: 7) "that Hispanics cannot become a 'nation' because they have neither a flag nor a land to fly it over. And if they did, where would it be? A secessionist chunk of the American Southwest? East Harlem? Miami?"

If there is a geographical Hispanic/Latino nation, it is a largely fragmented confederation of regional zones and nodes, not a unified area in any real sense. And it is precisely because Hispanic/Latino Americans are diverse and diffuse that we can best understand and appreciate their geographical identities through the lens of regional inspection, across settlement scales, and through time.

Finally, what might a future Hispanic/Latino American geography look like? I would contend that the fundamental geographical anatomy of this ethnic population is already in place. Although Hispanic/Latino Americans will no doubt increase as a percentage of all Americans, and while subgroup concentrations may increase or erode, it seems unlikely that the ratios of subgroup populations will change too greatly, because the homeland populations for many subgroups are small. Puerto Ricans who currently reside on the mainland are nearly equivalent to the total number of Puerto Ricans on the island, and Guatemala, Ecuador, Cuba, Dominican Republic, and El Salvador each have fewer than 15 million people today. Only Mexico, which counted some 104 million people in 2002, is a large country that also contributes significantly to the total number of Latin American emigrants. In 2000, Mexico accounted for more than half of the foreign born in the United States from Latin America ("Coming from the Americas" 2002).

California and Texas, the most Hispanic/Latino American states, and chiefly Mexican, are also states with the greatest number of Hispanic/ Latino elected officials (National Directory of Latino Elected Officials [NALEO] 2000). If political influence on a regional scale is to develop, it will likely emerge first in these areas.

It is not inconceivable, then, that Mexico, homeland to the largest share of Hispanic/Latino Americans, will continue to be the source of the greatest number of new Hispanic/Latino Americans. And this, in all likelihood, means that Mexicans (Mexican Americans and Chicanas/Chicanos) will, in the near future, continue to represent the vast majority of Americans of Hispanic/Latino ancestry.

In *Crossing Over: A Mexican Family on the Migrant Trail,* Rubén Martínez (2001: 136) relates his discussions with Purépecha migrants from the town of Cherán in Michoacán. The residents of this village, like villagers in so many other mountain valleys of these highlands, have been migrating to *el norte* (the north, i.e., the United States) for generations. One migrant who has journeyed to the San Joaquin Valley in California, then to Los Angeles, and finally to Arkansas remarked with optimism, "Within a decade . . . Hispanics will be the largest minority in the United States." That statistic, says Martínez, which is today cited with regularity in our media, has been a truth among Mexican migrants for years. A Latino American diaspora has been transforming this country for many generations, and as surely as a Hispanic American legacy has shaped the American Southwest, so, too, will it spread across and spice up the far corners of these United States. As the contributions to this volume attest, it is already happening.

CONTINUOUS COMMUNITIES

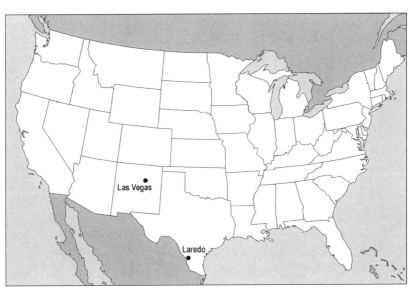

Map 1. Continuous communities.

2 | The Plaza in Las Vegas, New Mexico

A Community Gathering Place

Jeffrey S. Smith

In 1598, escorted by 130 soldiers and an untold number of women and children, Juan de Oñate spearheaded Spanish efforts to colonize what was to become present-day northern New Mexico (Nostrand 1992). On Spain's northern frontier, as in other parts of its New World colonies, the crown required all new settlements to adhere to royal planning ordinances. King Phillip II's codification of the Laws of the Indies in 1573 was intended to give order and a sense of familiarity to Spanish urban places (Crouch, Garr, and Mundigo 1982; Suisman 1993). Serving as the village focal point, the *plaza mayor* (main square) was to be the generative space for the entire community (Veregge 1997). The plan called for streets to radiate out in a centripetal fashion from the central plaza, forming a rigid grid pattern. Founding fathers of frontier settlements, however, rarely abided by more than the spirit of the laws (Arreola 1992). The realities of frontier life rendered many of the ordinances infeasible, and local conditions necessitated deviations.

Many of the early Spanish settlers in the upper Rio Grande region, for example, preferred to reside in ribbon-shaped settlements so they could be close to their fields (Jackson 1952; Knowlton 1969; Smith 1998). With increasingly frequent Indian raids, people were forced to congregate around fortified plazas (de Borhegyi 1954; Jackson 1988). Homes were built side by side and one room deep around an open square large enough to hold livestock and personal possessions. With windows facing the enclosed space, the outside walls offered fortresslike protection against invading forces.

When marauding Native Americans were finally subdued in New Mexico, many of these smaller plazas were abandoned and residents returned to a more diffuse settlement pattern. In governmental, ecclesiastical, or commercial centers, however, the plaza remained the focal point of the community. These plazas eventually evolved into public spaces that hosted celebratory events, including parades, community affairs, religious activities, and annual fiestas (Wilson 2001). Over time, these recurring events established the plaza's importance to the community. Serving as a cultural ligament holding the community together, the plaza became each town's principal *resolana* (Romero 2001).

In the *hermanito* (brotherhood) traditions of northern New Mexico, *resolana* is synonymous with *resolaneros:* men of all ages who gather in the warmth of the sun or under shady trees on hot summer days to share simple conversation (Romero 2001). Flora Romero de Herrera (2002) remembers the word *resolana* being used to refer to any place where people sat and talked about life. The word loosely translates to mean a place where people gather to while away their time, or a place of community gathering. Unfortunately, this essential part of community life is being lost as the New Mexico region undergoes cultural change (Carlson 1990). With the influx of Anglos into the upper Rio Grande region, many of New Mexico's Hispano urban plazas, especially those in Albuquerque, Santa Fe, and Taos, have become commodified spaces for tourists. No longer do these plazas serve as community gathering places. Local Hispanos have, instead, created other *resolanas*, including Wal-Mart and nearby Native American casinos. Levi Romero (2001: 27) recounts hearing a conversation between two longtime resident Hispanos of Taos. The first was overheard to say, "You know, I don't ever go [to the plaza] anymore. I'd rather come here [to Wal-Mart]." The other gentleman responded, "Yes, it's better here. The [plaza] is full of tourists and here one runs into a relative or neighbor."

In Las Vegas, New Mexico, however, the plaza continues to serve as the city's main *resolana*. The plaza is still the heart of the community and the space that attracts local residents. In this chapter, I demonstrate how the Las Vegas plaza continues to serve its traditional function as community gathering place. I begin with a snapshot of the historical evolution of the Las Vegas plaza and a comparative overview of the plazas in Albuquerque, Santa Fe, and Taos. I then present three aspects that illustrate how the Las Vegas plaza functions today as a community social space: (1) surviving commercial land uses; (2) sponsored community events; and (3) personal uses of the plaza.

I gathered a variety of sources to tell the story of the Las Vegas plaza. I conducted extensive fieldwork during the spring and summer of 2000 and 2001, employing personal observations and informal interviews with local residents, business owners, teachers, students, retirees, church officials, museum and library personnel, chamber of commerce employees, and local government officials. I used Sanborn Fire Insurance Maps from 1883, 1898, and 1930 to determine historical land use patterns on the Las Vegas plaza. Printed brochures from local chambers of commerce, tourism boards, and city governments were also amassed. I made daily notes and took countless photographs to document the project.

LAS VEGAS PLAZA

The first attempt, albeit unsuccessful, to settle the land now known as Las Vegas, New Mexico, was made by Luis Cabeza de Baca and his seventeen sons in 1821 (Fugate and Fugate 1989). By 1823, raiding Native Americans had driven off the pioneering settlers, and the land remained vacant for another twelve years. In the early spring of 1835, twenty-nine men from the nearby village of San Miguel petitioned the Mexican government for a new land grant to secure the 500,000 acres popularly known as Las Vegas Grandes en el Río de las Gallinas (Arrellano 1996). By April of that same year, the land grant was conferred and the community of Las Vegas, officially named Nuestra Señora de los Dolores de Las Vegas Grandes, was founded.

Following the traditions of the Laws of the Indies, the *plaza mayor* was established on a small hill at the center of the community, and streets radiated out from it in a grid pattern. According to Mexican governmental stipulation, the Las Vegas plaza was required to serve as a regional service center and focal point. For the next decade, resident Vegueños eked out a largely subsistence living on their small, long-lot plots northeast of the plaza (Arrellano 1996). Through the 1840s, the Las Vegas plaza had only two entrances so that residents could defend themselves behind the fortresslike barricades when under attack (Fig. 2.1).

By the mid-1840s, reports of commercial profits from trade quickly spread along the Santa Fe Trail, and Las Vegas was transformed from a simple agricultural village into New Mexico's leading commercial center (Arrellano 1996). The increased trade stimulated the local economy; it brought wage-paying employment and large quantities of affordable merchandise from the east. Soon, businessmen, including Don Miguel Romero de Baca, Charles Ilfeld, and Emanuel Rosenwald, established retail operations on the plaza. In 1860, the population of Las Vegas had grown to over one thousand (Citizens' Committee for Historic Preservation [CCHP] 1999), and six years later, at the height of trail activity, five thousand wagons passed through the Las Vegas area (Vander Meer 1999).

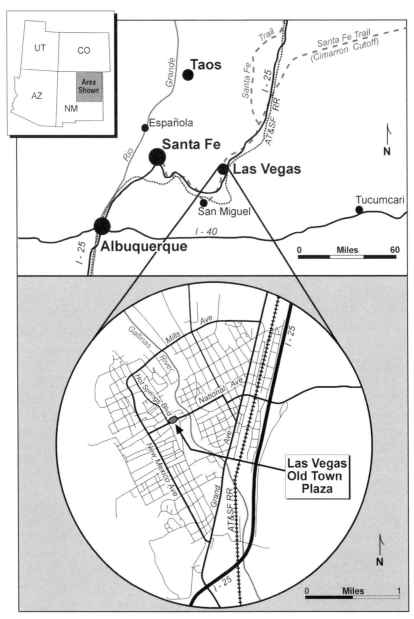

2.1.   Location of Las Vegas, New Mexico, and its plaza. *Cartography by J. S. Smith, 2002.*

2.2.   Wood vendor and burros on the Las Vegas, New Mexico, Plaza, ca. 1882–1883. The Plaza Hotel and The Great Emporium are in background on the right, facing the plaza. *Photo courtesy Museum of New Mexico, negative #52877.*

In 1879, the city's connection to national transportation routes changed again, when the Atchison, Topeka & Santa Fe (AT&SF) Railroad steamed into town (Meinig 1971). Even though railroad administrators decided to bypass the plaza in favor of a location one mile to the east, where an Anglo subdivision eventually emerged, the plaza's importance in regional trade and commerce was not diminished (Fugate and Fugate 1989; Gottschalk 2000). The plaza in Las Vegas had become too well established as a commercial center with strong connections to points beyond.

The arrival of the railroad did, however, accelerate migration from the east. Las Vegas grew in importance, and by 1882, its population had increased to six thousand, making it one of the most cosmopolitan cities in the region (Arrellano 1996). In that same year, the now-famous Plaza Hotel opened for business (Fig. 2.2). In 1883, Charles Ilfeld began selling goods in his three-story department store, The Great Emporium (Fig. 2.2). Within a decade, the *Las Vegas Daily Optic* called it "the largest and finest department house in all the Southwest (Gottschalk 2000: 36)." For the next thirty years, the Las Vegas plaza was a critical site in the economic development of the Southwest, and at the end of the 1800s, Las Vegas had become so important that it rivaled Denver, El Paso, and Tucson as the region's principal trade and commercial center.

By the early 1900s, that prominence was nearing an end. In the mid-1920s, the local region experienced a severe agricultural depression followed by the Great Depression of the 1930s (CCHP 1999). The area did not see signs of sustained economic recovery until the mid-1980s (Campbell and Strozier 1996). This extended economic slump helped shield Las Vegas from the wrecking ball and outside influences that diminished other Hispano urban plazas in the state. Today, 918 buildings in Las Vegas are listed on the National Register of Historic Places (more than any other city in the United States), and many of them surround the plaza (CCHP 1999). The town also boasts excellent examples of nearly every residential architectural style built in the United States between 1840 and 1940. In 2001, the National Trust for Historic Preservation ranked Las Vegas eighth in the United States among distinctive destinations because of its dynamic downtown, eye-catching architecture, and cultural diversity. Thanks in large part to the preservation of the architecture around the plaza and the innovative efforts of La Plaza Vieja Partnership, Ltd., the Las Vegas plaza continues to be the city's main gathering place.

Over the past century and a half, the plaza space has seen many transformations. In 1876, a windmill was erected on the space. The conspicuous structure not only provided a focal point for the community, it also served as gallows for local vigilante groups. By 1880, the symbol of the wild frontier was removed and replaced with a *kiosko* (bandstand) encircled by trees and a picket fence (CCHP 1999). Today's plaza with its gazebo under a canopy of mature trees reflects the success of the first historic preservation movement in the 1960s (CCHP 1999).

In the 1980s, a partnership of property owners provided the catalyst for today's thriving commercial space. The most recent plaza refurbishment was completed in 1991. Today the city invests considerable time and financial resources in maintaining the *kiosko* and surrounding plaza.

To appreciate the character of the Las Vegas plaza, I shall now inspect how plazas have evolved in other Hispano urban centers of northern New Mexico. While Las Vegas fell from the state's leading commercial center into economic ruin, the cities of Albuquerque, Santa Fe, and Taos (see Fig. 2.1) followed distinctly different paths. Due, in part, to the promotional efforts of Fred Harvey and the AT&SF Railroad in the 1870s, outsiders discovered the enchanted Hispano plazas in these communities (Cullen 1992). In the mid-1930s, the marketing of New Mexico's unique cultural imprints (including its Hispano plazas) was adopted by the state's newly founded Tourist Bureau (Andrés 2000). In a relatively short time, the success of its Heritage/Ethnic Tourism promotion scheme reinforced each city's unique cultural identity (Morley 1999; Mulligan 1992). Moreover, Santa Fe and Taos emerged as popular exotic destinations because of the reputations developed for these places by well-known authors like Willa Cather, Robert Frost, and D. H. Lawrence (Weigle and Fiore 1982). By the 1960s and the early 1970s, throngs of tourists had found the region's attractive climate, abundant sunshine, and rich culture appealing. The Old Town plazas in Albuquerque, Santa Fe, and Taos became primed for Anglo invasion. "Spatial mestizaje" aptly describes the cultural and racial blending that has become evident on the plazas in these cities (Wilson 1994).

The residential and commercial spaces around these plazas have experienced an invasion and succession of land uses. Newcomers, often Anglo, bought property for a fraction of its market value and built shops and expensive homes. This increased the value of the land around the plaza, which in turn caused property taxes to rise. Higher taxes combined with willing buyers convinced many Hispanos to sell their property and move out. Today it is rare to find commercial space that does not cater to the tourist industry on the plazas in Albuquerque, Santa Fe, and Taos. Most Hispano residents in these cities avoid the plazas because they have become theme malls and contrived, reconstructed tourist sites (Andrés 2000; Cullen 1992; Rodríguez 1998).

Unlike in Albuquerque, Santa Fe, and Taos, the plaza in Las Vegas, as I have noted, continues to serve as a gathering place for the local Hispano population. Three elements illustrate this function: (1) surviving commercial land uses; (2) sponsored community events; and (3) personal uses of the plaza.

COMMERCIAL LAND USES ON THE PLAZA

In 1993, Daniel Arreola found that the buildings and commercial activity surrounding plazas in San Diego, Texas, were strong indicators of the role these spaces played in community life. A 1902 map of the plaza in Old Town Albuquerque unquestionably reveals that the businesses around the square served the resident population. Of the eighteen spaces dedicated to commercial activity, four were saloons/bars, four were grocery stores/food markets, three were boardinghouses, two were barbershops, one served as a post office, and one as a public school (Andrés 2000).

While the San Felipe de Neri church continued to anchor the north side of the plaza, by the 1950s, commercial land uses around the Albuquerque plaza had changed dramatically. Barbershops, grocery stores, the post office, and the public school were replaced by restaurants and curio shops. In 1972, the number of eateries had increased to eight, with 85 tourist shops. By 1980, there were ten dining places, 104 curio shops, and eighteen art galleries (Andrés 2000).

Fieldwork in the summer of 2001 revealed that nearly all the commercial activity catered to tourists. Of the thirty-eight commercial units that fronted Albuquerque's plaza, twenty-six were curio shops, four were restaurants, four were art galleries, and one was a newly established visitor information center. Moreover, in the 1960s, 116 people resided on the plaza in Albuquerque. By 1980, that number had dwindled to about two dozen (Andrés 2000), and today it is hard to find any residential space on Albuquerque's Old Town plaza. Similar patterns of commercial succession and residential erosion are found on the plazas in Santa Fe (Cullen 1992; Morley 1999) and Taos (Rodríguez 1998).

By contrast, commercial activity around the Las Vegas plaza has consistently functioned as an integral part of the resident Hispano activity space. An 1883 map, for example, shows sixty-four commercial spaces fronting the plaza (Table 2.1). Of these, sixteen offered general merchandise/hardware, seven were saloons, six were grocery stores/food markets, and two were restaurants. No commercial establishments offered goods or services that catered to tourists. An 1898 map reveals that, with the exception of additional office space and fewer general merchandise stores, grocery stores, and saloons, the land uses around the Las Vegas plaza remained largely the same, suggesting that the commercial activity catered to the resident population. Analysis of a 1930 map reveals again that there were few changes in the types of businesses on the plaza, except for the lack of saloons, reflecting the influence of Prohibition (Table 2.1). Likewise, none of the specialty businesses identified were targeted at tourists.

Today, despite the fact that billboards sponsored by the Bridge Street merchants association and the Las Vegas Chamber of Commerce beckon travelers on Interstate 25 to shop at the Old Town Plaza, the space has not been transformed into a tourist site. Instead, fieldwork reveals that the commercial land uses around the plaza continue to serve as integral spaces for resident Vegueños.

The fifty-one spaces fronting the plaza in 2001 saw a variety of commercial and private uses, including seven general merchandise stores, five restaurants, three commercial offices, and six vacant spaces (Table 2.1). One of the best indications of the continued vitality of the plaza in serving the local population's needs is the prominent position of the church on the space. The original church of Nuestra Señora de los Dolores stood on the south side of the plaza until Archbishop Lamy sold the building in 1869

TABLE 2.1—LAND USE ON THE LAS VEGAS, NEW MEXICO, PLAZA

LAND USE	1883 (NO.)	1898 (NO.)	1930 (NO.)	2001 (NO.)
GENERAL MERCHANDISE/HARDWARE	16	9	28	7
GROCERY/FOOD STORE	6	3	—	1
RESTAURANT/CAFÉ	2	1	—	5
SALOON/BILLIARDS/DANCE HALL	7	3	—	3
OFFICE SPACE	5	11	10	3
APARTMENTS	12	10	7	15
HOTEL	2	1	1	1
BARBER/HAIR SALON	3	2	—	2
GOVERNMENT/COURTHOUSE	2	—	—	2
BANK	1	1	—	—
TAILOR/MILLINERY	2	—	—	—
CRAFTS/TRADE SERVICES	1	2	2	2
WAREHOUSE	1	2	—	—
LAUNDRY	1	1	—	—
DRUGSTORE	—	1	1	1
AUTO DEALER/REPAIRS	—	—	2	—
CHURCH PROPERTY	—	—	—	1
ANTIQUES/CURIOS	—	—	—	2
VACANT SPACE	3	6	—	6
TOTAL	64	53	51	51

Sources: Sanborn Map Company 1883, 1898, 1930; fieldwork, 2001.

(Gottschalk 2000). In 1938, space on the northwest side of the plaza that now houses the parish hall was acquired by the church and has remained in its possession since (Huchmala 2002). Equally telling is the fact that fifteen private dwellings are also found on the plaza. This is in stark contrast to the plaza spaces in Albuquerque, Santa Fe, and Taos, where apartments are all but absent. That both religious and residential land uses are still found on the Las Vegas plaza is remarkable, considering the prime space they occupy.

In 2001, only two businesses on the Las Vegas plaza offered goods that were even remotely targeted to tourists (Plaza Antiques and the Asian Showcase Imported Gifts). According to the Las Vegas Chamber of Commerce, a number of business proprietors on the plaza want to see more tourists frequent their shops, but they are much more concerned about keeping their loyal local customers and, therefore, have not converted their product lines to focus on curio items (Vander Meer 2001).

SPONSORED COMMUNITY EVENTS ON THE PLAZA

As land uses illustrate the distinctive character of the Las Vegas plaza, so, too, do community-sponsored events. In Hispanic American communities, the central plaza is the preeminent space for social interaction (Arreola 1992; Low 2000). Hosting public events and community activities such as parades, music performances, horse races, patriotic commemorations, religious celebrations, and even public executions has long been one of the recognized functions of a plaza. As individuals gather to witness and participate in activities, a strong sense of community and civic loyalty is fostered. Historically, all Hispano urban plazas of northern New Mexico served this multifaceted purpose. Today, however, in Albuquerque, Santa Fe, and Taos, plaza events sponsored by local governments and organizations are, by and large, directed at tourists. The plaza in Old Town Albuquerque hosts weekend Wild West demonstrations, including mock gunfights on Sundays. Moreover, each year all three cities host multiday arts and crafts festivals and creative arts events. Santa Fe's annual Indian Market and Crafts Fair is the plaza's largest public event, with well over one thousand vendors offering goods to thousands of tourists. With the increased popularity of these annual events, the cities of Albuquerque and Santa Fe outlawed non–Native Americans from selling jewelry under plaza awnings to preserve the authenticity of the tourist attraction (Andrés 2000; Morley 1999). Ironically, as Sylvia Rodríguez (1998) reports, these events were established by Anglo boosters decades ago for the explicit purpose of attracting customers to the plaza during the height of the tourist season.

The Las Vegas plaza, on the other hand, hosts numerous community-sponsored events intended for residents. In 2001, some eighteen community-wide activities were held on the plaza, including the Doggie-Do Days sponsored by the local Humane Society, Fire Prevention Awareness Week, car shows and road rallies, and various religious celebrations. Certainly, these events could be held in other public venues, yet the plaza is the first choice for all public events in the community, according to city officials (Garduño 2001).

An example of how the Las Vegas plaza serves as a community gathering place is seen every Fourth of July, when the city sponsors its annual American Independence Day celebration (Fig. 2.3). For more than eighty-five years, the plaza has served as the focal point for this event, which in-

2.3. People enjoying music, food, and conversation on the Las Vegas, New Mexico, plaza during the 2001 Fourth of July celebration. *Photograph by J. S. Smith, 2001.*

cludes, for example, music and dancing, food stands, novelty booths, a float parade, various entertainments for people of all ages, and the always popular Fiesta Queen pageant (Fig. 2.4). The multiday celebration has grown into the city's largest and most popular community event.

Pulsing music from a bank of loudspeakers is a cornerstone of the weekend. People dance and sing along with live bands, which play popular songs from a variety of genres, including rock, jazz, and Tejano, but the audience seems to come alive when the traditional Spanish New Mexican songs are played (Fig. 2.5). Of thirty-two bands that performed at the 2001 celebration, twenty were from the Las Vegas vicinity. On the final day, an open microphone session encouraged local bands to showcase their talent. Furthermore, some forty-eight booths lined the plaza; a vast majority of these stands offered novelty items or locally prepared food rather than arts and crafts.

The majority of the people who participate in the annual event, as either spectators or vendors, come from Las Vegas' immediate vicinity, and most of the people I spoke with reside in Las Vegas. However, many of the visitors from outside the region indicated they were former residents who returned each year to help maintain their ties to the community. Clearly, the

2.4.   Fiesta Queen of 1968 in the 2001 Fourth of July parade in Las Vegas, New Mexico. *Photograph by J. S. Smith, 2001.*

Las Vegas Fourth of July celebration is a product of local residents and intended to serve the local population. In addition to community-sponsored events, residents continue to use the space, a reflection of the plaza's distinctive character.

PERSONAL USES OF THE PLAZA

Arguably the best indicator of how well a plaza serves as a gathering place is the extent to which residents use the space on a daily basis. In Hispanic American communities, the daily lives of people unfold on the public plaza, and the space serves as an integral landscape that reinforces the local culture (Bressi 1993; Low 2000). In Albuquerque, Santa Fe, and Taos, however, the central plaza no longer holds the appeal it once had for local Hispanos. On one research trip to Old Town Albuquerque, I spoke with an unidentified elementary school teacher who was on a field trip with her students. She related that the annual field trip to Old Town was one of the most tangible ways for students to visualize and appreciate their cultural heritage. She added that few of the families of the students had ever been to the plaza.

In Las Vegas, by comparison, the plaza is used daily by resident Vegueños. Not only are people attracted to the surrounding commercial shops, but residents also use the open space for highly personal reasons (Fig. 2.6). On numerous visits, I have documented folks sitting on benches and conversing, people walking their dogs, kids playing on their way to and from school, older residents sitting on the benches soaking up the sun, and young adults cruising the plaza's perimeter. It is not uncommon during the warmer months to hear political groups call for action or see young couples getting married on the steps of the *kiosko* (Vander Meer 2001). The Las Vegas plaza, unlike the plazas in Albuquerque, Santa Fe, and Taos, daily continues to attract local Hispano residents.

CONCLUSION

A former editor of the New Mexico magazine *El Palacio* believes plazas are the heart of many New Mexico towns. Plazas contribute to the Old World ethos that pervades communities throughout the state, and they are

2.5.   Coro Reina del Cielo performs during the 2001 Fourth of July celebration on the plaza in Las Vegas, New Mexico. *Photograph by J. S. Smith, 2001.*

2.6.   Enjoying spring sunshine on the plaza in Las Vegas, New Mexico. *Photograph by J. S. Smith, 2001.*

the places where people converge to "participate in those activities . . . [to] express their membership within the community" (Nestor 1988). Unfortunately, the plazas in many of New Mexico's urban centers no longer serve the traditional function of community gathering place. In Albuquerque, Santa Fe, and Taos, the plazas have become contrived, appropriated, and commercially developed spaces directed to tourists more than to local residents. By contrast, the traditional character of the Las Vegas plaza has not been lost.

An analysis of maps from 1883, 1898, and 1930 helped me establish that the land uses around the Las Vegas plaza served the resident population during those years. Fieldwork in 2000 and 2001 revealed that little had changed on the Las Vegas plaza, despite efforts by the local chamber of commerce and a merchants' association to attract more tourists. The space still accommodates the demands of resident Vegueños.

While community-sponsored events could be held almost anywhere in the city, the Las Vegas plaza is the venue of choice. Residents are more strongly connected to the plaza than to any other parklike setting within the city. The important role that the plaza plays in community life is captured every year at the city's Fourth of July celebration. The multiday event attracts thousands of residents who come together as a community to listen to live music performed by local bands, consume food made by local vendors, witness the float parade, and enjoy the Fiesta Queen pageant.

Finally, local Hispanos continue to use the plaza for personal activities. People walk dogs, folks linger on benches, and young couples are wed on the plaza. Unlike the Hispano urban plazas in Albuquerque, Santa Fe, and Taos, where tourists reign supreme, the Las Vegas plaza remains the community's *resolana*. Asserted to be New Mexico's best-preserved plaza (CCHP 1999), Old Town in Las Vegas is the heart and soul of the community, and it remains an emblem of Hispano cultural identity.

SOCIAL GEOGRAPHY OF LAREDO, TEXAS, NEIGHBORHOODS

Distinctiveness and Diversity in a Majority-Hispanic Place

Michael S. Yoder and Renée LaPerrière de Gutiérrez

Studies of urban ethnic enclaves, or residential areas where minorities experience cohesion as a group, are growing in popularity in the present era of globalization, which is marked by historically high rates of migration. Such studies almost universally treat the ethnic groups in question in relation to the "host societies" or "charter groups" that constitute the historically dominant peoples of the regions in which migrants settle (Pacione 2001: 362–366). In the case of ethnic enclaves of the United States, the host society is usually, but not always, Anglo. Mike Davis (2000), for example, shows us that traditionally black inner-city areas can become Latino-dominant enclaves as blacks migrate to suburbs, as has occurred in greater Los Angeles, New York, and other northern cities. Thus, as demonstrated throughout this volume, most Latino communities, whether urban or rural, have recently been established and, in many cases, constitute a new phase of the filtering process in historically Anglo or black areas of cities.

Such is not the case, however, with Laredo, Texas, a historically Hispanic city comprising multiple generations of continuous occupation by Spaniards, Mexicans, and their offspring. This reality calls for a somewhat distinctive approach to the study of the Hispanic geography of Laredo, a city located directly on the border between Texas and Mexico. In Lower Rio Grande Valley cities of Texas such as McAllen, Brownsville, and Harlingen, Anglo majorities historically dominated the community's social and economic structure. A Hispanic underclass existed chiefly as labor, and, with few exceptions, a Hispanic middle class has only recently emerged. In Laredo, on the other hand, Hispanics have been dominant politically and socially for three centuries and, as a result, have constructed the social geography of the city and its surrounding rural hinterland (Arreola 2002).

Accordingly, this chapter examines the social geography of Laredo's neighborhoods and the increasing socioeconomic disparities that occur within the majority-Hispanic city. Such an approach will demonstrate the relatively unusual role that ethnicity and ethnic relations play in the social construction of this highly stratified community. Our study reveals that Laredo's historical isolation from other population centers in Texas and Mexico has created a geographical distinctiveness in this border city. Shared cultural traits transcend social class in Laredo, yet there are a variety of lifestyles and urban-design elements seen throughout the metropolitan area.

When Yoder recently announced in a lower-division college world geography class comprising predominantly Laredoans that the Latino population of the United States had reached parity with that of African Americans, surprisingly few of the students in the class reacted in any visible way. Follow-up questions posed on the spot produced the same result. It would be reasonable to regard this as an indication that the average worldview of students born in Laredo is framed more in terms of Laredo than of "mainstream" Anglo America. Ethnic identity among Laredo's Mexican Americans is quite unlike what is found in Los Angeles, Houston, or other American cities with sizable Latino populations.

One might argue that Laredo represents a departure from the cultural norms of mainstream America and, as such, exhibits a relationship between a distinctive group of people and their place that is typical of ethnic enclaves (Abrahamson 1996: 2). Many Laredoans identify with the particular place they occupy. Just as Latino enclaves within American cities are defined by language, local cuisine, family-run retail shops, architecture, and the like, Laredo is unique as an American city by virtue of such traits. Furthermore, despite strong kinship ties that bind the entire city, people nonetheless identify with particular neighborhoods in Laredo (Valdez 1993). This is especially evident in the dichotomy between the South Laredo of working-class barrios and low-income subdivisions and the North Laredo of middle- and upper-middle-class subdivisions and fast-paced, automobile-oriented commercial land uses that typify mainstream North American suburban style, or "suburbia Americana."

In this chapter, we provide a brief overview of Laredo's settlement history, particularly those aspects that underlie the city's unique character among Hispanic places. The discussion then turns to a description of the contemporary Laredo economy and the city's role in international trade insofar as these relate to social variability throughout the city. We describe the various sectors of the city and its neighborhoods and discuss pertinent aesthetic and lifestyle characteristics, such as housing, with attention to spatial patterns. Case studies of five neighborhoods, from working class to upper middle class, indicate the unique character of each of Laredo's many inner-city barrios and suburban subdivisions. Significantly, the case studies also shed light on the universality of many cultural practices throughout Laredo, lifestyle preferences, and kinship patterns that transcend social class. Examination of the social geography of neighborhoods enables researchers better to understand the dynamics that occur between and among the various social classes that make up a city whose citizenry is 94 percent Hispanic, 37 percent of whom lived below the poverty line in 1990 (U.S. Bureau of the Census 1992; Valdez 1993).

PHYSICAL SETTING AND SETTLEMENT HISTORY

Laredo is located along the Rio Grande in a semiarid portion of the Gulf Coastal Plain that is often referred to as the South Texas Plain. The city is approximately 150 miles inland from the barrier islands of the Coastal Bend of South Texas (Fig. 3.1). The Tamaulipan biotic province of which Laredo is a part is marked by xerophytic flora, gently rolling terrain with numerous arroyos and other small ephemeral streams that drain into the Rio Grande, and an annual rainfall just short of twenty inches (Everitt and Draw 1993: ix–x). The brushlike vegetation, referred to locally as *monte*, consists of short trees, shrubs, and numerous species of grasses and cactus. The region's limestone-dominated soils and dry climate, marked by 180 days a year of ninety-plus-degree temperatures (Fahrenheit), are agriculturally suitable for animal husbandry and not much else. The difficult environmental conditions account in part for the locality's relative isolation. Accordingly, sheep, goat, and cattle ranching, supplemented by small-scale irrigated agriculture, defines much of the region's economic history.

Spaniards established a permanent settlement at Laredo in 1755 after nearly a century of exploring the semiarid plains between the Spanish settlements of Monclova, in the present-day Mexican state of Coahuila, and San Antonio de Béxar, or present-day San Antonio, Texas (Arreola 2002). The Viceroyalty of New Spain felt it necessary to strengthen its presence in the region and to protect settlers against raids by the indigenous population. The riverbank location proved a worthy site to meet this objective. The meager indigenous population of the region practiced a largely migratory way of life that involved few permanent settlements. Thus, Spaniards were the first to bring urban culture to the region, on the north side of the river at present-day Laredo (Thompson 1986: 11).

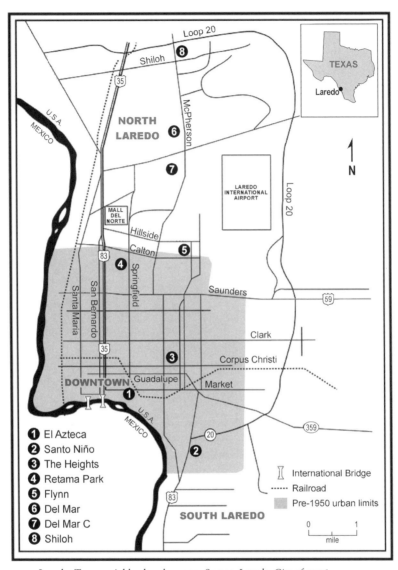

3.1.   Laredo, Texas, neighborhoods, 2002. *Source: Laredo, City of, 1996.*

José de Escandón, an explorer and the appointed governor of northeastern Mexico, was granted the authority in the 1740s to oversee settlement of
the region, including what would become the province of Nuevo Santander.
He gave authority to Capt. Tomás Sánchez in 1755 for the establishment
of the settlement of Laredo, adjacent to the Sánchez ranch (Laredo, City

of 1996: 6). In 1757, the population at Laredo included some sixty people who managed some ten thousand head of livestock. Land grants were long lots, called *porciones*, each of which was 9/13 of a mile in width along the river by eleven to sixteen miles long inland. Each had a rancho settlement, or small cluster of houses and buildings for the owners, landless laborers, and work equipment (Laredo, City of 1996: 36–37, 39–40). This early pattern of rancho social organization and settlement type, among other things, was the earliest version of a landscape of disparity that, in many ways, persists.

The Treaty of Guadalupe Hidalgo, signed February 2, 1848, established the border between the United States and Mexico at the Rio Grande, making Laredo an American town. Laredoans who desired to remain part of Mexico founded the adjacent city of Nuevo Laredo on the other side of the river. Combined, the two Laredos are known locally as "Los Dos" (The Two). Creation of the border initiated the binational trade between the two Laredos that today so strongly defines their character.

In 1881, rail traffic began to cross the Rio Grande, and the importance of the two cities in binational trade was enhanced (Thompson 1986: 259). Ever since, transborder trade, border security, and the interdiction of contraband and migrants have largely defined the Laredo economy. By the late twentieth century, Laredo/Nuevo Laredo had become a primary cargo crossing point between the United States and Mexico. In 2000, for example, 38 percent of all trade between the United States and Mexico, and about half of all overland trade between the two countries passed through Laredo and Nuevo Laredo (Laredo Development Foundation 2000a).

CONTEMPORARY ECONOMY

The dramatic increase in binational trade throughout the latter twentieth century stimulated the expansion of and improvements in transportation infrastructure in Laredo. This is particularly evident on the north and northwest sides of the city, where dozens of giant warehouses and truck-storage lots dominate the use of land. Two of the international bridges at Laredo and the surrounding area are chiefly oriented toward truck traffic. Intermodal shipping, with linkages between air, rail, and highway, is well developed in the locality. Mexico's Highway 85, which links Nuevo Laredo and Mexico City, is the only four-lane highway from Mexico's capital to the U.S. border. The railroad line between Mexico City and Nuevo Laredo is the only line between Central Mexico and the border with concrete-reinforced ties. Laredo is the southern terminus of the U.S. Interstate 35 corridor, a major freight artery between the south-central United States and the upper Midwest. The Texas Mexican Railway Company (TMRC) provides rail service from the two Laredos into Mexico and to the port of Corpus Christi, Texas. The Union Pacific Railway provides freight service between Laredo and the upper Midwest. The linkage of these railroads at Laredo accommodates the crossing of freight at the border. The convergence of multiple transportation modes, including rail, highway, maritime shipping, and air cargo, underlies the establishment of at least 210 trucking companies, 515 freight forwarders, and 91 customs brokerage firms in Laredo (Adams 2000; LDF 2000a).

The maquiladora sector of the economy at Los Dos Laredos benefits to some extent from the transportation advantages of the two cities. However, maquiladoras in Los Dos are relatively less important than in many other border metropolitan areas. While an inexpensive Mexican workforce exists in Nuevo Laredo, it is not as abundant as in other Mexican border cities ("Warehouses Are Booming in Laredo" 2000). Furthermore, maquiladoras established in Mexican border cities sometimes require a corresponding warehousing facility in the adjacent sister city of the United States for distribution of parts and assembled products (Wilson 1992). Three-fourths of Nuevo Laredo's seventy-six maquiladoras have corresponding warehousing facilities in Laredo (LDF 2001). The relatively high land costs in Laredo make the location somewhat less attractive than other border cities for in-bond manufacturing, but the transportation linkages partially offset that disadvantage.

While local government, business associations, and banks aggressively market Laredo/Nuevo Laredo as a viable location for the establishment of manufacturing plants, the business-government alliance emphasizes the port function of the cities even more. Nonetheless, civic boosters in Laredo estimate that blue-collar warehouse employees and maquiladora management personnel who live in Laredo number close to three thousand (LDF 2000b), though this number is probably overstated.

Transportation-related businesses seem more willing to invest in land-extensive warehousing and trailer-parking facilities in Laredo, which employ relatively few workers, but occupy large spaces and frequently require installation of paved areas and road maintenance. Warehousing employs fewer people than its physical domination of the landscape would suggest. The local government-business alliance pursues an economic development strategy, in part at taxpayers' expense, that is wasteful of land and does not generate a sufficient salary base to boost the standard of living to a noticeable extent (Yoder and Pisani, forthcoming).

The employment that international trade and its associated services generates, though modest, is regarded as crucial to Laredo's economy in light of the passage and implementation of the North American Free Trade Agreement (NAFTA) in the 1990s (LDF 2000a). Besides the storage of goods that pass in both directions over the border, other international trade-related activities include shuttling goods by eighteen-wheelers between the warehouses and trailer-storage lots of Laredo and trailer-storage lots in Nuevo Laredo. Customs brokerage houses clear parts and finished goods before they cross into Mexico. These activities result in a built environment dominated by warehousing and trailer storage, which might present the casual observer a false sense that abundant employment opportunities exist for unskilled and semiskilled labor. In reality, many companies are not Laredo based, and profits leave the area. Owners of customs brokerage firms, however, profit handsomely from the artificialities of the border (Giermanski 1997). Realtors frequently remark that many of these entrepreneurs purchase luxury homes in Laredo's suburban upper-middle-class residential neighborhoods on the city's north side.

Border retailing also defines the Laredo economy. Laredo's shopping centers and central business district cater to shoppers not only from the two cities, but also from nearby interior Mexican cities such as Monterrey and Saltillo (Arreola and Curtis 1993). In 1999, retail sales totaled nearly two billion dollars and employed a larger portion of the Laredo workforce than any other segment of the economy (Texas Center and Laredo Chamber of Commerce 2002: 9). The border-interdiction economy, involving a multitude of federal, state, and local law enforcement officials, is rapidly growing in light of the increase in trafficking of drugs and undocumented immigrants since the 1970s and the collective national unease in the wake of the events of September 11, 2001. In 1999, more than twelve hundred federal employees of the Immigration and Naturalization Service were stationed in Laredo (LDF 2000a). This number had reached 1,575 in February 2002 (LDF 2002). This segment of the workforce, which is largely Hispanic, increasingly represents a major component of the suburban population on the city's north side.

Despite the relatively poor local income-generating capabilities of the transportation and maquiladora industries, Laredo's high birthrate by U.S. standards and the continued influx of immigrants from Mexico have fueled a construction boom—two new hospitals, a fourth international bridge with a fifth planned, a university campus, a community college satellite campus, a sports arena, numerous new warehouses, and more than fifteen hundred new homes per year in the late 1990s. In 1998 alone, new warehouse construction increased warehousing space by 31 percent (LDF 2000a).

Compared with the Texas average, wage rates among Laredo's economically active population of seventy-five thousand are low and unemployment rates are high. The 37.0 percent of Laredo's population living below the poverty line in 1990 was more than double the state's average. The average weekly wage of $439 at the end of 1999 was approximately 40.0 percent below the state average of $713 (Texas Workforce Commission 2000). Laredo's per capita income of less than $13,000 was a meager 54.8 percent and 51.4 percent of the state's and the nation's per capita income, respectively (Texas Workforce Commission 2000). The unemployment rate of 8.0 percent in the summer of 2000 was higher than the national and state averages, though lower than that of other large Texas border communities. To add insult to injury, the cost of living, adjusted for median household income, was the highest in Texas, and the fifth highest in the United States at the end of 1998 (Demographia 1999). Such conditions hamper upward social mobility.

If we look at state and national norms, social disparities are evident in Laredo, and like the state's other border cities, it fares poorly in terms of standard of living. As the following discussion illustrates, however, disparities within the Laredo metropolitan area are even more dramatic.

Laredo exhibits a diverse social geography. This ranges from aging low-income inner-city barrios to new starter-home subdivisions in the working-class south side of the city, middle-and upper-middle-class "suburbia Americana" in North Laredo, and exurban *colonias* populated by an underclass that is sprinkled about the rural countryside east, south, and northwest of the city.

THE INNER-CITY BARRIOS OF EL AZTECA AND SANTO NIÑO

Despite Laredo's nearly 250-year history, the vast majority of the city's built environment emerged after 1935, including several neighborhoods that fit the category of inner-city barrios. Somewhat surprisingly, even though the city has Spanish origins, its urban geography strongly fits the quintessential pattern found throughout the United States of three primary and separate zones: the central business district, the inner-city zone in transition comprising neighborhoods with a mix of residential and light commercial land uses, and the suburban fringe, dominated by automobile-oriented and segregated subdivisions and commercial functions. According to a study commissioned in 1998 by the City of Laredo, the mean household income of nearly all inner-city barrios was less than $20,000, and most existed at or below the poverty level. In stark architectural and socioeconomic contrast were the upper-middle class subdivisions of the north side, nearly all of which averaged over $40,000 in mean income, and some of which averaged over $50,000 (Laredo, City of 1998).

The oldest surviving barrio is El Azteca, located immediately east of the historic central business district, or downtown (see Fig. 3.1). Natural boundaries on the south (the Rio Grande) and the east (Zacate Creek) and a rather intimidating artificial western barrier—the terminus of Interstate Highway 35, which leads directly by bridge to Nuevo Laredo—encircle El Azteca. One can drive through the city of Laredo and never actually encounter this barrio, which has been nominated for national historic neighborhood status (Myers 2000: 24). Often exaggeratedly designated as the city's first working-class barrio, the neighborhood, in fact, historically has supported a wide array of lifestyles, socioeconomic levels, and land uses, including both residences and family-run businesses.

Today the barrio exhibits architectural features dating from the latter nineteenth century to the present, though more than half the buildings are over fifty years old (Love and Duggan Real Estate Consultants and Appraisers 1989: 15; Myers 2000: 11). Typical street scenes include many examples of the prevalent board-and-batten working-class house. The neighborhood in general has a shabby, neglected appearance, but ethnic pride is exhibited on the walls of old brick buildings (Fig. 3.2).

Upon closer inspection, however, several obvious architectural features serve as strong indicators that the working-class designation of the neighborhood may be recent. To be sure, the 1900 City Directory of Laredo indicates that of 453 employed persons in the neighborhood, 35 percent were categorized as laborer, day laborer, farm laborer, or railroad laborer. Indeed, in 1900, the Mexican National Railway workshops were located immediately across Zacate Creek from El Azteca, and the neighborhood was home to many of its laborers. Railroad shop supervisors also lived in the neighborhood. Moreover, as the City Directory indicates, several merchants and ranchers lived in the neighborhood.

House types reflect the early economic diversity of the population. Spacious stone houses coexist alongside smaller wood-frame and brick houses.

Many small commercial businesses have also played an important role in the history of El Azteca. The neighborhood was originally named El Ranchero for a store that would grind corn and sell the masa (cornmeal) to local residents. The name changed to El Azteca once the Teatro Nacional (originally constructed in 1922 on Lincoln Street, a main thoroughfare linking the neighborhood with downtown Laredo) was changed to the Azteca

3.2.   Community mural on historic brick building in El Azteca neighborhood, Laredo, Texas. *Photograph by D. Arreola, 1997.*

Movie Theater in the 1930s (Laredo, City of 1996). Many of El Azteca's brick buildings are identifiably dual-purpose grocery stores with attached residences, either above or behind the store, to house the owner.

Architectural diversity, in combination with aesthetically, nonfunctional architectural details, reflects the attainment of a social level at which the mere provision of a roof over one's head had been achieved and surpassed. It is likely that some of the early neighborhood merchants who aspired to a middle-class sensibility lived in these houses. Today, however, the barrio is in fact closer to being homogeneously working poor.

Several issues collectively contribute to the identification of El Azteca as a working-class barrio. Very little visible gentrification has occurred, despite the persistence in the minds of Laredoans of the neighborhood's historically viable architectural features and streetscapes and efforts to promote the neighborhood as historic (Myers 2000: 24). The median income of the barrio in 1998 remained less than $10,000, and unemployment rose between 1990 and 1998 (Laredo, City of 1998). Abandonment of several homes is apparent, which may be both cause and effect of the increase in illegal drug activity that has plagued the neighborhood in recent years. According to sociologist Avelardo Valdez (1993), the Azteca neighborhood, located directly across the river from Nuevo Laredo's La Victoria neighborhood, is ideal for drug smuggling. El Azteca is also near downtown

Laredo, and smugglers can import both drugs and undocumented immigrants into the vicinity along the riverbanks, hide them there, and dispose of them downtown with little fear of getting caught by law enforcement officials. Further, Valdez (1993: 187) found that a notable portion of El Azteca's population consists of two poor groups: first-generation immigrants from Mexico who have lived in the neighborhood for forty or more years, and a new wave of recent immigrants.

It is quite likely that two additional phenomena served to gradually transform El Azteca into a more socially homogeneous working-class barrio during the twentieth century: the construction of the historically important upper-class and largely Anglo streetcar suburb of The Heights between 1890 and 1920 (discussed below); and the gentrification in recent decades of the largely Anglo St. Peters historic neighborhood, immediately northwest of downtown and named for St. Peters church, located in its midst. Both neighborhoods represent historically attractive places that could lure upwardly mobile citizens out of El Azteca.

Santo Niño, one of many working-class barrios of South Laredo (see Fig. 3.1), was laid out in the 1920s and settled through the 1940s on former dairy farm land and what was then the southern margin of the city, south of Chacon Creek (Laredo, City of 1996: 26). Santo Niño has been described as a close-knit community of working-poor Mexican American families (Valdez 1993: 191). Avelardo Valdez concludes that the high incidence of drug use, drug dealing, other forms of petty crime, and the reputation of the barrio as tough and dangerous are tied to its poverty. For example, automobile body shops and tire repair shops are common in Santo Niño. Many of these function as "chop shops" that dismantle stolen vehicles for the used automobile parts economy, and many harbor illicit drug trafficking. These enterprises have linkages that are national and extend beyond the Laredo area. Thus, Valdez (1993: 191–192) concludes, the neighborhood's crime rings are among the most sophisticated in all of Laredo.

The neighborhood generally has an unkempt look about it, with haphazardly parked cars, aging mobile homes, and poorly maintained houses constructed of wood, brick, or a mixture in those cases where rooms were added on at different times and under varying family-income conditions (Fig. 3.3). When improvements are made, they often include the use of burglar bars and brightly colored paint, which give the neighborhood a Mexican American feel. As in El Azteca, population densities are moderately high, in the range of 5,000–9,999 per square mile, and median household income is approximately $16,000, making it among Laredo's poorest neighborhoods (Laredo, City of 1998).

Valdez (1993: 191–193) found through interviews that longtime resi-

3.3.   Typical street-front housescape in Santo Niño neighborhood, Laredo, Texas. Note fence enclosure, yard shrine at left, and yard furniture. *Photograph by D. Arreola, 1997.*

dents of the neighborhood lament its deterioration since the 1960s. Prior to that decade, the neighborhood was poor, but had a largely suburban character to it, because it was then the southernmost point of Laredo's built zone. Neighbors interacted in positive ways with one another and looked out for each other's well-being. There has since been a diminishing of trust and other aspects of neighbor relations as crime and population have risen. A general feeling of suspicion pervades Santo Niño, and Valdez's interviewees felt crime was the culprit. Today one can still observe the unsightliness of the Zapata Highway (U.S. 83) commercial strip, lined in the early 1980s with, as Valdez describes them, unattractive commercial land uses that form a psychological barrier into the neighborhood.

THE HEIGHTS, A STREETCAR SUBURB

In 1888, seven out-of-town investors formed an entity called the Laredo Improvement Company (LIC), whose primary objective was to construct a streetcar system in Laredo. Laredo's city council granted LIC the rights to acquire the real estate and rights-of-way necessary for construction.

Once these rights were obtained, LIC created the Laredo Electric Railway Company. Among the routes established by this company by the end of 1889 was a lengthy line running east from downtown Laredo to Meadow Street, where the line turned north. Between 1889 and 1895, with the urging of management and other executives of the newly established Texas Mexican Railroad, most of whom were Anglos, LIC embarked on real estate development by creating Laredo's first streetcar suburb, known today as The Heights (Calderón 1993: 579; Devine 1967) (see Fig. 3.1).

The oldest and largest homes of The Heights are along Market Street and parallel streets adjacent to Market, along which ran the east-west portion of the trolley route. Today Market Street is the southern end of The Heights. The remaining streets of the suburb were constructed in proximity to the north-south trending portion of the trolley line, along Meadow Street. The earliest homes were built primarily of brick in the Victorian (Queen Anne) style. The decade 1900–1910 saw a boom in the construction of brick bungalows and prairie-style homes. Few Spanish surnames appear among the list of residents during this initial twenty years of development (Shanks 1993: 3). Another home-building boom in the 1920s occurred, with some large mission revival– and Moorish-style stucco homes adding a new architectural flavor to the neighborhood. In the 1930s, The Heights reached as far north as Clark Boulevard (Eastern Division Research 1981: 1–3). A lull in construction lasted during the later depression years and into World War II. After 1945, the building of homes resumed, especially in the north and northeast areas of the suburb. It was during these early postwar years that builders began to construct smaller, lower-cost tract houses in what is today the easternmost portion of The Heights (Beasley 1981: 42).

Among all of Laredo's neighborhoods, perhaps the greatest number of types of houses and market values exist in The Heights. One can observe a mobile home, a mansion, and multiple middle-class frame or brick houses within an area of two or three blocks. During the 1999–2001 period, for example, *The Real Estate Source: Laredo's Catalog of Homes*, a guide to residential real estate, listed some sixty-four homes for sale in The Heights, with prices ranging from $45,000 to $550,000. Nearly half were listed in the range of $100,000 to $200,000. The least-expensive houses tended to be located in the southwestern portion, often in areas with mixed commercial and residential zoning. Small apartment buildings, such as fourplexes, are scattered throughout the neighborhood, primarily in the southern section.

Professions and income levels of Heights residents vary widely. Interviewed in 1980, Luciano Guajardo, lifelong resident of Laredo's inner city and longtime director of the Laredo Public Library, said The Heights could no longer be regarded as a "gringo neighborhood." The shift from the initial Anglo dominance of the suburb occurred in the 1920s as Hispanic professionals, including doctors, merchants, and lawyers, moved into the neighborhood (Guajardo 1981). Data from the 2000 Census for the eight-block groups of the four census tracts that make up The Heights indicate that its population is 93.5 percent Hispanic, and 54.7 percent of the lived-in units are owner occupied (U.S. Bureau of the Census 2000).

Today, the northern and eastern portions of The Heights, for the most part, have retained the purely residential character they possessed more than fifty-five years ago. The few small businesses that exist, such as the occasional convenience store, are limited to the main thoroughfares, such as Meadow Street. The southern portion of The Heights, the oldest section, however, has been largely transformed into a mix of commercial and residential land uses. This can be quite unsightly, especially where setbacks separate commercial strip malls from the architectural flow of the streetscape. Guadalupe, Chihuahua, and Market Streets, the main east-west trending boulevards, contain banks, strip malls, a large supermarket, gas stations, franchise convenience stores, and fast-food restaurants. Locally owned businesses include flower and gift shops and auto parts stores, among others. The generic suburbia Americana style is increasingly dominating the appearance of these streetscapes. Any distinctive Mexican American flavor is limited to a few bilingual signs and the occasional use of bright paint, especially in the few cases where residential houses have been converted to businesses (Fig. 3.4).

DEL MAR AND SHILOH: SUBURBIA AMERICANA

The quintessential autocentric suburbia Americana style that defines the character of the post–World War II United States was relatively late to arrive in Laredo. Montrose (sometimes known as "El Monte"), Laredo's first controlled-access subdivision intended for motorists, evolved between 1900 and 1930 immediately southeast of The Heights (Laredo, City of 1996: 26). The first automobile-oriented subdivision that was separated by farm- or ranchland from today's zone-in-transition barrios was the neighborhood of Calton Gardens, developed in the mid-1920s in a grid pattern off the San Antonio Highway (now San Bernardo Avenue) immediately to the north of the city limits. At first, this type of detached suburb had only limited popularity in Laredo. By 1935, a decade after its establishment, only six homes had been built in Calton Gardens (Laredo, City of 1996).

3.4.   Commercial streetscape in Laredo, Texas. *Photograph by D. Arreola, 1997.*

The trademark curvilinear streets and cul-de-sacs of suburbia Americana first appeared in 1957 as Retama Park, a subdivision named after a local tree species (see Fig. 3.1). The neighborhood, which contains speculation houses built by local builders, adjoins the north side of the barrio of Las Cruces. Today, because it is aging, Retama and its predominantly brick homes somewhat resemble an inner-city barrio, but without the latter's preponderance of small-scale commercial land uses. Also established in the late 1950s was housing for the Laredo Air Force Base, a gunnery school that was operated from 1941 to 1945, and again from 1952 to 1973 (Guide to Laredo Air Force Base N.d.). Small brick ranch-style duplexes and single-family homes on curvilinear streets and cul-de-sacs housed the military personnel stationed at the base until its closing in 1973, at which time it was donated to the City of Laredo as the Laredo International Airport. Since that time, the single-family homes and some of the duplexes have become Flynn, a subdivision of privately owned residences (see Fig. 3.1). Some duplexes at the southern edge of Flynn are public housing units operated by the City of Laredo Housing Authority. What started out as a community to serve the relatively self-contained military base became one of the first automobile-oriented subdivisions detached from the city. Today it is a working-class neighborhood that is beginning to show signs of neglect and disrepair. Its contemporary North American design has remained intact, except for a few homes and duplex units on which burglar bars or brightly colored paint have been added to the exteriors.

The first suburb of significant size, Del Mar, was developed in the mid-1960s on a melon farm by the Trautmann family, whose fortunes derived originally from agriculture and investments in residential real estate (Guerra 2002; Moore 1996). Del Mar represents Laredo's first large-scale detached suburb (see Fig. 3.1). It was originally separated from the northern edge of the city's built zone by a nearly three-mile band of ranchland, which has since become nearly completely filled in with numerous other automobile-oriented subdivisions. It began as an unincorporated community, but was annexed in 1981 by the city. Its curvilinear streets, driveways filled with sport utility vehicles and minivans, palm and oak trees, green front lawns, and predominantly Spanish- and ranch-style brick and stucco homes make up the stereotypical suburban ensemble that is a familiar sight throughout the Sunbelt.

The Del Mar suburb had a somewhat difficult beginning. Bankers in Laredo were reluctant at first to provide credit for a community that was separated from the city by a large area of undeveloped land, and one marketed for the relatively small Anglo population, including officers from the air base. But the instant popularity of the planned community, with its relatively demanding deed restrictions on landscaping and its absence of commercial land uses, led to the growth of the community (Guerra 2002). Wealthy Hispanics as well as air force officers who preferred a more generic North American suburban way of life and isolation from Laredo proper felt at home in Del Mar (Herrera 2002).

Because Del Mar was unincorporated, and therefore separate from the jurisdiction of Laredo, it had to establish a municipal utility district, which was granted taxing authority by the State of Texas to provide and manage water and sewerage to the community. Del Mar established its own fire department, and Webb County's Sheriff's Department then served as the community police force (Guerra 2002). A private Catholic elementary school, a public high school, and a public elementary school all were constructed in the 1960s.

The original section is beginning to show signs of aging, but Del Mar's well-shaded homes can list at $110,000 to $135,000. Del Mar C, to the south, is the newest section with the highest income level and real estate values (see Fig. 3.1). Homes there carry a market price of approximately $170,000 to $250,000 (Cowley and Pechacek 2001).

At first glance, Del Mar, a sea of driveways, homes dominated by garages in the front, front yards planted in St. Augustine grass, and exotic trees, appears to merely replicate the generic architecture, landscaping, and spatial layout of suburban subdivisions throughout Texas. In short, Del Mar is architecturally and politically more Anglo Texan than Mexican American.

There are, however, some features of Del Mar that are uniquely Laredo. *Carnes asadas*—cookouts involving extended families—change the character of Del Mar on weekends, when streets become overcrowded with the cars of visiting relatives. The *palapa,* a gazebo-type open structure under which the grilling of meat occurs and a universal feature throughout Laredo, is common to the backyards of many Del Mar homes. Burglar bars mask the windows of many Del Mar residences. In a few cases, stucco or wood trim is painted aqua, yellow, or some other bright color. The local Tejano and accordion-based *norteño* styles of music that are commonly heard throughout Laredo blast from car radios and jam boxes in garages, driveways, and backyards.

In spite of its slow beginnings, Del Mar became a huge success and has served as a model for the subsequent suburban sprawling of North Laredo. The empty area between Del Mar and Laredo proper has since become almost entirely filled by such successful subdivisions as Hillside and Chaparral Village. Since the late 1980s, however, owing to the rapid growth of the middle class, most of the new growth has occurred north and northwest of Del Mar, where some two dozen additional subdivisions have emerged. Ironically, nearly half of this suburban sprawl has occurred since 1994, the year of a significant devaluation of the Mexican peso that, as widely reported in the popular press, adversely affected Laredo's economy, particularly retail sales to Mexican shoppers.

Among the sprawling new communities is Shiloh, a suburban sector that comprises six subdivisions and six condominium complexes and whose development began in the early 1990s and continues to the present (see Fig. 3.1). It was developed by the Arnulfo Santos family, which owned a large tract of land from I-35 eastward along what is now Shiloh Boulevard. Today the Santos and Associates Realty Company continues to be a major real estate and development firm in Laredo. Architecturally, homes in Shiloh are primarily variations of what realtors refer to as contemporary ranch style. Another appropriate description might be neoeclectic, or perhaps postmodern, to signify the blending of elements of ranch, contemporary, Spanish, mission revival, classical revival, Mediterranean, and even Mexican vernacular styles within the same house (Arreola and Curtis 1993) (Fig. 3.5).

Personnel required by the border-interdiction economy, as well as edu-

3.5.   "Suburbia Americana," with characteristic curvilinear streets, neotraditional housing, and St. Augustine lawns in Shiloh neighborhood, Laredo, Texas. *Photograph by D. Arreola, 1997.*

cators, skilled repairpersons, law enforcement officials, health-care personnel, and owners or managers of customs brokerage and freight-forwarding agencies are among the residents of Shiloh and other North Laredo middle-class subdivisions. On weekends, the aroma of Shiloh can change dramatically as extended families get together for *carnes asadas*. These events cause the suburban residential streets to become clogged with the parked cars of relatives, and the sounds of Tejano, cumbia, and *norteño* music resonate throughout, much as in Laredo's inner-city barrios. Thus, while north side residents earn more than do residents in the barrios, culture and extended family link the stark segregation that afflicts major multiethnic, multiracial metropolitan areas elsewhere in the United States.

Economically, the suburban fringe contains an array of neighborhoods, from the starter-home subdivisions of the Mines Road and aging first-ring automobile subdivisions like Retama Park to the Shiloh subdivisions and the wealthy Plantation development, with its attractive and well-maintained country club and golf course. As indicated in *The Real Estate Source*, listed prices for homes range from the mid-$70,000s to $150,000 in the older north-side neighborhoods; from the mid-$80,000s to $130,000 in north-side starter-home subdivisions; and from $95,000 to $150,000 in the Shiloh subdivisions. North-side condominiums in Shiloh range from $70,000 to $130,000. By comparison, new south-side starter homes range in price from the high $50,000s to the mid-$70,000s. Thus, not only is there a strong contrast in standard of living between inner-city barrios and the suburban fringe, but an almost equally striking contrast exists throughout the entire suburban zone circling Laredo on three sides.

Median household incomes also vary widely throughout the suburban fringe. In the starter-home subdivisions of the South Laredo suburban fringe, annual median incomes range from $10,000 to $39,000. Annual median household incomes of starter-home subdivisions and aging first-ring automobile subdivisions on the north side fall within the range of $30,000 to $39,000. Annual median household incomes of Shiloh and the wealthy Plantation development residents fall within the range of $50,000 to $75,000 (Laredo, City of 1998).

The north-south socioeconomic divide in Laredo is illustrated remarkably well by commercial real estate. Nearly all office space outside of the central business district is scattered throughout North Laredo. Mall del Norte, a major regional shopping mall with 1.19 million square feet of retail space and located three miles north of the central business district along I-35, serves as the city's primary retail and entertainment hub (see Fig. 3.1). Several franchise restaurants, some upscale, and motels line the freeway access roads from the mall northward for four exits. Strip shopping centers in the vicinity of the mall, along the north-south-trending McPherson Road two miles east of the interstate, and along the major thoroughfares linking I-35 and McPherson Road, house locally owned and franchise retail shops and offices for various consumer services. Comparatively speaking, South Laredo contains a much smaller number of retail outlets and very little office space. Pawnshops and automobile parts stores, and a few fast-food franchises stand out as the major occupants of strip shopping centers and stand-alone retail buildings along the Zapata Highway, South Laredo's primary commercial corridor. Retail businesses exhibit a stronger presence on the north side because of the higher income there and proximity to the interstate, which captures middle- and upper-class shoppers from Mexico.

EXURBAN *COLONIAS*

The most unfortunate visible evidence of socioeconomic disparity in the Laredo area lies beyond the suburban fringe in the nearly two dozen *colonias* in rural areas east, south, and northwest of the city. *Colonias* are rural subdivisions created on unused ranchland by landowners seeking a means to generate capital. Although they are not incorporated into the City of Laredo, as a source of low-cost labor and housing, they hold an important place in Laredo's social geography. Because they are remote and lack many basic services such as water, sewerage, natural gas, paved streets, and, in a few cases, electricity, lot prices are within the reach of many of Laredo's poorest citizens (Ward 1999). The lack of services and poor access to jobs in Laredo have prompted many passionate critiques of these neighborhoods and criticisms of the developers who create them and profit from the misfortunes of the region's poor. Housing ranges from makeshift clapboard shacks to mobile homes of various ages and levels of quality to brick homes. Abandoned and sometimes rusted-out vehicles and chickens and other livestock are not uncommon (Rust 1993). As in many of Laredo's barrios, nuclear families that are part of extended families frequently live adjacent to one another, with dwellings arranged in small groupings, giving *colonias* a Mexican American flavor. On the other hand, landscaping with exotic tree species and grass—the norm in Laredo's commodified suburban communities—is practically nonexistent in *colonias,* which, instead, make effective use of native vegetation.

Colonias have received much attention in political circles since the 1990s. In spite of this, they remain economically backward communities with high rates of unemployment. The driving factor of sustained misfortune, according to Smith (2000), is a vicious cycle that derives from remote location, associated cost and difficulty of transportation to jobs, the forgoing of education due to the time involved in commuting to low-paying jobs in Laredo, and the lack of on-the-job training. Because population densities in *colonias* are relatively low and they tend to be spread out, there is little economic feasibility in bringing manufacturing plants or other employment-generating facilities to the sites. The ability of manufacturers to establish low-wage maquiladora assembly plants in Nuevo Laredo precludes the creation of such plants in the *colonias* or in any other area of Laredo, for that matter. Instead, *colonia* residents tend to take on construction, warehouse, and domestic (housecleaning or gardening and landscaping) jobs in Laredo.

CONCLUSIONS

Laredo is a unique Hispanic place in the United States. It is intimately tied to its sister city of Nuevo Laredo economically and culturally through maquiladoras, freight forwarding, retail shopping, tourism, and even a binational baseball team, the Tecolotes (Owls) of Los Dos Laredos (Klein

1997). In contrast to conditions found in major Hispanic places throughout the United States, the stark social disparities that exist in Laredo are not racial or ethnic in nature. Shiloh, among the most racially diverse subregions of the city, is 88 percent Hispanic; Del Mar is 91 percent Hispanic; The Heights, 93 percent; El Azteca, 95 percent; and Santo Niño, 96 percent (U.S. Bureau of the Census 2000). Thus, there is little difference in the Hispanic percentage of the population between the poorest of inner-city barrios and the quintessential suburban upper-middle-class north.

A strong socioeconomic divide exists between working-poor Laredoans and the well-to-do. This dichotomy is apparent in spatial patterns of employment and income, disparities between North and South Laredo, and control over land use, planning, and zoning. Our empirical observations and an informal survey of students and faculty at Texas A&M International University corroborate Valdez' (1993) findings that the inner-city barrios largely comprise a blue-collar and low- to semiskilled workforce. The survey and our observations also substantiate the assertion that the northern suburbs contain households whose incomes derive from skilled or professional positions in such areas as law enforcement, border interdiction, public school teaching, medical care, and freight forwarding and customs brokerage. Freight forwarding and customs brokerage employ a sizable group of Mexican nationals who set up their operations on the U.S. side of the border so they may be paid in dollars and can reside in Laredo (De León 2002). The city's business and government elite, for the most part, live in north-side upper-class subdivisions and The Heights.

Questions linger about the social geography of Laredo in light of NAFTA, the war on drugs, and the catastrophe of September 11, 2001. Will the border, which has so strongly defined Laredo's character for more than 150 years, become more porous or less? Can the border ever become a catalyst for meaningful social and economic improvement in the city? The logic of NAFTA would suggest that traffic should cross the border in either direction more quickly and with less regulation, thereby diminishing customs and freight-forwarding operations (Giermanski 1997). Although binational trade has resulted in an economic landscape dominated by warehousing and truck-trailer storage, it employs only about 8 percent of Laredo's workforce, and NAFTA presumably could further reduce this source of outside capital (Giermanski 1998).

Increased attention to border security as long as international terrorism remains a threat makes this scenario less likely. Washington already is increasing its presence in Laredo in the form of federal law enforcement personnel. Can Laredo break its dependence on these two primary sources for generating outside funds, both of which are structurally tenuous? Can local enterprises develop that can draw sufficient income and sales from outside the region and lead to a more articulated economy and higher salaries?

Laredo's relative isolation from major population centers of the United States and Mexico underlies the unique character of the city's social geography. Thus, despite expanded free trade and geopolitical security concerns along the border, most likely, the stark inequities that challenge traditional community ties across Laredo will persist. Rapid population growth that continues, despite the discouraging persistence of lower-than-average income levels, remains largely Hispanic. The Anglo proportion of the population, 6 percent to 7 percent, has remained roughly the same for decades, so little need exists among Laredoans of Mexican descent to assert their ethnic identity in architecture or in urban design. Most likely, the consumption of suburbia Americana land-use styles will persist, and the spatial build-out of Laredo, following generic Sunbelt norms, will continue. Bilingual signs and Mexican decorative adornments undoubtedly will remain common features of Laredo's cultural landscape, as the residents of this remote area pursue as best they can their unique border version of the American dream.

II

DISCONTINUOUS COMMUNITIES

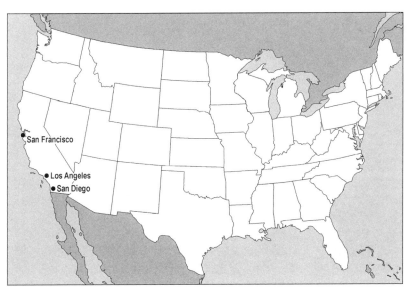

Map 2. Discontinuous communities.

BARRIO UNDER SIEGE

Latino Sense of Place in San Francisco, California

Brian J. Godfrey

San Francisco's Latino community does not rival in size or visibility such predominantly Hispanic metropolises as Los Angeles and Miami, but it boasts a long-term cultural contribution to an ethnically diverse and cosmopolitan city. Widely admired for its historic qualities, scenic charms, and social tolerance—and economically propelled by the Bay Area's high-technology boom—San Francisco became one of America's most expensive real estate markets in the late twentieth century.

This multicultural mecca has long attracted a heterogeneous mix of Latin Americans, mainly of Mexican and Central American origin. Although they have faced problems caused by gentrification and displacement in recent years, Hispanics have survived as a significant presence in San Francisco. The resilience of this vibrant Latino community raises issues of ethnic persistence amid neighborhood change that are relevant to Hispanic populations in other U.S. central cities. This chapter examines the Latino sense of place in San Francisco's Mission District, where a distinctive barrio has grown up despite—indeed, in part because of—the intense pressures of gentrification and urban redevelopment.

ETHNIC POPULATION AND HOUSING

According to the U.S. Census, which may undercount the number of undocumented residents, 14.2 percent of San Franciscans were of Hispanic origin in 1970, and 14.1 percent in 2000. Although the local Hispanic population did not explode, as did the Asian American population, which more than doubled through immigration, from 13.6 percent to 31.3 percent of the total population over the same thirty-year period, the fact that Lati-

TABLE 4.1—SAN FRANCISCO'S POPULATION, BY RACE AND HISPANIC ORIGIN

GROUP	1970		1980		1990		2000	
	POPULATION	% OF TOTAL	POPULATION	% OF TOTAL	POPULATION	% OF TOTAL	POPULATION	% OF TOTAL
WHITE	409,285	57.2	395,082	58.2	387,783	53.6	385,728	49.7
BLACK/ AFRICAN AMERICAN	96,078	13.4	86,414	12.7	79,039	10.9	60,515	7.8
AMERICAN INDIAN	2,900	0.4	3,548	0.5	3,456	0.5	3,458	0.4
ASIAN/ PACIFIC ISLANDER	95,095	13.3	147,426	21.7	210,876	29.1	243,409	31.3
OTHER RACES	10,415	1.5	46,504	6.8	42,805	5.9	83,628	10.7
HISPANIC ORIGIN/ LATINO	101,901	14.2	83,373	12.3	100,717	13.9	109,504	14.1
TOTAL	715,674	100.0	678,974	100.0	723,959	100.0	776,738	100.0

Sources: U.S. Bureau of the Census 1972, 1981, 1993, 2000.
Note: 1970 data regard Latino/Hispanic to be a racial category, while 1980–2000 statistics consider it an ethnic heritage overlapping other racial classifications.

nos remained demographically stable as a sizable minority is noteworthy in a popular city known for expensive housing. In contrast, the African American population declined from 13.4 percent of the city's total in 1970 to 7.8 percent in 2000, largely as a result of urban renewal in historically black neighborhoods (Table 4.1).

Although many San Francisco neighborhoods are racially integrated, each of the city's three major ethnic blocs exhibits a distinctive residential distribution. Non-Hispanic whites remain the city's largest racial group, but their percentage has dropped steadily since 1970, to about half the total population. Whites are the most likely to reside in homogeneous neighborhoods: twenty-four census tracts were over three-quarters white in 2000, as opposed to only four for Asian Americans, and none for Hispanics and African Americans (U.S. Bureau of the Census 2000). White residents cluster in the city's wealthy northern districts like Pacific Heights and the Presidio as well as in gentrified central neighborhoods like Haight-Ashbury, Noe Valley, and Castro. Chinatown remains over 95 percent Chinese, while upwardly mobile Asian Americans have dispersed into western and southern districts, such as Richmond, Sunset, and Outer Mission. The African American population has declined in recent decades, but it has retained residential nuclei from World War II–era migrations, most notably Bayview–Hunters Point and the Western Addition. Hispanics are the most concentrated of any major racial or ethnic group in San Francisco. From a central nucleus in the Mission District, Latinos concentrate along the Mission Street corridor toward Daly City (Fig. 4.1).

Housing affordability is a hotly contested political issue in the city. The contemporary renovation of "Victorian" housing, an influx of affluent whites, and a resultant rise in social status have transformed a series of historic ethnic neighborhoods in central and eastern San Francisco (Godfrey 1988, 1997). Apartment rental and home sale prices in the city escalated rapidly in the 1990s, along with the general markets for U.S. stocks and high-technology venture capital. San Francisco's combined median sale price of condominiums and single-family homes approximated $520,000 in 2001, when only 7.3 percent of the homes were affordable for those earning the city's median household income. Rental apartments, which accounted for 65 percent of the city's housing units, also reached stratospheric costs: the median advertised monthly rent for a two-bedroom

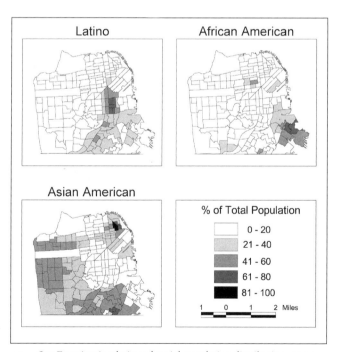

4.1.   San Francisco's ethnic and racial population distribution, 2000.
Source: U.S. Bureau of the Census 2000.

4.2.   San Francisco's Mission District, looking toward downtown, 2002. *Photograph by B. Godfrey, 2002.*

apartment in San Francisco reached $2,400 in 2001 (Bay Area Economics 2002: 67–68).

Despite such seemingly forbidding trends, Latinos have created a distinctive and enduring ethnic enclave in San Francisco's Mission District (Fig. 4.2). Once a working-class enclave of European immigrants, the core of the Mission District has been predominantly Hispanic since the 1960s. Here a multiethnic history of political organizing has long defied predictions of the imminent demise of a widely appreciated Latino neighborhood, or barrio. The sense of an external threat to community preservation has grown steadily over the years as surrounding neighborhoods such as South of Market, the Castro District, Noe Valley, Bernal Heights, and Potrero Hill have become expensive and socially exclusive (Curtis 1999; Nieves 1999, 2000; Rowen and Roth 1998). Although these neighborhoods are by no means homogeneous, generally they have become associated in the public mind with particular groups: new immigrants, established ethnic groups, white families or young singles, gay men and lesbians, artists, college students, and so on. Such social identities have acquired spatial connotations in the densely inhabited neighborhoods of eastern San Francisco, where many points of culture clash coexist within the space of a few blocks.

Given the Mission District's central location, ethnic charms, warm weather by local standards, and relatively cheap housing, rents and housing prices have tended to rise even faster than those citywide (Table 4.2). Once widely regarded as a poverty-stricken slum, the Mission District has become a popular place of residence and recreation among young urban professionals (Yuppies). Priced out of preferred but more expensive neighborhoods—such as Pacific Heights, the Marina, Noe Valley, and the Castro districts—by the city's overall housing shortage, Yuppies increasingly populate the Mission District. As a sign of the neighborhood's improved cachet, the median asking price of advertised homes (mainly condominiums) open for viewing in the Mission District reached $608,608 in May 2002 ("Open Homes" 2002: 22). Yet only 18.1 percent of District households own their homes, while 81.9 percent rent apartments (BAE 2002: 77). Despite a general decline in city apartment rents with the information-technology sector's decline and the general economic recession of 1991–1992, Mission District rental prices have held up better than those citywide. The increasing desirability of the area has shifted both housing costs and social status upward in a fundamental way.

Despite the city's expensive housing, the Latino population remained relatively stable during the 1990s and thus defied common predictions of demographic decline (San Francisco 1994). Even with the widely publicized "dot-com invasion" of internet-based firms during the late 1990s, the widely expected drop in the Latino population did not materialize. In 2000, the percentage of Latinos in the Mission District officially remained at more than 50 percent, and the percentage in the barrio's core census tracts at more than 60 percent (U.S. Bureau of the Census 2000). An analysis of how this barrio survives, even thrives, in the midst of the economic pressures, political complexities, and social diversities of a city like San Francisco suggests prospects for Latino neighborhoods in other historic, densely inhabited U.S. urban cores.

TABLE 4.2—HOUSING COSTS, SAN FRANCISCO AND THE MISSION DISTRICT

HOUSING INDICATOR	1997	2002	% CHANGE
MISSION DISTRICT: median advertised rent, 2 BR apt.	$1,330	$1,956	+47.1
SAN FRANCISCO: median advertised rent, 2 BR apt.	$1,714	$2,144	+25.1
MISSION DISTRICT: median sale price	$235,000	$410,000	+74.5
SAN FRANCISCO: median sale price	$332,500	$538,000	+61.8

Sources: Alejandrino 2000; Metrorent 2002; Apartment Association of San Francisco 2002; San Francisco Association of Realtors 2002.
Note: Median advertised rents for two-bedroom apartments are figured for all of 1997 and for April 2002; home prices include both houses and condominiums for all of 1997 and for the first quarter (Jan.–Mar.) of 2002.

LATINOS AND THE MISSION DISTRICT

Although the Latino community has deep roots, it has been historically discontinuous in San Francisco. Hispanic populations can be traced back to colonial times, but political vicissitudes and European immigration during the last two centuries transformed this maritime center. After the virtual abandonment of the Spanish settlement around Mission Dolores, the city's Latin American population clustered in North Beach during the gold rush. A community known initially as "Chilecito" (Little Chile) emerged on Telegraph Hill, due to the many South American immigrants who joined ships rounding Cape Horn en route to California. In 1875, the Mexican nationals' Catholic church in San Francisco, Our Lady of Guadalupe, was founded in North Beach. Yet the Hispanic community was unable to expand here. Italian immigration mounted in the early twentieth century, and development of the bohemian nightclub and restaurant complex after World War II raised rents and forced the growing Hispanic population to move into other parts of the city (Godfrey 1988).

The Mission District got its name from the original Spanish settlement, dedicated to Saint Francis of Assisi when it was founded in 1776. But it quickly became known as Mission Dolores, after a nearby stream. Despite the area's Spanish and, later, Mexican origins, European immigrants and their descendants urbanized it. Affluent classes built many impressive mansions in what was the late-nineteenth-century urban fringe. The 1906 earthquake and fire left the area largely unscathed and, subsequently, the developing district took on a working-class air, densely populated by residents of Irish, German, Scandinavian, and Italian origin. The founding of local churches reflected the neighborhood's mixed social character. The Irish came to dominate the area's Catholic parish churches. This abundance of Catholic parishes in the Mission District proved to be important in the Hispanic influx after World War II, when the churches converted to Spanish-language services for the predominantly Catholic Latin population.

Despite the relative ethnic stability of the interwar period, the Mission District became a low-income and dilapidated residential area during the depression. By the late 1930s, the core area, topographically the lowest-lying part of the Mission, was among the city's poorest, just a step up from South of Market. Latinos began moving into the Mission in significant numbers during this period, although residents of European stock still greatly outnumbered them. Construction of the Bay Bridge and its approaches during the 1930s displaced a growing Hispanic community, further accelerating this incipient Latin American influx into the North Mis-

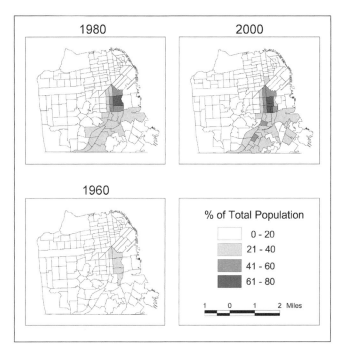

4.3.   Distribution of San Francisco's Latino population, 1960–2000.
Source: U.S. Bureau of the Census 1961, 1981, 2000.

sion. Apartments in this area were among the cheapest in San Francisco, renting for a third less than the city average. By 1940, the first Spanish-language religious congregation appeared in the North Mission.

Before World War II, increasing numbers of recent Hispanic immigrants gathered in the South of Market area, a traditional low-income point of entry for new arrivals to the city. Many Latin American males worked on the docks or in the nearby warehouses, food-processing companies, and light industry. Central American immigration to San Francisco mounted during this period. Companies based in the city—Folger's, Hills Brothers, and MJB—maintained contacts with Central America's coffee-producing areas. Once these links were established, social networks led to continuing migratory movements. The United Fruit Company also operated three freight and passenger steamships between San Francisco and Central America. Like previous European immigrant groups, Latin Americans followed the city's street pattern in moving from the gritty South of Market area into the Mission District after World War II (Fig. 4.3).

The influx of low-income Hispanic immigrants solidified the perception of the Mission District as a poverty area after World War II. As residents of European ancestry abandoned the area and rents remained low, the Mission District's Hispanic population grew steadily during the late 1940s and the 1950s. Latin American men labored at blue-collar occupations in small manufacturing shops, warehouses, and other locations close by in the North Mission, South of Market, and waterfront areas; Spanish-speaking women worked at the local packing plants and clothing manufacturers, such as the Levi Strauss plant. Sixteenth Street in the North Mission attracted Hispanic restaurants, bakeries, and specialty shops and became the first thoroughfare in the district with a significant Latin American cluster.

The Mission District was a working-class bastion before World War II, and with the postwar influx of Latin American immigrants, this social condition persisted. White residents of European ethnicity increasingly moved out. By the 1960s, the inner Mission District was a vibrant Latino barrio. By official count, the Mission core had become nearly 60 percent Hispanic by 1980, but given the presence of many undocumented residents, these official figures are probably conservative (Table 4.3). Door-to-door surveys conducted by local priests near St. Peter's Catholic church found about two-thirds of the population to be Hispanic during the 1970s. Along with the ethnic turnover, however, came problems of real estate disinvestment, linguistic barriers, and poverty (Godfrey 1988).

The Mission's continuing role as a reception area for Latin American immigrants stems largely from the presence of an existing Latino population with external family and social connections, which attracts newcomers in a dynamic of chain migration. Spanish continues to be widely spoken locally. Historically, Mission District housing has been relatively cheap. Although newly rented units are no longer inexpensive, longtime residents often have retained reasonable rent-controlled apartments. New immigrants tend to settle initially with relatives or companions from the same region of origin, which can entail considerable cramping of living quarters in the densely populated Mission. Numerous Latino immigrants, often single males, share two- or three-bedroom flats to reduce individual rent. Local housing advocacy groups have documented up to seventeen persons living in such apartments, with some residents even sleeping in closets. Approximately sixty single-room-occupancy (SRO) hotels offer short-term housing options in the Mission District. SRO rooms generally cost upwards of $500 a month, though they are plagued by hygiene problems in the common bathroom, communicable diseases such as tuberculosis, and safety issues (Arrieta 2001a, 2001b).

The saga of Albertina López, a Salvadoran immigrant in her early for-

TABLE 4.3 — HISPANIC POPULATION OF SAN FRANCISCO'S MISSION DISTRICT

CENSUS YEAR	WEST MISSION		NORTH MISSION	
	HISPANIC POPULATION	% HISPANIC POPULATION	HISPANIC POPULATION	% HISPANIC POPULATION
1950	644	5.7	1,344	17.7
1960	2,235	13.5	1,798	27.5
1970	5,361	32.6	2,333	39.8
1980	4,373	28.5	2,744	41.9
1990	5,218	31.7	3,285	48.6
2000	4,276	26.4	4,009	49.3

	MISSION CORE		TOTAL MISSION DISTRICT	
	HISPANIC POPULATION	% HISPANIC POPULATION	HISPANIC POPULATION	% HISPANIC POPULATION
1950	3,543	12.3	5,531	11.6
1960	7,589	26.9	11,622	22.7
1970	15,489	52.3	23,183	44.6
1980	15,862	55.9	22,979	45.7
1990	21,071	62.2	29,575	51.9
2000	21,860	60.9	30,145	50.1

Sources: U.S. Bureau of the Census 1952, 1960, 1972, 1981, 1993, 2000.
Note: Mission District core includes 2000 census tracts 208, 209, 228.01, 228.02, 228.03, 229.01, 229.02, and 229.03; North Mission District, tracts 177 and 201; and the West Mission, tracts 202, 207, and 210. Census tracts for previous decades are grouped for equivalent areas.

ties, illustrates common regional linkages and social ties. Albertina recounted in an interview that she was born of a poor family in the interior town of Chalatenango. Her parents both died as she was entering adolescence, so she moved to the capital, San Salvador, and worked as a domestic servant for about five dollars a month. Albertina became pregnant and had a son out of wedlock, but the boy was mentally retarded. (She did not marry the boy's father, and has never married.) As Albertina grew increasingly desperate about how to support herself and her newborn infant, a female Salvadoran friend living in San Francisco encouraged her to move there. Albertina left on a difficult, two-week odyssey in a chartered bus through Central America and Mexico, rarely stopping to eat or sleep. At the U.S.-Mexico border, Albertina crossed illegally in a car trunk. She arrived in San Francisco on May 1, 1985 (López 2002).

In San Francisco, Albertina quickly found work as a nighttime janitor at a downtown office, where she has worked ever since. On the trip to the United States, she met a Salvadoran man, Jesús, with whom she moved to an apartment on 21st Street, near Mission Street. The couple still lives together, but they have not married, since Jesús "has a commitment" to support a woman and children back in El Salvador. Through Fermín, a successful local Salvadoran entrepreneur originally from Jesús' home village, Albertina began working part time as a janitor in other offices and occasionally cleaning homes on the side. At present, she still lives with Jesús in the Mission District, where they pay about $500 a month for the same rent-controlled apartment. Albertina regularly sends money to her sister for the care of her son. In fact, Albertina bought a home in a suburb of San Salvador, where her sister and son now live, and where Albertina would like to retire someday. She has returned twice to El Salvador in recent years, now that she is a legal resident of the United States and can travel freely. After seventeen years in San Francisco, Albertina speaks little English and is worried that her linguistic limitations will prevent her from becoming a U.S. citizen (López 2002).

Many Latin American immigrants have not been so fortunate as Albertina, and the lack of steady employment remains a major problem. Recent arrivals typically toil in low-paying service jobs in restaurants, as office cleaners or domestic servants, and so forth. Informal employment in painting, construction, landscape gardening, and other household tasks is also common, despite frequent abuses of labor in such casual work. The Instituto Laboral de La Raza sees monthly about one hundred workers, predominantly Latino males, who find themselves unpaid after completing their jobs; about four hundred claims are filed annually with the city's labor commissioner or in small claims court. The most vulnerable workers are the male day laborers, mostly undocumented Mexicans and Central Americans, who gather at known locations and bid for jobs on a project basis. Large groups of men assemble daily along César Chávez Boulevard, waiting for job offers from passing motorists. Local residents have repeatedly complained of loitering, noise, drinking, and urinating in public, prompting police citations at times, though the San Francisco Day Laborer Program has provided an employment service and basic bathroom facilities for the casual workers. In addition, other local agencies—resettlement programs, social services, health clinics, community and church groups, and language and vocational training schools—struggle to support new immigrants.

INSIDE THE BARRIO: SOCIAL DIVERSITY AND LATINO IDENTITY

Spreading over an area of approximately 2.25 square miles, in 2000 the Mission District was officially home to 60,202 residents, housed in 22,025 dwelling units. The Mission District's median household income was $49,127 in 2000, nearly 10 percent below the citywide median of $53,630, but still much closer to the San Francisco norm than previously (BAE 2002; U.S. Bureau of the Census 2000). Nearly 19,000 people work in the District, including 6,500 employed in the leading production-distribution-repair (PDR) sector, particularly in apparel manufacturing, construction, auto repair, and utilities concentrated in the northeastern part of the Mission. In addition, more than nine hundred stores and restaurants dot the Mission, employing over 4,500 people (San Francisco 2002: 81–84). Mission Street is the major retail strip; other commercial thoroughfares of lesser importance include Valencia, 16th, and 24th Streets. With more than 26,750 residents, 8,400 jobs, and 9,788 housing units per square mile, the Mission District is one of the city's most densely inhabited and socially diverse areas (Fig. 4.4).

Spatial proximity seems to highlight the contrasting social identities in and around the Mission District. For example, Latinos predominate in the hustle and bustle of Mission Street between 16th and 24th Streets, congregating especially at the plazas serving the BART (Bay Area Rapid Transit) stations. On Mission Street, the District's principal retail corridor, the sidewalk and nearby arcades often feel like a *mercado*, or bazaar, as pedestrians mingle with associates and vendors. A daytime stroll along these frenetic commercial strips finds restaurants where Spanish is spoken, grocery stores, travel agencies, money-transfer operations, bars and nightclubs, music stores, and other establishments often identified with a particular country of origin (Fig. 4.5). Local establishments include Mission Cultural Center (Latino arts), Casa Guadalupe (products from Mexico and Central America), Acaxutla Restaurante y Panadería (Guatemalan and Salvadoran cuisine and bakery), and California Travel (money transfers to Mexico and El Salvador).

Upscale Valencia Street sits nearby, parallel to Mission Street. Here on the western side of the Mission District, a relatively affluent and young-ish clientele congregates in the cybercafés, trendy restaurants, fashionable bars and nightclubs, and vintage clothing stores. Along with the remaining Hispanic restaurants and other establishments along Valencia Street, new or reinvigorated venues now include Modern Times Bookstore (which advertises itself as a "progressive" resource), Psychic Horizons (a school for meditation and healing), Herbivore, the Earthly Grill, 2202 Oxygen Bar Organic Café, and New College of California (education for social change). On 18th Street, between Mission and Valencia Streets, sits the Women's Building, a community center decorated with colorful murals of global women's struggles.

Several blocks farther west sits the adjacent Castro District, symbolic axis of the city's highly visible gay community. Directly south of the Mission District lies Bernal Heights, where many lesbians have quietly settled in recent years. Despite their spatial propinquity and functional interdependence, these nontraditional communities seem culturally worlds away from the barrio of the Mission District. Still, these social worlds often overlap and intersect through commerce, work, transportation, housing, and other aspects of urban life.

The Mission District is too large and socially diverse to constitute a

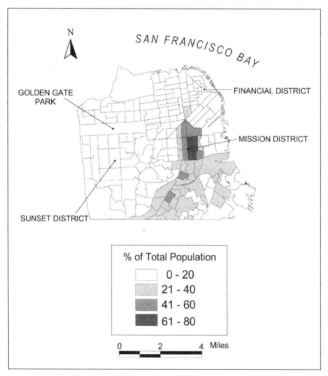

4.4.   Distribution of Hispanics in San Francisco neighborhoods, 2000.
Source: U.S. Bureau of the Census 2000.

4.5.   Mission and 24th Streets, a major crossroads of Latino San Francisco. *Photograph by B. Godfrey, 2002.*

single neighborhood. In reality, it comprises a series of small neighborhoods—often identified by proximity to major thoroughfares—which differ in land use and social composition. Table 4.3 divides the District into three basic and widely recognized social areas:

1. The West Mission, topographically elevated and socially upscale, encompasses the narrow, several-block strip between Valencia and Dolores Streets along the district's western edge. This transitional area has witnessed the most housing renovation in recent years, largely a spillover effect from prospering Eureka and Noe Valleys to the west. Only 26.4 percent of the West Mission's population was Latino in 2000, a significant decrease from the peak of 32.6 in 1970. The in-movers generally have small households; the 2000 Census indicates an average of only 1.9 people per household here. As a result, this popular area's residents declined by 245, or 1.5 percent, in the 1990s (Williams 2001).
2. The North Mission, which lies north of 17th Street, has long been composed largely of light-industry, warehouses, blue-collar services, and residential quarters. Historically, the North Mission has served

as a bridge, in both functional and social terms, between the Mission District and the industrial South of Market area. The North Mission remained about half Latino during the 1990s, but the area experienced an influx of relatively affluent white residents. Home to the Northeast Mission Industrial Zone, the North Mission has seen hundreds of live-and-work lofts constructed since the 1990s, along with a scattering of information-technology offices, trendy restaurants, and popular nightclubs (Mission Anti-Displacement Coalition 2002). As a result of the area's growing popularity, the resident population increased by 1,363, or 20.2 percent, in the 1990s; the 2000 Census indicates 2.5 people per household here (Willliams 2001).

3. The Mission core, which lies between 17th Street and César Chávez Boulevard and the 101 Freeway and Valencia Street, is the barrio's epicenter. It consists mainly of apartment buildings and single-family houses, along with two major commercial arteries. Mission Street serves the entire city, while lower 24th Street is more local and ethnic in quality. The Mission core's total population grew by 2,068 residents, or 5.6 percent, in the 1990s. Overall, there has been little additional housing built here in recent years, suggesting increasing crowding of the existing housing stock. The 2000 Census indicates 3.3 people per household in the Mission core, an increase over 1990, unlike what happened in the North and West Mission areas. While the Hispanic population in the Mission core grew by about 800 residents during the 1990s, the proportion of Latinos here actually decreased slightly, to 60.9 percent, over the decade, suggesting an influx by other ethnic groups (see Table 4.3).

The Mission District remains the heart of San Francisco's Latino community. The proportion of the city's Hispanic population residing in the district rose from 22.8 percent in 1970 to 27.5 percent in 2000. This increased residential concentration resulted partly from displacement in several nearby gentrifying neighborhoods. Yet the 1990s witnessed a stabilization of the Mission's Latino population, which grew by only about 600 residents and in relative terms slightly declined, to 50.1 percent of the district's overall population. The number of non-Hispanic whites increased by 2,667, to constitute 32.5 percent of the Mission's total population during the 1990s (Table 4.4). This racial shift attests to the growing popularity of the Mission District for non-Hispanic white residents.

Interestingly, recent growth in San Francisco's Latino population has

TABLE 4.4—RACE AND ETHNICITY IN SAN FRANCISCO'S MISSION DISTRICT

GROUP	1990		2000	
	POPULATION	% OF TOTAL POPULATION	POPULATION	% OF TOTAL POPULATION
HISPANIC ORIGIN	29,575	51.9	30,145	50.1
WHITE, NON-HISPANIC	16,914	29.7	19,581	32.5
ASIAN AMERICAN	7,448	13.0	6,800	11.3
AFRICAN AMERICAN	2,547	4.5	1,790	3.0
OTHER	533	0.9	1,886	3.1
TOTAL	57,017	100.0	60,202	100.0

Sources: U.S. Bureau of the Census 1993, 2000.
Note: Data on race are not strictly comparable with other decades, since the 2000 Census allowed individuals to select multiple racial categories. Hispanic origin is not considered a race, however, so it can be compared directly across census years.

taken place largely away from the barrio core: upwardly mobile Hispanics often move into middle-class, family-oriented neighborhoods in the Outer Mission and suburban areas, much as earlier European immigrants did. In the 1990s, the city's Hispanic population grew by over eight thousand (11.5 percent) in neighborhoods outside the Mission District.

Latinos in the Mission District are diverse in terms of country and region of origin, degree of cultural assimilation, and socioeconomic status. San Francisco's heterogeneous Latino population illustrates the complexities of ethnicity. Data from the U.S. Bureau of the Census and the Immigration and Naturalization Service, along with local interviews, indicate that Latinos of Mexican origin account for approximately 40 percent of the city's Hispanic population; probably about 20 percent have come from El Salvador; 15 percent from Nicaragua; and the remaining 25 percent from Honduras, Guatemala, Peru, and other countries. Recent years have witnessed the arrival of increasing numbers of Mayas and other indigenous groups from southern Mexico and Central America, for whom Spanish is often a second language. While Mexican Americans are the dominant cultural influence among Latinos in the Mission District, the presence of such a high proportion of Central Americans differentiates San Francisco from other parts of the Bay Area and California, where Mexican origin generally predominates.

Why such a large Central American population? Originally, given the city's historical position as a mercantile center of commercial interests on the West Coast, historical-geographic connections such as the coffee trade accounted for the large number of Central American immigrants to San Francisco. Social ties were established that became self-perpetuating through chain migration, by which family members and friends continued to pull associates from the sending countries. Then political events intensified the migratory currents. In the 1970s and the 1980s, the Central American political situation became oppressive and forced many to seek political refuge abroad. Many opponents of Nicaragua's Somoza regime fled to the United States before the strongman was overthrown in 1979; after this, many opponents of the Sandinista regime came to San Francisco. Internal crisis in El Salvador flared up in the late 1970s as well, leading San Francisco's Salvadoran population to swell. Significant numbers of Guatemalans also began to appear (Godfrey 1988).

Over time, San Francisco's diverse Latin American population has developed a broader pan-Hispanic cohesion. Faced with language, education, race barriers, and other problems, Latinos have tended to form a minority identity, as in other U.S. cities. In local politics, for example, it is important to have a Latino on the San Francisco Board of Supervisors. Ethnic identification also results from social ties and cultural commonalities within the local Latino community. Reliance on a common language is important, despite certain differences in Spanish vocabulary among the various national groups, as are shared cultural traits, religious traditions, communal festivals, and so on. Intermarriage among Latino nationalities is common, further encouraging ethnic amalgamation. For example, it is common to see marriages between Mexicans and Salvadorans, or between Salvadorans and Nicaraguans, given the prominence of these groups in the Mission District.

COMMUNAL FESTIVALS AND COMMUNITY ARTS: (RE)CLAIMING THE BARRIO

Latino ethnic solidarity is visibly displayed, and socially reinforced, by the cultural landscape of the Mission District. Communal festivals and community art help create a Latino sense of place with social, cultural, and political overtones. Visiting Mexicans often remark on how the Cinco de Mayo celebrations of U.S. Latinos surpass those in their homeland. Indeed, given their cultural dominance in the local community, such Mexican traditions often become the norm to which smaller Central American groups adhere. The Cinco de Mayo parade has been an annual event for the Latino community of the Mission since 1965. Although it celebrates a Mexican event—the defeat of the French at the Battle of Puebla in 1862—Central American groups have floats and are highly visible in the annual parade in the Mission District.

An annual Carnival festival, celebrated on Memorial Day weekend, also emphasizes the common cultural roots of diverse groups. Beginning in 1979 as a small procession in Precita Park, Carnival quickly grew to a major civic event. By 1983, when the festival was billed as "a gift of the Mission District to the San Francisco Bay Area," Carnival had become a multiethnic parade down Mission Street to the Civic Center, featuring twenty-seven marching groups and attracting between 50,000 and 100,000 people. One analyst claims, "The Mission District became home to Carnival because of its large, active artistic community and because many Mission residents had carnaval traditions in their home countries" (Sommers 1986: 163). Indeed, the royal court selected for Carnival 2002 represented different regional perspectives on the festivities: Queen Maisa Santana Duke, originally from Bahia, Brazil, performed with the Energia do Samba troupe; King Norberto Martínez, from Yucatán, Mexico, danced flamenco with the Grupo Andanza (Collins 2002: 6).

Community art is another sign of Latino ethnicity. Approximately one hundred major public murals, inspired by the great Mexican muralists and emphasizing the Hispanic presence in the barrio, have been painted in the Mission since the early 1970s. A children's book, *Barrio: José's Neighborhood*, depicts the colorful murals as representing the cultural history of the Mission's Latino population (Ancona 1998). Indeed, the major cultural centers in the Mission District—the Galería de la Raza, the Mission Cultural Center for Latino Arts, and the Precita Eyes Mural Arts and Visitors Center—were formed in the 1970s, inspired by the Chicano political movement. These cultural centers initially sought to define the Mission District as Latino cultural space, and in recent years, they generally have become more overtly political in depicting concerns about gentrification.

Although such organizations have their own particular missions, their shared focus on Latino cultural politics provides common cause. The Mission Cultural Center for Latino Arts, founded in 1977, provides studio space, an art gallery, and a theater for cultural performances. Precita Eyes Mural Arts and Visitors Center, which evolved from a mural workshop organized by director Susan Cervantes in 1977, teaches classes, organizes mural projects, and conducts tours of community murals (Fig. 4.6). The street art is generally created by amateurs in the community, not by professional artists, yet the resulting murals have proved immensely popular. For example, the murals lining Balmy Alley, started by the Mujeres Muralistas collective in the 1970s and continued by Precita Eyes artists, have become a major tourist attraction in the Mission District. Similarly, Galería de la Raza, founded in 1970 to increase public awareness and appreciation of

4.6.   The diptych *Family Life* and *Spirit of Mankind* on the Leonard R. Flynn Elementary School, San Francisco, painted by Precita Eyes Mural Arts Center artists under the direction of Susan Cervantes in 1976–1977. *Photograph by B. Godfrey, 2002.*

Chicano/Latino art and culture, sells reproductions of such cultural objects as candles, posters, piñatas, and postcards to visitors. More important, however, it displays original art for the community to enjoy. For example, the Galería has long sponsored a billboard outside the store featuring rotating murals by local artists expressing political concerns.

Poster art is another contemporary artistic form that takes explicitly political points of view. The San Francisco Print Collective, formed as a political action group in 1999, congregates a cadre of activist artists whose mission is "to increase public awareness and dialogue about local, national and international concerns by printing and pasting posters and large format banners and billboards throughout the city that are informative, memorable and thought provoking." The Print Collective uses the Mission Cultural Center's printmaking studio to create many of the political posters displayed on walls in the district in recent years. The collective's witty posters often satirize the trendiness of the "ethnic" Mission—as in a poster exhorting Yuppies to "Come Enjoy the Mission: Authentic Tacos!"—or take aim at the mayor, local landlords and developers, and others. An even more controversial group is the Mission Yuppie Eradication Project, a direct-action campaign started in 1998 "to save the Mission area in San Francisco from losing its character as a low rent working class neighborhood to an expensive playground for yuppies." The group's exhortation to vandalize expensive cars and restaurants caused local controversy and intense media attention in 1999.

Gentrification often starts with an influx of bohemian artists and other nontraditional elements who glamorize and popularize an area. In such New York neighborhoods as Soho and the Lower East Side, commercial artists paved the way for the real estate interests to market run-down, heavily ethnic areas as exciting and creative districts worthy of residential investment (Mele 2000; Zukin 1982). While many blame artists for gentrification, others see struggling artists as victims of the process. Rebecca Solnit's interpretation of the Mission's artists is quite sympathetic: "For decades, poor white kids—college students, musicians, artists, writers— have been moving into the Mission, which some poor whites never left, but many of the artists and radicals who were raised there or arrived as adults are Latinos (blaming gentrification on artists often presumes all artists are white)" (2000: 61).

Indeed, the Mission now boasts a growing cadre of successful non-Latino artists—such as Chris Johanson, Alicia McCarthy, Margaret Kilgallen, and Aaron Noble—who cultivate an aesthetic of the local streets in what the *San Francisco Bay Area Guardian* and other publications now call the "Mission School." This approach is evident in the Clarion Alley murals of the North Mission and emphasizes "pop-inflected murals painted in ways that take off from the more classic, '30s-influenced, Diego Rivera style found deeper in the Mission with a broader, postmodern range of subjects and sensibilities" (Helfand 2002: 32). Such Mission artists, some of whom have exhibited at New York's Whitney and other national art museums, have helped spark a local real estate bonanza reminiscent of Keith Haring's popularization of Manhattan's East Village.

On balance, community mural arts and the Mission School are inspired by Latin American folk practices and, even if influenced by popular contemporary currents, generally reflect an ethnically embedded and socially conscious expression of culture. Public art takes on political implications, given the heated debates surrounding gentrification of San Francisco neighborhoods such as the Mission District. Still, even where community mural art has sought to define the barrio's identity and protect the area from unwanted changes, local artistic preservation efforts have also made a low-income area more aesthetically pleasing and thus, in a sense, have contributed to gentrification.

A DEFENDED NEIGHBORHOOD:
ANTIDISPLACEMENT POLITICS

Community efforts to preserve the character of the Mission District date from the 1950s, when local residents fought against the construction of public housing projects. Although a few such projects were built, community activists were aware of the displacement of blacks and Japanese in the Western Addition and resisted massive redevelopment in the Mission District. During the 1960s, however, the construction of the BART subway line up Mission Street proved nearly as traumatic for the district as redevelopment had been in the Western Addition. The Mission Coalition Organization (MCO), active in the antipoverty programs of the late 1960s and the early 1970s, became a powerful voice for neighborhood preservation (Levine 2000). But the MCO became defunct during the mid-1970s, split apart largely by the unresolved conflicts posed by the Mission District's dual identity as both a Latino barrio and a working-class district of diverse groups (Castells 1983).

Subsequent resistance to gentrification among Latino young people has often taken informal, less-organized forms. The Mission District has a relatively high proportion of youth—about a third of the population—compared with the rest of San Francisco. With the general crowding of living quarters, a widely acknowledged lack of recreational facilities, and high unemployment, the street is a logical place for young people to congregate. Mission Street, for example, became infamous for lowrider cruising in the 1970s, as young Chicano men paraded their stylized cars on weekend evenings. The lowriders became associated with traffic congestion, vandalism, and violence, prompting the local police to crack down and order a curfew. Roberto Hernández later remarked, "I believe that the low-riders, and I was one of them, when we cruised down Mission Street, that it was what saved the Mission District from gentrification" (KQED 1994). Similarly, a local group called the Real Alternatives Program (RAP) claimed that "Mission youth by their presence are threatening the 'new' Mission; they are declaring that it is still the barrio. This is the real reason they are seen as such a threat" (Godfrey 1988: 159). Such views reflect the social polarization caused by gentrification and the emergence of a "defended neighborhood" (Suttles 1972), by which youth gangs and a forbidding reputation have served to protect the neighborhood population from displacement.

Despite the San Francisco barrio's defensive sense of place, rents in the Mission District have risen faster than the citywide average in recent years (see Table 4.2). The increased rents and low vacancy rates in the late

1990s contributed to a stabilization of the Mission's Latino population, as the District became less affordable for new immigrants. Fortunately for established residents, the vast majority of housing units in the Mission District are protected by rent-control legislation. In fact, the demographic stability of the Latino population in the Mission District suggests that many Latinos, like Albertina López, reside in reasonably priced rent-controlled apartments. In addition, the District has a large stock of permanently protected, often subsidized, rental housing. Governmental agencies and nonprofit community housing-development corporations control about two thousand units, or 10 percent of the total housing stock, thus providing an anchor favoring neighborhood ethnic stability. The most important local housing group is the Mission Housing Development Corporation, which owns or manages approximately one thousand units, about 60 percent of which have Latino tenants.

Fear of displacement has been widespread in the private-housing sector, despite the city's rent-control regulations and given landlords' ability to raise rents significantly with tenant turnover. In fact, the Mission District has consistently generated the highest numbers of Reports of Alleged Wrongful Evictions among all San Francisco neighborhoods in recent years. Data from the San Francisco Residential Rent Stabilization and Arbitration Board (2001) show that in the five-year period 1996–2001, an average of 150 such tenant claims were filed annually, about twice as many as in any other neighborhood in the city. Certainly, increasing cost and scarcity of rental units have fueled antidisplacement politics in the Mission District. As Bruce Williams has speculated in this regard, "That may explain why change, although not apparent statistically, was so hotly contested in the Mission even though it was so much more pervasive in many other San Francisco neighborhoods . . . In a neighborhood like the Mission, tenants, commercial or residential, lived in fear that a gold-rush economy would displace them into a market that had become unaffordable" (2001).

Since the early 1990s, community activists have been concerned about protecting the PDR sector from an influx of offices, dot-com firms, and biotechnology companies in the northeast Mission. In 1991, the Planning Department (San Francisco 2002) created the Northeast Mission Industrial Zone, where restrictive policies encouraged the location of industrial and service businesses, such as automobile repair and business support, though critics lamented the loss of much-needed jobs from new and more lucrative firms. Nonetheless, the steady influx of software and computer professionals, many taking advantage of good freeway access to Silicon Valley, renewed long-standing debates about displacement in the late 1990s.

A related controversy arose surrounding live-and-work housing, initially designed for artists, which became hot real estate properties in many run-down industrial areas. As of spring 2002, 389 live-and-work units had been built in the Mission and another 267 were either under construction or in possession of a permit to build. The Mission District is second only to South of Market in the number of live-and-work units, which are almost always market-rate sale or rental units. While these new live-and-work units brought affluent residents to the northeastern Mission District, critics claimed that this type of housing displaced lower-income residents and PDR businesses (San Francisco 2002).

Local anger at the rising pressures of increased rents, evictions of long-term residents, loss of space for community nonprofit groups, and un-bridled live-and-work residential development for the affluent led to an explosion of neighborhood activism in the summer of 2000. Large-scale marches by the Mission Anti-Displacement Coalition (in 2002), a coalition of several community organizations, made local headlines. Fueled by rising indignation about the escalating rents and mounting evictions in the district, the controversies fused radical housing advocates, artists, and Latino community activists in common cause. Under pressure from the Mission Anti-Displacement Coalition, the Mission Planning Council, and other community organizations, the San Francisco Board of Supervisors approved interim controls on development in the Mission District in July 2001 and renewed them in July 2002. Passed over the protests of private housing developers and some housing advocacy groups, the interim controls prevented large-scale office development, live-and-work projects, and market-rate housing with fewer than 25 percent affordable units while encouraging nonprofit community groups to locate or remain in the Mission District.

In a belated response to contemporary development pressures and community protests, the Planning Department in early 2002 embarked on a community-planning process in the Mission District and several other neighborhoods in eastern San Francisco—South of Market, Bayview, Visitacion Valley, and Showplace Square/Potrero Hill. Community workshops attempted to involve the public and to achieve consensus on new zoning controls as a way to guide future development in these areas (Kim 2002). The Mission Anti-Displacement Coalition proposed a "People's Plan" that included restrictions on private commercial and residential development to ensure equitable growth without displacement of the existing population (Fig. 4.7). Critics claimed that this activist approach favored housing development corporations and other community-based organizations over for-

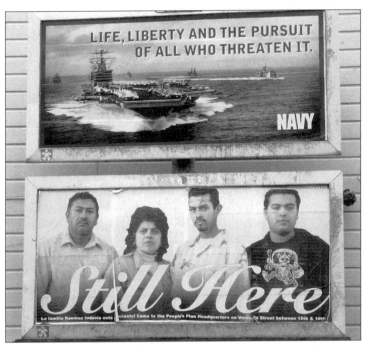

4.7.   "Still Here," a billboard designed by the San Francisco Print Collective to advertise the People's Plan for rezoning San Francisco's Mission District, 2002. *Photograph by B. Godfrey, 2002.*

profit developers and that it would hinder economic growth in the long run (Garofoli 2002). In any case, the political organizing around the People's Plan indicated the presence of a savvy activist community with an intense commitment to neighborhood preservation at all costs.

CONCLUSION: COMMUNITY PLANNING AND THE LATINO BARRIO

How can we account for the demographic stability of San Francisco's Latino population in the face of significant odds? I have argued that a sense of Latino territoriality has arisen that is defensive in its cultural landscape and assertive in its political activities. In the Mission District, Latino settlement history, social networks, cultural activities, community art, and local politics have prevented large-scale displacement so far. In fact, despite the citywide pressures of gentrification and redevelopment, which have displaced many African Americans, San Francisco's Latino population has stabilized in recent years and even grown in some areas. Ethnic patterns of immigration, work and housing, community art and public space, and anti-displacement politics have created a defensive sense of place in the city's primary Hispanic barrio. Constraints on social mobility for recent immigrants and competition with non-Latino groups over such scarce resources as jobs, housing, and inner-city territory increase pan-Hispanic solidarity. The community's sense of being under siege heightens the feelings of ethnic and social solidarity.

This case study of San Francisco's Mission District also suggests the strengths and weaknesses of social resistance based largely on cultural politics. Community mural art establishes a Latino place identity, for example, but also makes the neighborhood more attractive to in-movers. Political activity relies on popular mobilization of an ethnically and socially diverse district in which affluent residents have more inclination to get involved than do recent working-class immigrants. Consequently, the presence of an established Hispanic minority in the barrio checks but certainly does not prevent neighborhood revitalization. So far, erosion of Hispanic territory has been limited mainly to the western and northern flanks of the Mission District. This suggests that social networks and cultural traditions, as well as economic status, become bound up with an area's spatial structure, giving a locale an enduring sense of place. Whether community-planning processes currently under way can prevent the continued displacement of Latinos and other low-and moderate-income residents of San Francisco's Mission District remains to be seen.

GLOBALIZATION OF THE BARRIO

Transformation of the Latino Cultural Landscapes of San Diego, California

Lawrence A. Herzog

This chapter explores cultural landscapes and the nature of change in two barrios in San Diego: Barrio Logan, just south of downtown; and San Ysidro, the border gateway to Mexico lying twelve miles south of the city center. Two ideas traditionally have been used to explain barrio landscapes in Mexican/Latino communities in the United States: (a) the "barrioization" paradigm; and (b) the "barriology" paradigm. The former seeks to explain the formation of barrios as an experience of a less-advantaged Latino population staking out a territory which is then overwhelmed by urban diseconomies—poverty, crime, negative land uses, and so on. The latter describes the process by which Latinos began to reassert control over their neighborhoods through acquisition of political power, mastery of the process of urban planning, and the use of art and muralism to create identity.

I will argue that a new paradigm is needed to understand Latino barrios in the context of changing urbanism—and its new complexities. New forces permeate urban landscapes. They include postmodernity, globalization, privatization, and simulation. How will these new forces affect existing Latino enclaves? I take the position that globalization represents a critical new paradigm for understanding Latino barrios in the United States. It is particularly noteworthy as a defining force in Latino barrios in the southwestern U.S. border region, due to the influences of nearby Mexico and the increasing exchanges of workers, cultural practices, goods, services, capital, and technology. The San Diego/Baja California border region offers an ideal laboratory because of its location on the international boundary. The border imposes a set of global forces on the region, from transnational manufacturing to immigration, cross-border trade, and smuggling. I offer six "ecologies" that seek to capture some critical dimensions of the changes in Latino landscapes I have determined through interviews, site visits, archival study, and transient observation of Mexican American barrios in San Diego over the last decade.

TRADITIONAL PARADIGMS

The cultural landscape of Mexican American barrios in the southwestern United States can best be viewed as dialectic, a clashing of two sets of forces. The first results from external pressures of urban development, capitalism, and anti-Mexican sentiment. These pressures tended to restrict Chicano populations to marginal spaces within the larger city, leading scholars to speak of a process of "barrioization." The second is an internal response by people of Mexican heritage to create a homeland, a distinct ethnic space that is valued by those who occupy it, a notion that has been termed "barriology" (Villa 2000).

The gradual spatial concentration of the Mexican/Latino populations into barrios of the urban Southwest border region left behind a set of distinct cultural landscapes over the last century and a half. The idea of barrioization cannot be traced to any single decision or conspiracy of actors, but, rather, to an unspoken theme that unified all of the built-environment decisions made by powerful actors in the history of southwestern urban development.

Barrioization, in Southern California and parts of the Southwest, may be said to comprise the 1900–1945 era of Mexican built-environment history. During this period, the region continued to grow, cities expanded, more immigrants from Mexico arrived, and the process of barrioization intensified. These immigrants experienced increasing segregation into less and less desirable parts of the city.

Various forces were at work. On the one side, as noted, increasingly larger waves of Mexican immigrants arrived in the American Southwest in the early decades of the twentieth century. As they flowed toward urban labor markets, a second force—the economy—took over. Like other unskilled immigrants before them, Mexicans did not have the resources to pay very high rents.

As cities like Los Angeles industrialized and developed, land values increased. Enclaves of cheap rental housing formed, typically in the least-desirable parts of town: adjacent to factories, near noisy railroad stockyards, or on the far edges. Language and social accommodation also played a role in the process. Mexican immigrants became more comfortable living near the old "Sonoratowns" and "Little Mexico" enclaves, where they could find others who spoke Spanish. By 1950, barrios were well entrenched in cities like Los Angeles (Griswold del Castillo 1978; Romo 1983), Santa Barbara (Camarillo 1979), El Paso (García 1981), Tucson (Sheridan 1986), and San Diego (Herzog 1990).

The 1950s and the 1960s were a period of frenzied urban development, particularly in the largest southwestern cities, most notably, Los Angeles. Here the barrios that had existed for several decades were threatened by massive urban redevelopment. Land was seized for building freeways and other public facilities. Many unwanted developments—factories, freeways, stadia—invaded what had been the primary living spaces for Mexican immigrants. The cultural landscape soon became one of distress.

Examples of this process of barrioization are evident throughout the southwestern United States. In East Los Angeles, the building of freeways substantially disrupted the landscape of Mexican American neighborhoods like Boyle Heights and Chavez Ravine. In San Diego, a freeway and bridge sliced the Barrio Logan neighborhood into fragments. Some observers went as far as to argue that freeways allowed more freedom of movement, a truly democratic development (Banham 1971). But too many freeways destroyed the sense of place and endangered the quality of life in Mexican American neighborhoods.

In the twentieth century, the Latino population's consciousness shifted. Latinos began to view their neighborhoods as a kind of valued cultural and social space. It has been argued that the period of the 1930s, during which the economic depression spurred massive deportations of Mexican immigrants, sparked greater determination in those who remained to construct permanent spaces in the Latino community (Villa 2000). This determination, termed "barriology," began with the creation of symbolic activities—parades, holiday festivities, and cultural events—that ritually celebrated not only Mexican culture, but also Mexican American place/community.

One specific form of intervention by Chicano community activists materialized as a battle to preserve parkland being usurped by freeway and other development. In Los Angeles, activists and preservationists fought to protect several public spaces on the east side, including Obregon and Elysian Parks. In other cities of the Southwest, "Chicano Parks" and community centers were created in Mexican American neighborhoods. In San Diego, an unused water tank lying in Balboa Park was transformed into a Mexican American cultural center called Centro Cultural de la Raza. On the otherwise uninspiring exterior, stark, colorful, powerful murals were painted. Nearby in Barrio Logan, the oldest Mexican American neighborhood in the city fought to create a neighborhood park under the Coronado

Bridge. In 1970, the neighborhood mobilized a political action in the form of civil disobedience when it learned that land under the bridge was to be given to the California Highway Patrol for use as a substation and parking lot. Latino residents responded by occupying the space, remaining on it, first, as an act of protest, and, later, to construct their own park. Eventually, city and state governments backed off and allowed the community its park, a site that today commands enormous symbolic pride in the community. Surrounding the park are vivid Mexican murals covering the otherwise imposing pillars of the Coronado Bridge. Each spring, a special Chicano Day celebration takes place here to honor the history of the community's struggle to create this important place.

Thus barriology represents a kind of collective decision to find ways to Mexicanize the bland spaces that had become home to the Chicano population. This growing social place consciousness produced a contemporary generation of artists, community organizers, architects, store owners, schoolchildren, and others determined to inscribe their cultural origins on the built landscape of their neighborhoods. This impulse can be seen both as a response to the crisis of barrioization and marginalization and as a way of enriching their community experience. It is noteworthy that the neighborhoods occupied by people of Mexican descent usually consisted of buildings in the Anglo tradition—wooden bungalows, Victorian mansions, or simple brick and concrete apartment houses. Ironically, the buildings designed with Mexico in mind—the mission revival and Spanish colonial revival structures—were usually not occupied by people of Mexican descent. These turn-of-the century building styles were largely created and financed by Anglo promoters and investors concerned not so much with the preservation of Latino culture as with the propagation of a romantic image of California that would attract residents and consumers.

Although Latinos could not alter permanent buildings and large infrastructure projects, they could transform the landscapes to make their communities more livable. It would be a mistake to restrict discussion of Latino barrio landscapes to the buildings alone. Landscapes in cities are strongly defined by buildings, but the spaces between the buildings are often equally or more important to the overall cultural landscape. This is quite noticeably the case in the Latino barrio. As Mexican Americans established territorial control over these places, they also established their own cultural landscapes. They personalized many of these spaces, transforming them, in part, from hopeless ghettos into vital living spaces, moving from a condition of being barrioized to one in which they felt a sense of belonging, a sense of place, a barriology.

THE NEW PARADIGM OF GLOBALIZATION

Like the larger city, Latino barrios in the United States are increasingly influenced by an emerging set of global forces. Over the last decade, globalization has become a catchall phrase that seeks to capture the process
in which exogenous forces—global investment, global corporate decision making, transnational labor markets, global production, international
smuggling, and other world processes—affect nations, regions, and cities
(Sassen 1991, 1998; Sklair 1991).

Globalization has a specific and particularly striking influence on Latino
barrios, especially those located in the Southwest U.S. border region (especially the states of Texas, New Mexico, Arizona, and California), because
of the proximity of Mexico and the international border. By its very nature,
the borderland is an inherently globalized region. The proximity of Mexico
has accelerated socioeconomic and cultural integration between Mexico
and the United States, in part as a reaction to the increasing regionalization
of product and labor markets in a global economy. The signing of the North
American Free Trade Agreement in 1993 created an institutional affirma-
tion of this process. The subsequent decade saw growth in cross-border
flows of people, goods, capital, and culture spurred by several global phenomena in the region (Herzog 1990, 1999). Chief among these have been
the maquiladora (assembly plant), which ties U.S. capital to Mexican labor
enclaves in the manufacturing of goods (Sklair 1994), and the immigration process, which involves a cross-border supply-demand relationship in
which U.S. companies recruit workers from south of the border. This has
expanded not only U.S.-Mexican ties, but also global connections between
Mexican American barrios in the Southwest and the original homeland,
Mexico, through the latter's geographically contiguous zone—the northern
Mexico border.

San Diego, California, the case study analyzed in this chapter, is an important example of a globalizing region. Some 3 million people reside in
the San Diego region, and about one-half million are Latino. Add in over
2 million Mexican inhabitants in Tijuana-Rosarito-Ensenada and you have
a demographic space of 2.5 million Latinos/Mexicanos out of an overall
population of 5 million. Over the last two decades, San Diego's connection to Mexico and its urban neighbor, Tijuana, has dramatically expanded
across the spectrum of economic, functional, and cultural ties. Economically, NAFTA has cemented connections in the retail sector, manufacturing,
high tech, services, and tourism. Joint-venture capital is now moving freely
back and forth across the border. Assembly plants exist on both sides of

the border. Cultural events are commingled on a weekly basis as part of the cross-border tourism industry's attempts to expand markets in both nations. All of these connections mean greater functional integration of people, goods, communications, and money traveling north and south of the boundary. Many of these contacts reach directly into the barrio, as will be discussed below. Family ties, cultural connections, common language, and perhaps most critical, economic opportunity are now bringing Mexicans and Chicanos into greater contact, and thus bringing the barrio back into touch with Mexico.

Global connections across the border have reinforced the changing relationship between Latino/Chicano barrios and Mexico. Traditionally, Mexican immigrants to the United States were looked upon by Mexican citizens as *pochos*, people who abandoned the homeland and lost their cultural identity with Mexico while falling into a state of marginality in the host nation, the United States (Paz 1961). They became trapped in a liminal space between Mexico and the United States: in Mexico, they were the forgotten family outcasts, divorced from the homeland; as Mexican immigrants to the United States, they were generally held in low esteem.

But since the mid-1980s, this pattern has seriously begun to reverse. Mexico discovered the political and economic value of maintaining relations with its more than ten million immigrants in the United States (de La Garza and Vargas 1992). Politically, Mexican immigrants might be granted voting rights back in Mexico, thus suddenly having the power to change the outcome of important elections. Economically, Mexican Americans represented a stunning market for Mexican entrepreneurs, a market that had been ignored for too many decades. In specific subsectors — health services, food, design products, art, furniture, and household goods — Mexican suppliers had a built-in market among Latino immigrants, but that market had not been tapped sufficiently. Globalization facilitated the expansion of that market, through advertisement and direct marketing to barrio populations.

On several other levels, the globalization paradigm has changed the way the barrio functions. Under the two previous paradigms — barrioization and barriology — an "us" (Latinos) versus "them" (Anglos) polemic dominated. Globalization has created marginality on both sides of the border. Thus new alliances may form, between marginal people across the border and between supporting liberal factions on both sides of the line. Some Latinos in Mexico may not agree with these alliances. Thus old stereotypes about Mexicans fall away, as democratic choices give them a sense that they can honestly vote for what they think is right and not base their electoral choices simply on the ethnicity or cultural background of politicians. This liberates residents in Latino communities by giving them more autonomy over decisions made about the world beyond their borders.

SIX ECOLOGIES FOR LATINO BARRIOS IN THE SAN DIEGO–TIJUANA BORDER REGION

Given the relative newness of the globalization phenomenon, it is too early to predict social outcomes. An antiglobalization movement has formed, but it remains unclear whether it will become strong enough to topple cross-border trade. How significant the pro-globalization trend will be is also unclear. What is clear is that some combination of the forces of barrioization and barriology, combined with the new forces of globalization, commodification, and global production, will exercise a greater impact on the barrio. Below, I propose six ecologies that define the San Diego–Tijuana and surrounding region. These ecologies synthesize the effects of various social, political, economic, and geographic factors that have blended to create a new urban-cultural landscape in the Mexican barrio.

Ecology I. Barriers

Globalization imposes new hierarchies on the city. Exogenous investment will tend to exacerbate the pattern of place destruction begun in the twentieth century. Thus the city will grow as a function of corporate machines like skyscrapers, freeways, and mega-shopping malls. Exogenous actors, like global investors, national governments, corporations, or large-scale commercial developers, can have a big impact on barrios. One of the ways they transform the barrio is by imposing new built-environment elements that can be destructive to the barrio. For example, corporate investors often build structures out of character with the surrounding neighborhood; these structures often become barriers that impede the flow of people and the quality of life for Latino residents. Such barriers may range from concrete walls to poorly designed freeways to international fences.

In San Diego, barrios have been particularly impinged upon by freeway construction and, of course, by the great globalization icon—the border fence, which rises over San Ysidro's Latino community. Freeways are fundamental to the mobile lifestyle of Southern Californians, yet their placement in the urban landscape can be unfortunate. Mega-shopping malls innocently sell products, but they also define a certain set of values and completely transform neighborhood spaces by their disproportionate scale. These new "corporate landscapes" (Relph 1987) destroy the sense of place in a neighborhood.

Two examples of barriers in Latino barrios in San Diego include the Interstate 5 freeway and its Coronado Bridge on/off ramps in Barrio Logan, and the border fence in San Ysidro. In the early 1960s, freeways were being built all over Southern California. The I-5 freeway runs north and south and was extended from downtown San Diego to the border. The site decision for I-5 caused it to slice through the heart of Barrio Logan, effectively cutting the neighborhood in half, disrupting daily activities, and forcing hundreds of people out of their homes. Several years later, the barrio was again hit by a divisive facility, the new Coronado Bridge, which extended from the mainland to nearby Coronado Island. Once again, planners chose the path of least resistance, locating the bridge, as well as on and off ramps, in the heart of Barrio Logan. Once again, numerous homes were torn down, families were forced to leave the barrio, and, more important, a parade of ugly columns and pillars supporting the bridge now laced through the center of the community (Fig. 5.1).

In effect, the two new freeways sliced through the barrio from two directions, causing it to fragment spatially. Worse still, this accelerated the impulse of city officials and local industry to view the barrio as expendable. During the 1970s, vacant land was rezoned for industrial use, and noxious waterfront industrial users—recycling yards, chemical storage facilities, sheet metal shops, welding yards, and the like—began infilling spaces between and around the traditional residences.

San Ysidro, an important Mexican and Mexican American enclave in South San Diego, experienced a similar disenfranchisement through local and state government decisions to build two freeways (I-5 and I-805) directly through the community and to build public housing in a community already overloaded with low-income residents. But perhaps most destructive of all have been the facilities imposed on the San Ysidro community by the federal government, in the form of ugly fences and walls along the international boundary, as well as an unattractive immigrant detention facility sited in the heart of San Ysidro.

The building of fences along the border is part of the federal government's strategy to convert the border area into a high-security zone for protecting the sovereignty of the United States and keeping illegal immigrants and drug smugglers out of the country (Fig. 5.2). Agencies such as the General Services Administration (GSA), the Immigration and Naturalization Service and U.S. Customs, and the U.S. Army Corps of Engineers see the border as a place of surveillance, not a vibrant residential community. Yet the fact is that San Ysidro has more than twenty thousand mostly Latino residents, while more than triple that number reside in close prox-

5.1.   Pillars of Coronado Bridge slice through San Diego's Barrio
Logan. *Photograph by D. Arreola, 1984.*

imity on the Mexican side of the border in Colonia Libertad and other
downtown neighborhoods of Tijuana. Further, this is a space in which hundreds of thousands of people travel each day, to jobs, school, shopping, or
social visits. San Ysidro's border zone is a vital residential space.

   Nevertheless, federal security agencies have designed facilities that are
completely out of sync with San Ysidro's sense of place. The GSA designs border-crossing facilities in the form of stark, concrete, windowless
bunkerlike structures surrounded by high chain-link fences. INS and the
U.S. Army Corps of Engineers designed the border fences to be imposing
and stark. The San Diego–Tijuana wall is forty-seven miles long and built
from corrugated metal landing mats recycled from the Persian Gulf War.

5.2.   Corrugated steel fence, San Ysidro, California, border, Mexican side. Each cross symbolizes a Mexican immigrant who died traversing the border. *Photograph by L. Herzog, 2002.*

Migrants have punched it full of holes, so a second, parallel, wall is under construction a few hundred feet north. The new wall includes eighteen-foot concrete pilings topped with tilted metal mesh screens and an experimental cantilevered wire mesh–style fence being developed by Sandia Labs. The fence/wall runs toward the Pacific Ocean, where it becomes a ziggurat of eight-, six-, and four-foot metal tube fence knifing into the sea. The fence zone is also buttressed by six miles of stadium lights, twelve hundred seismic sensors, and numerous infrared sensors used to detect the movement of people after dark. The overall effect of this landscape is to render the San Ysidro border space into a war zone, with corrugated walls, chain-link fences, and helicopters patrolling at night.

Ecology II. Recaptured Space

Both Barrio Logan and San Ysidro began to fight back against their destruction as early as the 1970s. In Barrio Logan, the conflict between corporate industrial users, backed by government, and the residential/commercial sector reached a crescendo in the late 1970s, when the California Highway Patrol decided to build a police station directly under the bridge in the barrio. Residents erupted in mass protest, occupied the land under the bridge, and began spontaneously building a community park. To avoid confrontation, the City of San Diego and the state transportation agency (CALTRANS), as well as the California Highway Patrol, finally agreed to give the land over to the community. Thus was born Chicano Park, a public park that commemorates the moment when the community finally began to fight back against its destruction by local and state government. It is an illustration of the concept of barriology.

There is also evidence that this social movement was globalized, as Mexican artists and architects began to cross the border and participate in the rebuilding of the barrio. In the 1970s and the 1980s, backed by a statewide coalition of Chicano and Mexican artists, the community redesigned the space under the bridge by commissioning Mexican/Chicano artists to paint giant murals on the pillars of the Coronado Bridge; many of them became nationally recognized for their work. Indeed, Chicano Park has become a kind of international landmark for the use of muralism as a form of community protest as well as an icon of cultural identity (Arreola 1984; Barrera and Mumford 1988; Ford and Griffin 1981). Further, when the community decided to build a kiosk in the center of Chicano Park, it hired a Mexican architect from Tijuana to design it. The subsequent use of a pre-Columbian, Aztec-style raised platform cemented the connection between Chicano Park and Mexico. Also, numerous murals on the pillars of the bridge made visual references to Mexican as well as Latin American history. Chicano Park is a good example of the quest to recapture lost space in the barrios. This process is accompanied by what might be termed a "global cross-border solidarity" with Mexico.

In San Ysidro, the new plan for redevelopment, especially at the interface with the border crossing, seeks to erase the negative imagery imposed by the federal government and recapture the space for local residents. In a globalizing world, international border zones like San Ysidro can no longer be thought of merely as buffer spaces, defensive edges, or appendages to states. Nations now understand that border zones can house people, industry, trade infrastructure, and other economic activities. Borders, therefore, can physically become more than pass-through spaces; border zones can become destinations, dynamic urban centers, or satellite villages near major population agglomerations. The enormous density of pedestrian visitor flows and automobiles through border zones offers a ready market for trade and tourism.

The San Ysidro–Tijuana border crossing is the main gateway between Mexico and the United States, and the most heavily populated border metropolis in the world, with some 5 million to 6 million people. It is also the most dynamic NAFTA gateway in North America. The town of San Ysidro has a population of about 20,000, about 90 percent of Mexican origin. The social character of the town ranges from working and middle class to poor; statistically, it is one of the poorer subregions of San Diego. Downtown Tijuana lies a few hundred yards to the south of the San Ysidro border crossing, and that subdistrict of the city alone houses over 100,000 inhabitants within a radius of one mile of the border.

Thirty-four million vehicles and over seven million pedestrians cross this gate each year. But the port of entry and surrounding zone on both sides of the border are fragmented by a variety of land use and design problems—traffic congestion, poor circulation routes, disorganized land uses, conflicts between local interests, crime and public safety concerns, and unresolved land development plans. San Ysidro–Tijuana has been saddled with an abundance of negative land uses—border security agencies like the Border Patrol and Customs, warehouses, parking lots, and barbed-wire fences. If a single thing can be said to characterize the San Ysidro–Tijuana crossing zone, it is its unattractive image.

San Ysidro has been engaged in a process of recapturing its identity for two decades. In the late 1980s, the community was chosen by the American Institute of Architects (AIA) as a site for investigating planning problems. The subsequent study and report, *Adelante San Ysidro* (AIA 1988), marked the first time the community had had a plan to help guide its future.

Following the signing of NAFTA, the business community began to show interest in San Ysidro's revitalization. The City of San Diego designated San Ysidro a redevelopment area, thus opening it to millions of dollars of federal support funds.

In the late 1990s, a number of investors, community advocates, and others believed it might be possible to create an urban village at the San Ysidro–Tijuana border crossing. Border monitoring would continue to have a function within the district, but steps might also be taken to create better public places within a more cosmopolitan setting supported by careful landscape design. These groups debated methods for reinventing San Ysidro's border crossing zone.

One private firm purchased large tracts of land adjacent to the San Ysidro crossing and, with the Redevelopment Authority of the City of San Diego, put together a large-scale commercial development called Las Americas. The plan was a metaphor for the future of land along the border—an integration of pedestrian walkways, gardens, plazas flanked by private retail, entertainment, hotel, and office buildings (Fig. 5.3). The initial idea was to create a complex of mixed retail uses, a public plaza, a land-

5.3.   Artist's rendering of the Las Americas complex, San Ysidro, California. *Courtesy LandGrant Development, Las Americas, proposal brochure, 1997.*

mark pedestrian bridge linked to a new pedestrian crossing, a world trade center, a market facility, and links to a regional trolley, as well as across the border to Tijuana's downtown artery, Avenida Revolución. Here was recognition that the boundary itself could be a space of community life, rather than a space of instability, conflict, and smuggling. But, unfortunately, it also reinforced the pattern of creating new public spaces via the private sector, and in the long run will create a border zone that is a privatized place.

A reinvented and well-planned San Ysidro gateway could ignite a regional reconfiguration in the distribution of wealth. As San Ysidro becomes a destination in and of itself, more tourists and local residents may simply come to the border, and not necessarily cross it. Like Old Town in San Diego, San Ysidro and the surrounding South Bay could become a surrogate for a Mexican/border cultural experience, where consumers would feel comfortable coming to the border without having to deal with the perceived inconveniences of crossing into Tijuana.

Meanwhile, a new cast of global public spaces will be previewed here. While projects designed to recapture lost space are intrinsically worth celebrating, we must be sure that they are properly designed. For example, we can ask the following questions: Is Las Americas going to be a village that will feature pedestrian-scale public spaces with heavy use, or is it going to consist of suburban, freeway-oriented privatized spaces? Are the developers sincere in their claims of wanting to create a "village," or are they propagating a "myth of village," which will then be spread by private sector publicity agents, even though the private spaces will turn out to be artificial spaces oriented toward enhancing consumption? Will the quality of life for pedestrians and community members be enhanced? The conversion of the border into a theme park of artificial, consumer-oriented public spaces would not be entirely surprising, given the nature of public spaces in neighboring Southern California and the historical experiences with these types of spaces in other borderland locations (Arreola 1995, 2001).

Ecology III. Global Tourism

Tourism is one of many late-twentieth-century industries increasingly controlled by large multinational corporations. Global tourist enterprises like airlines, travel agencies, advertising firms, and investment groups exert a monopoly over the tourism industry (Britton 1982; De Kadt 1979; Jenkins 1982; Urry 1990). These corporate entities offer such profitable deals to local operators that they make it almost impossible for them not to participate, even if there are subtle, long-term negative environmental impacts.

Globalized tourism has a particularly important local impact and could substantially alter the quality of life of Latino barrios in San Diego. Global tourism reaches into the barrio when business entrepreneurs begin to see Chicano/Latino culture as a commodity that can be sold to tourists. Further, barrio residents are aware that tourism could improve the economy of their community. The problem lies in the tradeoffs between expanding the economy through large-scale tourism and perhaps losing cultural identity in the process. Development has a way of destroying the human scale of a barrio.

Scholars have argued that global corporations tend to want to homogenize products and consumer behavior; this enhances the degree to which they can control this behavior through global advertising and through iconographic images and products that are universally recognized, like golden arches and Mickey Mouse (Sklair 1991). When this homogenization is transferred from consumer products to consumer places such as barrio communities, as happens in the case of tourism, the effect is to homogenize and destroy not only authentic cultural spaces, but also the physical environment surrounding them (see, for example, Arreola 1995).

The commodification of place offers perhaps the most vivid illustration of how tourism development exposes the placeless objectives of its global corporate stockholders and boards of trustees. The main goal of tourism development is enhancing marketability and the volume of clients through the construction of landscapes that satisfy the needs of users. Studies have shown that tourists prefer comfort, reliability, and pleasure, especially in foreign settings. Urry (1990) speaks of "the tourism gaze," a socially constructed tourism landscape that brings to mind the comparison to Foucault's "medical gaze," another systematic, controlled design for an economic interest group.

Tourism becomes just another commodity, albeit a large one, for consumption, and thus part of the world market. The distinct marketing strategies of the international tourism industry have been shown to lead to the production of placeless landscapes, devoid or destructive of culture and nature (Eckbo 1969). If tourism is more profitable in built landscapes that are homogeneous, then what incentive can there be for tourism developers to preserve the original landscapes of the places where they invest?

Tourism can also create enclaves where the tourism activity becomes isolated from the surrounding community. Enclave design is now the driving force of most tourism development (as it is in the design of residential development in much of the western world, for example, in the form of gated communities). Common fixtures in tourism landscapes are fences, walls, and other elements that deliver the message that outsiders are not really welcome.

Both Barrio Logan and San Ysidro are currently embroiled in community debates about tourism development. An experiment to create a Mexican Disneyland just across the border in Tijuana failed, but some Latinos are wondering, Will it reemerge in the barrios of San Diego? Barrio Logan has not traditionally been a major tourist destination in the San Diego region; it could never rival the big-ticket tourism destinations such as Seaworld, the San Diego Zoo, and Old Town. However, the City of San Diego has recognized that it has been remiss in promoting Latin cultural heritage sites as part of the tourism experience. There is greater interest in San Diego in providing the visitor industry with more destinations in the area of cultural tourism. Mexican and Mexican American destinations fall high on the list of expanded tourism in the San Diego region. Barrio Logan would be a logical site for enhanced tourism. The Chicano Park murals could become part of a packaged tourism experience, as could visits to several outstanding local Mexican restaurants. Local Latino leaders, however, have been debating the tradeoffs between economic gains from the tourism economy and the potential loss of identity in the neighborhood if the barrio opens itself to tour bus circuits and packaged tourism.

San Ysidro has never been a tourism destination, but, rather, a gateway into Mexico. However, a reinvented San Ysidro could become a destination in its own right. Like San Diego's Old Town, San Ysidro could package itself as a border town that has long been connected to Mexico. It could house any number of Mexican tourism activities, which visitors could enjoy on their way back from Mexico—destinations such as museums, media experiences, and even mini theme parks. One local group has mentioned the idea of building a Museum of Immigration on the border west of the main business district of San Ysidro. Community leaders would also have to grapple with the loss of cultural identity brought on by having so many tourists stream through the district. However, since San Ysidro is already fragmented by a proliferation of money exchange houses, Mexican insurance agencies, and ninety-nine-cent stores, tourism activities, if strategically located, might not be so harmful to the community.

Ecology IV. Global Consumerism

As mentioned above, one of the central critiques of globalization is its tendency to reduce consumption behavior to a ritualistic and controllable activity that multinational corporations can manipulate through their vast empires of media, communications, and advertising. The systematic promotion of a fast-food consumerist culture is one example of this kind of global behavior manipulation (Ritzer 1996). The culture of the shopping mall is another example (Kowinski 1985). In both cases, global corporations have used the media, graphic design, and sophisticated marketing techniques to promote a culture of consumerism that defines specific kinds of spaces (malls, festival spaces, etc.) and specific kinds of experiences (fast-food consumption, mall promenading, etc.) as the primary forms of consumption. This culture of consumerism ultimately produces a very narrowly defined built environment, one dominated by suburban, freeway-oriented shopping malls and big-box retailers, and strip development corridors lined with fast food and small shopping centers. Much of this consumerist cultural landscape is, among other things, automobile, not pedestrian, oriented and largely placeless.

As Latino barrios enter into strategies of redevelopment and economic expansion, they are invariably faced with the prospect of developing consumerist spaces. This kind of development, like the tourism development mentioned above, could have the effect of sacrificing the neighborhood-scale way of life that has become fundamental to the barrio. Once again, barrio leaders will need to guide the community through the morass of decisions, land use, zoning, and other details necessary to protect communities from ugly, placeless shopping center development when better designs could be utilized.

The Barrio Logan neighborhood historically has been devoid of any significant commercial sites, such as supermarkets or shopping centers. Latino developers recognize this gap and have located space for a new commercial facility to be named the Mercado Shopping Center. One challenge for the project is how to create a neighborhood design and architecture scheme that respect the distinct Mexican/Latino qualities of the barrio, from its pedestrian scale to the existence of murals, gardens, and other elements. Developers of this project have reported difficulty in securing corporate loans; sources claim that the Mexican barrio is too risky for building a major supermarket chain. Further, they claim that the design for the center has watered down many of the original barrio-friendly design elements, effectively leaving an essentially suburban-style shopping mall with little reference to the barrio (Juárez 2002).

In San Ysidro, the community faces a massive shift toward the construction of retail outlet malls and new shopping centers to capture the large market of Mexican consumers and visitors passing through the region. The first new shopping mall, Las Americas, built literally adjacent to the international boundary line on the edge of San Ysidro, offers a glimpse of both the possibilities and the concerns embedded in this kind of enterprise.

Las Americas is a three-phase, mixed-use, retail-office complex located about one-quarter mile west of the San Ysidro–Tijuana border crossing. Phase I is 375,000 square feet of open-air retail and restaurant space. The second phase will add another 270,000 square feet of retail and restaurant space, and a Phase III is expected to add a pedestrian bridge to Tijuana, a new port-of-entry facility, a transit center, hotel, conference building, office space, and more retail shops. While the Las Americas project advertises itself as having an urban village atmosphere at a pedestrian scale, the empirical reality of the center in its first year of existence was at odds with this picture. First, the project is entirely tied to automobiles, since that is the only form of transportation that allows people into the center. In fact, the project's site plan has it set back from the main road, with a mega-parking lot separating the road (and town of San Ysidro) from the commercial center.

Second, the project is not really a public space in the traditional sense. A private security team patrols the shopping mall and is quick to intervene if users engage in any behavior that appears not to be oriented to shopping, for example, taking photographs, sitting and writing, sketching, or any sedentary activity on site. In short, the village engages in many forms of exclusion of public-space users, unless they fit the consumerist model desired by the private center.

Further, while the project calls itself mixed use, in fact, there is no residential space on the site, which adds to the problem of its overstated pedestrian-oriented village quality. In addition, while the construction of Phase I appears to have a second floor, closer inspection reveals that, for now, no second floor exists; rather, there are merely fake façades and imitation windows.

A project where users arrive by car is less likely to become an urban village. Without a permanent population on site, supplying instant markets for economic uses of the land, the space may have mediocre success and possibly substantial losses of revenue during times of international crisis. More important, the false architecture, lack of housing on site, and high level of security make this an unappealing public space, and one with limited positive spillover effects for the community. The rampant commercial investment element of the project seems to have overshadowed its potential impacts on San Ysidro.

Ecology V. post-NAFTA Housing

In post-NAFTA Southern California, neighborhood change is challenged by free trade and by more open borders between the United States and Mexico. Styles of architecture and tastes in housing cross north and south of the border as part of the larger diffusion of cultural practices along the international frontier (Herzog 1999). More critical, the continued flow of Mexican migrants, both legal and illegal, into San Diego has put greater pressure on the region to provide affordable housing for immigrants. But rising land costs and skyrocketing demand for property have driven housing prices beyond the reach of lower-income families. This has been especially hard on Latinos, especially immigrants arriving since 1980.

Latino immigrants have always filtered toward immigrant reception zones and traditional barrios. Both Barrio Logan and San Ysidro were immigrant-recipient communities for most of the last century. As housing costs have risen around the region, Latino barrios have been forced to seek innovative approaches to affordable housing. One important approach is for Latino nonprofit developers to build market-rate, lower-income housing in the barrio. In Barrio Logan, with the support of various social service and housing advocacy groups, Latino developers and a coalition of Latin and U.S. architects designed affordable housing units in a high-density, but well-crafted, residential complex called Mercado Apartments (Fig. 5.4).

Completed in the early 1990s, Mercado Apartments were designed with elements that would maintain the identity of the Barrio Logan neighborhood. First, the use of bright colors on the façade of the building was in-

5.4.   Mercado Apartments, San Diego's Barrio Logan, an example of housing designed to preserve cultural identity in the barrio. *Photograph by D. Arreola, 1998.*

tended to conform with the Mexican tradition of bright colors in urban settings—from markets and street murals to the tints in paints used on buildings and homes (Arreola 1988). Second, the architectural style of the complex was deliberately chosen to be similar to the simple, clean "pueblo-adobe" look, rather than the more ornate Spanish colonial revival. The latter is seen in the barrio as being less authentic, a product of Anglo Santa Barbara rather than something truly Mexican. Third, the building was intentionally not set back from the street, and it incorporated patios and balconies facing the street. This maintains the tradition of front porches seen in the older wooden cottages in the barrio and also the custom of Latino connection to the street and to street life.

There are 144 units in the Mercado Apartment complex. Over six hundred people live here, 90 percent Latino, and more than 50 percent come from the Barrio Logan/Logan Heights community. The project has been a successful model of how post-NAFTA barrios can create affordable residential living spaces under the right conditions.

Meanwhile, in San Ysidro, a Latino community group—Casa Familiar—has begun to buy land with the idea of building higher-density, affordable housing units. Several of these projects allow the architect to make a larger contribution to the urban design of South San Ysidro by creating new parks, plazas, and other walking spaces. Here the idea is not only to create affordable housing, but also to enhance the quality of life of the barrio.

Ecology VI. Invented Connections

In order to survive, I will argue, the barrios have to consolidate their healthy linkages to the larger city and, in the case of San Diego, to the border. Barrio Logan has discovered that it has many linkages to the region, through transportation infrastructure like the San Diego–Tijuana trolley, through joint participation in local development projects, and through its connection to new downtown facilities. The example of the San Diego Padres' new ballpark is illustrative.

Although a neighboring district of downtown San Diego (called East Village) actually houses the new ballpark, the Padres team has made a point of courting the Latino residents of two nearby barrios, Sherman Heights and Barrio Logan. A debate is raging inside the Latino community over this relationship, and it has not been resolved. Latinos wonder how sincere the Padre ownership has been in courting their community. They feel they were left out in the planning of the ballpark and were brought in only after the fact to mollify community concerns about the relationship between the ballpark and surrounding Latino barrios. The fact that Padres baseball has approached the Barrio Logan community shows that Latinos have increasing power. The Padres, in the end, do not want to alienate Barrio Logan.

Transit connections have been utilized to better link Latinos to the city. The San Ysidro trolley runs from the border into downtown San Diego (Fig. 5.5). Completed more than a decade ago, it facilitates commuting from both Barrio Logan and San Ysidro to jobs in the South Bay area and to the agglomeration of employment in and around downtown San Diego and the nearby Port District. Latinos in San Ysidro use the trolley to commute to work in National City, Chula Vista, and downtown. Many recent Mexican immigrants living in San Ysidro also use the trolley to reach the federal courts and immigration-related offices in the downtown business district. Finally, the new downtown ballpark will utilize the trolley extensively to bring Latino fans to ball games. Tijuana residents will be able to walk across the border and travel on the trolley from San Ysidro directly to the ballpark. South Bay Latinos will also be able to utilize the trolley to arrive car free at Padres ballgames. The trolley could become a key marketing tool for baseball and for other downtown economic activities seeking to expand their market to Latinos.

In San Ysidro, as mentioned previously, a huge new urban activity cen-

5.5.   The San Diego–San Ysidro trolley is an invented connection linking Barrio Logan
and downtown San Diego with Tijuana and northern Baja California. *Photograph by
L. Herzog, 2002.*

ter is being appended to the existing community. Las Americas, a giant
multi-use center, when its three phases are complete, will include shopping,
offices, community facilities, park space, and public plazas. It will eventually connect to Tijuana via a new pedestrian bridge. In its current form, Las
Americas is entirely reliant on automobile access. Missing is a connection
to the trolley line into San Diego and to the village of San Ysidro itself. Las
Americas lies nearly one mile west of the last trolley station. Discussions
to continue the line toward Las Americas have not moved forward to date.
While the San Ysidro Latino community has supported the project, there
is still concern about what the long-term impacts of this undertaking will
be, and whether the developers can be counted on to follow through with
promises to the community.

CONCLUSION

These six "ecologies" are as important to Latino barrios as they are to
the Mexican communities south of the border. I have suggested, first, that
global players like state and federal governments or corporate investors

tend to impose walls, freeways, and other barriers across the barrio land-scape. In response to these kinds of external developments, barrios have fought to recapture their social ecologies by constructing parks, murals, innovative housing, new urban villages, and other positive land uses.

Meanwhile, two new ecologies loom over the barrio—global tourism and global consumerism. Both stem from outside investors wanting to expand the barrio economy by creating artificial consumption spaces for tourists or shoppers. These spaces could compromise both barrio identity and the quality of pedestrian life, which has been so important to the character of the barrio.

But good news comes in the form of two other emerging ecologies: post-NAFTA housing, and invented connections. In San Diego, the construction of well-designed, appropriate, affordable housing is an important development in a city with a housing shortage. New housing designed to enhance the identity of the barrio is a further positive sign. Equally, the ability to invent new connections between the barrio and the rest of the city is key to the former's survival. The barrio cannot exist in a vacuum; it should retain its identity, but at the same time, it must find ways to connect to the metropolitan regional economy.

Globalization brings new problems to the Latino barrio, not the least of which is dealing with political actors and decision makers who are based far from the region, such as investors in global enterprises whose headquarters are in New York, Chicago, London, or Tokyo. Globalization connects the local to negative global phenomena. Drug smugglers' activities have been linked to Chicano gangs in San Diego, or to the children of some wealthy Mexican border families (O'Connor, 2002). The Latino barrio's success in transcending the era of barrioization must now come up against a new set of forces and a new kind of urbanism. How the barrio embraces and organizes itself in the face of this new urbanism will determine its fate in the twenty-first century.

6 BARRIO SPACE AND PLACE IN SOUTHEAST LOS ANGELES, CALIFORNIA

James R. Curtis

Four miles south of downtown Los Angeles, in the "exclusively industrial" city of Vernon, there is an extraordinary mural that sprawls more than eight thousand square feet across the high white walls and fences that surround Farmer John's meatpacking facility. Like the colorful pages of a 1950s illustrated children's storybook, the Leslie A. Grimes trompe l'oeil mural whimsically depicts Tom Sawyer–like farm boys—and no less than 709 pigs—frolicking merrily about a lushly bucolic countryside that is the very epitome of our romanticized image of nineteenth-century rural America. The block-long-plus mural is at once as illusionary as it is anachronistic. Not only does it put a happy face on the death and butchering executed on the kill floors behind those painted walls, it also seems hopelessly out of touch with both this time and this particular place: the old railroad-oriented industrial corridor and working-class communities of southeastern Los Angeles County, now home to one of the largest and highest concentrations of Latinos in Southern California. But as spatially and temporally incongruous as it may be, the naïve if nostalgic mural seems nonetheless a fitting artistic symbol for a resilient urban area that has endured in its traditional role, despite having undergone a truly profound economic and ethnic metamorphosis.

A little more than a generation ago, the southeast region was L.A.'s surprisingly robust answer to Detroit, Pittsburgh, Akron, and Chicago all rolled into one. Its gritty, smokestack economy was dominated by such Fordist assembly-line industries as automobiles, steel, glass, tires, and consumer durables, as well as meatpacking. Many of the jobs were unionized, with correspondingly good wages and fringe benefits. The blue-collar suburbs that surrounded the factories, while likely not conforming to anyone's conception of the suburban ideal, quietly emerged for their residents as places of meaning, identity, and memory. Here working-class people could afford to purchase a modest home, raise a family, and pursue their vision of the good life in a small-town setting that offered a healthful, civic-minded mix of commercial, social, and governmental institutions and organizations. But unlike their "frostbelt" counterparts in the Northeast and the Midwest, areas that were complex mosaics of ethnic and immigrant diversity, these working-class communities were composed almost exclusively of native-born whites. Conforming to a xenophobia that was pandemic in Southern California during the era, this Anglo archipelago embraced the array of discriminatory policies and practices that systematically promoted racial and ethnic segregation.

In this exclusionary fashion, it contributed to the hanging of a "cotton curtain" that extended along the railroad tracks paralleling Alameda Street, which dramatically, if precariously, formed the quarter's western edge. Just across the street was South Central L.A., an area predominantly of blacks and Latinos that suffered from critical housing shortages, high population densities and unemployment, poverty, and mounting social discontent. Prior to the mid-1960s, few could have foreseen the impending urban upheaval and economic implosion that would shortly reorder not only the area's economy, but also its social geography, transforming these solidly white communities into solidly Latino barrios.

In this chapter, I examine the factors and processes responsible for the formation, growth, and contemporary character of Southeast L.A. as a Hispanic space and a Latino place. I argue that while the area has seemingly reinvented itself over the past three decades, it nonetheless has retained much of its essential historical form and function as an important industrial workplace and a home of substance for working-class people.

Second, I contend that from a metropolitan-wide perspective, the southeast region represents the newest barrio type in an evolving sociospatial pattern of Latino settlement and culture in the greater city. Toward that end, I introduce a four-stage barrio typology that conceptualizes in a space-time continuum the historical Hispanization of the Los Angeles metropolis.

Finally, I maintain that while the Latino tenure has altered the Southeast's cultural landscape, the material and infrastructural legacy inherited from preceding occupants was generous and continues to exert a pervasive influence on the area's built environment and sense of place.

SOUTHEAST LOS ANGELES

It has been variously called L.A.'s "empty quarter," its "rustbelt," its "great underbelly," its "armpit" (Davis 1994; Donahoe 1987: 70). Such pejora-

6.1.   Hard-edged industrial landscape of Southeast Los Angeles, looking northwest across the Los Angeles River toward downtown. *Photograph by D. Arreola, 2000.*

tive terms paint a bleak picture indeed of the Southeast as a kind of vanquished industrial wasteland, an urban eyesore, and a civic embarrassment (Fig. 6.1). But like the popular images and stereotypical portrayals of all places—whether positive or negative, historical or contemporary—these mask a reality on the ground that is decidedly more complex and dynamic, from both the economic and the social perspectives. Although the Southeast has been an area of considerable significance to the Los Angeles economy since the 1920s, it seems fair to suggest that it has suffered from a citywide apathy, disinterest, and outright avoidance, all of which have probably contributed to misconceptions and trite generalizations about it.

Although its boundaries are vague, the Southeast broadly includes an area that lies immediately south of downtown L.A., separated from it by a maze of freeways and railroad tracks as well as the fenced and concrete-encased Los Angeles River, which flows south, southeast, and then south again as it skirts the district (Fig. 6.2). For the purposes of this study, the quarter's northern edge is Vernon, an illusory "city" that reported ninety-one residents in the 2000 Census, but employs more than fifty-five thousand workers. The eastern edge is taken as the Los Angeles River and the 710 Freeway that parallels it. Although certainly more permeable than it once was, the western boundary remains chiefly along Alameda Street and the Southern Pacific Railroad tracks that connect with the harbor at Long

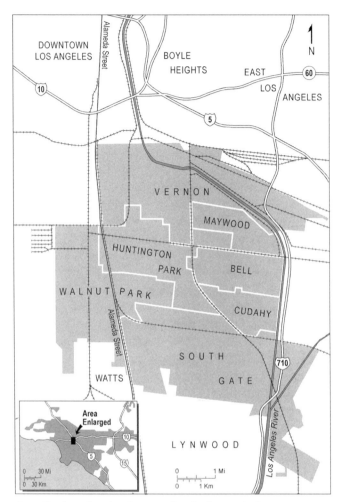

6.2.   Southeast Los Angeles area of study. *Source: Author.*

Beach about fifteen miles distant. The southern edge is defined for convenience here as the political boundaries that separate the cities of South
Gate and Lynwood, just north of the 105 Freeway. A compelling case could
be made for inclusion of Lynwood as well as other predominantly Latino
communities east of the river, including Bell Gardens, Commerce, and
Pico Rivera, but physical, land use, and perceptual barriers, coupled with
slightly contrasting histories and socioeconomic factors, argue against such
inclusion.

As thus delimited, the Southeast encompasses a flatland area in the heart
of the Los Angeles basin that is about 3.5 miles wide by 4.5 miles long. Po-

litically, it consists of several modest-sized cities with populations of fewer than 100,000, including Bell, Cudahy, Huntington Park, Maywood, South Gate, Vernon, and the unincorporated community of Walnut Park. South Gate is the largest of the cities in both area and population; Huntington Park is the commercial and cultural core; Vernon is the industrial axis; Bell, Cudahy, Maywood, and Walnut Park are mainly residential.

According to the 2000 Census, the Southeast as defined above had a total population of 262,858. As reflected in Table 6.1, even by Southern California standards, it is an area of extraordinarily high concentrations of Latinos, ranging from a low of 90.0 percent in the city of Bell to a high of 96.3 percent in Maywood. These communities are, in fact, so predominantly Hispanic that they rank among the least ethnically diversified urban places in the greater Los Angeles area. Among the Latino cultures, residents of Mexican descent constitute between 67.0 percent and 77.0 percent of the total population in each of the communities. There are, however, locally significant concentrations of other Latino national-origin groups, including, most notably, Peruvians, Cubans, Puerto Ricans, and Central Americans, especially Salvadorans. The small non-Hispanic populations consist primarily of diverse Asian groups as well as Anglos, mainly longtime elderly residents. The African American population remains negligible.

Growth of the Latino population in the area is revealed in Table 6.2, which documents the increasing percentage of Latinos residing in the two largest cities, Huntington Park and South Gate, between 1960 and 2000. From a nascent base of less than 5 percent of each city's total population in 1960, within twenty years Latinos ballooned to 46 percent in South Gate and to an astounding 85 percent in Huntington Park. In the next twenty-year period, from 1980 to 2000, growth of South Gate's Latino population accelerated relative to Huntington Park's, resulting in both cities achieving

TABLE 6.1—SOUTHEAST LOS ANGELES POPULATION, 2000

CITY	TOTAL POPULATION	LATINO POPULATION	% LATINO
BELL	36,664	33,328	90.0
CUDAHY	24,208	22,790	94.1
HUNTINGTON PARK	61,348	58,636	95.6
MAYWOOD	28,083	27,051	96.3
SOUTH GATE	96,375	88,669	92.0
WALNUT PARK	16,180	15,496	95.8

Source: U.S. Bureau of the Census 2000.

TABLE 6.2—PERCENT LATINO POPULATION, HUNTINGTON PARK AND SOUTH GATE, 1960–2000

CITY	1960	1970	1980	1990	2000
HUNTINGTON PARK	4.5	35.9	85.0	92.0	95.6
SOUTH GATE	4.0	17.3	46.0	83.1	92.0

Sources: Arreola 2000, table 4.3; U.S. Bureau of the Census, 2000.

similarly high percentages by 2000. Explanations for the initially contrasting rate of Hispanization for the two cities illuminate the broader pattern for the area as a whole.

At the inception of rapid Latino growth in the 1960s, Huntington Park was a comparatively poorer community with a larger stock of older, more-affordable housing that became increasingly available as a consequence of escalating white flight. Moreover, at that time, most of the incoming Latinos were moving into the Southeast in classic spillover fashion from the overcrowded barrios of Boyle Heights and East L.A., located only a couple of miles north of Huntington Park and neighboring Maywood. The latter were over 80 percent Hispanic in 1980. This suggests that, at least early on in the process of ethnic transition, Hispanic settlement of the Southeast occurred in a general north-to-south progression, reflecting social, economic, and geographical factors. As time went by, however, the entire Southeast became a receiving area for Latinos relocating from elsewhere in the metropolitan area, and also, increasingly, for newly arriving first-generation immigrants from Latin America. This group reportedly now constitutes close to 50 percent of the area's Hispanic population (Rocco 1996: 375).

A TYPOLOGY OF BARRIOS IN THE HISPANIZATION OF LOS ANGELES

Before examining more specifically the catalysts for and circumstances of the growth of Latino populations in the Southeast, it is instructive to consider how the area fits into the broader historical and contemporary context of Hispanic settlement in the greater Los Angeles area. As a consequence of the long tenure of Latinos in the region—in concert with high population growth, increasing internal diversity, and great areal expansion of settlement—Hispanic communities in L.A. have evolved and changed over time. In an attempt to frame such change into a conceptual format that might facilitate critical historical and geographical analysis, I offer a typology of four barrio types that assesses the evolving growth, form, and character of

Latino communities in Los Angeles (Fig. 6.3). For each of the barrio types, I identify a phase and dominant spatial process. These include the general time period, a hypothetical barrio form, an associated geometric representation, a dependent or independent status based largely on socioeconomic conditions and linkages, and, finally, an inward or outward orientation, also based primarily on socioeconomic factors.

Mindful that the limited intent of this section is to suggest for contextual purposes only that the Southeast represents the most recent stage in the sociospatial evolution of barrios in Los Angeles—not to be an exhaustive explanation of either the concept or the subject matter—only an abbreviated analysis of each barrio type is proffered here.

For most of the history of Los Angeles, the barrio was a rather small, insular Mexican enclave that focused on the city's main plaza; it was a marginalized community that had evolved as a consequence of Spanish colonial town planning, limited population size, and socioeconomic factors, including poverty and racial segregation (Griswold del Castillo 1979: 141). Indeed, from its founding as a civil pueblo by the Spanish in 1781 through the first decade of the twentieth century, the plaza-based community—or "Sonora Town" as it came to be called—housed most of the Mexican popu-

Barrio Type	Phase & Spatial Process	Time Period	Hypothetical Form	Geometric Representation	Dependency-Orientation
Plaza-based	Inception/ Constriction	1781-1910			Independent, Inward-oriented
Urban *Colonias*	Transition/ Nodality	1911-mid-1950s			Dependent, Outward-oriented
Hierarchical	Maturity/ Primacy	Mid-1950s-mid-1980s			Dependent, Inward-oriented
Metropolitan Realms	Emergent/ Expansion	Mid-1980s-present			Independent, Inward- & Outward-oriented

6.3.   Typology of Los Angeles' evolving barrios. *Source: Author.*

lation, close to 90 percent as late as the 1880s (Acuña 1984: 7–8). The centripetal pull of the city center, coupled with land-tenure restrictions, economic limitations, and difficult living conditions in the surrounding rural areas, spatially constricted the barrio from extending much beyond a mile or so of the plaza. Because of the nucleated or monocentric nature of the settlement, the barrio could be classified as independent, meaning that it did not chiefly rely for its economic livelihood on either outside communities or external resources. Because it was a cohesive community with extensive internal social and economic networks, it was largely inward oriented.

After 1910, the historic plaza-based barrio was supplanted by numerous urban *colonias,* or small Latino enclaves, occupied almost exclusively by residents of Mexican ancestry (Allen and Turner 1997: 92–109). Lasting perhaps until the mid-1950s, this transitional form emphasized a spatial process of multiple nodality, facilitated technologically by mass adoption of, first, the electric streetcar, and, subsequently, motor vehicles, including public buses as well as private automobiles (Brodsly 1981). *Colonias* were dispersed widely throughout the aggressively expanding metropolitan area, especially in relatively inconspicuous, undesirable places or zones of disamenity. These zones, despite their shortcomings, afforded employment opportunities, especially in agriculture, railroads, and industry (Ríos-Bustamante and Castillo 1986: 104–109).

The area most immediately and significantly affected, however, lay just east of the Los Angeles River. As the streetcar lines pushed out of downtown L.A. and over the river after 1910, several *colonias* were established, including Boyle Heights, Brooklyn Heights, Lincoln Heights, City Terrace, Belvedere, and Maravilla (Romo 1983). Although these and related *colonias* shared characteristics, each evolved quite separately and had its own distinctive identity. That identity was buttressed by a strong social bond that was a product of poverty, the construction of family life, minority status, and shared histories, as well as Mexican national origins and culture (Sánchez 1993). Because of their relatively small size and limited functions, they may be considered dependent, outwardly oriented communities that relied upon external areas and resources for employment and most necessities of daily life.

Over the ensuing twenty-five or thirty years from the mid-1950s, the *colonias* on the east side coalesced through a process of what might be labeled "superbarrioization," creating a single dominant or primary Latino place—East L.A. East L.A.'s extraordinary growth was fueled by high natural population growth rates and soaring immigration, especially after passage of new immigration laws in 1965 (Allen and Turner 1997: 37–41). As the preeminent port of entry, it attracted immigrants not only from Mexico but also, increasingly, from other Latin American countries. In keeping with the basic geographical conceptions of a central place, East L.A. sat atop the barrio hierarchy, sprawling over fifteen square miles, undoubtedly the largest and most renowned Latino community in Southern California, if not the nation. Below it was a nesting of primary and secondary barrios of varying size, Hispanic composition, and levels of social and economic importance. Although several of these achieved significance in the Latino experience as places of residence, activity, and identity, they all were, directly or indirectly, wittingly or unwittingly, oriented toward and conceptually dependent on the collective Latino symbolism and resources of East L.A.

By the mid-1980s, the Hispanic population in the four-county Los Angeles megalopolis surged over four million and expanded widely in all directions. An emergent phase became evident as critical thresholds of population, physical size, and social and economic activities were attained in several large barrio complexes throughout the greater urban area. These metropolitan barrio realms were relatively self-sufficient, independent Latino communities no longer functionally or symbolically oriented toward East L.A. Indeed, East L.A. had itself become one such realm, albeit the largest. A partial list of other realms at present might include San Fernando–Pacoima in the San Fernando Valley; the Central American core of Pico-Union just west of downtown L.A.; Long Beach–Wilmington–San Pedro in the south Los Angeles County harbor area; Culver City–Mar Vista in West L.A.; Santa Ana in central Orange County; and the Southeast L.A. industrial quarter. Although inwardly oriented and sustained by a strong internal sense of community and daily activity spheres revolving around home, work, schools, shopping, and recreation, the cultural space and networks of the mobile individuals and families within these realms typically embrace other barrios and Latino places of congregation throughout the urban area (Rocco 1996: 369). Despite overarching similarities, each of the realms is distinctive in the specific ways in which it evolved as well as in the character of its cultural landscapes and place personality.

DEINDUSTRIALIZATION OF SOUTHEAST LOS ANGELES

The Hispanic settlement of Southeast L.A. evolved as a consequence of the intersection of both endogenous and exogenous factors that fundamentally altered the district's economic and social underpinnings. Beginning in the late 1960s and accelerating into the early 1980s, the most compelling of the exogenous, or external, factors that galvanized the ethnic transformation was the phenomenon of deindustrialization (Bluestone and Harrison 1982). Deindustrialization was a component of global economic restructuring (Scott 1998), which changed the nature of industry and industrial employment in the area (Soja 1989: 190–221). In essence, through this convoluted and, at times, bitter process of economic decline, stagnation, and then reorientation, the area was poised to return full circle, back to its original role as an incubator of industry and a source of employment for an ethnically segregated working class.

From its origins in the 1920s, the Southeast had traded on a fortuitous combination of geographical site and situation factors to capture much of L.A.'s non-defense-related industrial and manufacturing output (Hise 2001). In addition to its close proximity and ease of access by road and, especially, rail to the harbor, downtown, and the transcontinental railroad switching yards, the district benefited from the availability of inexpensive land, cheap utilities, low tax rates, accommodating zoning laws, few and relatively toothless environmental regulations, and highly supportive local governments; it also enjoyed a large, skilled, and reliable labor force (Nicolaides 2002: 23–26). Utilizing these and other advantages, including the emergence of a colossal and voracious consumer market in Southern California, the Southeast amassed an impressive and diversified base of industrial, manufacturing, processing, and distribution activities that included literally hundreds of factories and firms, ranging in number of employees from only a few to several thousand. Among the largest were those in the dominant industrial triad of auto assembly, rubber and tires, and metallurgy and machinery. Corporations included, most notably, General Motors, Firestone Tire and Rubber, Bethlehem Steel, Consolidated Steel, Aluminum Company of America, Continental Can, Owens-Illinois Glass, and Weiser Lock, each employing at its peak between several hundred and five thousand workers. Meatpacking was another area specialization, a development that stemmed from location there of the Union Stock Yards from 1922 to 1963 (Nelson 1983: 215). Vernon alone counted more than forty-five plants that employed thousands of workers. In addition, the district had significant concentrations of factories or outlets in several other industries, including furniture, chemicals, clothing and apparel, food processing, and trucking.

As an "open shop" region that had staunchly, even violently, opposed organized labor, wages and working conditions in the district initially were not always good, and in some plants were abysmal (Donahoe 1987: 996). But the situation improved enormously in the mid-1930s with passage of the National Labor Relations Act (the Wagner Act) and associated legislation, which facilitated the formation of labor unions. Although not all of the industries were unionized—and even in those that were, relations between the trade unions and corporate management were often contentious—the Southeast nonetheless developed a reputation as a place where a working-class person could earn a decent wage.

Moreover, demand for labor at all skill levels rose significantly, even spectacularly in some sectors, through the Depression, the Second World War, and into the era of postwar prosperity in the 1950s and the early 1960s. Such sustained demand was a product not only of burgeoning industrial growth, but also of critical labor shortages that stemmed from the massive repatriations of Mexican workers during the Depression, the flight of labor due to the war effort, and mounting competition from nonindustrial employers after the war. Consequently, beginning in the 1920s and gaining momentum into the 1950s, a steady stream of workers poured into Southeast L.A., coming mainly from the Midwest and the upland South. This flow bolstered the area's prodigious employment ranks and populated its aspiring, if rather insular and severely segregated, suburbs.

Although the prospects for continued growth and prosperity seemed assured in the glow of impressive industrial output and employment gains, as early as the 1960s, small but ominous cracks in the structure of industry could be detected. Almost imperceptibly at first, production workers, ostensibly victims of industrial automation and other labor-reducing technological innovations as well as management initiatives, were laid off in some factories. Then into the 1970s, slowly but inextricably over the decade, one after another, the plants themselves began to close. Mirroring trends that had surfaced earlier in Detroit, Youngstown, Gary, and other old-line industrial cities in the traditional manufacturing belt of the upper Midwest, it soon became apparent that the catalysts for such unexpected and extraordinary change were not isolated to Southeast L.A. Rather, they sprang from an enormous and unprecedented national economic restructuring that was itself the product of a radically evolving international economy. At issue were declines in older basic industries verses the growth of newer technology-oriented industries; but even more deep-seated were fundamental considerations of the changing roles of capital and labor in a postindustrial global economy (Sassen 1988).

If this trend began as a trickle in the late 1960s, it ended as a proverbial flood in the early 1980s. In the five-year period 1979 through 1983, many of district's largest plants closed, including Norris Industries, with over two thousand workers; Firestone Rubber, with more than one thousand workers; Bethlehem Steel, with more than two thousand workers; and General Motors, with nearly five thousand workers. In addition to the closures and serious layoffs in countless smaller plants, other major closures soon followed, including the Dial Corporation's Purex plant and the Oscar Mayer meatpacking company (Rocco 1996: 375). Literally tens of thousands of jobs were lost, more than 12,500 in South Gate alone (Nicolaides 2002: 329). Drastic change was afoot in Southeast L.A., which would culminate in the formation of a new industrial economy and a sweeping ethnic transformation of its suburbs.

If the process of deindustrialization had evolved over time, a second exogenous factor that contributed to the Hispanization of Southeast L.A. occurred with dramatic suddenness: the Watts riots of August 1965. By the time African American anger and frustration had been vented and civil order restored, 34 people had perished, more than 1,000 had suffered injuries, nearly 4,000 had been arrested, and some 6,000 buildings had been damaged (Soja 2000: 135–140). For the Anglo residents of the district—many of whom lived within gunshot range of Watts and had, as the riots raged, stood armed guard over their homes as the local police barricaded the streets leading into their communities from South Central L.A.—this rebellion was a startling and unmistakable declaration that their racialized, segregated way of life was fast coming to an end. As Nicolaides (2002: 64) points out in her detailed and illuminating account of South Gate, among the white working class a mentality had evolved that united the area "most tenaciously around the shared identities of race, homeownership, family status, and nativity." Indeed, she argues, not only "racial separatism" was embraced with the same vigor as was "self-reliance, independence, Americanism, [and] familism," but the new agenda in the postwar period was explicitly "to segregate, protect, and defend the suburb" (Nicolaides 2002: 5, 182). The Watts riots shattered those values and the racist agenda. So when the job layoffs and plant closures came, coupled with the new social environment, most Anglos accepted that it was time to move on: as many as 200,000 or more left the area between the 1960s and the end of the 1980s (Davis 1994: 57).

REINDUSTRIALIZATION AND BARRIOIZATION

The Southeast L.A. communities were devastated, not only by the massive loss of jobs and corresponding disruption of their traditional social fabric, but also by a serious erosion of their tax base and hence their ability to provide critical services. In the difficult transition to a new order, the Southeast was aided by several endogenous, or internal, factors that affected the process of barrioization and contributed to a reindustrialization of the area's economy. Initially, it seemed, the Southeast would become a very different place from what it had been historically. But now as a certain level of stability, if not necessarily commensurate prosperity, has been achieved, the characteristics that defined the area as a working-class district with considerable attributes as well as persistent problems remain intact: it has changed by degrees, but not in essence.

Typical of rapid ethnic residential succession, the flight of Anglos from the Southeast created a significant housing opportunity for incoming Latinos. Houses and apartments were readily available, and home prices and rents plunged, at least initially. An important endogenous factor that facilitated this filtering-down process was the existence in several of the communities of small Mexican *colonias* that dated from as early as the 1930s. These historical cores of Hispanic population, together with a small but influential nucleus of middle-income Latinos who had arrived by 1950 and had purchased homes in the upper end of the local housing market (Nicolaides 2002: 194), fostered the establishment of kinship, social, and employment networks that eased and promoted the continuing settlement of Hispanics.

By the mid-1980s, and earlier in the northern tier of communities, however, explosive Latino growth had already pushed the existing housing stock to the threshold of saturation. Nevertheless, in response to critical housing shortages in barrios throughout the metropolis, in-migration to the Southeast continued, increasingly of poorer first-generation immigrants. To accommodate the demand and to help marshal sufficient financial resources to acquire housing, a host of adaptive housing and survival strategies were employed. In addition to conventional densification or in-filling practices, such as replacing old single-family homes with new multifamily complexes or building small apartments on the back property of existing homes, the most common approach was for two or even three families—or several single men—to jointly purchase or rent a dwelling. Indeed, three-bedroom, one-bathroom detached houses were routinely advertised by real estate companies as "two-family homes" (Donahoe 1987: 101). Another widespread, though illicit, practice was to convert garages and other domestic structures, such as toolsheds, into rental units (Nicolaides 2002: 330–332). Not only had the housing market become saturated, but because the incoming families were typically larger than earlier generations, the average household size also increased substantially, rising to over five in some of the communities. Moreover, reflecting high demand and limited supply as well as profit taking on the part of landowners, prices in the housing and rental markets had become hyperinflated.

Understandably, the municipal governments were overwhelmed. Not only were they buffeted by soaring population growth, extraordinarily high densities and crowded conditions, double-digit unemployment rates, a large and growing concentration of low-income groups with pressing social service needs, and a rapidly deteriorating physical infrastructure, they also were reeling from a crippling loss of revenues. Tens of millions of dollars annually were lost as a result of plummeting sales, property, corporate, and personal taxes due to the plant closures and downsizing in those that remained in operation. This loss was coupled with the folding of many established retail outlets that had catered to the departed Anglo population. Moreover, in 1978, state Proposition 13 had passed, which slashed California property taxes, greatly reducing the budgets and causing fiscal chaos in municipal governments statewide. Consequently, the Southeast communities were forced to drastically cut expenditures for basic services, including police and fire protection; hospitals, clinics, and health-care programs; water, street, and sewer operations; the array of social services; libraries; as well as educational institutions. Because of the heavy influx of children, the schools, in particular, were hard hit by the dual problems of diminishing budgets and enrollments that often exceeded by two or three times a school's official capacity.

In their desperation, some of the cities sought quick-fix financial solvency in questionable ventures, including establishment of gaming facilities, especially card casinos; ill-conceived or poorly planned redevelopment projects; and tax subsidization and financial incentives to attract new retail trade, especially car dealerships. Although well intended, most of these brought little long-term financial relief. Complicating the fiscal dilemma was the fact that political leadership still rested primarily in the hands of longtime Anglo residents who were not always aware of, or sensitive to, the needs and concerns of the new majority of the area's citizenry (Davis 1994: 67–68). Strict code enforcement and heavy use of the power of eminent domain, for example, had resulted in a serious reduction of the housing stock and the consequent displacement of low-income populations.

In sum, by the mid-1980s, the overall quality of life in the Southeast had seriously declined, and the prospects for improvement appeared discouragingly bleak. But despite forecasts of impending municipal and economic collapse, the nadir had, in fact, been reached. Better times were coming, if only incrementally.

A second endogenous factor that affected the area's contemporary economy and Latino character was the process of reindustrialization. As a corollary of deindustrialization, reindustrialization is predicated upon the production equation of deep reductions in labor costs, resulting in the formation of primarily low-wage, semiskilled and unskilled, nonunion jobs. Although it certainly was not unique, Southeast L.A. nonetheless possessed a distinctive and attractive ensemble of factors that promoted such development. In addition to its locational advantages and existing industrial infrastructure, the area offered relatively inexpensive leases, tax incentives, subsidized utilities, and, most critical, an abundant supply of cheap and dependable Latino labor. As the traditional heavy industries departed, local and foreign entrepreneurs, especially Asians, converged on the area to introduce a plethora of smaller-scale "replacement industries," most notably, textiles, apparel, and dyeing; furniture making and upholstery; food and beverage processing; paper manufacturing and recycling; warehousing and storage; petrochemical refining and pharmaceuticals; light metals fabrication and recycling; wrecking and welding operations; toys and novelties manufacturing; and industrial–toxic waste disposal. As a consequence of this bittersweet process of industrial transformation, aggregate employment levels have rebounded to nearly the 1970s peak; the area remains an impressive generator of jobs. Of course, wages, benefits, and working conditions are generally at levels substantially below those previously enjoyed by union workers, and in some less-enlightened plants, virtual sweatshop environments prevail. But while certainly less than ideal, the wage structure for similar work is comparable to averages throughout the metropolitan area, and employment in the district has proved to be stable through the 1990s and into the new millennium. It also bears noting that, as in the past, a substantial majority of the Southeast's working residents are not employed in the district; these communities are not now, and never have been in the classic sense, company towns.

Two additional endogenous factors have influenced the Latino character of the area and improved its quality of life since the late 1980s. First has been the emergence of more fiscally sound and responsive local governments, led predominantly by Latino elected and appointed officials. Although city coffers remain modest, revenues have both increased and stabilized. More important, the cities have successfully sought and secured external funding, including federal government block grants and a host of redevelopment monies and low-interest loans. These resources have been used primarily to expand public transportation; build new parks, community centers, and recreation facilities; fund social programs; and attract new industries. New schools have also been built.

The second factor has been the revitalization of the area's commercial districts and strips, which now offer a large and diverse range of retail and service activities. These services cater to the local population and, in-

6.4. Revitalized and Latino-reoriented commercial core of Huntington Park, California, along Pacific Boulevard. *Photograph by D. Arreola, 1997.*

creasingly, to a citywide Latino clientele by providing not only shopping and entertainment, but also employment and entrepreneurial opportunities (Fig. 6.4).

PLACE PRÉCIS AS CONCLUSION

Through the process of barrioization, the Southeast L.A. area has been imbued and enlivened with a distinctive Hispanic personality and verve. But like all communities, its built environment and sense of place are evolving composites of both past and present influences. Although the Anglos may have departed, the physical, institutional, and symbolic legacy they left was generous and remains visually and structurally pervasive. In assessing these communities both materially and as places to live, one is struck not only by their manageable size, but, more critically, by the breadth and solidity of their institutional framework. Compared with most barrios in Southern California, these historically blue-collar suburbs are relatively well endowed with civic center complexes, parks, playgrounds and recreational facilities, community centers, libraries and schools, public auditoriums and fraternal halls, churches, medical facilities, and shopping areas. As inadequate or overcrowded as they may have become, the sheer existence of such institutions immeasurably enhances the quality of personal and social life and contributes to a strong sense of order, stability, and identity.

Likewise, despite high densities and signs of deterioration in some neighborhoods, the district's residential areas are relatively stable and attractive when compared with their metropolitan counterparts. Many are being well maintained if not upgraded. Here, as in Latino communities nationwide, traditional Hispanic housescape elements, including the placement of fences and yard shrines as well as the use of bright house colors, have been grafted onto their inherited Anglo structures (Arreola 1988) (Fig. 6.5). Through such forms of Latino cultural expression, a kind of place consciousness and sense of spatial attachment have been engendered that contest the socioeconomic and environmental marginalization of these barrios. As Villa (2000: 4–6) has persuasively argued, a "barrio is a complex and contradictory social space" with a "recurring dialectic" of positive and negative qualities. That seems abundantly true of the barrios in Southeast L.A.'s industrial corridor.

6.5.   Curbside view of a Tudor-style house with Hispanic embellishment in Huntington Park, California. *Photograph by D. Arreola, 1997.*

III

NEW COMMUNITIES

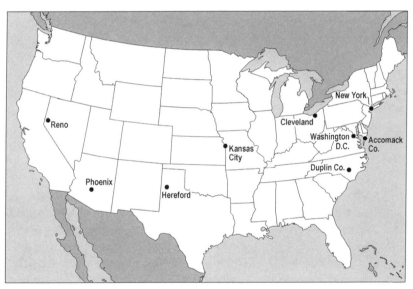

Map 3. New communities.

CHANGING LATINIZATION OF NEW YORK CITY

Inés M. Miyares

A *New York Times* article entitled "Latino Culture Wars" (2002) featured the story of a young girl who was to represent her school in Jamaica, Queens, by singing a solo at the twenty-fifth anniversary conference of the New York State Association for Bilingual Education. The lyrics of the song focused on pride in Puerto Rican heritage. Ironically, though, the nine-year-old singing the song was from Guatemala. The article argued that, despite the increasing diversification of the city's Latino community, the dominant culture to which all Latinos were assimilating was a Caribbean culture, particularly a Puerto Rican one.

New York City's Latino community has long been dominated by a Caribbean presence, and that has affected the definition and perception of Latino culture in numerous ways, including the cultural curriculum of the school system. The two largest Latino communities, Puerto Ricans (2000 population of 830,123) and Dominicans (2000 population of 579,269) account for 65.2 percent of the city's 2.2 million Latinos. However, the other 35 percent are diversified and both culturally and spatially differentiated from the Caribbean community. While some New York–based scholars and politicians suggest that non-Caribbean Latinos in New York assimilate toward a Caribbean identity and culture, in this chapter I will argue that the manifestation of Latino identity varies by borough, by neighborhood, by era, and by source country and entry experience. This process of differential identity illustrates the dynamics of international and transnational movement and affirms the geographical concept of invasion and succession.

Currently, what are perceived to be established Latino landscapes in the city are experiencing significant transformation through the arrival of immigrants from new source countries. In Manhattan, for example, where the two largest communities dominate the Latino landscape, "Latino" means Caribbean, whereas in Queens, where the Latino population is both more diverse and heavily Andean, the Latinization of the landscape has taken on a character that reflects the diversity of the community. The newest arrivals, the Mexicans, are transforming the Latino landscapes of all the boroughs, and some groups, both old and new, have no clearly identifiable landscape.

Three issues are explained in this chapter. First, it is necessary to understand how to interpret New York's ethnic landscapes. Since emigration from Latin America began in the mid-to-late nineteenth century and did not become a dominant force until the mid-twentieth century, I discuss criteria for identifying and interpreting a Latino streetscape in the context of immigration to a previously existing built environment. I then describe the evolution of New York's Latino community, with particular emphasis on the shifts in source regions and source countries between 1990 and 2000. Third, I discuss how these shifts are now visible on the city's landscape, especially the social and economic streetscape.

Ford (1995) has challenged geographers to examine the interplay between new concerns and existing generalizations in cities experiencing rapid change. New York is an ideal location in which to explore this tension. Latino ethnic patterns in New York are diverse, yet Latinos are more numerous here than in any other metropolitan area in the nation. Although the city's history and built environment differ significantly from those of most other major Latino centers, it is important to examine whether there are common characteristics in New York that have allowed Latinos to adapt to the city.

New York's built environment differs in two major ways from that of cities in the West and the Southwest with large Latino populations. First, many western and southwestern cities were founded during the Spanish colonial era or prior to the cession of northern Mexico in 1848. Thus, Spanish/Mexican settlers formed the initial layers of the cultural landscape, and subsequent waves of settlement reinforced earlier patterns. Settlement locations and cadastral patterns (Arreola 2002; Arreola and Curtis 1993; Nostrand 1987), housescapes (Arreola 1988), public spaces such as plazas (Arreola 1992), and other cultural signatures used to identify Latino landscapes cannot be applied directly to Latin American neighborhoods in New York. Except for the symbolic construction of "*casitas*" by Puerto Ricans (Aponte Parés 1997), the housing stock of New York City is dominated by multiple-unit structures and not by houses, and Latin American immigrants were latecomers into an already built environment.

There are landscape signatures that parallel those found in the South-

7.1. Mexican-owned grocery store on 8th Avenue in Sunset Park, Brooklyn, incorporating the Mexican flag, the Virgin of Guadalupe, the Mexican coat of arms, and El Cerrito de Tepeyac, the site of the apparition of the Virgin of Guadalupe in 1531. *Photograph by I. Miyares, 2002.*

west and the West, however. These are the adaptations made by Latinos to existing streetscapes. Arreola (1988), for example, argues that the use of color on exterior façades, a practice initiated by the Spanish during the colonial era, can be used to identify a Mexican American housescape, as can placement of religious shrines, perhaps to the Virgin of Guadalupe, in front of a house. In a city like New York, where residents have little control over residential façade hue, the use of color and other public symbols such as religious iconography are incorporated into the economic streetscape rather than into the house. Colors from national flags, national shields, and emblems; stereotypes like the use of saguaro cactuses by Mexican businesses; and religious iconography, particularly of the Virgin of Guadalupe, are commonly incorporated into façades and on the awnings of businesses (Fig. 7.1).

Historically, the plaza as social space has served a critical role in Latin American geography and culture (Arreola 1992). Although New York is not a plaza town, neighborhoods are salted with small parks and playgrounds that have assumed the role of plaza. Additionally, many Latino neighborhoods have wide sidewalks that have become social spaces, whether through placement of permanent street furniture such as benches or of temporary furniture such as lawn chairs and card tables for domino games. Informal economies common to Latin American plazas, such as churro, tamal, and fruit drink vendors, have also emerged on these sidewalks. Loud music, lively conversation, and playing children, too, fill these public spaces. What varies from neighborhood to neighborhood is the source and style of the Latino music, the topics of conversation, and the colloquial variations of Spanish or indigenous language spoken.

Even within these generalizations, three types of Latino streetscapes have evolved in New York. The first is the enclave streetscape, which is dominated by a single group. Once the prevalent streetscape, this type is found in very few areas of the city today. The second is the multiethnic streetscape, which adapts and redefines itself regularly as a reflection of demographic changes among both the entrepreneurs and the communities being served. The third is a streetscape of invasion, where new immigrants take advantage of site and situation to establish an economic banner street. Finally, there are also groups, both old and new, that are either invisible on the landscape or have only relic or commemorative landscapes comparable to those identified by Jeffrey Smith (1999) in Colorado.

FROM CARIBBEAN ROOTS TO A PAN-AMERICAN COMMUNITY

Although it is probable that there was a significant Latino presence in New York City prior to the mid-nineteenth century, it is during the latter half of that century that the roots of today's Latino community took hold. Initial waves, though quite small relative to immigration from Europe, comprised principally businessmen, entrepreneurs, artisans, merchants, white-collar professionals, and their dependents. Very few Central and South Americans were part of those early waves. The majority were Cubans who came either to establish a business or to work in the growing number of cigar factories in Lower Manhattan and nearby Elizabeth, New Jersey. New York also drew Caribbean leaders such as José Martí from Cuba and Dr. Julio Henna from Puerto Rico. Martí, for example, who ultimately became the father of Cuban independence, worked for Joseph Pulitzer's *New York World*. The 1890 Census enumerated the Latino population at approximately six thousand, of which 57.5 percent were from Cuba and the West Indies (Haslip-Viera 1996).

Settlements at the turn of the twentieth century were defined by a series of *colonias* that emerged near places of employment. The populations at these locations tended to follow from source towns in the homeland during the early decades of this process (Herbstein 1983; Sánchez Korrol 1983). Cubans and Puerto Ricans were employed especially in some five hundred cigar factories congregated in Lower Manhattan, the city's Lower East Side, and Chelsea, areas occupied by concurrent immigrants from eastern Europe and Italy. A significant Puerto Rican community developed near the Brooklyn Navy Yard, where waterfront jobs were readily available. Puerto Rican–owned commercial establishments emerged in Greenpoint, Brooklyn, drawing settlers to that neighborhood. As Jews moved out of East Harlem—which had been occupied by immigrant Jews through the late nineteenth and early twentieth centuries—Puerto Ricans filled the void, finding affordable housing in a neighborhood where they could also establish a local economy. This led to the transformation of East Harlem into Spanish Harlem, or El Barrio, the city's dominant Puerto Rican neighborhood. Spanish Harlem eclipsed the older center near the Brooklyn waterfront (Sánchez Korrol 1983).

Although the Cuban population grew from its nineteenth-century beginnings, it was outpaced by the growth of the Puerto Rican community. Once the dominant group, Cubans declined in both relative proportion of the total number of Latinos and economic and political importance. Cuban settlement and commerce became increasingly directed toward New Jersey and, subsequently, to South Florida. Cubans continue to have a presence in the city, but there is no longer a visible Cuban community or landscape.

The movement of earlier waves of immigrants into unskilled and lesser-skilled jobs in the garment industry and other light industries in New York from the 1930s to the 1950s coincided with declines in the sugar industry and resultant unemployment in Puerto Rico (Herbstein 1983). Additionally, the nascent commercial airline industry made travel between San Juan and New York affordable for the working-class population on the island. As U.S. citizens, Puerto Ricans were not subject to visa restrictions imposed on potential immigrants. This led to continued growth of the city's Puerto Rican community, both in number and economic strength.

Early on, it was the lesser skilled and lesser educated who came to New York, while the better educated and better skilled tended to migrate elsewhere, particularly to Sunbelt cities (Ortiz 1986). As the various New York enclaves matured, entrepreneurial and professional classes developed, providing goods and services to members of the community. A unique barrio politics developed and political leadership emerged, raising issues of concern beyond those solely of the island. Puerto Rican and Nuyorican (New York Puerto Rican) arts, music, and culture took new form, creating a Latino landscape with a distinctive Caribbean flavor that penetrated beyond the confines of the enclave. As the Puerto Rican population grew, new neighborhoods emerged, such as those in the Bronx, and followed similar patterns of invasion and succession.

The Dominican presence in New York also dates to the late nineteenth and early twentieth century, but as a small, invisible population. Large-scale Dominican migration to the United States in general and to New York City in particular began in 1965 with the co-occurrence of three critical triggers. First, out-migration was seen as a potential solution to the problem of dissent following the 1965 revolution and the U.S. military invasion and subsequent installation of a puppet government. Entry visas to the States were granted to would-be or actual revolutionaries. Second, large-scale direct and indirect foreign investment in the Dominican Republic had so restructured the economy that significant proportions of the population were unemployed (Hernández and Torres-Saillant 1996). Third, the Immigration and Nationality Act of 1965 had removed family-reunification visas from the annual visa ceilings. Thus, Dominicans who received the initial post-revolution visas were able to obtain visas for networks of immediate family members. By the 1980s, Dominicans made up the single largest group of immigrants to New York, a position they held until 1996, when their total was slightly surpassed by immigrants from Russia (Kraly and Miyares 2001; New York City Department of City Planning 1992, 1996, 1999).

Although there are Dominicans residing throughout the city, the largest concentration in both New York and the United States is in the Washington Heights/Inwood area of Upper Manhattan (Fig. 7.2). The neighborhood has plentiful housing, many affordable apartments large enough to accommodate families, as well as good access to public transportation and parks. Waves of immigrants have passed through the area since the turn of the twentieth century, including Jews, African Americans, Puerto Ricans, and Cubans during the early 1960s. Dominicans entered through the process of invasion and succession and soon became the dominant population of the neighborhood (Jackson 1995).

Washington Heights developed both an enclave-based and a transnational economy and political culture. Immigrants ranged from educated professionals and entrepreneurs to lesser-skilled laborers, and within a rather short time, the retail landscape of Washington Heights was dominated by Dominican-owned businesses providing a full spectrum of goods and services to the community. Through the redistricting that followed the 1990 Census, Washington Heights was able to elect a Dominican, Guillermo Linares, to the U.S. House of Representatives. Circular migration and transnational households retained social, cultural, and even po-

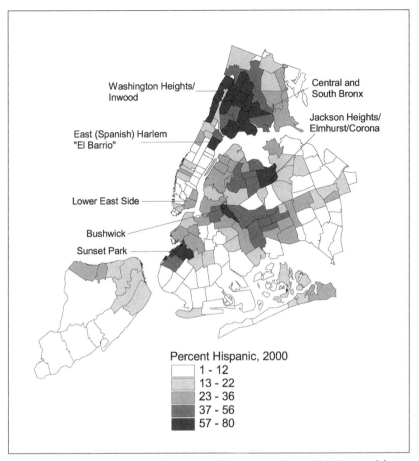

Washington Heights/
Inwood

Central and
South Bronx

Jackson Heights/
Elmhurst/Corona

East (Spanish) Harlem
"El Barrio"

Lower East Side

Bushwick

Sunset Park

Percent Hispanic, 2000

1 - 12
13 - 22
23 - 36
37 - 56
57 - 80

7.2. Percentage Latino by ZIP Code, New York City, 2000. *Source: U.S. Bureau of the Census 2002b.*

litical ties, resulting in the election of Leonel Fernández Reyna, a resident of Washington Heights, as president of the Dominican Republic
(1996–2000). During Fernández Reyna's presidency, his family remained
in Washington Heights, and at the end of his term, he returned to the neighborhood as well, making him the first U.S.-based transnational president.

Similarly, political events in South America and the Caribbean coincided with changes in immigration law in 1952 and 1965. In the 1950s,
middle-class Colombian entrepreneurs seeking to escape the chaos and violence in their homeland came to New York in growing numbers, as did
Cubans escaping Batista's tyranny and, later, Castro's Communist regime.
Unlike previous waves of Latin American immigrants, even earlier co-

nationals, the Colombians and many of the Cubans settled in the Jackson Heights neighborhood of Queens (see Fig. 7.2). By the 1960s and the 1970s, the Colombians were followed by Ecuadorian and Peruvian entrepreneurs seeking better opportunities in the United States.

The Immigration and Nationality Act of 1965 introduced numerical limits on Western Hemisphere immigration (Kraly and Miyares 2001), and the first major waves of South American immigrants did not have immediate family resident in the United States. Thus they had to qualify for visas as skilled professionals who could later facilitate the entry of extended family members through family reunification. Although settling throughout the city, the South Americans concentrated in the Jackson Heights–Elmhurst-Corona corridor of Queens (Fig. 7.2), establishing a multinational economy and providing the community with the full spectrum of goods and services for the Andean-region immigrants. However, since this corridor is a major transportation route through what has become the most ethnically diverse region of the country, the South American entrepreneurs expanded their products and services beyond solely the needs and wants of Andean immigrants. Successful entrepreneurs quickly learned to extend their businesses beyond the confines of the enclave.

During the 1980s, Central Americans, hoping to attain asylum status subsequent to the various civil wars occurring in the region, migrated to the New York metropolitan area. The largest group was from El Salvador, but there were migrants from Guatemala and Nicaragua as well. Unlike in Washington, D.C., San Francisco, Los Angeles, and other major settlement regions for Central Americans, enclave economies and streetscapes developed in nearby suburbs of Nassau County and in New Jersey, not within New York City itself. The Central American population tends to settle in neighborhoods with other Latino populations and to enter lesser-skilled labor niches. They seek goods and services from Spanish-speaking entrepreneurs and professionals, but travel to Long Island or New Jersey for specifically co-national products and services (Coutin 2000; Mahler 1995; Wright et al. 2000).

The most recent waves of arrivals to New York are Mexican. Although there was a Mexican presence in the city in the nineteenth century (Haslip-Viera 1996), the contemporary waves of Mexican immigrants began in the mid-twentieth century (Méndez and Miyares 2001; Smith 1996). The explosion of the Mexican population in New York, however, is a phenomenon of the 1990s. Informal accounts of the waves of Mexicans coming to New York City suggest that surpluses in historical labor niches in Southern California were the root of the earliest documented and undocumented migrants to the metropolitan area. For example, there are stories about Mexicans recruited as laborers in the landscaping industry in New York who settled in the upper Bronx near the Westchester County line, or in eastern Queens near Nassau County. Others argue that the migration of Mexicans from Los Angeles to New York is related to the greater social acceptance of undocumented immigrants, coupled with the loose INS inspection at La Guardia Airport in Queens at the time. A significant proportion of these Mexicans who came to New York in the 1990s are from the Mixtec regions of the State of Puebla (Méndez and Miyares 2001; Smith 1996), and since 1990, the Mexican population has increased by at least 235 percent. Since many undocumented Mexicans were not enumerated in 2000, the actual number is probably substantially higher.

Mexicans have settled in all five boroughs, and their growth has outpaced the growth of all other Hispanic groups in the city. Their settlement is typically an invasion into both Hispanic and non-Hispanic immigrant neighborhoods. The population comprises both recent arrivals from Mexico and internal migrants from other U.S. states. Thus in a short period of time, the Mexican community in New York has established a significant economic presence along the city's streetscapes. In some neighborhoods, such as Brooklyn's Chinatown in Sunset Park, they are a readily accepted curiosity; in existing Puerto Rican neighborhoods, such as Spanish Harlem ("El Barrio") or Bushwick, they are seen to be taking over the neighborhood.

DEMOGRAPHIC CHANGE, 1990–2000

As reflected in Table 7.1, between 1990 and 2000, New York City's total population grew by 9.4 percent, while the city's Hispanic population grew by 16.9 percent. Part of that growth can be accounted for by the city's improved efforts to identify housing units, resulting in a better enumeration. However, while it is clear that substantial growth did occur, this growth was not evenly distributed among the national-origin groups, nor was it evenly distributed among the boroughs. Since the boroughs differ greatly in both total population and national-origin composition, it is important to look at both the enumerated populations and the relative changes over the ten-year period.

How the Hispanic-origin question was reported makes comparing the 1990 and the 2000 data challenging. A change in wording resulted in an increase in the proportion of Latinos who did not indicate a specific country of origin, and thus an explosion of the "Other Hispanic/Latino" popula-

TABLE 7.1—CHANGES IN LATIN AMERICAN POPULATIONS, BY NEW YORK CITY BOROUGH

POPULATION SUBGROUP	BRONX			BROOKLYN			MANHATTAN		
	1990	2000	% CHANGE	1990	2000	% CHANGE	1990	2000	% CHANGE
TOTAL	1,203,789	1,332,650	10.7	2,300,664	2,465,326	7.2	1,487,536	1,537,195	3.3
HISPANIC	531,575	644,705	21.3	474,878	487,878	2.7	405,821	417,816	3.0
% HISPANIC ORIGIN	44.2	48.4		20.6	19.8		27.3	27.2	
MEXICAN	12,273	34,377	180.1	18,512	58,825	217.8	10,948	30,391	177.6
PUERTO RICAN	336,367	319,240	−5.1	263,424	213,025	−19.1	149,464	119,718	−19.9
CUBAN	9,209	8,233	−10.6	9,481	6,755	−28.8	18,671	11,950	−36.0
DOMINICAN	87,261	133,087	52.5	55,301	65,694	18.8	136,696	136,283	−0.3
CENTRAL AMERICAN	19,847	21,408	7.9	37,452	32,111	−14.3	11,872	9,433	−20.5
SOUTH AMERICAN	43,909	20,782	−52.7	63,435	33,451	−47.3	53,046	25,193	−52.5
OTHER HISPANIC/ LATINO	22,709	107,578	373.7	27,273	78,017	186.1	25,124	84,848	237.7

POPULATION SUBGROUP	QUEENS			STATEN ISLAND			ALL BOROUGHS		
	1990	2000	% CHANGE	1990	2000	% CHANGE	1990	2000	% CHANGE
TOTAL	1,951,598	2,229,379	14.2	378,977	443,728	17.1	7,322,564	8,008,278	9.4
HISPANIC	403,563	556,605	37.9	32,734	53,550	63.6	1,848,571	2,160,554	16.9
% HISPANIC ORIGIN	20.7	25.0		8.6	12.1		25.2	27.0	
MEXICAN	12,794	55,481	333.7	1,171	7,798	565.9	55,698	186,872	235.5
PUERTO RICAN	94,395	108,661	15.1	17,472	28,528	63.3	861,122	789,172	−8.4
CUBAN	18,406	12,793	−30.5	1,252	1,392	11.2	57,019	41,123	−27.9
DOMINICAN	52,309	69,875	33.6	1,146	1,867	62.9	332,713	406,806	22.3
CENTRAL AMERICAN	30,375	34,183	12.5	1,676	1,964	17.2	101,222	99,099	−2.1
SOUTH AMERICAN	163,047	152,696	−6.4	6,716	4,252	−36.7	330,153	236,374	−28.4
OTHER HISPANIC/ LATINO	32,237	122,916	281.3	3,301	7,749	134.8	110,644	401,108	262.5

Sources: U.S. Bureau of the Census 2002a, 2002b.

tion. While there appears to be some decline in several Latino communities, it is unlikely that a drastic decline actually occurred, particularly among the Puerto Ricans and the South Americans.

Settlement in particular boroughs and neighborhoods is affected by New York's real estate business. Despite laws against overt steering in the real estate market, some agents continue covertly to direct clients to particular neighborhoods based on their race or national origin. Those most affected are Afro-Caribbean Latinos and Mexicans (Miyares and Gowen 1998).

The Bronx has been a majority-minority borough for several decades, with the proportion of the borough's Hispanic population increasing from 44 percent to 48 percent between 1990 and 2000 (Table 7.1; Fig. 7.2). Puerto Ricans continue to dominate the population, accounting for at least half of the enumerated Hispanic population and nearly a quarter of the borough's population. However, the borough witnessed substantial growth in Dominican and Mexican populations during the decade. The Central American population, with the exception of Hondurans, is small. The Bronx hosts a growing Garifuna population — Afro-Caribbean/indigenous Hondurans from the country's Caribbean coast. Since people of color, whether Latino, African American, or Afro-Caribbean, make up the overwhelming majority of the borough's population, it is not surprising that growth has continued among these groups. Housing in most of the Bronx is still quite affordable, and housing discrimination is much less prevalent than in the other boroughs.

Brooklyn has historically been the city's most populous borough, but its Hispanic population is substantially smaller than that of the Bronx. Approximately half of that population is Puerto Ricans who continue to reside in the earlier settlements along the waterfront, in Greenpoint/Williamsburg and in Bushwick. However, redevelopment along the waterfront has led to a greater scattering of the Puerto Rican community in Brooklyn. The second-largest group is the Dominicans, but they compose a much smaller share of the total and have tended to co-reside with Puerto Ricans.

Mexicans are third and appear to be settling in historically immigrant but not Latino neighborhoods. A growing agglomeration has appeared in Sunset Park, where Mexicans are coinvading a Jewish and Polish neighborhood along with recently arrived Chinese immigrants (Fig. 7.2). The Mexican population grew by 300 percent, from 896 in 1990 to 3,591 in 2000, in the Sunset Park–Industry City 11232 ZIP code (U.S. Bureau of the Census 2002b).

Another Brooklyn neighborhood that has seen explosive growth in its

Mexican population is Bushwick (Fig. 7.2). This neighborhood is 80 percent Hispanic, the majority of whom are Puerto Ricans. However, the Mexican population grew by 260 percent over the 1990–2000 decade, from 1,262 to 4,544 (U.S. Bureau of the Census 2002b).

Hispanics constitute just over a quarter of Manhattan's population and, as in the Bronx, they are principally Caribbean in origin (Table 7.1). As in Bushwick, growth in the Mexican community has occurred primarily in existing Latino areas—principally "El Barrio", or Spanish (East) Harlem (Fig. 7.2). The economic redevelopment, gentrification, and subsequent higher rents that affected many other Manhattan neighborhoods during the 1990s, including Central and West Harlem and Washington Heights/Inwood, has yet to spread to East Harlem. Many middle-class Puerto Ricans moved to other neighborhoods in search of better housing and schools, opening the door to Mexican settlement. Mexican entrepreneurs established businesses in storefronts vacated by Puerto Ricans, thus attracting more Mexicans to the area. A popular nickname, which describes this area, is "Little Puebla," Puebla being the state in East-Central Mexico that appears to be the *patria chica,* or little homeland, of this Mexican immigrant subgroup.

Although there are Hispanics from all regions of Latin America in Washington Heights and Inwood (Fig. 7.2), there is no question about the dominance of the Dominican community in that neighborhood. Unlike many parts of East Harlem that continue to be landscapes of poverty and blight, Washington Heights exudes a Caribbean energy and youth regularly rejuvenated by daily flights to and from Dominican homeland towns of Santo Domingo and Puerto Plata. The presence of Yeshiva University is a significant remnant of the once-dominant Jewish population. In some ways, though, the remaining Jews who reside here seem to be guests of the Dominican community.

Most of Queens was developed in the twentieth century, and its housing stock is more suburban in size and density than that of the previously discussed boroughs (Miyares 2001). Queens' largest Latino source region is also the Caribbean, but its most visible population is from South America (Table 7.1). The borough population tends to be more middle class, even among immigrants. The Caribbean population in Queens tends to be middle class and often co-resides with the South Americans. A quarter of the population is Hispanic, and South Americans embody at least 27 percent of all Hispanics in Queens. Colombians and Ecuadorians form the largest groups and tend to co-reside in the Jackson Heights–Elmhurst-Corona corridor of northwestern Queens (Fig. 7.2). Mexicans have settled in this heavily Latino neighborhood, but they are found increasingly in every immigrant neighborhood where the previous residents have moved to the suburbs, thus providing access to the housing stock and storefronts.

Staten Island is unlike the other boroughs in that it is the most suburban area of the city. The majority of the housing stock is single-family detached dwellings. Its physical and infrastructural separation from the rest of the city, coupled with its limited public transportation, attracts a middle- to upper-middle-class population, and like suburban populations elsewhere, they depend on cars. There are less-expensive apartments and housing projects in close proximity to the Staten Island Ferry dock. However, most of the Latinos, chiefly Puerto Ricans, who live in Staten Island are in middle-income households that have moved into home ownership. The suburban nature of the borough has attracted Mexicans, now the second-largest subgroup, to fill residential labor niches such as landscapers, housekeepers, and nannies.

LATINO STREETSCAPES

Since the overwhelming majority of New York City's population lives in apartments as opposed to houses, it is often difficult to discern the presence of an ethnic group by looking at residential housescapes. However, every neighborhood has a principal commercial street, and this is often converted into an ethnic main street. It is commonly through business signs that immigrants make their presence known. Names of businesses reflect place names from the home country or key cultural artifacts. Colors of the national flag are common in store awnings, and the flags themselves and national crests abound in store décor. Key religious symbols are also common. Immigrants are so prevalent and diverse that coethnic proprietors use many kinds of visual clues to attract potential customers.

Within the Latino community in New York there are currently three types of economic streetscapes. The first is the "enclave streetscape," where a single national group dominates the landscape. Although goods and services may be advertised to all groups in the immediate neighborhood, there is no question about the dominant group. The second is the "multiethnic adaptive streetscape." This emerges on a commercial street where multiple groups take advantage of site and situation, particularly access to transportation. No single group dominates. Instead, the retail landscape is fashioned to mirror the ethnic dynamic of the city. Entrepreneurs who establish firms on such a street tend to be adaptive to their clientele as they expand their businesses out of the initial ethnic main street. Third is the "landscape of invasion." Since immigration in New York has historically exemplified invasion and succession through neighborhoods, new groups typically create landscapes of invasion as they establish businesses on ethnic main streets.

There are also groups that have not established an economic streetscape or whose landscape is a relic of an earlier era. In New York, two groups fall into this category of "landscapeless" Latinos—Cubans and Central Americans. During the nineteenth century, the heyday for New York–based Cuban cigar manufacturing, there was a clear Cuban landscape (Haslip-Viera 1996). However, with the decline in this industry and subsequent decline in New York's Cuban population, that landscape disappeared. The 1950s saw the establishment of several Cuban businesses along 82nd Street in Jackson Heights, but by the turn of the twenty-first century, most of those businesses had closed and the Cubans had moved to the suburbs. While there are still a number of Cuban-owned businesses, they are dispersed throughout the city, and with the exception of Cuban restaurants, they are very difficult to identify as Cuban owned. A statue of José Martí may stand at the Avenue of the Americas entrance to Central Park, but unlike in Miami, where even parking structures are named after the Cuban leader, the average New Yorker would be hard-pressed to say who Martí was or why his statue was there.

The Central American population in New York is also an invisible streetscape population, but for very different reasons. Central Americans, principally Salvadorans, have established an economic enclave in Hempstead in Nassau County east of Queens, and numerous Salvadorans have businesses in Pan-American areas of northern New Jersey. Salvadorans in the city tend to fill particular labor niches, such as helpers at greengrocers owned by Koreans and as bussers or waitstaff in restaurants.

ENCLAVE STREETSCAPE IN DOMINICAN WASHINGTON HEIGHTS/INWOOD

In Washington Heights, there are still Jewish bakeries and delicatessens, the main campus of Yeshiva University, and several synagogues, but this is no longer a Jewish landscape. It is clearly a Dominican one, strongly connected transnationally to its home country. Since it is common knowledge that Dominicans dominate the population and culture of the neighborhood, symbols of national pride create the streetscape. Few stores, however, specify that they are Dominican owned, and most of the signs are in Spanish and commonly use the red, white, and blue of the Dominican

7.3.   A typical multiservice travel agency in Washington Heights, Manhattan. The neighboring store, Santo Domingo Records Shop, is one of the few with a Dominican place name. *Photograph by I. Miyares, 2002.*

flag. Since the Dominican community controls so much of the neighborhood's economy, Dominican place names are rare as business names. One key exception is the use of Quisqueya, the Taino word for the island of Hispaniola.

Whether on a residential or a commercial street, Caribbean music and the voices of children fill the air. The language of trade is Spanish, as evidenced by signs and conversations. Nearly every billboard, regardless of what it is advertising, is in Spanish. During warmer seasons, the streets are filled with men playing dominoes and discussing local and global events. Transnational connections are reinforced in multiple ways, particularly through businesses that facilitate *envíos* and *cargas* (shipments of money and packages), and through international telephone calling centers. Many Latino New Yorkers do not have long-distance, especially international long-distance, service from their residential telephone providers. Instead, they take advantage of storefront businesses where one pays for a certain number of minutes to make an international call at a prearranged time. Since these types of telephone centers are common in many sending countries, they have become lucrative businesses in the city. American Airlines, which serves Santo Domingo and Puerto Plata with daily flights, is very visible on the streetscape through travel agency signs and ticket offices throughout the neighborhood (Fig. 7.3). Public art, such as murals, reflects pride in community and culture, and the themes evidenced in murals target the next generation, calling for pride and strength in the transnational character of Washington Heights.

While Dominican place names are unusual on signs in Washington Heights, other symbols of national identity and pride are prevalent. One of the neighborhood's major streets, Saint Nicholas Avenue, has been renamed for Juan Pablo Duarte, the founding father of the Dominican Republic. One restaurant, 27 de Febrero, is named for Dominican Independence Day. Most restaurants in Washington Heights serve goat on May 30, the date in 1961 when former dictator Gen. Rafael Trujillo—known as El Chivo, or The Goat—was assassinated.

Food, a key part of every culture, is central to the Dominican-ness of this neighborhood. Street vendors sell tropical fruit, peeled and sliced for immediate consumption, as well as *empanadas de yuca, pastelitos,* and *kipes* —various types of fried pastries. Fresh tropical juices and *batidos* (milkshakes) are available on every block. As the community has matured economically, it has expanded its marketing of Dominican foods. The first Washington Heights–based Dominican restaurant chain, Caridad, now has a dozen locations across Upper Manhattan and the Bronx. The sights, scents, and sounds of the Dominican Republic are so much a part of the Washington Heights landscape that one is vicariously taken to the island.

MULTIETHNIC ADAPTIVE STREETSCAPE IN PAN-AMERICAN JACKSON HEIGHTS-ELMHURST-CORONA

When it was originally developed in the early twentieth century, Jackson Heights was to be an exclusive pseudosuburb modeled on the Garden City concept and designed to attract Park Avenue residents with its large apartments, formal English gardens, quality boutiques, social clubs, tennis courts, and other similar amenities constrained by space in Manhattan. Although a master plan for Jackson Heights was never developed, connections to as many forms of public transportation as possible were intentionally developed in order to allow the targeted population to commute to jobs in Midtown or Lower Manhattan. Commercial streets were designed to run parallel or perpendicular to subway and bus lines, and subway routes connected Jackson Heights to similar developments such as Sunnyside Gardens and Forest Hills. It was not until the 1950s that residential infill development connected Jackson Heights to neighboring and more working-class Elmhurst and Corona (Miyares 2001).

The exclusionary covenants that governed the original deeds (no Jews, no blacks, no Catholics) became moot when the real estate market crashed in the 1930s. Jews and Irish were the first to break through the covenants controlling Jackson Heights real estate, soon followed by Colombians and Cubans, but no single group established an enclave beachhead. Certain commercial streets have attracted Indian, Pakistani, Korean, Filipino, and other Asian businesses; thus the economic streetscape is not even exclusively Pan-American. The Latino American economy is focused on Roosevelt Avenue, approximately between 74th Street and 90th Street.

Since so many countries of origin have located their businesses on Roosevelt Avenue, country-specific toponyms and symbols are prevalent. Travel agencies, telephone centers, money-transfer centers, and similar businesses specifically designed to maintain transnational connections advertise services to all of Latin America, whereas the name of the business and the awning color communicate the proprietor's place of origin. The perceptive eye notes the difference between the shades of yellow and blue of the Colombian and Ecuadorian flags. Bakeries named for Cali, music stores named for Guayaquil, and Poblano grocery stores are common sights. With the entry of Mexican businesses, one now sees icons of the Virgin of Guadalupe as well as saguaro cactuses incorporated into storefront decorations.

With each new source country, Roosevelt Avenue seems to adapt and reinvent both its formal and its informal economies. Informal Mexican tamal and churro vendors dot various intersections along the street. Sometimes, unexpected partnerships develop. An example of this is a small Korean-owned shopping center where the owners have leased storefronts to Mexicans. Upstairs from Taco-Landia one finds Ko Seguros, and the *botánica* next door, which serves the various forms of syncretistic Catholicism, Santería, and *curanderismo* (folk healing) practiced in this neighborhood, has a Korean tarot card reader (Fig. 7.4). During the summer, a taco wagon, common to California and the Southwest but new to New York, locates itself in the small parking lot in front of these stores, next to the Korean street-based sundries vendors.

Since early arrivals from South America would have needed to qualify for highly skilled professional visas prior to entry, a number of well-established entrepreneurs have expanded their businesses across the city. Restaurateurs, for example, have opened second and third locations on "restaurant row" streets in other parts of the city, whether or not in Latino neighborhoods, taking advantage of the location's reputation for good restaurants, regardless of type of food. The most visibly adaptive Jackson Heights–based business is Delgado Travel. Delgado is an Ecuadorian busi-

7.4.   *Botánica* in the Korean/Mexican plaza on Roosevelt Avenue in Jackson Heights, Queens. *Photograph by I. Miyares, 2002.*

nessman from Guayaquil who has established a transnational travel agency that now has branch offices throughout the city, but its main office and *casa de cambio* (money-exchange house) is on Roosevelt Avenue. Even in Jackson Heights, Delgado is adapting his marketing strategies to attract the growing Mexican market (Fig. 7.5).

The key component of a multiethnic adaptive streetscape is its dynamic response to the ethnic composition of the immigrant stream. The Roosevelt Avenue section of Jackson Heights is currently multiethnic Latino and reflects the migrant streams of the past two decades. However, since no group dominates, and since the Latino area abuts a Pan-Asian adaptive streetscape, a change in the immigrant pool could result in significant neighborhood change. Additionally, unlike in areas such as Washington Heights, if an ethnic politics develops, it would need to be led by someone with a pan-ethnic vision who could represent the dynamic among the neighborhood's ethnic communities, both Latino and non-Hispanic.

STREETSCAPES OF INVASION:
THE NEWLY ARRIVED MEXICANS

A few years ago, it was the Koreans who seemed ubiquitous on the streetscape through their dominance of the greengrocer industry. One of the first labor niches to be taken over by Mexicans in New York is the staffing of these fresh fruit and vegetable markets as Koreans find the practice of employing coethnics increasingly cost prohibitive. Now, not only are Mexican laborers omnipresent, so are Mexican businesses.

Mexicans are the fastest-growing Hispanic community in the city and have developed a viable economy in a very short period (Méndez and Miyares 2001; Smith 1996). These businesses have been established in commercial districts of historically immigrant communities, whether Latino or another ethnic group. For example, an expanding streetscape of invasion is along 8th Avenue in Sunset Park, Brooklyn (Fig. 7.6). In the 1990s, recent immigrants from China established a third Chinatown in an area previously occupied by European immigrants. Although there are a few relic Polish and Italian businesses on 8th Avenue, nearly every business that is not Chinese is Mexican.

A neighborhood where the invasion may be seen as a threat is East Harlem, "El Barrio." Here, boarded-up storefronts are reopening as Mexican-owned and operated enterprises. Puerto Rican murals, flags, and other cultural icons are still prevalent on the streetscape, but growing Mexican settlement in the neighborhood is changing its character from Caribbean

7.5. A typical block on Roosevelt Avenue in Jackson Heights, Queens, includes an Ecuadorian business next to two Mexican businesses. The largest advertisements in the window of this office of Delgado Travel are for special rates to Ecuador and Mexico. *Photograph by I. Miyares, 2002.*

7.6. Mexican-owned fruit stand in Sunset Park, Brooklyn, is an example of invasion into both an existing ethnic neighborhood (Fukianese-speaking Chinatown) and an existing niche economy (Korean-dominated greengrocers). *Photograph by I. Miyares, 2002.*

7.7. The Puebla México Restaurant has opened in the shadows of this historic Puerto Rican mural on Lexington Avenue and 103rd Street, East Harlem, Manhattan. *Photograph by I. Miyares, 2002.*

to Mexican. Although one could argue that Mexicans are creating a Little Puebla by resuscitating blighted, depressed blocks along East Harlem's commercial streets, some longtime residents are comparing this revitalization to the negative aspects of gentrification in Harlem (Fig. 7.7). They fear that the Puerto Rican community is losing control of the neighborhood. Although the neighborhood was blighted, it was the Puerto Rican community that established "El Barrio" as a port of entry and center of community pride and culture.

A streetscape signature common to California and the Southwest but recently introduced as part of the Mexican landscape of invasion is the *esquinero* (from *esquina*, corner; Smith 1996). *Esquineros* are itinerant day laborers who line up on selected street corners in the hope of being hired, typically for off-the-books landscaping and construction jobs. *Esquineros* are found in the same neighborhoods where Mexican businesses are located, but they are also appearing in middle-class areas of the city. Residents in such neighborhoods are as likely to condemn the "Mexican invasion" as not-in-my-backyard blight as they are to hire *esquineros* to maintain their lawns and remodel their homes. The love-hate relationship between *esquineros* and the host community, long a feature in Southern California (Valenzuela 2000), has advanced eastward as the Mexican population has exploded.

CHANGING LATINIZATION

New York is unlike any other city in the United States or, possibly, the world. It is an ever evolving, ever changing social mega-experiment that reinvents itself regularly as a manifestation of global events. Caribbean leaders, scholars, and politicians argue that Latino immigrants are assimilating toward a Caribbean identity, yet "El Barrio," the stereotypical Puerto Rican community, is being infiltrated by Mexican residents and businesses. Washington Heights has not developed a generic Caribbean streetscape, if one could exist, nor is it becoming Puerto Rican. It is distinctly Dominican. The Jackson Heights–Elmhurst-Corona corridor has been multiethnic throughout most of its history, and currently there is a spatial interplay between Pan-American and Pan-Asian streetscapes.

Neighborhoods that have never had significant Latino populations are becoming increasingly Latinized, whether middle-class Puerto Ricans are buying homes in Staten Island, or Mexicans are settling in Chinatown–Sunset Park. Political leaders, ranging from city council members to borough presidents to congressional representatives to transnational presidents, are rising out of the Latino community. The key to understanding the dynamics of the geography of Latinos in New York is to recognize that it is not a static process, because New York itself is not static. Even established streetscapes can change seemingly overnight, adding to the adventure of reading the city's landscape.

Soccer and Latino Cultural Space

Metropolitan Washington *Fútbol* Leagues

Marie Price and Courtney Whitworth

September 2, 2001, was a bad day for the coach of the U.S. national soccer team. His team had lost a World Cup qualifying match to Honduras at Washington's RFK Stadium before a sell-out crowd of over fifty-four thousand fans—with half of the fans supporting the Honduran team! Coach Bruce Arena complained that his team could never have the home-field advantage in Washington, even though the stadium is in the nation's capital. He observed, without irony, that "it would be virtually impossible to hold a World Cup qualifier in this stadium anymore . . . We want to put on away games at home? I think that's very difficult" (Goff 2001).

Albeit symbolically, the Honduran fans had deterritorialized the U.S. team, making them feel "not at home" in their own country. This is all the more remarkable considering that Honduras is a small Central American country with fewer than 7 million people. Moreover, according to the 2000 Census, only 217,000 people of Honduran ancestry reside in the United States. Part of the explanation for this territorial instability is that Latino fans, especially recent immigrants, are far more passionate about soccer than the average native-born American (Galeano 1998). Honduran fans traveled from across the country to cheer their national heroes, whereas the average U.S. fan came from the Washington metropolitan area.

Many recent Latino immigrants consider soccer a "cultural necessity," according to Don Garber, the head of Major League Soccer. The success of professional soccer in the 1990s was made possible by aggressive targeting of the "ethnic fan" (Wilbon 2000), especially recent immigrants from Latin America. Yet this symbolic battle over home turf and identity is revealing in other ways and shows the complex ways in which the perception and conception of physical space is constantly reworked by cultural practices.

8.1.   Recent immigrants in metropolitan Washington play soccer in a Latino league while fans from their home country look on. Immigrant-run recreational leagues are a vital, albeit ephemeral, cultural space for Latinos in Washington. *Photograph by M. Price, 2001.*

This chapter explores how Latino immigrants in the United States, through soccer, carve out cultural space for themselves. In particular, we argue here that homegrown immigrant soccer leagues in cities all over the United States are vital yet underappreciated nodes of immigrant social networks and place-making activities (Fig. 8.1). These nodes become especially important when one considers that many new immigrants do not live in neatly defined residential enclaves among coethnics. The more common pattern, at least in metropolitan Washington, is one of decentralized suburban living, which makes the maintenance of ethnic identity through enclaves unlikely (Singer et al. 2001).

Immigrant-run soccer leagues selectively link immigrants (mostly men) with their communities of origin. Leagues create a cultural space that is familiar, entertaining, practical, inexpensive, transnational, and ephemeral, where immigrants gather to reaffirm their sense of identity and belonging. Soccer leagues are multigenerational social centers that supply participants with information about employment and legal status and news from home, and may both facilitate and preclude immigrant assimilation into the dominant U.S. society. Yet, because soccer leagues do not create formal structures, as a church, an ethnic restaurant, or a neighborhood does, their imprint and legacy are easily ignored.

This is why we consider the spatial patterning of soccer leagues to be a dynamic expression of "Thirdspace," as defined by Edward Soja. The social networks that evolve around the leagues arise from a "sympathetic deconstruction and heuristic reconstitution of the Firstspace-Secondspace duality" (Soja 1996: 81). For our purposes, Thirdspace is best understood as a transnational conception of space. It is constituted from the tensions that exist between the lived-in space in Washington (Firstspace) and a perceived or remembered space of the country of origin (Secondspace). Immigrant soccer leagues actively redefine space and identity through networks that are predicated on being neither here nor there, but someplace in between (Luna 2000). It is the betweenness-of-place demanded by the transnational realities of immigrant life that begs for a different understanding of space. The trialectics of spatiality, especially the concept of Thirdspace, offers a conceptual handle with which to theorize about the complex spatiality of global cities such as Washington or Los Angeles. At the same time, soccer leagues are highly visible and a flexible form of place making used by Latino immigrants. As such, their existence is changing how lived space in Washington is used and perceived.

METHOD AND SOURCES

To document the spatiality of soccer leagues, we used both quantitative and qualitative techniques. To map the flow of immigrants into the Washington metropolitan area, administrative data from the Immigration and Naturalization Service were used to show intended residence of legal immigrants by country of origin and ZIP code. This map indicates the dispersed and diverse nature of the Latino immigrant flow to Washington from 1990 to 1998. Second, we mapped some of the locations of soccer leagues and compared those with Latino residential concentrations to see how well the two distributions matched.

Information about the leagues came from the *Washington Post*, Spanish-language newspapers, player interviews, and our attendance at games. The leagues are covered extensively by all of the community's Spanish-language newspapers, such as *La Nación, El Tiempo Latino,* and *El Pregonero*. When it is soccer season, from May through October, the *Washington Post* publishes articles written in Spanish every Friday in the sports section. These articles usually cover some aspect of a specific local league or professional soccer news from the United States and abroad. This in itself is an interesting indication of Latino prevalence in Washington and the demand for information about soccer.

We visited five leagues and interviewed some sixty players using a survey that had both closed and open-ended questions. All of the leagues were based in Virginia, although for comparative purposes it would be useful to study Maryland leagues. While the players in the leagues are exclusively men, women and children participate as fans and vendors. Although women were not included in the formal survey, we informally interviewed several women about the significance of the leagues in their lives. Ultimately, we selected two Bolivian leagues for closer study of transnational ties between the leagues and the sending communities, in this case, located in the Valle Alto in the Department of Cochabamba. In the summer of 1999, the senior author traveled to Bolivia to interview village leaders and return migrants from the villages that had teams in northern Virginia (Price 2000).

SPORTS, IDENTITY, AND SPACE

For many, the study of sports or games lies on the margins of academic respectability (Dyck 2000). With the publication of *Sports Geography,* John Bale (1989) defined a subdiscipline in human geography and gave it visibility. Years later, the literature on sports as an expression of culture, politics, and landscape has grown and diversified within geography as well as the social sciences (Armstrong and Giulianotti 1997; Bale 1994, 2001; Cronin and Mayall 1998; Dyck 2000; Eichberg et al. 1998; Galeano 1998; Raitz 1995). Initially, geographers tended to look at the impact of sports on the landscape. Over time, the literature has broadened to consider how sports may shape both political and cultural identity, blur racial lines, confer status, maintain community, and reflect the processes of globalization.

John Bale was also a leader in linking an interest in sports to international migration (Bale 1991; Bale and Maguire 1994). When one considers the vast literature about Latino immigration and immigrants produced in the last few years (Fox 1996; Massey 1998; Massey, Durand, and Malone 2002; Suro 1998; Waldinger 2001), it is rather astounding that immigrant soccer leagues have received so little attention. If they merit mention at all, it is usually at the anecdotal level to illustrate the workings of social networks. Part of the reason for neglecting them is that they are difficult to document. Given the cultural value assigned to soccer by many Latin Americans, the transfer of soccer to the United States by Latino immigrants would seem worthy of more careful consideration (Lamb 2001; Luna 2000; Rosaldo and Flores 1997).

In one of Douglas Massey's many studies of Mexican migration, he surveys two Mexican communities, in Michoacán and Jalisco, and supplements these data with surveys from sixty immigrant households that settled in Southern California. He describes a soccer club created by one of the communities in which nearly all of the immigrants from one town participated. Every Sunday, townspeople who had relocated to Los Angeles gathered to watch soccer and socialize. Massey notes that "this weekly reunion not only breaks the routine of work, but also provides a regular forum for communication and exchange. By sponsoring the regular interaction of townspeople, the soccer club serves as a clearinghouse for jobs, housing, and other information" (1998: 204). Through soccer, information and a sense of community are provided to people who need them.

Cecilia Menjívar's book *Fragmented Ties* examines Salvadoran social networks in San Francisco. She, too, addresses the significance of sports clubs, especially for male immigrants. In addition to providing camaraderie, soccer networks made information about jobs, housing, used cars, and ride sharing readily obtainable. She cautions that these networks link people with similar levels of resources and information, which helps them survive, but may not provide the more extensive social networks needed to improve their social status. Menjívar (2000: 182) claims that some female migrants dislike the sports clubs, complaining that they "provided ample opportunities for men to get together and drink," something that the women despise.

Journalists have been more willing than academics to write about the rise of immigrant soccer leagues. For example, a 2001 story in the *Arizona Republic* describes the growth of Latino leagues in Phoenix. In the late 1970s, there was only one Latino team playing in the entire Phoenix metro league. By 2001, the Liga Latinamericana had 125 adult and 40 youth teams. "When Hispanic immigrants arrive in the United States, many immediately search for jobs, homes, churches—and soccer teams. For the last, they venture to city parks such as Encanto, Marivue, Starlight and Tempe Diablo, places where new arrivals can make friends and feel comfortable" (Thomas 2001). The story relates various social and informational roles the leagues play in Arizona, but it is the fundamental psychological appeal of soccer that registers. "It is something we need to live. It's in our blood," insists one of the coaches (Thomas 2001).

It is indisputable that immigrant leagues provide many important social and cultural functions. But they also require space to exist. In the Washington metropolitan area, one of the most visible expressions of the Latino community is the growth of adult amateur soccer leagues. Next, we describe the Latino leagues, how they fit into the overall story of Washing-

ton's rise as a Latino-immigrant destination, and the people who participate in the leagues. We address the search for space, specifically how fields
are allocated and the issue of access that many immigrants must overcome.
Throughout the remaining narrative we conceptualize the spatiality of soccer leagues and how they force us to envision space anew.

WASHINGTON'S LATINO SOCCER LEAGUES

Immigrant-created soccer leagues are an active expression of cultural identity for Latinos in Washington. According to the 2000 Census, there were
over 432,000 Hispanics in the Washington metro area, the majority of
whom were foreign born (U.S Bureau of the Census 2000). In 1998, it was
estimated that there were more than 30 Latino leagues of over 450 soccer
teams in the Washington region, and every weekend over 7,000 players
participated in these leagues (Escobar 1998a). Eleven players are on the
field during a soccer game, and the average number of players on a team
in these leagues is between 14 and 20. Leagues are organizations of teams,
and leagues in the Washington region have between 8 and 20 teams. These
leagues, according to *Washington Post* journalist Gabriel Escobar, are "the
only home-grown industry for Latinos that directly affects most members
of the community" (Escobar 1998a). Escobar explains that "leagues have
existed for decades and in many ways mirror the growth of the Latino community, expanding from modest beginnings in Northwest Washington and
following the migration into the suburbs, where most of the more than 30
leagues are now based. The soccer boom of the last few years is described as
unprecedented by long-time participants, fueled by the community's matu-
rity and its relative affluence, particularly in the Latino business sector that
sponsors leagues and teams" (1998a).

Examples of leagues in Washington, northern Virginia, and Maryland
include the Liga Guatemala de Fútbol, Liga Salvadoreña, Liga Unión Salvadoreña de Fairfax, Liga INCOPEA, and the Arlington Bolivian Soccer
League (Table 8.1). The teams in these leagues often organize by town or
district of origin in the home country. Other teams take the names of professional clubs found in members' native country. Teams may also be of
mixed origin, with players from various Latin American, Caribbean, and
African countries.

Many of the teams from these leagues compete in the Taca Cup, an annual championship game between the two best Latino teams in the metro
area. The Cup is sponsored by the Central American airline, Taca, and
the leagues begun by Central Americans are the most active participants.

TABLE 8.1—METROPOLITAN WASHINGTON SOCCER LEAGUES

LEAGUE	NO. OF TEAMS	YEAR ESTABLISHED	COUNTRIES REPRESENTED
ALEXANDRIA SOCCER LEAGUE	8	1989	El Salvador, Honduras, Peru, Mexico, Guatemala
ARLINGTON BOLIVIAN SOCCER LEAGUE	16	1988	Mostly Bolivia
AMERICAN SOCCER LEAGUE OF ARLINGTON	9	1985	El Salvador, Peru
LIGA INCOPEA	17	1991	Bolivia
LIGA TARATA	6	1996	Bolivia
LIGA BOLIVIANA DE VETERANOS	8	1998	Bolivia

Sources: Interviews of key informants, 2000 and 2001.

Taca spends about $50,000 a year sponsoring the event. In addition to referees and space, the airline also flies the Copa Taca winning team (all twenty players) to El Salvador and Guatemala to play against professional teams there (Díaz 2000). The stakes are so high that teams sometimes field semiprofessional players and recruit professional coaches from their home country to help them train. Some of the most competitive teams have even begun to pay their superior players. Herbert Mayorga, the president of the one of the area's best teams, El Salvador de Maryland, says that he spent over $40,000 in 1997 in direct salaries to his players. His investment paid off because they won the Cup that year (Escobar 1998b).

The vast majority of league players, however, are in it for the love of the game. The players we interviewed had lived in the United States for a little less than eight years on average, which underscores the age of this community. Moreover, all of the men surveyed came directly to the Washington area, either with family or because they had family members living here. The number of years in the United States varied substantially; one man had lived in the Washington area for twenty-five years and another had moved to the area from Argentina just two weeks before. Typically, they were young men in their twenties and early thirties (the average age was twenty-nine). They tended to work in the construction industry in skilled and semiskilled jobs such as drywall, painting, carpentry, and general day labor. Others worked in food service. Several of the men from South America (Peru and Bolivia) were college educated. Typically, however, they were not employed in their field (such as architecture), but worked in construction instead.

Players have different reasons for participating in the leagues, but every player we interviewed agreed that playing in the leagues was either important or very important. Eighty-eight percent of the players surveyed concurred that *fútbol* leagues were "very important" for the individuals involved and for the community. The Latino leagues provide young immigrants a safe, family-oriented environment and, since the leagues play in public parks, no alcohol is consumed. The leagues police the players, because drinking or leaving excessive garbage could jeopardize a league's permit to use the space. Older men who coached or played in the veteran leagues (for men over thirty-five) also stressed the importance of soccer as a wholesome activity that kept young men healthy and away from drugs. Most players also recognized the fact that the leagues were a place to gather with people from their native countries and stay in touch with friends and family from "back home."

In our initial interviews, most players were surprised by our interest in the leagues. Sometimes there was even distrust when we approached for an interview. Once players started talking about the leagues, however, their excitement grew, and many admitted that they had never realized how many roles these leagues created for Latinos in the region. For them, the leagues were first and foremost about playing *fútbol*. One of the players expressed this best when he said that soccer was "part of the culture. Like football or baseball in the U.S., soccer *is* the Latin community." For most of the men we interviewed, soccer leagues were the only immigrant organization to which they belonged.

FIRSTSPACE: IMMIGRANT METROPOLITAN WASHINGTON

Washington emerged as an immigrant gateway in the 1980s and the 1990s, when the region underwent incredible growth. The 2000 Census reveals that 832,002 foreign-born individuals resided in the Primary Metropolitan Statistical Area (PMSA), which equals 16.9 percent of the total population. This figure is more impressive when one considers that in 1970 the foreign born were only 4.5 percent of the total metropolitan population (Singer and Brown 2001: 979). Slightly more than one-third (38.6 percent) of the foreign-born residents in 2000 were from Latin America, making that region the leading source area for immigrants (U.S Bureau of the Census 2000).

Another way to appreciate the growing influence of Latinos in the region is to track the increase in Hispanics (a figure that captures both foreign-born and native-born Hispanics). In 1980, Hispanics accounted for just 3 percent of the total population for the Washington PMSA. By 2000, Hispanics were 9 percent of the population and totaled over 432,000 (Suro and Singer 2002). The composition of the Latino community in Washing-

TABLE 8.2 — RECENT LATIN AMERICAN IMMIGRANTS TO METROPOLITAN WASHINGTON, 1990–1998

COUNTRY OF ORIGIN	% OF TOTAL IMMIGRANTS	NO. OF IMMIGRANTS
EL SALVADOR	33.4	25,263
PERU	9.3	7,029
BOLIVIA	7.5	5,644
JAMAICA	6.7	5,082
GUATEMALA	5.0	3,774
NICARAGUA	4.1	3,103
MEXICO	4.0	3,004
TRINIDAD & TOBAGO	3.6	2,747
DOMINICAN REPUBLIC	3.5	2,631
COLOMBIA	3.3	2,513
OTHER LATIN AMERICAN	19.6	14,825
ALL LATIN AMERICA	100.0	75,615

Source: U.S. Immigration and Naturalization Service, 1990–1998.
Note: Based on administrative data for 75,615 Latinos admitted as legal permanent residents during the period and those who indicated their intended residence to be the metropolitan Washington area.

ton is also distinct from the national picture. Although country-of-origin data was not available from the 2000 Census when this study was conducted, administrative data from the INS suggest the makeup of Latino immigrants during the 1990s. Table 8.2 shows the country of origin for legal immigrants from Latin America and the Caribbean by intended residence in the Washington area from 1990 to 1998. The leading source country is El Salvador, representing one-third of all Latinos in the data set. Next are Peru and Bolivia, accounting for nearly 17 percent of the flow. Jamaica is the largest sending country from the Caribbean. The small number of Mexicans, only 4 percent of the Hispanic group counted, is a striking difference from the national trend, in which Mexico is the leading source country for all immigrants to the United States.

For many recent immigrants, day-to-day life in Washington is restrictive. Most work long hours in construction or food service, five or six days a week. Not all are documented, and thus they live among a close circle of friends and try not to attract the attention of authorities. Undocumented immigrants often live for years in the United States without the ability to return home for fear of losing whatever status they may have acquired toward permanent residence. Figure 8.2 maps the settlement of recent Latino immigrants by ZIP code as well as the location of various soccer leagues.

This map is based on administrative data from the INS that show the

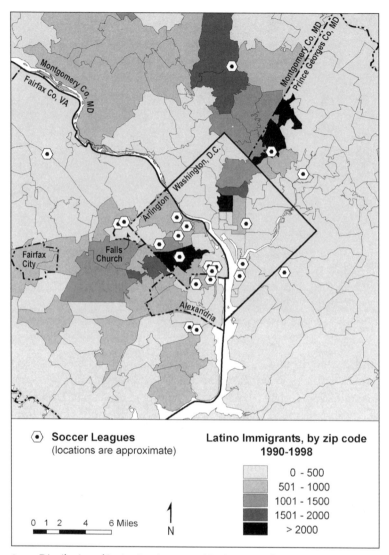

8.2.   Distribution of Latino immigrants and Latino soccer leagues, metropolitan
Washington, 1990–1998. *Source: U.S. Immigration and Naturalization Service,
1990–1998; cartography by C. Whitworth.*

country of origin and intended residence of legal permanent residents who
entered the country or had a change in status from 1990 to 1998. Since
these data do not include undocumented immigrants, they do not account
for all recent Latino immigrants. The general pattern, however, is probably
accurate, as research suggests that the residential patterns of the undocu-

mented are similar to those of the legal immigrant population (Newman and Tienda 1994). Latinos are found in nearly every ZIP code in the region. Most of the highest concentrations (ZIP codes with over fifteen hundred recent immigrants) are close-in suburbs of Virginia and Maryland and not in the District of Columbia (with the exception of the Adams Morgan and Mount Pleasant neighborhoods).

While there are areas with high concentrations of Latino immigrants, such as South Arlington in Virginia or Langley Park and Silver Spring in Maryland, there are few ethnic areas where one country of origin dominates. For example, one South Arlington ZIP code contained immigrants from 128 countries in 2000. The Langley Park–Hyattsville ZIP code had immigrants from 125 countries (Singer et al. 2001: 5).

Shifting scale to the neighborhood rather than a ZIP code, one is still hard-pressed to find distinct ethnic enclaves. An exception is the South Arlington neighborhood called Chirilagua, filled with Salvadoran immigrants and named for their community of origin. One of the leagues whose players we interviewed, Alexandria Soccer League, drew many of its players from nearby Chirilagua.

The combination of recent immigrant flows to Washington from diverse sending countries and a tight housing market contributes to a dispersed pattern of residential settlement that is not conducive to the formation of ethnic enclaves. Immigrants tend to find housing where they can in the Maryland and Virginia counties that surround the District of Columbia. Certainly, some immigrants have the resources to purchase single-family homes, but many newcomers do not. It is not uncommon for new arrivals to share small apartments with four to six other people. Food is bought in bulk and cooking duties are shared so that the maximum amount of money can be saved or sent to family back home. Lack of space, both private and public, is a serious problem.

There are few inexpensive public places where immigrants can gather. If large numbers of Latino youth congregate in a parking lot or an open lot, they are bound to draw attention from authorities. Thus for many newcomers, a few hours on the green fields of greater Washington marks the social and cultural highpoint of the week. As Figure 8.2 demonstrates, the location of a league is usually not in the area of highest immigrant concentration. Fields are not evenly distributed throughout the region, and access to them is tightly controlled. Thus the first step in creating a Latino cultural space is to find a field.

FINDING SPACE: THE SEARCH FOR FIELDS

Leagues exist for an important institutional reason: without them, players would be unable to get access to fields. The concept that one has to sign up with a county bureaucracy to play in an open field is outside of the realm of experience of many Latino immigrants, yet fields are highly regulated and sought-after spaces. Players have to play by the county's rules, or they do not play at all.

Fairfax County officials were first confronted with the problem of Latino leagues in 1990, when residents complained to officials about Latino teams taking over fields. Bilingual officers were sent to talk to the players and explain the protocol required to obtain permits to play on these fields. Officers also made it clear that absolutely no drinking would be allowed in these public facilities and that permits would be revoked if violations were discovered.

Fields are supposed to be used by county residents only, but many of these leagues have players who live outside of the county in which they play. Fairfax County charges $20 for each out-of-county resident, which generated $126,000 in revenue in 1997. In Arlington County, where the charge is $15 per out-of-county player, revenue from this source totaled $150,000 in 1997 (Escobar 1998b).

A common complaint from players is the limited number of fields, or more precisely, restricted access for immigrants. In informal chats with players, we found that many thought that there were enough fields, but that somehow immigrants were being discriminated against. A typical story told in interviews is that of playing on an open field, only to be chased off by the police, who threatened to arrest them if they did not vacate the field.

Fairfax County has 875 fields, which to the casual observer might seem like a large number. Yet if one considers that the county has over one million residents and that these fields are used by youth soccer, American football, and lacrosse, it becomes clear how access to play space must be tightly scheduled. The league structure, of course, enables Latino organizers to navigate the system, to gain access to space. Without the leagues, many Latino men would never get a chance to play.

Immigrants rather quickly accept the need for leagues, but they take the idea one step farther. Rather than play in existing adult recreation leagues, they create their own leagues, organized by shared identities and perceptions of places far way.

8.3. Men from Achamoco, Bolivia, play on a soccer team named after the town. *Photograph by M. Price, 2001.*

SECONDSPACE: SOCCER LEAGUES AS PLACES REMEMBERED

The soccer leagues offer a much-needed space where recent immigrants can gather to spend time with coethnics, speak their native language, and enjoy cuisine from their native countries. The organization of the leagues, and the very names of the teams, suggests that this cultural practice is also about memory of home, or at least some idealized perception of home.

Typically, teams are named for the home communities of the majority of players (Fig. 8.3). Team names such as Achamoco, Chirilagua, Tiataco, and Mogotillo are place references that evoke both loyalty and rivalry. Other immigrants pay homage to the professional teams from their home country by wearing an identical uniform, purchased in San Salvador or Lima, for example, and sometimes using the same name. For example, Estrella del Sur in the American Soccer League of Arlington is named for a lower-division team in El Salvador. One of the Peruvian teams in the same league dresses in the exact uniform of the Peruvian national team.

The Alexandria Soccer League was created in 1989, and was composed entirely of players from El Salvador. Since then, teams from other countries have joined the league. Honduras, Peru, El Salvador, Guatemala, Mexico, and even African nations are represented in the league. Games are played in Alexandria, Virginia. According to the league president, the league feels that it is a family-oriented program, "where people come together to get a chance to see themselves."

We visited this league on a sunny day in April, the first day of the season. There were at least three hundred people in the bleachers and standing along the sidelines; most of the fans were young Latino men. The first three men we talked with were from Honduras, where they knew each other growing up. All of them lived in the Washington metropolitan area, and they agreed that it had been much easier to adjust to life in Washington because they knew each other when they arrived. All came directly to Washington from Honduras and have lived in no other metropolitan area. None of these men were on a team that played that day, but they were there to support other friends from Honduras who were playing.

We talked with a nineteen-year-old from Honduras who lived in Washington with his parents, who immigrated eight years ago. His grandmother had nineteen children, and he estimated that at least half of them and their families now lived in the Washington area. He graduated from high school the year before we interviewed him, and he was repairing boats for a living. He was from a town in Honduras called Macuelizo, and he mentioned that there was a team in another league that was made up entirely of members of his family, all of them from this town.

The young Honduran explained that relatives who had come to the United States earlier sponsored his citizenship and, in his words, "everyone sponsors everyone." He claimed that all of his friends from Honduras lived here now. As we were talking, his cousin walked by and said hello. Our interviewee eventually left with his friends to watch a televised soccer game between Honduras and Nicaragua at a nearby Latino restaurant.

We spoke with a man from El Salvador who had lived in Alexandria for eleven years. He was from Olímpia and played on Team Olímpia in the Alexandria Soccer League. He had started playing in this league three years earlier, after learning about it from his friends. His teammates were all from El Salvador, and he socialized with them regularly after games. He worked as a dishwasher and sometimes as a busboy at the Kennedy Center, something he was proud to share with us. When asked how important soccer was to the Latino community, he smiled and said that "it is very, very important, and everyone plays and loves the sport."

The Arlington Bolivian Soccer League is widely recognized as one of the most-organized Latino soccer league in the Washington metropolitan area. The president of the league, Félix Sandoval, estimates that two thousand to three thousand participants come out every Sunday to either play or watch the league's many teams. Games are played from 8:00 A.M. until 5:00 P.M. at two locations in South Arlington. Most of the players are from Bolivia, but every team is allowed to have five foreigners on its roster, although only three can take the field at one time. According to Arlington County Parks and Recreation regulations, 50 percent of the team must reside in Arlington County, but Sandoval estimates that over 70 percent of the participants live in the county. The league strictly adheres to FIFA (Federación Internacional de Fútbol Asociación) and Bolivian Federation rules and regulations, which are published in a comprehensive rule book for all of the referees and coaches. The players take the league very seriously, and some of them are former professional players and coaches from Bolivia, many of whom have participated in the World Cup and Bolivia's famed Tahuichi Soccer Academy.

Each team in the Arlington Bolivian Soccer League is sponsored, typically by a local restaurant, company, or hotel. The sponsor pays for all of the uniforms, field fees, new equipment, and insurance for the team. Many of the team uniforms are sent directly from Bolivia, as these teams are named for professional Bolivian teams. Extra money goes into a pool for unexpected expenses, such as medical care for injured players and even money for their families if they are the primary breadwinner and are unable to work because of soccer-related injuries.

The league has an accountant, and all of the money raised is on the books. Women are allowed to write to the league for permission to sell Bolivian food and drinks on the sidelines, and a portion of the money made from this goes into the pool of extra money. Players and spectators line up hours early for homemade *salteñas*, a traditional Bolivian pastry filled with meat and vegetables.

On Sunday mornings in Reston, Virginia, hundreds of Bolivians gather to watch men from their native country play in the Liga INCOPEA. Reston is one of the celebrated planned communities of Fairfax County. It is the embodiment of a middle-class suburban ideal—not a likely setting for three hundred to four hundred Bolivian immigrants playing soccer. Yet the league is there because enough of its members live in Fairfax County to apply for a permit, and it was the only field they could find to play their matches.

INCOPEA stands for Incorporación del Pueblo de Esteban Arce, and the league consists of players from the district of Esteban Arce in the Department of Cochabamba, Bolivia. The league was established in 1991 and began with six teams. Today seventeen teams participate. Each team is named for and represents the *comunidad* (village) from which the players originate. Santa Rosa, Achamoco, Arbieto, Tiataco, and Villa La Loma have seen substantial numbers of their young men and women migrate to metropolitan Washington. Players on these teams grew up playing *fútbol* in their villages. Although they now live in metropolitan Washington, they continue to play *fútbol* together in their new home.

The structure of INCOPEA consciously replicates village structures in rural Bolivia. The league is fairly closed, including only players with ties to the small villages in Esteban Arce. In such a rural district, most people still earn their livelihoods from the soil or from remittances sent by faraway family members. Older people prefer to speak Quechua, the major native Andean language, rather than Spanish. The district seat, Tarata, is not involved in this league, but has its own smaller one. This, too, mirrors the social structure in Bolivia, where rural villagers and townspeople may know each other, but tend not to socialize. It is a division that has subtle racial undertones, with people from the district capital (in this case, Tarata) identifying with their European roots while those in the *comunidades* align themselves with their Amerindian heritage.

Most INCOPEA games take place between 8:00 A.M. and noon on Sunday. There are many more men sitting on the sidelines than women. Many of the players have not worked in the United States long, and some are probably undocumented. Their wives, sisters, and parents are in Bolivia, yet they are unlikely to return home anytime soon because of their precarious legal status. Their goal is to work hard, make money, and either return to Bolivia or have their families join them in the States.

Unlike other leagues, INCOPEA's primary purpose is to raise money to send back to villages in Esteban Arce. In 2000, the league president told us, "The mission of INCOPEA is to help our communities in Bolivia. It is not about socializing with other groups." Travel by Price to the villages of Esteban Arce in the summer of 1999 showed that this league played a prominent economic role. INCOPEA's leadership estimated in 2000 that villages received between $20,000 and $30,000 a year from league revenues in Virginia. This money is used to build churches and sports facilities like basketball and soccer fields. It also improves schools and town plazas and provides electricity. Money is raised through dues paid by every player. Some of the money is earned from concessions sales on game day.

It is the most vivid example we have found of a transnational network that evolves around soccer, but results in a grassroots development strategy. As one player told us, "We have to do this; if we waited for the Bolivian government to do something, we would not have even one brick for our communities."

In our cross-league survey, 90 percent of the players interviewed played on teams with people from their native country, and of those, 88 percent knew some of their teammates when they were living in their native countries. Families come to watch them play, which gives family members the opportunity to visit with friends and relatives. The leagues do more than create a social outlet; they actively assemble a shared memory of place, a Secondspace. This is all the more compelling because the people involved often have not returned to these places for years. They may have children who have never seen these homeland places, who know them only as a point on a map, a team on a soccer field. And yet this Secondspace has meaning because it exists in the shared memories and perceptions of league organizers and players.

A TRANSNATIONALIZED THIRDSPACE

On a brisk November afternoon with the autumn leaves ablaze, golden light filtered down on the final minutes of the Liga Tarata's last game of the season. Not only the league champion would be determined, but an elaborate closing ceremony would follow to venerate a three-quarters-sized replica of the patron saint of Tarata, St. Severino, which rested in a glass coffin on a nearby basketball court (Figure 8.4). Folk dancers in elaborate costumes were milling about on the tennis courts as they waited for a small procession to begin from the edge of the park to the place were St. Severino lay in repose.

At the end of the procession, one of the dancers led her small son by the hand. He also wore a folkloric outfit (Figure 8.5). The boy had never been to Bolivia, let alone Tarata, but he was dancing and paying his respects to the patron saint of this small town in the Valle Alto. One has to wonder what place this child was experiencing. Why did being part of this place mean so much to his parents? Cecilia, a young Bolivian woman, summarized her life experience in Arlington, Virginia: "Until I went away to college, I lived Bolivian, I ate Bolivian. I had never been to a Bennigan's or a Ruby Tuesday. In Arlington, this is possible."

The Tarateños had produced this wonderful spectacle to affirm their identity and to celebrate their place. Two hours later, everything was folded

8.4.   Statue of St. Severino, the patron saint of Tarata, Bolivia, is honored on a basketball court during the last Liga Tarata soccer game of the season. *Photograph by M. Price, 2001.*

8.5.   Dressed in folkloric costumes, Bolivian immigrants celebrate the saint's day of St. Severino at the championship match of the Tarata League. *Photograph by M. Price, 2001.*

into pickup trucks, minivans, and sedans and stored away until the next event in spring. The quiet neighborhood park was left spotless, as if nothing had happened there.

Through soccer leagues and other immigrant organizations an intricate transnational world is woven. This Thirdspace comes from the duality of immigrant existence, a tension between a lived-in space—Washington— and a distant, remembered space, in this case, Tarata, Bolivia. The reconciliation between these different worlds leads us to someplace in between. Given the limited resources and spaces available to many Latino immigrants, that Thirdspace is often a soccer field.

There is a final need that soccer leagues satisfy, and that is the very human desire for status, not a flashy, superficial status, but status that validates one's life as significant and meaningful to others. Given that many immigrants experience a sharp drop in social status after moving to the United States and taking on menial jobs, it makes sense that league organizers and star players acquire status within their social worlds. Luin Goldring (1998: 167) makes this point very well based on her research on transnational social fields among Mexicans. She notes how transnational social fields, and their localities of origin in particular, provide a special context in which people can improve their social position and perhaps their power. From this position, they can make claims about their changing status and have that status recognized. They can participate in changing their place of origin so that it becomes more consistent with their changing expectations of status. In this way, transnational social communities are also communities of meaning in which status claims are interpreted via shared histories and understandings of practices, rituals, goods, and other status markers. Thus it would seem that creating a transnational Thirdspace is also about affirming one's status to oneself, one's family, and to a broader locality-based social network.

CONCLUSION: SPATIALITY AND SOCCER

Fútbol leagues in the Washington metropolitan area serve a number of purposes for the Latino community: they provide a safe place for Latinos to gather and socialize with members of their native countries; they give Latinos the opportunity to watch soccer played well, by people like them; and they even raise money to send back to their towns and villages in Latin America. The leagues touch the lives of most recent Latino immigrants, and thus they also have the power to convey status on those who excel as players or organizers. We asked players if they belonged to other Latino organizations, and besides a few Spanish-oriented churches, most of them told us that they did not. In a metropolitan area like Washington, which has only recently experienced a substantial influx of Latin American immigrants, there are few immigrant enclaves for new arrivals to engage. Soccer leagues, therefore, form vital social networks that sustain communities of immigrants.

On most Sunday mornings, thousands of men and women from El Salvador, Bolivia, Honduras, and Peru stream into the county parks to create a cultural space that is neither here nor there, but grounded in betweenness. The formation of such communities is an unanticipated and a relatively understudied outcome of the globalization of labor markets. Such leagues are concrete expressions of transnational communities and the Thirdspaces they create.

9 | THE CULTURAL LANDSCAPE OF A PUERTO RICAN NEIGHBORHOOD IN CLEVELAND, OHIO

Albert Benedict and Robert B. Kent

Popular nightclubs featuring merengue and salsa music are common on Cleveland's Near Westside. *Arroz con habichuelas, tostones, alcapurrias,* and *mofongo* are often on the menus of many small restaurants in the neighborhood. Spanish is spoken at the local McDonald's. Corner grocery stores feature Goya products as their main food line. Spanish-language newspapers are available. Pirate radio stations broadcast in Spanish and compete with legal stations for space on the airwaves. Small Puerto Rican flags hang from the rear-view mirrors of many cars. These signs suggest the presence of a Puerto Rican community.

Amos Rapoport (1982: 88–89), in *The Meaning of the Built Environment,* characterizes two types of feature elements that combine to form the cultural landscape of an area: "fixed feature elements" and "semi-fixed feature elements." Fixed feature elements do not change very often—or slowly at best. Examples include the architectural style of a building, from its interior walls and ceiling to its exterior. The costs of modifying fixed feature elements often exceed the reach of those who occupy preexisting housing or already developed neighborhoods.

A more appropriate measure of an evolving cultural landscape is semi-fixed feature elements. Semi-fixed feature elements may include a storefront sign, lawn ornaments, specific house colors, or the display of a national-origin flag or symbol. The lower costs associated with altering such features makes them accessible to individuals of all socioeconomic levels. Moreover, since ethnic groups or immigrant communities typically move into ready-built-environments, the adoption of these elements is the easiest way to create familiarity and personal identity in a particular area. When a number of individuals of the same ethnic background in a particular geographical area collectively use a set of shared semi-fixed feature elements, these combine to create a distinctive cultural landscape.

The Puerto Rican community in Cleveland's Near Westside occupies a ready-built environment. As a consequence, most of the landscape elements that reinforce the Puerto Rican presence in the neighborhood take the form of semi-fixed feature elements. Previous research among Mexican American and Puerto Rican Hispanic subcultures suggests that this type of element is often a religious shrine placed in the yard, a house painted in bright pastel colors, perimeter fencing, or a well-kept front yard flower garden. These landscape elements have roots in Mexican American and Puerto Rican cultures.

While these two cultures are different in many respects, there are also strong similarities, and those become evident in the cultural landscapes of these Hispanic subgroups in the United States. As an example, both the Puerto Ricans and the Mexican Americans may use religious shrines in front of their homes. However, Puerto Ricans choose to display the Virgin of the Milagrosa (la Virgen de la Milagrosa), whereas Mexican Americans most commonly venerate the Virgin of Guadalupe (la Virgen de Guadalupe). The use of bright paints on a home's exterior is another common feature. Arreola (1988) notes that in the Southwest, brilliantly painted houses combine with other elements to create the Mexican American "housescape." Jopling (1988) notes that Puerto Ricans also paint houses bright colors and even suggests that color preference may be an indicator of socioeconomic level.

This study broadly examines the assumption that semi-fixed landscape elements associated with Hispanic populations occur with greater frequency in areas where Hispanic population concentrations are high. First, we investigate the relationship between variations in the percentage of Hispanic population in specific geographic areas and the frequency of semi-fixed landscape elements associated with Hispanics. Second, we use a temporal approach to study landscape change by documenting the evolving patterns of use and the frequency of semi-fixed landscape elements compared with Hispanic population change in a neighborhood. Our study area is the Near Westside of Cleveland, Ohio, where Puerto Ricans and other Hispanics have settled in some neighborhoods since the 1970s. Two field surveys, one administered in 1996 and another in 2002, measured the occurrences of Puerto Rican landscape elements in residential, religious (churches), and commercial spaces. Data from the 1990 and 2000 U.S. Censuses provided population numbers and characteristics in the neighborhood at the block-group level for the study area. We briefly review Hispanic population growth, settlement, and community formation in Northeast Ohio and in Cleveland. This is followed by a review of the method we used to complete the survey and the presentation of the survey findings.

PUERTO RICAN COMMUNITY IN NORTHEAST OHIO

Cleveland developed as an industrial city because of its location along the shores of Lake Erie, the construction of the Ohio and Erie Canals, and an extensive rail network to the East and the Midwest. Industrial cities in the Midwest have historically drawn a large foreign-born population, and Cleveland was no exception. In the 1920s, over half of all Clevelanders (200,000) attended nationality churches, where services often were held in languages other than English, and more than twenty nationality newspapers, often published in foreign languages, circulated in the city. Cleveland received large numbers of immigrants from Central and Eastern Europe. Notable among these were Italians, Germans, Hungarians, Serbians, Slovenians, and Croatians. Many of these ethnic groups formed homogeneous neighborhoods that served as safe havens for immigrants, who identified closely with their country of origin (Miggins 1984: 19–20). While some of the early ethnic neighborhoods remain in Cleveland, most of the second- and third-generation European immigrants have moved to the suburbs. Although eastern Europeans still immigrate to Cleveland in large numbers, recent decades have brought new immigrants to the city, including Asians and Hispanics—principally Puerto Ricans, Mexican Americans, and Mexican nationals.

Mexican nationals were the first Spanish-speaking group to settle in Cleveland, appearing in small numbers in the first decades of the twentieth century (Santana 1999). However, tightening of immigration policies in the 1930s had a major impact on the Mexican labor force. At the same time that Cleveland was losing its Mexican population, the demand for labor continued after World War II, during the city's industrial boom years. As U.S. citizens, Puerto Ricans made an ideal choice to fill these labor needs. Recruiters were sent to Puerto Rico to entice workers with the promise of employment and a better life, and Puerto Ricans migrated to Cleveland in large numbers (Bonutti and Prpic 1977: 179; Pap 1973: 282–283).

In northeastern Ohio, the influx of Puerto Rican immigrants occurred not only in Cleveland, but also in nearby Lorain. Lorain lies on the western edge of the Cleveland metropolitan area. As happened in Cleveland, labor recruiters coaxed Puerto Ricans to work in Lorain's steel mills in the 1940s and the 1950s. Even after the contracts of these early immigrants to Cleve-

**TABLE 9.1—PUERTO RICAN POPULATION GROWTH IN
THE GREATER CLEVELAND AREA**

YEAR	PUERTO RICAN POPULATION
1960	4,595
1970	16,050
1980	24,110
1990	34,053
2000	47,444

Sources: Meléndez 1997; Pap 1973: 282. U.S. Bureau of the Census 1990, 2000.

land and Lorain expired, many stayed in the continental United States and sent for their families and friends from the island (Zentos 1987: 509).

After 1960, the Puerto Rican population increased steadily in the region. In 1960, there were only 4,595 Puerto Ricans living in Cleveland. Forty years later, there were 47,444 Puerto Ricans in the greater Cleveland area, a tenfold increase (Table 9.1). Much of this growth occurred in the 1990s, with the Puerto Rican population increasing nearly 41 percent in that decade.

The region's Puerto Rican population is concentrated in two nodes, Cleveland and Lorain. Over half are located in Cleveland (25,385), with the city's only significant concentration occurring in the Near Westside, an area just to the west of Cleveland's urban core. In Lorain, the city's southeastern neighborhoods, adjacent to a large steel works, are home to about one-quarter of the region's Puerto Ricans (10,536). Puerto Ricans represent 15.3 percent of the total population in Lorain and only 5.3 percent of the total population in Cleveland. The remaining Puerto Rican population is widely distributed in the region's suburban towns and periphery. In Cleveland and Lorain, Puerto Ricans are the dominant Hispanic group, accounting for 73 percent of the total Hispanic population (U.S. Bureau of the Census 2000).

The Puerto Ricans who first migrated to Cleveland located near the Lady of Fatima Catholic Church on the east side of the city. Subsequently, competition for housing with African Americans prompted Puerto Ricans to move to the Near Westside, especially to the neighborhoods of Ohio City, Clark Fulton, and Tremont. Immigrant groups, including Germans, Hungarians, Italians, Irish, and others, initially resided in these near-downtown neighborhoods. Proximity to industrial jobs located on the Flats along the Cuyahoga River made these neighborhoods attractive to immigrants (Zentos 1987: 509). Remnants of this diverse immigrant past are still visible throughout the Near Westside, particularly in the architecture of the churches, as religion and religious institutions played a central role in the community life of new immigrants.

Religion and religious institutions have also represented a key element in the establishment of the Puerto Rican community and the creation of a Puerto Rican neighborhood in Cleveland. Early Puerto Rican immigrants turned to the Catholic Archdiocese of Cleveland. In an effort to cater to the new immigrants, a few Roman Catholic churches offered services in Spanish, and the Archdiocese created the Spanish Catholic Mission in 1954 (Bonutti and Prpic 1977: 185). In 1975, Puerto Rican Catholics established their own church when they purchased the church building that formerly housed the West Side Hungarian Reformed Church in the Near Westside's Ohio City neighborhood. This building became the new home for the congregation of San Juan Bautista (Zentos 1987: 509).

Steady increases in the city's Puerto Rican population during the ensuing twenty years caused the San Juan Bautista congregation to outgrow its church. Subsequently, it joined with a smaller Puerto Rican Catholic congregation, the Capilla Cristo Rey, which operated from a storefront, and together the two congregations financed and built a new church, completed in 1998. The new church, La Sagrada Familia (The Holy Family), is built in a Spanish colonial mission style reminiscent of many traditional churches in Puerto Rico. At a cost of $1.7 million, the project represents a major investment for the Puerto Rican community in Cleveland (Long 1997). This church is one of the few new structures that the Puerto Rican community has built in a neighborhood in which it has otherwise adapted and reused existing buildings.

Evangelical Protestant churches have played an important role in Latin America in recent decades. This has also been the case in the Puerto Rican community in Cleveland's Near Westside. Many of these churches have appeared, often in storefronts, residences, or sometimes in recycled churches. The Spanish Assembly of God was the first Protestant church to serve the Puerto Rican community of Cleveland. Opening its doors for worship in 1952, it quickly formed a congregation of over two hundred (Bonutti and Prpic 1977: 186). Others followed, and by the late 1990s, thirteen of the twenty-three Hispanic-oriented churches on the Near Westside were Evangelical Protestant churches serving the Spanish-speaking population (Benedict 1998).

Clubs and social groups also played critical roles in the development of the Puerto Rican community in the Near Westside. The Sons of Borinquen, a benevolent society, opened its doors in 1951. For eleven years, the club served as a social meeting place, but more important, it provided a support

base for those Puerto Ricans who needed food or financial assistance (Bonutti and Prpic 1977: 188). With its demise, other social clubs and service-
oriented organizations were established to fill the needs of the Puerto Rican
community. One of the most important of these is the Spanish-American
Committee, located in the Ohio City neighborhood. The organization was
founded in 1966 and operates today with a small staff. It offers services
including day-care facilities, English as a second language instruction, immigration support services, and employment and discrimination counseling. A large mural decorates the exterior wall of its headquarters; the mural
illustrates the history of Puerto Rico from the period of Spanish colonial
rule to the present day.

Today, community-service clubs advocate the preservation of Puerto
Rican culture in the local community. For example, in 1991, an elementary school teacher founded the Centro Cultural Julia de Burgos to teach
Puerto Rican children about their island homeland and its culture, because
many residents had never visited the island. The Escuela Popular, another
community-service organization, bridges the gap between Puerto Ricans,
other Hispanics, and non-Hispanics who live in the rapidly changing neighborhoods of the Near Westside. While much of the effort of the Escuela
Popular is directed at bettering the life of recent Spanish-speaking immigrants, it also offers a wide range of classes, including Spanish-language
instruction, cooking, and dance, and Spanish-language films. Other social
clubs, such as the San Lorenzo Club, have created Little League baseball
teams in an effort to engage the neighborhood's youth in positive social
activities (Meléndez 1997).

During the 1980s and the 1990s, the Puerto Rican community in the
Near Westside gradually established a commercial base in the neighborhood that provides a range of products and services targeted to Puerto
Ricans and other Hispanics. These services include Latin nightclubs, small
bars, restaurants serving traditional Puerto Rican fare, grocery stores, music stores, and a few *botánicas*, specialty shops selling religious articles like
shrines, medicinal plants, and prayer candles. The small commercial area
is centered along West 25th Street and Clark Avenue and creates a bit of a
Latino cultural oasis where Puerto Ricans and other Hispanics can shop,
eat, and socialize.

SURVEY METHOD

The goal of our study is to measure the presence of landscape elements in
the Near Westside neighborhood and to assess the relationship between

TABLE 9.2—POPULATION PROFILE OF CLEVELAND'S NEAR WESTSIDE

SUBAREA	TOTAL POPULATION		HISPANIC POPULATION		HISPANIC % OF TOTAL		OCCUPIED HOUSING UNITS	
	1990	2000	1990	2000	1990	2000	1990	2000
CORE	1,084	1,082	601	588	55	54	400	338
DOMAIN	4,896	6,025	1,899	2,860	39	47	1,838	2,140
PERIPHERY	4,082	1,109	1,101	352	27	32	1,428	375
TOTAL	10,062	8,216	3,601	3,800	36	46	3,666	2,853

Sources: U.S. Bureau of the Census 1990, 2000.

their presence and the distribution and concentration of Hispanic population. In addition, the study examines how the occurrence of Hispanic landscape elements changed over a six-year time period (1996–2002) as the area's Hispanic population grew.

Using 1990 Census block group–level data for percentage Hispanic population, we divided the study area into three subareas: a core, a domain, and a periphery. In 1990, total population in the study area was 10,062, with Hispanic population accounting for 3,601 of the total, or about 36 percent. At the time of the 2000 Census, the total population in the study area had declined nearly 18 percent, to 8,216, with Hispanics representing 3,800 of the total, or about 46 percent (U.S. Bureau of the Census 1990, 2000) (Table 9.2). In the core block groups, Hispanics were the dominant ethnic group, over 51 percent of the population. In the domain block groups, Hispanic population ranged from over 34 percent to 51 percent, whereas in the periphery, it was between 17 percent and 34 percent in the respective block groups (Fig. 9.1). Two block groups fell in the core group, five in the domain, and three in the periphery in 1996 (Fig. 9.2). Because of changes in the percentage of Hispanic population between the two census periods, changes occurred in the categorization of the block groups into the three areas. In 2002, the number of block groups in the core remained the same as in 1990, but the number of blocks categorized as falling in the domain increased by three, and those in the periphery dropped to one.

We conducted a survey of Hispanic landscape elements in the block groups identified above in 1996 and then repeated it again in the same area in 2002. The consolidation by the U.S. Census of two block groups, two in the domain and two in the periphery, between 1990 and 2000 reduced the official number of block groups between the two periods; however, the geographical areas surveyed remained the same.

The landscape survey developed and utilized in this study benefited

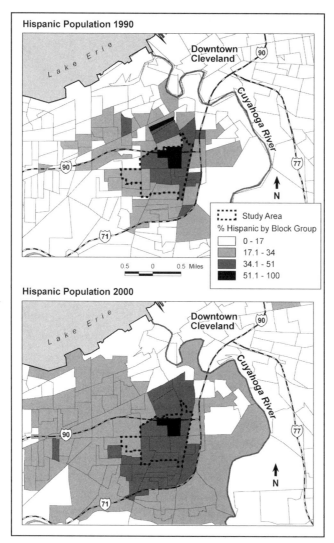

9.1.   Percentage Hispanic population by block group, Cleveland's Near Westside, 1990 and 2000. *Source: U.S. Bureau of the Census 1990, 2000.*

from earlier work on Hispanic landscapes by several researchers, including Curtis (1980) on Little Havana in Miami, Arreola (1981, 1988) on Mexican American landscapes in the Southwest, and Kent and Gandia-Ojeda (1999) on Puerto Rican yard complexes in Lorain, Ohio. Our Hispanic landscape survey sought to examine Hispanic landscape elements in three distinct land-use categories: commercial, religious (churches), and residential.

The survey examined all commercial land uses in the study area. We recorded the business type (restaurant, grocery, gas station, convenience store, nightclub, tavern, music store, pharmacy, and other) and the use of language on the signage associated with a business. Signage was classified as Spanish, Spanish/English, or English. These observations included language use on the main business sign as well as language use on secondary signs and announcements on the property and in windows. Particular attention was directed to the presence of advertisements for Goya products,

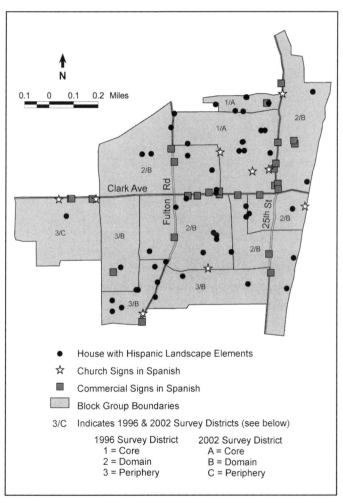

9.2.   Cleveland's Near Westside and the distribution of semi-fixed Hispanic landscape elements, 2002. *Source: Field survey, 2002.*

a brand of foods particularly popular among Puerto Ricans; political signs promoting Hispanic candidates for local office; and signs promoting Hispanic community events. The type and number of all signs were recorded.

The survey included all churches in the study area. As was the case with commercial properties, attention was focused principally on the use of language in promoting the church to an ethnic population. Language use on the principal congregation sign as well as on any secondary signs or announcements was noted, as was the religious affiliation of the church.

The analysis of the residential landscape varied from that of the commercial and religious surveys, because only those residential properties that exhibited one or another of three key landscape features commonly associated with Hispanic-occupied dwellings were included in the tabulations. Thus, only those dwelling units displaying a religious yard shrine (the Sacred Heart of Jesus, the Virgin of the Milagrosa, or the Virgin of Guadalupe), a Puerto Rican flag, or a political campaign sign promoting a candidate with a Hispanic surname were included in the survey and led to categorization as a Hispanic residence. Secondary data were also collected for those dwelling units falling into this category. These elements included paint colors used for the house exterior and trim, front yard fences, front yard gardens, and potted plants in the front yard or on the porch.

Findings from the field surveys offer insight into landscape elements displayed in the Puerto Rican community. They suggest how population concentration and change in the Puerto Rican community influence the use of semi-fixed feature elements. In this manner, we can begin to see what characteristics suggest a Borinqueño, or Puerto Rican, landscape in Cleveland.

COMMERCIAL SIGNAGE

Spanish and/or Spanish and English signage accounted for about 15 percent of all commercial signs in the study area at the time of both surveys (Table 9.3). In both 1996 and 2002, the presence and relative frequency of use of Spanish-language signage on commercial buildings followed a somewhat predictable pattern. In the core block groups, where the percentage of Hispanic population was over 50, signs in Spanish and Spanish and English represented between 33 percent and 22 percent of all signs, respectively, for 1996 and 2002. In the block groups of the domain, where the Hispanic population was less significant, the percentage of signs in Spanish and Spanish and English was between 17 in 1996 and 12 in 2002. For peripheral block groups in 1996, Spanish and Spanish and English signs accounted for just 4 percent of commercial signs, but this number increased

TABLE 9.3—LANGUAGE OF PRIMARY COMMERCIAL SIGNAGE, CLEVELAND'S NEAR WESTSIDE

LANGUAGE SUBAREA

	CORE				DOMAIN			
	1996		2002		1996		2002	
	No.	% OF TOTAL	No.	% OF TOTAL	No.	% OF TOTAL	No.	% OF TOTAL
SPANISH	5	15	2	11	7	6	4	3
SPANISH & ENGLISH	6	18	2	11	13	11	12	9
ENGLISH	22	67	15	79	97	83	112	88
TOTAL	33	100	19	100	117	100	128	100

	PERIPHERY				TOTAL			
	1996		2002		1996		2002	
	No.	% OF TOTAL	No.	% OF TOTAL	No.	% OF TOTAL	No.	% OF TOTAL
SPANISH	0	0	1	5	12	5	7	4
SPANISH & ENGLISH	3	4	2	10	22	10	16	10
ENGLISH	68	96	17	85	187	85	144	86
TOTAL	71	100	20	100	221	100	167	100

Source: Field surveys, 1996 and 2002.

to 15 percent in 2002. This increase is somewhat misleading, because the number of signs in Spanish and Spanish and English remained the same between the two surveys—three in each instance. However, the total number of commercial signs in the periphery declined precipitously in 2002, causing the percentage of signs in Spanish or Spanish and English to increase markedly. Indeed, there was an overall drop of nearly 32 percent in the number of signs in the study area between the two periods. These declines occurred principally in the peripheral block-group areas and, to a lesser extent, in the core block-group districts.

Most of the commercial establishments surveyed in this study were located along two main arterial streets, West 25th Street and Clark Avenue (see Fig. 9.2). These streets are close to the center of the study area, where the block groups that form the core and the domain intersect. The most common businesses with Spanish or Spanish and English signs included restaurants, music stores, *botánicas,* and grocery stores (Fig. 9.3). Often, businesses that use Spanish or Spanish and English signage offer the Puerto Rican community goods and services that would be difficult to find in a

9.3.   *Bodega* in a Near Westside neighborhood, Cleveland. Signs in Spanish and English and Puerto Rican motifs like the national flag, the palm tree, and the *coquí* (frog) are common semi-fixed features in the landscape. *Photograph by the authors, 2002.*

typical franchise or non-ethnic-oriented store. One of the most interesting, and indicative, of these businesses is the neighborhood grocery store, or *bodega*. Only three neighborhood grocery stores with Spanish-language signs existed in the study area, and all of these were located in the core. One of the stores was nestled between houses on a secondary street, and the other two were located on major arterial roads amid other retail and residential mixed-use entities. Characteristically, these stores are tightly packed from floor to ceiling with food products ranging from plantains to homemade picante, or hot sauce. One may also find nonfood items associated with Puerto Rican culture, like the güiro, a traditional percussion instrument, or ceramic figures of the *coquí*, a frog native to Puerto Rico that is often used as the unofficial symbol of the island.

CHURCH SIGNAGE

Just over half of all churches in the study area used Spanish and/or Spanish and English signage on the building exterior at the time of each survey (Table 9.4). The patterns of language use in the study area generally reflected the relative concentrations of Hispanic residents in each of the three zones. Although there were comparatively few churches in the block groups of the core area, signs in Spanish predominated in both 1996 and 2002. In the block groups making up the domain, where Hispanics were between 34 percent and 51 percent of the total population, the use of Spanish and Spanish and English signage on churches reached 66 percent in 1996 and 40 percent in 2002. In the census block groups of the periphery, where Hispanics were one-third or less of the population, Spanish-language signs were used by only 18 percent of the churches in the 1996 survey. Surprisingly, in the survey conducted in 2002, this percentage jumped to 67. However, a closer examination shows that this percentage fails to represent the actual situation. The number of churches using Spanish-language signs actually remained the same between the two survey periods—two in 1996 and two in 2002. However, the total number of churches in the block groups of the periphery declined from eleven in 1996 to just three in 2002. Many of the churches in the study area operate out of rented storefronts and, as a consequence, their congregations are often highly mobile and the churches impermanent. This may explain the steep drop in the number of churches between the two survey periods. Hispanic congregations also often pur-

TABLE 9.4—LANGUAGE OF PRIMARY CHURCH SIGNAGE, CLEVELAND

LANGUAGE	SUBAREA							
	CORE				DOMAIN			
	1996		2002		1996		2002	
	No.	%	No.	%	No.	%	No.	%
SPANISH	3	100	3	75	2	33	3	30
SPANISH & ENGLISH	0	0	0	0	2	33	1	10
ENGLISH	0	0	1	25	2	33	6	60
TOTAL	3	100	4	100	6	100	10	100

	PERIPHERY				TOTAL			
	1996		2002		1996		2002	
	No.	%	No.	%	No.	%	No.	%
SPANISH	2	18	2	67	7	35	8	47
SPANISH & ENGLISH	0	0	0	0	2	10	1	6
ENGLISH	9	82	1	33	11	55	8	47
TOTAL	11	100	3	100	20	100	17	100

Source: Field surveys, 1996 and 2002.

chase old church buildings from other denominations and adapt them to their particular needs.

The use of Spanish-language signage and the recycling of older church buildings are examples of adaptive reuse and the succession of cultures in the Near Westside. The church building that once housed St. Matthews Lutheran Church, built in the 1880s by German immigrants, now is home to the Iglesia Sinai—Asamblea de Dios (the Sinai Church—Assembly of God).

RESIDENTIAL LANDSCAPE

Residential landscape elements associated with Hispanic neighborhoods occurred with some frequency in some block groups and were nearly absent in others (see Fig. 9.2). In each of the surveys, 1996 and 2002, more than fifty homes in the study area displayed a Catholic religious shrine, a Puerto Rican flag, or a campaign sign supporting a candidate with a Hispanic surname (Table 9.5). This represented 1.5 percent of all occupied housing units and about 5 percent of all housing units occupied by Hispanics. Religious shrines, usually to the Virgin of the Milagrosa, were the most common Hispanic landscape element, and these accounted for at least half of all residential landscape elements tabulated in each survey.

Unexpectedly, political signs showed up as notable landscape elements in each survey period. These represented about one-quarter of the landscape elements in both survey years. Usually, these supported Nelson Cintrón Jr., the first Hispanic elected as a city council member in Cleveland, in the mid-1990s.

Puerto Rican flag displays also occurred with some regularity in the study area, although this varied considerably between the two surveys. In 1996, only six residences flew the island's flag, but this number jumped to fifteen in the 2002 survey (Table 9.5).

The frequency of homes with Hispanic landscape elements did not entirely demonstrate the patterns originally anticipated. The core block groups did not have the highest occurrences of residential landscape elements. Rather, in both survey periods, it was the domain, with a Hispanic population between 34 percent and 51 percent, where Hispanic landscape elements occurred most frequently. In the 1996 survey, even the block groups designated as belonging to the periphery had an appreciable number.

These results might seem counterintuitive; however, this may not be the case. The core's block groups likely have so few residential landscape

TABLE 9.5—SEMI-FIXED RESIDENTIAL LANDSCAPE ELEMENTS, CLEVELAND'S NEAR WESTSIDE

RESIDENTIAL ELEMENT SUBAREA

	CORE				DOMAIN			
	1996		2002		1996		2002	
	No.	% OF TOTAL	No.	% OF TOTAL	No.	% OF TOTAL	No.	% OF TOTAL
SHRINE	4	57	4	36	14	54	24	52
FLAG	1	14	4	36	2	8	11	24
POLITICAL SIGN	2	29	3	27	10	38	11	24
TOTAL	7	100	11	100	26	100	46	100

	PERIPHERY				TOTAL			
	1996		2002		1996		2002	
	No.	% OF TOTAL	No.	% OF TOTAL	No.	% OF TOTAL	No.	% OF TOTAL
SHRINE	15	75	1	100	33	62	29	50
FLAG	3	15	0	0	6	11	15	26
POLITICAL SIGN	2	10	0	0	14	26	14	24
TOTAL	20	100	1	100	53	99	58	100

Source: Field surveys, 1996 and 2002.
Note: One house may display multiple landscape elements. In 1996, forty-nine houses were surveyed: six in the core, twenty-four in the domain, and nineteen in the periphery. In 2002, fifty-five houses were surveyed: ten in the core, forty-four in the domain, and one in the periphery.

elements because land use is more commercial, and a much larger percentage of the population is living in small apartment buildings or subdivided houses, where the opportunities for adding semi-fixed symbols are less common than for single-family dwellings.

The large number of landscape elements recorded in the periphery in the 1996 survey seems unusual, as does the dramatic disappearance of these in the survey data six years later. This is explained by the fact that one block group with a low percentage of Hispanics in 1990 was classified as being in the periphery in the 1996 survey. Population data for 2000 showed a dramatic increase in the Hispanic population of this block group, and for the 2002 survey it was reclassified as falling within the domain. The survey results suggest that it is likely that, by 1996, a significant Hispanic population had already moved into the block group, but because the block groups were classified using the 1990 data, the Hispanic population was judged to be much smaller than it actually was.

9.4.   Near Westside home, Cleveland, with elements often associated with Hispanic residential landscapes. These include a religious statue in the yard, a crucifix under the eaves, ornate wrought iron on the door, a neatly tended front yard garden, and the chain link fence. *Photograph by the authors, 2002.*

The presence of secondary landscape elements was noted for those houses that displayed a shrine, an ethnic flag, or a political sign. These elements included house color, house trim, front yard gardens, potted plants, and the use of perimeter fencing. Perimeter fencing, almost always chain link, is the most common secondary landscape element, with nearly two-thirds of all houses with primary landscape elements also having a perimeter fence. Front yard flower gardens, the use of potted flowers in the front yard or on the porch, and homes painted in bright pastel colors often characteristic of Puerto Rican homes occurred comparatively infrequently. However, the handful of houses that were brilliantly painted in the study area almost always displayed multiple landscape elements (Fig. 9.4). The house shown in Figure 9.4 is painted light blue, has a crucifix hanging from the gable, a shrine to the Virgin of the Milagrosa, a front yard garden with potted plants, and a decorative, yet secure, wrought-iron frame over the door.

CONCLUSIONS

The use of Spanish- and Spanish and English–language signage by businesses and churches as well as the use of Hispanic residential landscape markers in the survey area generally followed expected patterns. In areas where Hispanic population concentrations were greatest, the use of semifixed landscape features associated with Hispanics, particularly Puerto Ricans, was also high. Commercial signage in Spanish and/or Spanish and English occurred with the greatest frequency in the core, where the proportion of Hispanic residents exceeded 51 percent. These features were less frequent in the domain and were largely absent in the block groups of the periphery, where the percentage of Hispanic population fell to between 17 and 34. Church signage also followed this basic pattern, and signs in Spanish or Spanish and English occurred with the greatest frequency in the core.

The presence of Hispanic residential landscape elements followed a slightly different pattern. Comparatively few of these elements appeared in the core block groups, while the greatest numbers occurred in the block groups constituting the domain. Because the block groups that embodied the core had more commercial land uses and because more apartments and multifamily units were found in these block groups and their occupants were less likely to have the ability to modify these buildings or yards, semifixed landscape elements were less common.

Despite a modest increase in the study area's Hispanic population and a large percentage increase in the city's Hispanic population between 1990 and 2000, the survey data did not show any increase in the presence of Spanish-language signage or residential landscape elements in the six-year period between 1996 and 2002. Indeed, between the two survey periods, there was little change in either the relative frequency or the absolute number of Spanish-language signs or Hispanic residential landscape elements. This is explained by the timing of the surveys. They did not correspond with the dates of the population censuses, and it is likely that much of the Hispanic population increase on the Near Westside and in Cleveland in general occurred prior to 1996, when the first landscape survey was conducted.

This study assumed that when Hispanic population percentages and numbers increased in a particular area or neighborhood, the absolute numbers and frequency of Spanish-language signs and residential landscape markers associated with Hispanic populations would also increase. The findings show that this generally is the case in Cleveland's Near Westside Hispanic neighborhood. But this pattern may not necessarily hold in other cities or with other Hispanic populations. In Cleveland, most Hispanics are of Puerto Rican origin, and for many who have come directly or recently from the island, Spanish is their language of preference. However, as Hispanic populations continue to move to midwestern cities, immigrants may already have acculturated to life in the United States and the use of the English language. In other instances, variations may exist where second- or third-generation Hispanics whose use of Spanish may be limited or non-existent and whose Latino cultural affinities may have been somewhat diluted. Additional Hispanic residents with such characteristics would seem unlikely to have much use for the Spanish language and might be less likely to use semi-fixed Hispanic landscape elements on their homes or in their yards.

The study also suggests that the use of comparatively few semi-fixed landscape elements can create the appearance of an ethnic neighborhood. In the case of Cleveland's Near Westside, Puerto Ricans and other Hispanics have used Spanish-language signs on businesses and churches and a range of yard and garden ornamentation, especially Roman Catholic religious shrines, to create the beginnings of a Puerto Rican enclave. A review of the survey data underscores the small number of businesses or churches using Spanish-language signage to create the impression of an emerging Latino neighborhood. Fewer than thirty-five businesses (about 15 percent of the total) and just nine churches (slightly more than 50 percent of the total) used Spanish-language signage during the period under study. Semi-fixed residential landscape elements occurred even less frequently: only about 1.5 percent of all occupied housing units in the one-square-mile study area incorporated one of these elements on the house or in the yard. The survey and census data suggest that, even among those housing units occupied by Hispanics, only about 5 percent use semi-fixed landscape elements on their house or in their garden.

This study's method, like that employed by many cultural geographers, uses the published literature, census data, and an observational survey to track landscape creation and transformation. While these approaches allow one to document the characteristics of the landscape and its changing nature, they provide little insight into the motivations of those neighborhood actors who employ Spanish-language signage or use Hispanic landscape elements in their yards or gardens. While it may be reasonable to conclude that businesses and churches use Spanish-language signage to communicate more effectively with potential Spanish-speaking customers or parishioners, the rationale for using semi-fixed Hispanic landscape elements in yards or on homes is less apparent. Indeed, some might reasonably argue that the Hispanic landscape elements observed in this study have little to do with expressing any kind of Puerto Rican or Latino cultural identity or solidarity. For example, one might speculate that campaign signs in yards and houses supporting a Democratic Party city council candidate with a Hispanic surname are more about personal political preference than about Hispanic cultural attachment.

Nevertheless, other landscape diagnostics are perhaps more telling. The presence of the statues of the Virgin of the Milagrosa in Near Westside neighborhood yards appears to signify a Puerto Rican association, because no other Hispanic subgroups in the study area revere this particular saint. And what message does flying the Puerto Rican flag convey to neighbors and the public at large? Is it a political statement about independence, statehood, or the island's commonwealth status? Or does it mean something else? In any event, there is little doubt that it reinforces some level of Puerto Rican identity, regardless of its exact intent.

Thus, in future studies of the creation and evolution of Hispanic neighborhood landscapes, researchers should combine observational field surveys with in-depth interviews. Robust interview data, once collected, will permit an even richer interpretation of the evolving Hispanic landscapes in neighborhoods of urban areas in the United States.

10 | LATINOS IN POLYNUCLEATED KANSAS CITY

Steven L. Driever

The Midwest usually appears in discussions of the United States' Latino population only in passing. The numbers of Latinos there are rather modest compared with those for places such as California, Texas, and the southwestern border counties long recognized for heavy concentrations of Hispanic population. For 1990, the U.S. Bureau of the Census counted some 1,727,000 Hispanics in the Midwest; they constituted 2.9 percent of the population (Driever 1996). For 2000, the census counted some 3,125,000 Hispanics in the region, accounting for 5.0 percent of the population (Guzmán 2001). What is sometimes overlooked in the analysis of such summary statistics is that the Midwest is a very large region (Ohio, Michigan, Indiana, Illinois, Wisconsin, Iowa, Minnesota, Missouri, Kansas, Nebraska, and North and South Dakota). Within its vast domain, there are noticeable concentrations of Hispanic population in some large metropolitan areas and even in smaller cities with meat-processing industry.

The Kansas City area has had a significant Hispanic population for many years. As the twenty-first century unfolds, a number of signs suggest that greater Kansas City has emerged as the main center of Latino population and activity between Chicago and Dallas. In 2002, the Mexican Consulate in St. Louis, the largest metro area in Missouri, relocated to Kansas City, Missouri, so that it could better serve its clientele. Also in 2002, for the first time in many years, the beleaguered Kansas City, Missouri, School District gained, rather than lost, students because of a large increase in Latino enrollment.

This chapter will discuss why the Kansas City area has attracted Latino residents and the vital roles they have played in its economic development and prosperity. The discussion will address their relationship with the larger community as well as interrelationships within the Latino community itself. The Kansas City metro area encompasses a broad expanse of rolling plains almost equally divided between Missouri and Kansas and further divided into many local political units. Urbanization has sprawled in all directions as the metro area's labor market has proven in recent years to be one of the nation's strongest. At the same time, the city has witnessed a resurgence of Latino immigration and the formation of new clusters of Hispanic settlement, both in the core area and in the suburbs. Political barriers and sheer distance divide Latinos across this urban area, yet they share a sentiment that their future in Kansas City is secure and promising.

MEXICANS IN EARLY KANSAS CITY

The Kansas City area has a long history associated with Latinos, and it has from the beginning depended on them for its economic development and prosperity. Two of the earliest towns in the area—Independence and Westport—served as starting points for the Overland Trails to the West in the 1830s (Serl, Lanterman, and Sheaff 1944). Along one of the trails, the Santa Fe, Mexicans usually drove and cared for the animals in the wagon trains and the pack trains. There are newspaper accounts of Mexicans trading around the levees of Kansas City in 1850 and living at least temporarily in the city while they traded their goods (Laird 1975: 29). One native Mexican, Miguel Antonio Otero Sr., operated one of the largest wholesaling and overland freight companies in America from 1861 to 1877 in Westport (now part of midtown Kansas City, Missouri), and there were other wealthy Mexican traders as well (Chávez 2001; Driever 1996).

By 1884, Kansas City was directly connected to Mexico via the meeting of the Mexican Central Railroad and the Atchison, Topeka & Santa Fe Railroad at El Paso. It is inconceivable that this railway system and other contemporary railroads linking Kansas City and the Southwest did not bring Mexican labor to Kansas City to support railroad operations in the late nineteenth century. However, the earliest documentation of Mexican railroad workers residing in Kansas City appears for 1905, when the Atchison, Topeka & Santa Fe Railroad recruited 155 Mexicans, later joined by their families, to lay track to Wichita and Fresno, California. After the job was completed, the Mexicans returned to live in Kansas City, mainly in old boxcars (Chávez 2001).

The 1910 Census is the first federal census documentation of Mexican residents in the Kansas City area, and it grossly undercounts them because of their mobility and indifference to being counted. Some simply stayed in

Kansas City temporarily because of the instability and seasonality of the available railroad work. As a railroad center, Kansas City served as a distribution point of Mexicans to fields and factories to the north and to the east (García 1996; Valdés 2000: 32).

Nevertheless, by the 1920 Census, Kansas boasted the fifth-largest Mexican population of any state in the United States (Mendoza 1997: xviii). Young Mexican males first came to the Kansas City area to work on the railroads, which hired them in crews, usually from April to October, to lay and repair track, especially in Kansas, where the oven-hot summers scared off most American laborers. An estimated 75 percent of the first-generation Mexicans employed in Kansas City worked for the railroads. Most of the rest worked for the meatpacking plants as killers, skinners, salters, renderers, and freezer operators; however, their contributions to this once-important Kansas City industry have hardly been documented (*Kansas City on Parade* 1950).

That they are almost anonymous in the annals of Kansas City written before the 1950s reflects blatant discrimination. Not only were Latinos segregated in housing and in public spaces (schools, movie theaters, public swimming pools, etc.), but they suffered from the widespread assumption that, no matter how long they resided in the area, they were somehow not real Americans.

The first-generation Mexicans lived mainly in three districts: Argentine and Armourdale in Kansas City, Kansas, and the Westside in Kansas City, Missouri (Fig. 10.1). Argentine was south of the Kansas River and originally just south of the tracks of the Atchison, Topeka & Santa Fe Railroad; it essentially developed as a company town, with the Mexicans dominating the east end. Armourdale was north of the Kansas River and just to the northeast of Argentine. It was surrounded by railroad tracks and had good accessibility to the five major meatpacking plants in Kansas City, located in the bottomlands of the Kansas River. One can assume that the smelly, greasy packing plants became the community's main employer, for by 1908, a federal study concluded that meatpacking was "not only the principal industry" in Kansas City, Kansas, but "the only industry [there] of importance" (Montgomery and Kasper 1999: 102).

The Westside was a large district in Kansas City, Missouri, just to the east of the Kansas River bottomlands. Mexicans formed two small clusters there, one of mainly single transient men in the north and one of families in the center and south. The northern cluster of Mexicans, along with many of the buildings there (from Wyandotte to Grand and Third to Fifth Streets), has disappeared, but the central and southern concentrations gradually

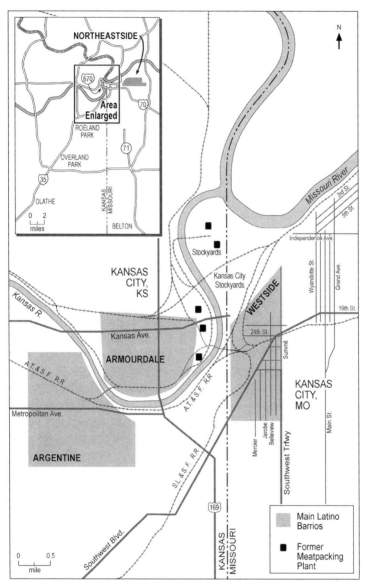

10.1.   Four major Latino barrios in Kansas City metropolitan area core.
*Sources: Adapted from 1914 Map of Greater Kansas City; Greater Kansas City
Map; U.S. Bureau of the Census 2000b.*

took root. By the 1920s, they supported the first strip of Latino commercial services, along 24th Street, very close to the present-day Latino business strip that stretches for several miles along Southwest Boulevard.

The early Latino businesses provided places where Westsiders could shop in comfort, but what sustained the community were two institutions: Our Lady of Guadalupe Church, founded in 1914 by exiled Mexican Father Joseph Muñoz; and the Guadalupe Center, a social-service agency founded in 1919 by a Catholic women's club. The center began with a school run by volunteers and a clinic for Mexican immigrants (Guadalupe Centers, Inc. 2001). By the 1930s, with the support of the Works Progress Administration, it offered language classes for adults, and drama, folk dance, fiestas, and other cultural activities in a new mission-style building constructed on 23rd Street (Valdés 2000: 124).

THE NEW WAVE OF LATINO IMMIGRANTS

Today, most Kansas Citians still picture the Latino community as it was back in the early twentieth century and assume that the vast majority of Hispanics in the Kansas City area still live and work in the same three communities. Nothing could be further from the truth. The U.S. Bureau of the Census (2000a) puts the Latino/Hispanic population of greater Kansas City at almost 93,000; however, local leaders estimate that the real figure is at least 130,000 to 150,000. The Latino proportion of the area's total population thus approaches 8 percent. In the 1990s, the Kansas City area witnessed a very impressive increase in Latinos, most of it due to immigrants late in the decade seeking higher salaries and better job opportunities. Of the recent immigrants from Latin America, nearly 90 percent have come from Mexico, about 6 percent from Central America and the Caribbean, and only 5 percent from South America (Lewis 2001: 4). In addition, many immigrants have come to Kansas City from California and South Texas. They are aware that Kansas City's relatively tight labor market ensures that they will almost certainly receive more than the minimum wage. Juan González (2000: 199–205), the award-winning New York journalist, predicts that the migration of Latin Americans to the United States will continue in record numbers, and there is every reason to believe that the Kansas City metropolitan area will become an increasingly attractive destination for all Latinos.

According to the U.S. Bureau of the Census (2000a), about 76 percent of all Hispanics in the Kansas City metropolitan area identified themselves as being of Mexican origin. Although the Mexican proportion of the total Latino population in the area appears to be increasing with the recent surge in immigration, this does not mean other Latino voices are mute or drowned out. For example, on June 25, 2002, Dominican Night was held at the Kansas City Royals baseball stadium. This unlikely event was scheduled because the president of the Dominican Republic, Hipolito Mejía, flew into Kansas City to honor two Dominican managers whose teams (the Kansas City Royals and the Detroit Tigers) were playing against each other, a first for Major League Baseball. As Dominican flags waved and merengue tunes filled the stadium, press from throughout Latin America and Kansas City recorded the event (Harlow 2002). In a quieter but no less effective way, the Legión Hispánica of North America, an organization founded by Prof. Joel Balam de Escalante, a local educator, frequently brings together Latinos and non-Latinos to discuss Spanish and Latin American art history and literature.

THE KANSAS SIDE: NEW LATINO WAVE MEETS HEARTLAND AMERICA

According to conservative census figures, Wyandotte County, which contains mainly Kansas City, Kansas, now has a population that is 16 percent Latino; the county's Latino population grew 130 percent from 1990 to 2000 (Lewis 2001: 3). In Kansas City, Kansas, the Latino community has expanded from Armourdale northward some two miles to the downtown of Kansas City, Kansas, and from Argentine southward another two miles to the Johnson County border. Wyandotte County is currently and for the foreseeable future the metropolitan area's most dynamic Hispanic zone.

Most of the adult immigrant Hispanic population shares the American Dream, and a 2001 survey reveals that about 80 percent of that group aspires to open their own businesses in the Kansas City area (Lewis 2001: 16). About half of all new business licenses issued each year in Wyandotte County go to Hispanics (Murguia 2002). This trend might persist for years because of continuing high levels of Latino immigration and because of El Centro, Inc., a dynamic Kansas-side social-service organization. Among other things, El Centro operates an entrepreneurial development center, or incubator, in the Argentine community, which now houses nine small businesses and is expanding to make room for more tenants (Sendorff 2002). Even some retail businesses in the part of Johnson County near the Wyandotte County line proximate to Argentine changed their mix of goods and marketing strategies in the 1990s to appeal primarily to Hispanic customers. For example, the Price Chopper grocery store just south of the

10.2.   Anthony Estrada, grocery manager of Roeland Park, Kansas, Price Chopper
Supermarket, checking large display of cookies in the Mexican food aisle. Behind Estrada
is the Tex-Mex aisle. These aisles are the busiest in the store at most times of day.
Photograph by S. Driever, 2002.

county line in Roeland Park has a complete Tex-Mex aisle and an authentic Mexican food aisle (Fig. 10.2) and has special displays supplied with
staples trucked in directly from suppliers in Mexico and their U.S. subsidi-
aries (Estrada 2002). Although the company will not divulge the store's net
revenues, it is no secret that the Roeland Park store is one of Price Chopper's most profitable locations.

Johnson County, an area that includes Roeland Park, Overland Park,
and Olathe (see Fig. 10.1, inset), is one of the wealthiest counties in the
United States. It is experiencing an explosion of growth in its Hispanic
population. According to census figures, the Latino population there grew
some 158 percent between 1990 and 2000 compared with an overall population increase there of only 27 percent. Perhaps as many as thirty thousand Hispanics now reside in the county, making up over 6 percent of the
county's total population. Recent immigrants have been attracted to Johnson County's strong labor market, particularly in retail and personal services, construction, and landscaping.

The county was quite unprepared for the influx of immigrants not only
working there but also often living there in large apartment complexes or

duplex subdivisions that can be found near almost any major intersection in older areas. To deal with the new population, the chief of police of Overland Park, the largest city in the county, spearheaded the establishment of an El Centro, Inc., office in vacant space in a shopping center in the city. The Johnson County El Centro office refers clients, almost entirely first-generation immigrants from Mexico, to appropriate service providers. In addition, the office, in partnership with the local community college, offers English as a second language (ESL) classes four nights a week.

Olathe, the Johnson County seat, is an old city located in the southwestern corner of the urbanized part of the metropolitan area that, nevertheless, has a sizable Latino population. It is likely that Hispanics have worked and possibly resided there almost from the city's beginning. The city was founded in 1857 and quickly became the first overnight rest stop on the Overland Trails leading west from Kansas City, and stage lines taking passengers from Kansas City to Lawrence and Fort Scott, Kansas, stopped there regularly (Burns 1957). After the Civil War, the St. Louis and San Francisco and the Atchison, Topeka & Santa Fe Railroads connected Olathe with Kansas City. Today, the southwest section of Olathe (south and west of the courthouse) has so many Latinos that locals refer to it as "Little Mexico." Most of the community is relatively new, a result of unprecedented local expansion (Danneberg 2002).

Olathe is the most rapidly expanding city in the Kansas half of the metropolitan area. Between 1970 and 1980, it more than doubled its land area and population, and between 1980 and 1990, the city almost doubled in area and population again (Olathe Planning Commission 1990). Latinos there work in various places, including local housing construction sites, in new retail shopping centers and box stores in the more affluent southeastern corner of the city, and in light industry along the I-35 corridor that bisects Olathe. Although the Latino community there probably numbers about nine thousand, it has as yet no recognized community leader or, despite a number of small Hispanic businesses, a Hispanic Chamber of Commerce (Ramero Brown 2002).

Despite the efforts of enlightened Johnson County residents, the mix of suburban affluence and the immigrant poverty on which it depends can be volatile. Nowhere can this potentially explosive mixture be studied more readily than in the fast-food industry, which likes to hire immigrants because of their willingness to work hard for low pay and because they will serve as "go-betweens" in the cultivation of new markets (Talwar 2002). Unfortunately, ethnic tensions can erupt into open conflict among workers and between workers and management.

In 2002, 15 Latino workers at an Overland Park McDonald's brought discrimination allegations to the attention of regional-level management. Reportedly, a new manager had addressed the protesting workers in a disparaging manner, pushed them, and shoved meat trays on the holding cabinet hard enough to cause injury (Lambert 2002). The manager was transferred to a new store, but an investigation (Operation Vanguard) by the Immigration and Naturalization Service of I-9s, the Employment Eligibility Verification forms for new hires, led to the arrest of apparently all the protesters at their homes (Cardona 2002). In fact, the INS investigation of the employment records of all fifteen Kansas City–area McDonald's restaurants revealed that 230 of 559 employees had "discrepancies" such as invalid Social Security numbers in their hiring records (Sánchez 2002a).

This unfortunate but by no means isolated incident was traumatic for many Latinos. The board of the League of United Latin American Citizens (LULAC) convened in Washington to discuss the situation, and several of its officials as well as more than a few local activists met in Kansas City with regional and corporate headquarters officers of McDonald's and regional officials of the INS. Usually in such situations, the corporation will strive to restore its image by using one or more local Hispanic organizations to convey its goodwill and good deeds to the Latino community via newsletters, reports, and public events in exchange for corporate financial support. Such a process of "amplification" has characterized the relationship between Hispanic organizations and corporations since the early 1980s (Ortiz 1996: 118–119). In this instance, McDonald's Heartland Office insisted that the corporation had not initiated the investigation carried out by the INS. It further vowed to "build a bridge to move forward" by promising to establish three Hispanic franchises; promote three Hispanic staff members to management; find a supplier in the Hispanic community; initiate sensitivity training for all its employees; use bilingual labeling; join the Kansas City Hispanic Chamber of Commerce; and help sponsor Hispanic events (Coalition of Hispanic Organizations 2002).

THE MISSOURI SIDE: POLYNUCLEATION
OF THE LATINO COMMUNITY

Although there are two Latino communities in Kansas City, Missouri, the old Westside (see Fig. 10.1) is the sentimental, if not exactly the historical, heart of Hispanic settlement. By 1915, the main cluster of Mexicans there, bounded by 23rd and 25th Streets on the north and south and by Mercier and Belleview on the west and east, supported a commercial district with eighteen businesses, six run by Mexicans and others welcoming them as customers (Mendoza 1997: 146). Since then, many of the local Hispanic leaders have been rooted in the Westside, the predominantly Latino part of which also has expanded north and south well beyond the original Mexican nucleus. Most of the expansion occurred soon after July 1951, when the Kansas River flooded surrounding lowlands, including the Argentine and Armourdale districts. Some fourteen thousand people were evacuated from those two districts, and many of the Latino families relocated to the Westside, transforming the area south of Southwest Boulevard from an Irish American/German American community into a predominantly Latino one (Callon 2002).

The Westside, however, has suffered from interstate highway construction. In the 1950s, I-35, with extensive overpasses and short tunnels, literally cut the Westside in half (Fig. 10.1, inset). In the 1960s, I-670, the so-called Crosstown Freeway, was a below-street-grade highway dividing the north end of the Westside with a huge trench. The land clearing, demolition, and barriers associated with those projects, traffic noise, and general deterioration of usually outdated buildings all contributed to a population decline in the Westside from 1940 to 1970: from an estimated thirteen thousand residents to seven thousand (Valdés 2000: 136).

Today, most of the residents of the Westside are second- and third-generation Latinos, and a significant number believe that their barrio, the oldest residential neighborhood in the metropolitan area beyond downtown Kansas City, must be rehabilitated if it is to remain viable. They have been active in garnering public support for restoration of the residential areas and for revitalization of its business and commercial areas. Since 1973, the Westside Housing Organization (WHO), a private nonprofit community development corporation, has overseen the rehabilitation of many rundown single- and multifamily dwellings and the construction of new homes where suitable space is available (as in the 2500 block of Mercier). WHO works with local, state, and national organizations to revitalize housing for low- and moderate-income families; it is the organization Westside residents can turn to for help in repairing and improving their homes. For example, homeowners who do not qualify for conventional loans can ask WHO for assistance in finding grants and low-interest loans; they can even rent tools from WHO for a nominal fee. The Westside Community Action Network (WCAN) is a 501(c)(3) corporation that works with the Kansas City, Missouri, Police Department to improve the quality of life for Westsiders, focusing on what might be called self-help programs. For example, WCAN organizes neighborhood cleanups, issues neighborhood crime alerts through its bimonthly newsletter (which is hand-delivered throughout the Westside), and instructs newsletter readers about ways to maintain and improve their homes and yards.

The revitalization of Westside business and commercial areas has received considerable attention because the residential area cannot prosper without an economic base of support and without adequate services. For many years, the main focus has been on improving the business-scape along Southwest Boulevard. At first, the idea was to beautify the several blocks of small Latino businesses from about Summit to Jarboe with plantings, a fountain, and other amenities. Although these goals were modest, not all were met.

Since 1990, the emphasis has shifted to job creation and community sustainability through the construction of the Westside Business Park. With federal enterprise-zone grant funds, the Hispanic Economic Development Corporation (HEDC) purchased, over several years, an idle twenty-two-acre site in the 2600 block of Southwest Boulevard. The site, where the roundhouses of the Kansas City Terminal Railway were located to service and repair trains at nearby Union Station, remained idle for several years as HEDC sought an appropriate anchor willing to invest in the park. Finally, DST Output, a subsidiary of DST Systems, Inc., approached HEDC about using the site. The company was operating in old, scattered facilities in the Westside and it was seriously considering relocating to another city, if necessary, where it could consolidate its production operations. Finally, it offered to invest in restoring the roundhouse buildings for office space (about 55,000 square feet) and building a large production facility (about 227,000 square feet) to process financial statements and related business forms. This huge facility is DST's biggest operation in the Midwest, handling more than 60 percent of all mutual fund statements mailed in the United States. DST Output's goal is to have about half of its projected 750 employees hired from within a twenty-square-mile enterprise zone that stretches west into Kansas and east into traditionally African American neighborhoods in Missouri.

The HEDC project, at this point, is operational and is considered a success. Its officials understand the local community and have built a truly stunning facility. The restored roundhouse would be a rare historical landmark anywhere. On Southwest Boulevard, it speaks to the unique and vital role that the Westside and the Latino community played in making Kansas City the nation's premier railroad center after Chicago. More important, perhaps, the entire complex and the many ancillary businesses with which it will contract will anchor the Westside economically for many years to come.

The other Latino community in the core area of Kansas City, Missouri, is the Northeast Side, a formerly predominantly Italian American area that appears to be making the transition to becoming very Hispanic while expanding its boundaries at the same time (Fig. 10.1, inset). In the late 1970s, it appeared that the Northeast Side would have a mix of Italian American families and young professional newcomers interested in restoring homes in Kansas City's second-oldest residential neighborhood, especially along the boulevards. Today, however, the area is becoming noticeably Latino. Of the five census tracts of the original Northeast Side, four have Latino populations of more than 30 percent of the total, according to the conservative census figures. Moreover, three census tracts south of Independence Avenue (formerly considered the southern boundary of the neighborhood and currently running east-west through the middle of the community) now have populations over one-third Latino (U.S. Bureau of the Census 2000b). This entire area has experienced rapid rates of immigration in the last several years.

All the census tracts discussed above have male-female ratios higher than that for Kansas City, Missouri (51.7 to 48.3), have a median age below the city's (34.0), and have more Hispanics claiming Mexican ancestry than for the entire city—83.0 percent versus 73.0 percent. These numbers indicate relatively high rates of recent immigration, chiefly from Mexico.

In April 2002, for the first time, a meeting was convened in the Northeast Side for the purposes of discussing these recent changes and to encourage local leaders and activists to begin to work together on issues related to the local Latino community. Several dozen service providers for the Latino community and for the Northeast Side have since met monthly to address the unmet needs of the local Latino residents in health services, education (especially secondary and higher), housing, and language (especially ESL classes and computer accessibility). The Northeast Side is large and sufficiently dynamic that these service providers are trying to form a coalition to oversee the development and provision of community services.

The commercial streetscape is always quick to respond to changes in consumer demand, particularly when there is ethnic turnover. One need only drive along Independence Avenue, the Northeast Side's main thoroughfare, to observe the evolving retail structure. There are numerous Latino shops, most providing convenience goods to local residents, and a few large Latino establishments have market thresholds that encompass most of the other Latino barrios as well. Along Independence Avenue one can purchase tickets to catch a daily bus to El Paso and Chihuahua; shop for Mexican foods, herbs, and party supplies; enter a Latino sports bar; consult an Asian American dentist with a Spanish-speaking staff; sign up for cable TV in Spanish; send money to Mexico; dance in a Latino nightclub; eat in more than a few Mexican restaurants; and attend church services in Spanish.

There are so many first-generation Latino families in the Northeast Side that its Northeast High School was designated in 2001 as the only ESL high school in the Kansas City School District. Moreover, the LULAC National Education Service Center (NESC) is piloting a parents in quality education program for a group of parents at a Northeast Side elementary school, Scarritt. The program shows the parents how to work more effectively with the schools and teachers on behalf of the academic interests of their children. The parents meet weekly in the school cafeteria to interact with teachers, to role-play situations, and to learn how to raise the educational and career expectations of their children. At the same time, NESC is running a Young Readers after-school tutorial program at Scarritt and another elementary school (García) in the Westside; that program has proven so successful that the Kansas City School District provided funds to expand it to other schools (Sánchez 2002b).

The Northeast Side is a dynamic community that has replaced the Westside, the heart of the entire Latino community, as the center of Hispanic population on the Missouri side of the metro area. However, whether this community can ever replace the Westside as the location to which most area Latinos attach the greatest sentiment and symbolism remains to be seen.

The Missouri side has also experienced suburbanization of a significant part of its Latino population. Cass County has seen rapid population growth in response to a low cost of living and low taxes. The City of Belton, which sits on the southern edge of the metropolitan area (Fig. 10.1, inset), has about two thousand Hispanics out of a total population of a little more than twenty thousand. Considerable new construction, golf courses, a large tree nursery, a nearby assisted-living facility, and a nearby Wal-Mart distribution center employ numerous Latinos, many of whom moved north from Texas in search of better-paying jobs (Ruiz 2002). One recent inmigrant from Texas, Guillermo Gómez, worked for $5.20 an hour at an assembly plant in El Paso; while visiting a friend in Kansas City, he decided to stay and found part-time work as a cook in a Mexican restaurant, where he now earns over $9.00 an hour. Despite the expense of attending a local college, he is able to send money to his family in El Paso (Mayer 2002).

Like Johnson County's Olathe, Belton is an edge city with a mainly new Hispanic population that has not yet formed its own community institutions or leadership. Nevertheless, city officials seem determined to embrace the changing demographic landscape and have worked out a sister city agreement that includes student exchanges and internet–digital camera connections with Manzanillo, Mexico.

UNITY AND DISUNITY IN THE LATINO COMMUNITY

In an urban area as vast as metropolitan Kansas City, one might wonder whether the polynucleated, geographically dispersed, and culturally diverse Hispanic community can retain its sense of solidarity. Already there is something of a rivalry between the Kansas side and the Missouri side, no doubt reflecting the political realities that have divided the larger society since the events associated with the Civil War. Because of spatial mismatch between places of residence and places of employment, the average Kansas Citian now travels twenty-nine miles per day in a vehicle; there is no reason to believe that Latinos are an exception to this statistic (Lewis 2001: 7; Mid-America Regional Council 2001: 59). Without a better system of public transportation, extensive travel times will soon create a rift between the older Latino neighborhoods in the core area and the newer, younger Latino communities in the suburban edge cities.

Finally, there has been some conflict between the second- and third-generation Latino Americans and the first-generation immigrants because of different cultural norms, class membership, and life experiences; over time, this conflict could intensify, as the newcomers are susceptible to downward assimilation (López 2000). A 2002 editorial in one of Kansas City's bilingual newspapers is a sobering reminder that the Latino community itself is changing and that although many second- and third-generation Latino Americans identify with American middle-class values, newly arrived Latino immigrants may not:

> Fitting in hasn't always been easy for Hispanics. Thus, those who've endured discrimination or have had parents of family members who've endured hardships aren't happy to see that many newcomers who come to the United States aren't interested in fitting in or making their way. They perpetuate the belief that Hispanics are here to impose their ways on others and don't wish to be part of the overall society. Such people aren't here to assimilate, but come to the United States to continue their lifestyles as they did in Mexico or Latin America, so much so that they make nuisances of themselves . . . It's up to decent Hispanics to let the rude newcomers know how to act . . . it's the only way that everyone can learn to live together. ("Hispanic Newcomers Should Show Proper Social Conduct" 2002)

For the community to remain viable, its best interests must be championed by key metropolitan-wide institutions. Two major nonprofit organizations—El Centro, Inc., and the Guadalupe Center, Inc.—offer a full range of services to Latinos and many low-income non-Latinos as well. They essentially provide the same services and activities to either side of the state line. Kansas City is also fortunate to have the Coalition of Hispanic Organizations (COHO), which has been revitalized and meets monthly to coordinate responses to issues that affect local Latinos (Coalition of Hispanic Organizations 2001).

Even nonprofit organizations oriented toward the larger urban community can provide invaluable tangible and moral support to the Latino community. For example, the University of Missouri–Kansas City (UMKC), in the not-so-distant past, was accused of ignoring the local Latino community; these charges helped create a climate that resulted in a new university administration. Now, UMKC addresses the needs and aspirations of the local Latino community in a variety of ways: it has provided office space and institutional support to COHO since 2001; and it houses and jointly sponsors (along with the Institute for Human Development and University of Missouri Outreach and Extension) Program Alianzas, a collaborative effort to facilitate partnerships in support of Latino community development. Program Alianzas is spearheading the effort to coordinate the Northeast Side service providers to better meet the needs of Latinos there.

The role of so-called niche media is very important, because the large media outlets ignore Latinos or simply report events (Cinco de Mayo, Fiesta Hispana in September, Mexican folkloric presentations, etc.) that, however noteworthy, tend to reinforce traditional stereotypes. Private for-profit niche media focused on Latinos are the entities that can best overcome the differences and distances separating Hispanics in Kansas City. The city is fortunate to have two bilingual newspapers, a Spanish-language weekly, and two Spanish-language radio stations.

A milestone occurred with the publication of the first issue of *KC Hispanic News* on September 16, 1996. This newspaper was the first focused on news about Kansas City's Hispanic community; initially, most people thought there would never be enough local news and events to report (Ramírez 2002). Not only was that concern unfounded, but so many small businesses, corporations, and ad agencies requested advertising space that the problem became one of deciding which local news stories could be covered in the biweekly.

The radio stations, of course, required a bigger capital investment and so are more telling evidence of the power of the local Hispanic market. One, La Super X (KKHK 1250 AM), is the result of two local entrepreneurs,

Paul and Frank Ramírez, trying to promote their businesses in Kansas City, Kansas. The station depends on leased airtime and broadcasts primarily traditional Latin music only during the day. The other, La Doble Z (KCZZ 1480 AM), is a twenty-four-hour radio station owned by non-Hispanic Arkansas investors; it broadcasts more contemporary Latin music, although most of the music programming is *norteño* in order to appeal to the many listeners from Texas and northern Mexico.

All of these niche media serve to form a panethnic identity focused on issues and events that affect the entire Latino population. The print media cater to common concerns (such as profiling and discrimination), fears (of violence, e.g.), and ethnic pride (in festivals, special awards, etc.). The radio stations can cover virtually any subject and maintain a larger audience than the print media as long as they play the right mix of music. Whereas radio has the potential to reach large segments of a Spanish-speaking audience, only about 11 percent of Americans in general read the daily newspaper (Calderón 2000; Moore 2001: 86). The better radio personalities can make their listeners feel like part of a large family at any time of the day or night. The announcer is often acting in loco parentis, and just through modulation of the voice and careful choice of words, repeated often, can persuade listeners to relax and to form a common, positive identity. For example, Saul Hernández (Fig. 10.3), an announcer on La Doble Z, has an on-air voice that is avuncular, and he repeatedly refers to his listeners as "mi raza" (my race) or "mi raza bonita" (my beautiful race)

CONCLUSION

Latinos have long played a vital role in the economic development and prosperity of the Kansas City metropolitan area. Whereas in the past they mainly kept the railroads running and put meat on the tables of Americans around the country, today they, like other Americans, are enmeshed in the service economy. The new wave of Latino immigrants into the area is like a vast army of recruits called up to handle mainly unskilled jobs that, nevertheless, are an essential ingredient in the new economic order that was established in the 1990s. Kansas Citians wanted to dine out, they wanted to buy affordable new housing on the outskirts of the metropolitan area, they wanted someone else to mow their lawns; all of these things would have been difficult or perhaps even impossible without Latino immigrant labor.

Class exploitation in the context of a new global order of the division of labor might have been the end of the story, but the Latino community has grown too large in Kansas City to be a stepping-stone to someone else's satisfaction. The community is now large enough to be self-sustaining and

10.3.   Saul Hernández ("El Piporrazo," a nickname in honor of the
Mexican comedian-singer Eulalio González, "El Piporro") broadcasts
from KCZZ 1480 AM (La Doble Z), Kansas City, every Monday through
Saturday afternoon. The signal is strong enough to reach most of the
Kansas City metropolitan area. *Photograph by S. Driever, 2002.*

to provide for many of its own needs. Yet the community is also becoming
sufficiently savvy in grassroots politics to demand from society at large satisfaction of other unmet, higher-level needs (more educational opportunities, better jobs, more respect, etc.).

At the same time, the larger community has spread out over the metropolitan area so that one nucleus or focal point no longer exists except in
the minds of some individuals. Space and geographic and political barriers
divide the community. Even within barrios, the community is riven by class
conflict associated with the different life experiences and cultural values
of first-generation immigrants and the second and third generation descendants of immigrants. These problems notwithstanding, the future looks
bright for the polynucleated Latino community in the area. Kansas City
appears to have a critical mass of talented Hispanics who are committed to
preserving and enriching their changing community and to articulating its
role within the metropolitan area. Through their efforts, there is an emerging collective sense that "our time has come," that the Latino will soon be
accorded equal status with other Kansas Citians, and that Latinos' part in
Kansas City's progress will finally be recognized and appreciated by all.

11 | LATINO COMMERCE IN NORTHERN NEVADA

Kate A. Berry

From the mid-nineteenth century through the early twentieth century, Nevada attracted few Latino settlers. Among these few were those lured by opportunities in gold and silver mining; others came to work as vaqueros on sheep and cattle ranches, and some stayed on to secure jobs in railroad construction (Martínez 2001; Miranda 1997; Shepperson 1970). Most were from Mexico and California, yet a few came from as far away as Chile. From just over three hundred Latinos statewide in 1875 to over a thousand in 1920, Nevada supported relatively few Latinos until the 1980s, when the state experienced dramatic population increases, and the number of Latinos rose significantly (Miranda 1997). The number of immigrants from Mexico increased by nearly 400 percent during the decade of the 1980s, and immigrants from Central and South America increased by 300 percent. By the end of the twentieth century, over a third of a million Latinos lived in Nevada, making up approximately 20 percent of the state's total population.

Perhaps because the population changes have occurred so recently, there has been very little scholarship concerning Latinos in Nevada, particularly those in the northern part of the state. This chapter spotlights the Reno metropolitan area in northern Nevada to examine how small businesses and commercial establishments represent the city's growing Latino presence and culture. During the 1990s, Reno experienced a dramatic surge in Latino population as immigrants moved into northern Nevada from Mexico, El Salvador, Guatemala, and other Latin American countries as well as from cities in the U.S. Southwest and the Pacific Coast. As a result, new demands for products and services have developed; even advertising and marketing have changed to accommodate people who are more comfortable conversing in the Spanish language. Some entrepreneurial Latinos have become owners of small retail and service businesses that cater to current demands among Latino and non-Latino consumers. This chapter examines the business-scapes (landscapes created by, for, and around businesses) created by Latinos within the Reno metropolitan area as a gauge of the evolving population and cultural dynamics associated with the recent wave of Latino migrants and considers how the city's economic pulse has been influenced.

The chapter is divided into two major sections. The first section outlines the contours of Latino Reno and provides glimpses of Latino presence and Spanish language throughout the city's business-scapes. In the second section, attention turns to Latino-owned businesses, with a focus on a single business corridor in Reno, South Wells Avenue, and associated streets.

OPENING UP SPACE: CONTOURS OF LATINO RENO

Reno is in a constant state of becoming—caught up in ever increasing demographic shifts as people move into, around, and out of this city of one-third of a million residents. The greater Reno metropolitan area in northern Nevada includes the City of Reno along with its sister city, Sparks, and portions of unincorporated Washoe County. Reno is the second-largest metropolitan area in the state, after Las Vegas in southern Nevada. Despite the rural, cowboy image of the state, about eight of every nine Nevadans reside in Reno, Las Vegas, or one of their suburbs. Reno's population growth contributes to Nevada's being the nation's fastest-growing state (based on proportionate population increases between 1990 and 2000), although the population increases in the north are not as spectacular as those in the southern portion of the state (U.S. Bureau of the Census 1990, 2000). Census estimates suggest that the population of the greater Reno metropolitan area itself grew by 33 percent over the decade of the 1990s, while the state as a whole grew 66 percent. It is particularly striking that between 1990 and 1999, Reno attracted more than twice as many foreign immigrants (22 percent of the population growth during this time period) as the state as a whole (9 percent) and about three times as many international immigrants as the greater Las Vegas metropolitan area (7 percent). More than half (60 percent) of all foreign immigrants in Reno were from Latin American countries (U.S. Bureau of the Census 2000).

An increasing number of Reno's residents are Latino. Census estimates (which are likely to be conservative because of high undercounts) show that 17 percent of the population in Reno identified itself as Latino or Hispanic in 2000, more than double the proportion a decade earlier (U.S. Bureau of the Census 1990, 2000). Reno attracted more than thirty-three thousand Latinos in the 1990s, accounting for approximately 40 percent of the overall population growth in the city, a higher proportion than for the state as a whole (34 percent). Reno is, as geographer Terrence Haverluk (1998) suggests, a new Latino community—that is, an urban area that was originally settled by Anglos that has only recently experienced significant migration of Latinos. Furthermore, foreign immigrants make up an increasingly significant portion of the city's growing Latino population.

Latino residences are neither randomly scattered throughout Reno nor tightly clustered into distinct ethnic enclaves; rather, there is a combination of both scattering and clustering within the metropolitan area. While many Latino residences can be found in various parts of the metro area, several neighborhoods are predominantly Latino, and this pattern seems to have been in place since at least the early 1970s (Miranda 1997). Latino neighborhoods can be found west of the airport, east of the University of Nevada at Reno (UNR), and in central Sparks (Fig. 11.1).

As Reno's Latino population surges, businesses of many types have started to take note of the potential for new marketing targets. As a result, signs in Spanish are becoming increasingly commonplace throughout the city's business-scapes. Some businesses have adapted by adding Spanish-language phrases or information to their signage to expand their potential customer base without displacing their existing clientele. The office of a national insurance company and a nearby gas station, for example, post the sign "Se Habla Español" (Spanish spoken here), as do a growing number of other businesses, large and small, in an effort to attract more Latino customers. The signs "Open/Abierto" and "Bienvenidos" (Welcome) are also becoming increasingly popular with local retailers and service companies as an unobtrusive means of indicating a Latino-friendly environment.

In order to expand their Latino clientele while minimizing the risk of offending other customers, another popular approach has been to include Spanish as a language option along with English. In service-oriented businesses, such as banks, this has occurred during the past few years as customers are given a choice of making ATM transactions in Spanish or English, although Spanish-language ATM services have been widely available in adjoining California and Arizona for much longer. Language choice is also emphasized by the Regional Transportation Agency, which posts detailed instructions in Spanish as well as English at the downtown bus hub. Retail stores incorporate this approach in their storefront signage. The clothing store Casa Joy's, for example, clearly identifies itself as a family

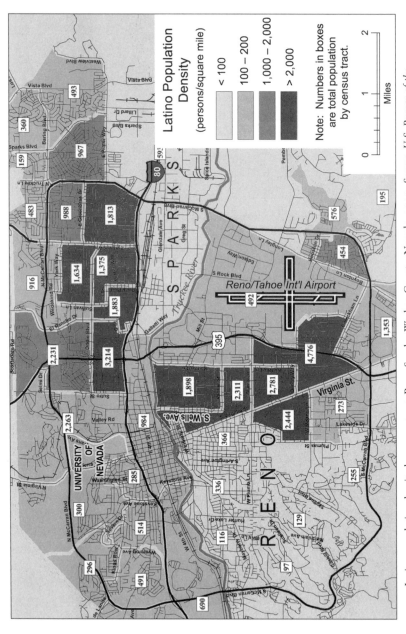

11.1. Latino population density by census tract, Reno-Sparks, Washoe County, Nevada, 2000. *Source: U.S. Bureau of the Census 2000.*

clothing store in both Spanish and English. Some signs target pedestrians, as in the case of window signs in retail stores, service establishments, banks, and bus facilities, while others are aimed at drivers and riders, as in the case of major storefront signs and billboards. Regardless of the scale, these examples illustrate the gradual diffusion of Spanish-language phrases within existing business-scapes and serve as indicators of the increasing significance of Latinos in a city that encourages enterprise and where people cultivate options and reject reliance on mandates.

Some businesses have opted for a more assertive approach by offering (and advertising) products and services that target a wide variety of Latino tastes. For example, small *taquerías,* such as Tacos de Acapulco, carve out success by catering to Anglos as well as Latinos. They offer such items as breakfast burritos, menudo, and specialty dishes from Mexico's central Pacific coast. Multinational food chains, as well, are working to secure a stronger Latino customer base. After the recent success of Dulce de Leche McFlurries in an area McDonald's, Dulce de Leche M&Ms are now marketed to attract young Latino customers and their parents. Even a national cellular phone company, Cricket, has developed a major Spanish advertising campaign in Reno that directly targets prospective Latino customers. International phone cards and money-courier services are increasingly popular products that many local small businesses, such as Murillo's Store, advertise because of their appeal to customers with family or business ties in Mexico or countries in Central America (Fig. 11.2).

Another business promotion strategy is the use of national colors on storefronts and signs to attract customers who identify with that country. One example is Yerania's Salón de Belleza/Beauty Salon in central Sparks, which uses the blue and white colors of the Salvadoran flag in the color scheme for the store and as a sign to indicate the owner's affiliation with El Salvador. The most common color schemes are Mexico's national flag's hues of green, red, and white, which are selectively used on storefronts and signs, and even occasionally on signs indicating commercial space for lease. A few stores display actual or replica flags, often posted alongside a U.S. flag.

Some businesses choose decorations for the inside of their stores that reflect ties with a particular community, state, or country in Latin America so as to attract and retain customers from these places. Maps of Mexico or the State of Jalisco, for example, are not uncommon as interior wall decorations in restaurants and small retail stores. Murals are another type of interior decoration used to convey idealized places and establish connections to these Latin American locales. A very large mural on an interior

11.2.   Exterior walls of Murillo's Store, Reno, alert customers that phone cards (*tarjetas telefónicas*) and international money-courier services(*envíos de dinero México a todo el mundo*) are available. *Photograph by K. Berry, 2002.*

wall of the restaurant Así Es Mi Tierra, for example, shows idyllic scenes of the Salvadoran countryside.

After a field exercise conducted for a geography class at UNR, one student noted that "as Reno becomes more culturally diverse, so do the tiendas y negocios that comprise Reno's economic landscape." Reno's business-scapes are beginning to open up space for Hispanics. By the standards of the Southwest, this has been a slow process and late in coming, but Reno is an inherently conservative place (Price 1972)—in many respects, more like Boise than Tucson. So despite the omnipresent gaming industry and the façade associated with tourism, significant cultural changes to Reno's business-scapes have been minimal and somewhat erratic until the 1990s. Today, the presence of Latino cultures is extending throughout a wide range of businesses in the metropolitan area and may be seen in the growing presence of Spanish-language signs, the selection of products and services advertised, the use of national colors, and choice of decorations.

TRANSFORMING PLACE: THE LATINO BUSINESS CORRIDOR

There has been very little research done on Latino small businesses in the United States (Harries 1971; Shim and Eastlick 1998). The U.S. Economic

Census estimated that in 1997, nationwide, Latinos owned 40 percent of all minority-owned firms, the largest proportion of any minority group in the country. Most Latino-owned businesses were sole proprietorships (83.0 percent) and most were small—with about two-thirds having annual receipts of $25,000 or less and about eight out of every ten having no paid employees (U.S. Department of Commerce 2001; U.S. Bureau of the Census 2002). These businesses were strongly concentrated in the four states with large Latino populations—California, Texas, Florida, and New York—but Nevada was ninth, with 5.1 percent of all firms being Latino-owned businesses (U.S. Department of Commerce 2001). According to the 1997 Economic Census, about 16.0 percent of Nevada's Latino-owned businesses were situated in Reno. Estimates are that about half of the Latino-owned businesses in Reno were in the service industries and one in seven were in wholesale or retail trades; only about 28.0 percent of these businesses had paid employees (U.S. Bureau of the Census 1997).

Like Latino residences in Reno, businesses owned by and catering to Latinos may be found throughout the city, but there are clusters of businesses, business corridors with numerous Latino small businesses in proximity to one another. One such corridor is along South Wells Avenue. The South Wells Avenue corridor is surrounded by neighborhoods with high concentrations of Latino households. The 2000 Census indicates that the neighborhoods surrounding South Wells Avenue—east of Virginia Street— had Latino population densities of over two thousand per square mile (Fig. 11.1).

South Wells Avenue has not always been a small-business corridor. This area gradually converted from a mixed residential and business area. Forty-five years ago, 40 percent of the addresses were residences and 60 percent were businesses. By 2000, it had become principally a small business strip, with 93 percent of the addresses listed as businesses (*Reno City Directory* 1957, 2000). Many of the older brick homes have been remodeled and adapted to meet the needs of new business owners; even detached garages have been employed as business spaces. In other cases, older residential buildings have been removed and new structures built on the site for the business.

In addition to a proliferation of small businesses catering to Latinos along South Wells Avenue, there is an eclectic mix of other businesses. Fast-food drive-throughs, delicatessens, bars, and expensive restaurants are situated within this business strip, along with crystal and bead stores, tarot card reading places, pet stores, antiques shops, spy supply shops, insurance agencies, health-care facilities, and formal wear shops. The growth in the number and variety of Latino small businesses, however, has been particularly impressive. During the two-year period between 1998 and 2000, the number of business permits requested by individuals with Hispanic surnames for the ZIP code area including South Wells Avenue rose 168 percent, based on the University of Nevada Small Business Development Center estimates (Fig. 11.3). This business district, like others in the Southwest abandoned by Anglos, has seen a succession of Latino merchants (Arreola 2000). On South Wells Avenue, new business development and turnover seem to be accelerating for many types of business—Latino and non-Latino alike—but the increase in small businesses owned by Latinos and those catering directly to Latinos has been particularly notable.

During April through June 2000, thirty-five Hispanic-owned businesses in the South Wells Avenue corridor and associated side streets were identified as potential participants in a pilot study. Nineteen of the business owners agreed to work with UNR faculty, students, and Hispanic Chamber of Commerce members to complete a survey questionnaire which included fifteen questions about business description, business owner's characteristics, customer profiles, and business financing. Tables 11.1 and 11.2 summarize results from the pilot study.

Five general types of businesses were identified: clothing stores, food stores (restaurants and grocery stores), variety stores (videos, gifts, and general merchandise), household services (beauty salons, phone card stores, money-courier services, diet-control programs, and tax preparation services), and automotive repair shops. These categories were not absolute, as many of the small businesses diversified their products and services for financial security. For example, one of the clothing stores not only carried apparel and shoes, but had diversified to include herbal medicines, diet supplements, music CDs, prepaid phone cards, videos, and books. Figure 11.4 shows another example of product diversification in a Christian bookstore on South Wells Avenue that advertises bibles, videos, tapes, CDs, and gifts in addition to its mainstay of Christian-oriented books.

The small businesses participating in the study were largely family owned and operated, with less than one-quarter hiring any paid employees outside the family (Table 11.1). The vast majority were new businesses. Seven years was the longest time that any business had been at its current location, and 84 percent had been opened at their present location for five years or less. Bank loans were rare, with four out of five owners relying on personal savings or loans from family or friends to finance business needs. Lack of access to cash for business operations seems to be a long-standing problem and widespread concern for Latino small business owners. Almost twenty years ago, a nationwide survey sponsored by the U.S. His-

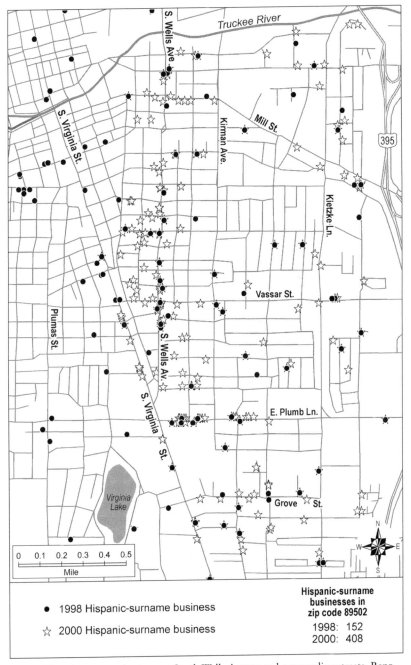

Truckee River

S. Wells Ave.

S. Virginia St.

Kirman Ave.

Mill St.

[395]

Kietzke Ln.

Plumas St.

• Vassar St.

S. Wells Av.

S. Virginia St.

E. Plumb Ln.

Virginia
Lake

• Grove ☆ St.

N
W ⊕ E
S

| 0 | 0.1 | 0.2 | 0.3 | 0.4 | 0.5 |
Mile

• 1998 Hispanic-surname business

☆ 2000 Hispanic-surname business

**Hispanic-surname
businesses in
zip code 89502**
1998: 152
2000: 408

11.3. Hispanic-surname businesses, South Wells Avenue and surrounding streets, Reno, 1998 and 2000. *Source: City of Reno, 1998; Field study, 2000.*

TABLE 11.1—RENO'S SOUTH WELLS CORRIDOR BUSINESS AND OWNER CHARACTERISTICS, 2000

BUSINESS TYPE	%
CLOTHING STORE	11
FOOD STORE	26
VARIETY STORE	32
HOUSEHOLD SERVICES	26
AUTOMOTIVE SERVICE	5
TYPE OF OWNERSHIP	
FAMILY OWNED	89
NOT FAMILY OWNED	11
TYPE OF FINANCING	
BANK LOANS	20
LOAN FROM FAMILY OR FRIEND	13
PERSONAL SAVINGS	67
EMPLOYEES	
NO PAID EMPLOYEES	79
ONLY 1 EMPLOYEE	5
2–5 EMPLOYEES	11
OVER 5 EMPLOYEES	5
TIME AT CURRENT LOCATION	
LESS THAN 1 YEAR	42
1–5 YEARS	42
6–10 YEARS	16
RELOCATION	
RELOCATED	17
SAME LOCATION	83
OWNER'S RESIDENCE IN NORTHERN NEVADA	
5 YEARS OR LESS	26
6–10 YEARS	42
11–15 YEARS	16
MORE THAN 15 YEARS	16
GENDER OF BUSINESS OWNER	
MALE	50
FEMALE	44
CO-OWNERS (M&F)	6
EXPERIENCE IN SAME TYPE BUSINESS	
PRIOR EXPERIENCE	58
NO PRIOR EXPERIENCE	42

Source: Field study, 2000.

TABLE 11.2—RENO'S SOUTH WELLS BUSINESS CORRIDOR PRODUCT AND CUSTOMER INFORMATION, 2000 (%)

ARE CUSTOMERS LOCATED NEAR BUSINESS?		
	LOCATED NEARBY	78
	NOT LOCATED NEAR BUSINESS	22
IS CUSTOMER'S PROXIMITY IMPORTANT TO BUSINESS SUCCESS?		
	IMPORTANT	82
	NOT IMPORTANT	12
	UNCERTAIN	6
HOW FREQUENTLY IS SPANISH SPOKEN IN BUSINESS TRANSACTIONS?		
	HALF THE TIME	27
	PRIMARY LANGUAGE	73
HOW MANY BUSINESSES STOCK PRODUCTS FROM ___?		
	MEXICO	86
	CENTRAL AMERICA	50
	SOUTH AMERICA	29

Source: Field study, 2000.

panic Chamber of Commerce identified access to capital as the number-one problem facing Latino small-business owners. Access to the cash needed to develop a small business was also considered to be a concern more specifically in Nevada (Rodríguez 1984), and the pilot study suggests that this may continue to be an issue for many of the Latino small business owners in the South Wells Avenue corridor.

Several business owners mentioned that, prior to opening a business on South Wells Avenue, they acquired business skills, developed a customer base, and established key business contacts through selling products in booths at a local flea market or through their work contacts on the side. This finding seems to align with the idea that Latino immigrants create employment niches and networks that become invaluable social capital in the acquisition of new skills and leveraging financial resources (Davis 2000). The role of social networks in business origins and development deserves more extended study in the Reno setting and where Latino business enterprise is significant.

While product diversification was found to be popular among these small businesses, there was a clear sense of selecting products that would be of interest to Latino customers. Eighty-six percent of the businesses participating in the survey stocked products from Mexico (Table 11.2). Half the small businesses stocked products from Central American countries,

11.4.   Jesús Rey de Reyes Librería Cristiana (Jesus King of Kings Christian Bookstore), Reno, offers and advertises a wide variety of products in addition to books. *Photograph by K. Berry, 2002.*

and over one-quarter stocked products from South American countries. The top reasons for selecting a particular mix of products were that customers bought or had expressed an interest in these products and that the price was right.

Customers for these businesses were primarily Latinos whose transactions occurred in Spanish (Table 11.2). Each of the business owners suggested that half or more of the customers were Latinos. About one-third of the businesses said more than 95 percent of their customers were Latinos. Spanish was the primary language used in business transactions for nearly three-quarters of the small businesses in the pilot study.

Furthermore, most business owners depended on customers who lived close to their business (Table 11.2). Over three-quarters of the business owners said that their customers lived nearby. Many of the business owners (82 percent) identified that proximity of customers was important to the success of their business.

To give a personal sense of the findings of the pilot study for Latino small businesses on South Wells Avenue, an excerpt from a student's report is included because it suggests the ways business owners have created a niche by starting family businesses, diversifying their products, and welcoming their customers.

A woman named Juanita from El Salvador warmly greeted us. The store was filled with everything under the sun. Glancing around I noticed she had shelves filled with food and medicines. There were also racks of CDs and tapes. In the front glass case she had jewelry, toys, cards, etc. You name it she had it and if she didn't have it, she would get it for you. Juanita works the store by herself and her young son helps her out on the weekends. She told us that it was important to be surrounded by Latinos since most of her business comes from the people that live near by.

CONCLUSIONS

In one of the last issues of the journal *Landscape*, Joe Chilango wrote about Yakima, Washington, describing it as "a city in transition, and much of this transition comes from Chicanos" (Chilango 1994: 41). While many of Reno's newer and more conservative residents prefer to call themselves Latinos, Hispanics, Guatemalans, Mexican Americans, or even simply as being from El Salvador, rather than as Chicanos, the idea of transition holds true for Reno just as it does for Yakima. The economic and political pulse of the city has been engaged as Latinos move into Reno and change the surrounding urban landscapes.

The business-scapes of Reno represent these changes. Business owners with a few years of success, such as those at Beto's *taquería*, work hard to keep up with their current surge in popularity. Others have expanded, such as El Mundo Latino clothing store, which now has two stores on South Wells Avenue. While some businesses close, others open up in their wake. For example, El Pescador restaurant is soon to open in the remodeled building where another Mexican restaurant had been located, not far from South Wells. A sign for El Pescador in English and Spanish reaches out to passersby, in hopes that the restaurant will develop a clientele of both Latinos and non-Latinos alike.

People are beginning to take note as more Latino-run business operations come online and more services and products catering to a wide variety of Latino tastes become available. During the spring and summer of 2002, a Reno newspaper raised the awareness of non-Latino readers by running a dozen or so articles concerning Latino population change, the growth of Latino small businesses, leadership in the local Hispanic Chamber of Commerce, and changes along the South Wells Avenue corridor. Other evidence of the force of change comes from the City of Reno, whose Planning Department is moving forward with plans to revitalize South Wells Avenue through road and sidewalk reconstruction designed to slow traffic and create a more pedestrian- and cyclist-friendly corridor. Some Latino business owners have proposed that Latino themes be incorporated into the design and construction, thereby making visible the growing influence of Latinos in northern Nevada.

12	SE VENDEN AQUÍ

Latino Commercial Landscapes in Phoenix, Arizona

Alex Oberle

In his definitive study of the American Southwest, Donald Meinig (1971) delineates the region based on its combined Anglo, Hispanic, and Native American heritage. This tricultural influence situates the Southwest within the boundaries of New Mexico, Arizona, and Far West Texas. Meinig's Southwest encompasses several major cities that strongly reflect the region's Spanish and Mexican roots. Santa Fe, with its world-renowned plaza and centuries-old Palace of the Governors, is often characterized as the prototypical southwestern city. In Albuquerque, Old Town represents the city's Spanish colonial heritage. El Paso's landscape has been distinctively influenced by its common border with Mexico and connections with its sister city, Ciudad Juárez. Tucson contains a number of Hispanic landmarks, such as the San Xavier del Bac Mission and the flat-roofed adobe buildings that line the narrow streets in its Mexican-era central city barrio neighborhoods.

Phoenix, however, is quite different. Its history is dominated by the achievements of more contemporary Anglo settlers and entrepreneurs whose canal building, agriculture-based prosperity, and business influence are part of urban lore. While there are Mexican and Mexican American neighborhoods in the city, these landscapes are decades rather than centuries old and are not very visible in a city where rooftop air conditioning units, palm-lined golf courses, and glass and steel office buildings dominate not only the skyline, but also street corner vistas.

Yet even this landscape is not what it once was. While Phoenix's large expatriate midwesterner and easterner populations quietly worked through the economic boom of the go-go 1990s, the city's population structure was rapidly changing. Even before the U.S. Bureau of the Census released the official numbers in 2000, Phoenix's Anglo residents suddenly awoke and found a transformed landscape of *panaderías* (bakeries), *discotecas* (record stores), and *carnicerías* (meat markets); restaurants that specialized in *posole, birria,* and *mariscos de* Sinaloa; and other strange, previously unseen business establishments. People began to notice a proliferation of Spanish-language check-cashing and money-wiring outlets along with Latino day laborers lined up along block after block of certain thoroughfares. Some of these features of Phoenix's Latino landscape certainly existed ten or twenty years ago, but they were not as visible because there were fewer of them and because those that did exist were largely confined to the traditional Hispanic core of the city. In today's Phoenix, the Latino landscape is increasingly evident in the suburbs and on the urban periphery. Residents have become keenly aware that Phoenix has evolved into an international city and is no longer the sleepy cow town it once was.

This chapter explores the recent impact of Hispanic Americans in Phoenix by investigating their influence in commercial enterprise. I conducted this research by collecting field data on Latino businesses and comparing these data with spatial patterns of Hispanic settlement. Information from secondary sources further supplements this study.

LATINOS IN PHOENIX

Employment in agriculture attracted the first Latinos to the Phoenix area. As early as the late 1800s, Mexicans from Sonora and Mexican Americans from southern Arizona settled adjacent to the Salt River, near what is now downtown Phoenix. The construction of dams along the Salt River in the first half of the twentieth century allowed for the rapid expansion of agricultural lands, which increased the demand for farm laborers. These employment opportunities, combined with political and economic uncertainty in Mexico, drew substantial numbers of Mexican immigrants to Phoenix and the surrounding area. Although many Mexicans were forced to return to Mexico during the Great Depression, a steady stream of immigrants arrived in Phoenix throughout much of the early and middle 1900s (Dimas 1999).

Despite the early existence of a significant Latino population, Anglos maintained control of Phoenix's power structure and ensured that Hispanics would remain an invisible minority. Intermittent flooding along the Salt River, however, forced Anglo homes and businesses to relocate several miles north of the river. As a result, property in the floodplain was inexpensive, so de facto segregation occurred when the poorer Latino population settled along the river (Dimas 1991). This area became the core of Phoenix's Hispanic population and attracted Mexican immigrants throughout much of the first half of the 1900s. The original settlement expanded over time, and new neighborhoods appeared along its periphery. Barrios such as Golden Gate, Cuatro Milpas, and El Campito extended from the Salt River floodplain to the south side of present-day downtown Phoenix. Collectively, these neighborhoods are called Nuestro Barrio, which is still the oldest concentration of Latinos in the city (City of Phoenix Planning Department 1992). Hispanics also settled in other adjacent areas to the west and south of Nuestro Barrio (Our Barrio), and this contiguous area of Latino residence is known as South Phoenix.

Since the 1970s, Latino residents have expanded from South Phoenix into other areas of the city, most of which are no more than a few miles from downtown. Older Hispanic neighborhoods exist in the Garfield neighborhood just northwest of downtown and to the southwest along Buckeye Road. Since the 1980s, as Phoenix's Latino population has increased rapidly, Hispanics have settled in more distant parts of the city (Fig. 12.1). Concentrations of Latinos have emerged in West and North Phoenix and in portions of suburban cities like Glendale—to the northwest—as well as Mesa and Chandler—to the southeast—that had small incipient barrios.

A rapidly increasing Latino population is sustaining this expanding settlement. In 1980, Phoenix's Hispanic population composed 13 percent of the city's population (Luckingham 1994). According to the U.S. Bureau of the Census (1990, 2000), this percentage increased to almost 20 in 1990 and skyrocketed to 34 in 2000, so that today about one in three Phoenix residents is of Hispanic ancestry. This represents a 14 percent increase in Phoenix's Latino population. No other southwestern city has experienced such a dramatic increase, not Las Vegas, Los Angeles, Tucson, El Paso, Albuquerque, or Denver. Remarkably, Phoenix's 34 percent Latino population is almost as great as that of Tucson (36 percent), where Mexican influence has long been a hallmark of the city's heritage (Fig. 12.2). Of all of the cities of the greater Southwest, only Los Angeles (1,719,073 Latino residents in 2000) has a greater total Hispanic population than Phoenix (449,972 Latino residents).

Other cities in the Phoenix metropolitan area are also experiencing an influx of Latino residents. As of 2000, approximately one out of five residents in both Mesa and Chandler were Hispanic. In Glendale, one of four residents was Latino. The Hispanic populations of Mesa and Glendale grew by around 9 percent between 1990 and 2000 (U.S. Bureau of the Census 1990, 2000) (Fig. 12.3).

The majority of the Latino population in the Phoenix area is of Mexi-

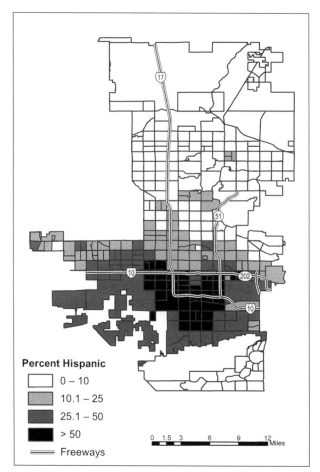

12.1.   Phoenix's Hispanic population, by census tract, 2000.
Source: U.S. Bureau of the Census 2000.

can ancestry. In the City of Phoenix, 83 percent of the Hispanic population identifies itself as Mexican or Mexican American, while approximately 15 percent of Latinos in Phoenix claim other Hispanic ancestry (U.S. Bureau of the Census 2000). After conducting research in Phoenix, Skop and Menjívar (2000) noted that other Latino groups were increasing the diversity of the city's Hispanic population. It is likely that Central American immigrants from El Salvador and Guatemala account for a growing portion of this non-Mexican Latino population. These authors also suggest that Phoenix, like Los Angeles and Miami, has become a "gateway" city that attracts large numbers of Hispanic immigrants directly from Latin America and then redistributes some of this population to other areas of the United States.

While the waves of Latino immigrants who settled in early- and mid-twentieth-century Phoenix arrived largely to seek employment in agriculture, contemporary Hispanic immigrants are likely a mixture of sojourners and permanent residents who have arrived to find jobs in the booming service economy. Phoenix's rapid population growth has spurred a frenzy of new-home construction, which has created a multitude of entry-level jobs in home building and landscaping. The city's strong tourist industry also demands a vast employee base to staff positions in janitorial, food, and resort services.

LATINOS IN THE COMMERCIAL ECONOMY

To assess the Hispanic business and commercial landscape, I discuss both small, often Hispanic-owned, businesses like *carnicerías* or *discotecas* and large corporate chains and franchises like check-cashing and money-wiring outlets, which frequently tailor their services to Latino immigrant populations. I also discuss Hispanic day labor. Although not a bricks-and-mortar landscape, block after block of day laborers lining certain city streets has become as permanent a part of the visible Hispanic commercial landscape as any traditional business. Furthermore, Latino day labor in several Phoenix-area cities will become truly material as municipal governments begin to establish actual day labor centers. I conclude with a discussion

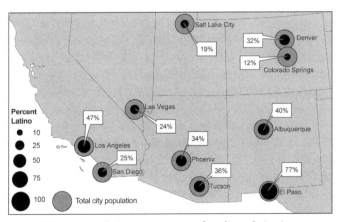

12.2.   Hispanic population as percentage of total population in some southwestern cities, 2000. *Source: U.S. Bureau of the Census 2000.*

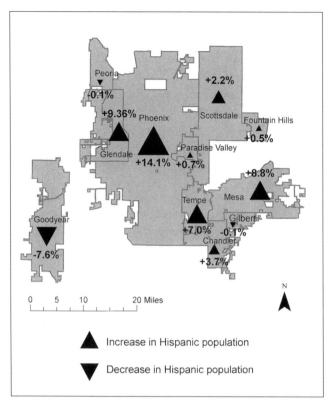

12.3.   Hispanic population change in select Phoenix-area
municipalities, 1990–2000. *Source: U.S. Bureau of the Census
1990, 2000.*

about how Hispanic business landscapes can serve as indicators of the
expansion and composition of local Latino populations across the Phoenix area.

Check-cashing and Money-wiring Outlets

Check-cashing outlets, money-wiring services, pawnshops, and employment agencies are frequently associated with the urban underclass. These
businesses reflect a landscape that is marked by a lack of economic opportunity, where residents often have low-paying, short-term employment that
requires them to quickly convert paychecks to cash, liquidate assets, and
shift jobs. Such economic problems are representative of the inequalities
that manifest in the social geography of American cities. However, there is
evidence to indicate that landscape features like check-cashing and money-

wiring businesses may be associated more with the geography of immigrant populations than with that of general urban poverty.

Check-cashing outlets (ccos) and money-wiring outlets (mwos) are visible aspects of the Hispanic immigrant landscape. As local populations change, these businesses seem to materialize almost overnight. Although they take many forms, ccos and mwos commonly exist in grocery stores as separate businesses or in strip malls. In some cases, they even occupy free-standing structures that were previously other well-known business establishments; check-cashing outlets that, curiously, resemble Taco Bell restaurants or gas stations are notable examples. These businesses certainly do not serve an exclusively Latino immigrant clientele, yet much of their customer base is likely Hispanic immigrants. Most ccos and mwos advertise in Spanish and use various marketing tools to target certain populations. Some business names, such as Casa de Cambio (money exchange house) and Giros a México, Centro y Sudamérica(money wire to Mexico, Central and South America), unequivocally indicate the intended clientele (Fig. 12.4).

Other forms of advertising may be subtle. Posters in the windows are sometimes displayed in red, white, and green, the colors of the Mexican flag. Western Union advertisements frequently depict the geographic outline of Mexico in the background. Exchange rates between dollars and

12.4.   Money-wiring outlets are unequivocal testaments to services demanded by immigrant Hispanic populations. *Photograph by A. Oberle, 2001.*

TABLE 12.1—CHECK-CASHING AND MONEY-WIRING OUTLETS, PHOENIX, BY CENSUS TRACT, 2000

% HISPANIC BY CENSUS TRACT	NO. OF CENSUS TRACTS	NO. OF CCOS AND MWOS/CENSUS TRACT	CCOS AND MWOS/PERSON
<50	195	109	1/8,945
>50	31	46	1/3,370

Sources: U.S. Bureau of the Census 2000; Qwest Communications International 2000; MoneyGram Website 2000; Western Union Website 2000.
Note: CCO = check-cashing outlet; MWO = money-wiring outlet.

pesos are often prominently exhibited. Money-wiring or check-cashing paperwork is in a bilingual format, but some customized money-wiring forms are available only in Spanish and are titled "Envíos a México" (remittances to Mexico).

Research conducted in Phoenix supports the assertion that CCOs and MWOs are features of the Latino immigrant landscape. By comparing the locations of these businesses with census data about Hispanic population distribution, one is able to discern a spatial relationship between Hispanic populations and the existence of check-cashing/money-wiring outlets. CCOs and MWOs generally exist in greater numbers in or adjacent to census tracts with a majority Hispanic population. For example, in the thirty-one census tracts in Phoenix that have a majority Hispanic population, there are forty-six CCOs and MWOs. Assuming that the average census tract has 5,000 residents, it is possible to determine that there is one CCO/MWO per 3,370 people. This is considerably higher than the 1:8,945 ratio found in tracts with less than 50 percent Hispanic population (Table 12.1).

Additional field and census research corroborates these findings and provides more details about the relationship between these types of businesses and the Latino community. There are five locations across the City of Phoenix where CCOs and MWOs tend to cluster in groups of five to six. Three of these clusters occur adjacent to traditionally Hispanic neighborhoods in downtown, South, and West Phoenix. Each of these clusters is surrounded by census tracts that have a majority Latino population. A survey of the landscape in these areas reveals an enduring yet evolving Hispanic presence. Some of the homes exhibit fenced front yards, brightly painted exteriors, and even yard shrines, all of which are indicators of the Mexican American housescape (Arreola 1988). These older, more established homes exist in conjunction with apartment complexes and rental units, housing that likely accommodates recent Latino immigrants (Arreola et al. 2002).

The remaining two CCO/MWO clusters occur in areas of North-Central and even peripheral Far North Phoenix, which, according to census data, have only small Hispanic populations. Yet an examination of the local landscape illustrates that these areas do indeed have emerging Latino populations, as revealed by the presence of Hispanic businesses such as *carnicerías, discotecas,* and *taquerías.*

Caskey (1994) refers to CCOs as "fringe banking," because these businesses are often poorly regulated and serve marginalized populations to whom standard commercial banks are not available or accessible. The core business of a CCO is to convert a customer's check to cash and offer short-term loans. In addition to these basic services, many CCOs sell money orders, offer money-wiring services, and provide for the electronic payment of utilities like water, electric, and telephone services.

I interviewed local bank and CCO officials, who told me that the proliferation of check-cashing and money-wiring outlets in Latino neighborhoods was the result of several factors. Convenience was the most widely cited reason for using a CCO instead of a bank. The hours of operation at banks are often quite limited, as they are generally not open in the evenings, on Sundays, or on holidays and have limited service on Saturdays. Many Hispanic immigrants work longer than eight-hour days or have inconsistent transportation to and from job sites, so the extended hours offered by CCOs are crucial. Banks also require various forms of identification and documentation in order to open an account. Many immigrants, especially those here illegally, likely lack this type of paperwork and would be discouraged from establishing an account. Finally, many immigrants do not trust banks and would rather do business with a CCO that charges a consistent, flat fee for cashing checks.

Money-wiring services are common in Latin American immigrant communities because of the widespread practice of remitting money to one's home community. Worldwide, immigrant remittances to homelands approach an estimated $67 billion (Castles and Miller 1998: 5). Remittances from the United States to Mexico alone are estimated to be approximately $2 billion annually (Durand, Parrado, and Massey 1996: 423). My interviews with MWO employees suggest that many Latino immigrants in Phoenix also commonly send money to and receive from family members living in other states.

Until recently, the money-wiring business was dominated by a few large corporate entities like Western Union and MoneyGram. Now, however, other institutions, especially American and Mexican banks, are gaining a foothold in the market and offer their own money-wiring services.

In order for these large numbers of check-cashing and money-wiring outlets to be viable, abundant capital must be readily available. Phoenix's vibrant economy has made it easy to meet these economic conditions. Latino immigrants are an integral part of Phoenix's labor market, either as formal employees or as members of the burgeoning informal employment sector. Hispanic day laborers are the most visible constituents of this "hidden" economy. In the Phoenix area, stretches of city streets, often several blocks long, have been converted into staging areas for Latino immigrants seeking short-term employment. In the morning twilight, well before rush hour, job seekers line up in parking lots or in front of businesses in hopes of finding work for the day. Commuters nervously watch small groups of young Latino men shuffling and loitering, and often wearing ragged sweatshirts and worn-out hats that bear the colors and logos of professional sports teams that have not won a championship in decades. Potential employers, however, do not view these activities as suspicious; instead, they see capable workers ready for a variety of labor-intensive jobs. They see one less person to add to their Workers' Compensation coverage, one less check to cut, and one less W-2 form to send out in January.

Day Laborers

Although little formal research has been conducted on day laborers in Phoenix, Valenzuela (2001: 44–45) analyzes this phenomenon in greater Los Angeles and presents findings that are likely transferable to the Phoenix area. He discovered that day laborers were predominantly younger male Latino immigrants who had recently arrived in the United States and did not have legal immigration status. Most illegal immigrants were from Mexico and had arrived within the past five years. Their median age was thirty-three, and approximately half were single men who had never married. Valenzuela describes day labor as fluid, flexible, and informed, with individuals constantly entering into and exiting the market. His surveys suggest that some day laborers engage in this type of employment on a permanent basis while others perceive it as more temporary. A small proportion have other employment and tend to solicit day labor on their days off, but for the majority, these sorts of jobs are their only employment. The surveys further indicate that a lack of immigration documentation and an individual's inability to speak English are the two primary reasons why Latino immigrants seek day labor instead of joining the formal job market.

Valenzuela concludes that there are many public-policy implications related to the day labor phenomenon. He identifies three strategies that communities in Southern California have selected as their method of interacting with day laborers. First, some communities choose to do nothing, to allow day labor sites to go unregulated. This decision may be problematic, as home and business owners often object to day laborer gatherings and pressure police departments and local officials to monitor and possibly prosecute those involved in this sort of activity. Second, some municipalities explicitly prohibit day laborers from gathering in public places. This decision causes the relocation of day labor staging areas. However, this decision has little effect because a court can overturn it as a violation of people's First Amendment right to gather in a public place, or a community may simply lack the police necessary to consistently enforce such regulations. Third, communities establish legitimate day labor sites where people are able to gather without fear of police or neighborhood action. Some of these sites regulate laborers by limiting the number of participants, charging a small upkeep fee, or checking for immigration documentation. Other permanent sites are not controlled and simply serve as sanctioned gathering places.

Many municipalities in the Phoenix area are currently deciding how to respond to day laborers. Phoenix constructed a permanent site at Bell Road and 24th Street, and day laborers and immigrant activists are requesting at least one additional site. Chandler plans to use private donations rather than tax dollars for a permanent site along Arizona Avenue, a major thoroughfare. In Cave Creek, a bedroom community to the north of Phoenix, businesses convinced a local church to establish a site for day laborers (Díaz 2002a, 2002b). Mesa, Phoenix's largest suburb, has been involved in a protracted discussion about a potential site, but the city has now postponed that decision until after city council elections (Díaz 2002b).

The day laborer debate in Mesa is not unusual. It illustrates citizens' evolving perceptions of their city in light of a rapidly changing population. In recognition of these changes, the Mesa City Council in early 2000 appointed a twenty-two-member citizen task force to evaluate the city's day labor situation. Council members suggested that the task force make recommendations that considered the impact of the day labor situation in Mesa. The city council purposely selected task force members who would represent diverse opinions on the topic: merchants affected by day labor gatherings, day laborers, local neighborhood residents, day laborer employers, Hispanic community representatives, school officials, and others. Task force members solicited a variety of information and testimony to develop their recommendations. They collected newspaper articles on Hispanic immigration issues, particularly those that dealt with local populations and day labor. Representatives from the Immigration and Naturalization Service, the Mesa Police Department, various attorneys, nonprofit groups, and California municipalities that had established day labor sites spoke to the task force (Kurtz et al. 2000).

Although the Day Labor Task Force contributed several policy recommendations, it reached consensus on only one of the proposals, that the City of Mesa should support state and federal government efforts to establish the necessary laws to allow day laborers to work legally. All agreed that some sort of guest worker program was necessary, but that this could not be achieved at the municipal level. Essentially, some members were concerned that the existence of a day labor center would violate federal laws against the hiring of undocumented immigrants. Several experts assured the task force that the creation of a day labor center would not break any laws, so long as the center itself was not actively hiring individuals who lacked appropriate documentation. Regardless, some of the task force members expressed unease and uncertainty about the implications of establishing a day labor center.

These reactions elucidate the complex relationship between longtime residents and newly arrived Latino immigrants. Local officials understand how important day laborers are to the city's economy, but do not want to sanction activities that violate the law. Governments rally against the abuse of day laborers, but dread any legislation that would mandate the payment of the minimum wage or insurance coverage. Most everyone enjoys the prosperity of an economically vibrant community, but many also fear the cultural and social changes that accompany it. The resulting mixed messages and almost paradoxical policy decisions are indicative of the Phoenix area's coming of age in an increasingly globalized world.

Latino Business Enterprise

The global economy allows for the relatively unfettered flow of goods back and forth between distant locales. For Latino immigrants, this means that merchants in Phoenix can easily and rapidly obtain specialized products from across Latin America. As a result, many entrepreneurs have established small businesses that stock specialty items and cater to emerging niche markets. The transformation of strip mall spaces into Mexican bakeries and of minimarts into Latin American regional restaurants is testament to Phoenix's evolving ethnic landscape. Specialized Hispanic businesses are emerging across the city, not only in the Hispanic core, but also in peripheral and suburban areas. The nature of these establishments provides clues about both the diffusion of the city's Latinos over time and space and the internal heterogeneity of its Hispanic population.

An analysis of common Latino business types in the City of Phoenix yields some useful information about how these types of establishments can serve as indicators of a neighborhood's ethnic characteristics. By comparing the locations of various Hispanic businesses with census population data about Latino ancestry, one is able to approximate the relationship between certain types of establishments and the nature of the populations they serve. Some enterprises tend to be among the first to pioneer a new Latino immigrant neighborhood, while others exist primarily in older, more traditionally Hispanic neighborhoods. Field observations of the businesses and the surrounding area support these initial assertions.

Carnicerías not only sell fresh cuts of meat, but they also often provide other grocery items and specialty products. In Phoenix, more *carnicerías* are located in census tracts with less than 25 percent Hispanic population. In fact, three are located on the relative periphery of Far North Phoenix. The widespread existence of *carnicerías* in suburban areas some distance from traditionally Hispanic neighborhoods likely is due to these establishments being among the first types of Hispanic-oriented businesses to locate in recent Hispanic immigrant communities. There are several factors that possibly explain this pattern.

First, the variety of products at a *carnicería* specifically caters to the needs of the Latino immigrant population. Because certain cuts of meat are unavailable at a supermarket, a local butcher can create a niche market for these types of specialty products. Compared with other types of Hispanic-oriented businesses that sell products that are only infrequently purchased, *carnicerías* require a lower threshold population and, therefore, a smaller clientele.

Second, many *carnicerías* also fill the role of a "general store" that provides Mexican or Latin American groceries and other basic goods. These sorts of establishments serve as a point of contact for Latinos living in adjacent neighborhoods; people can come to the local *carnicería* to contact other people, gain access to important information, and seek other specialty goods and services.

Discotecas, shops that sell Mexican and Latin American cassette tapes and compact discs, are also evident in areas with an emerging Hispanic immigrant population. Although almost two-thirds of the *discotecas* in Phoenix are found in census tracts with a greater than 25 percent Hispanic population, the rest are found in areas with a smaller proportion of Hispanics. *Discotecas* also seem to be one of the first types of businesses to appear in newer Hispanic neighborhoods. Unlike meat markets, *discotecas* do not sell products that are consumed on a daily basis. However, because most of these businesses are housed in small minimall spaces, their overhead is low, which allows them to remain viable in spite of a relatively small Hispanic target population. Furthermore, these shops sell music that is popular with Spanish speakers, and that may make them more accessible to Hispanic immigrants than to Mexican Americans, who may not speak Spanish or appreciate Latino music.

Yerberías are specialty shops that sell medicinal herbs and religious items like prayer cards, rosaries, and votive candles. Most *yerberías* are confined to Phoenix's traditional Hispanic core, yet a few exist in other parts of the city. *Yerberías* require a larger, more established population of potential clients than do meat markets and music shops. Medicinal herbs are typically purchased in bulk, so customers may need to replenish their supplies only a few times per year. Similarly, religious items are purchased no more than a few times per year, perhaps only for a saint's feast day, near Christmas, or during Lent.

Panaderías are Mexican or Latin American bakeries that sell baked goods like tortillas, breads, and wedding cakes. Because *panaderías* sell items that are consumed on a daily basis, one would expect that they would be located in the Hispanic core and also in smaller, more recent Hispanic neighborhoods. Yet, in Phoenix, all but two are found within the traditionally Hispanic part of town. *Panaderías* may actually be more of a specialized business. Some Hispanic immigrants may make their own tortillas, do their own baking, or purchase these products at specialty supermarkets. Therefore, the bakery typically attracts clientele for special occasions such as parties or weddings. *Panaderías* thus have a very different niche from a business such as a meat market or a music store.

Llanteras market new and used tires and wheel rims to a specifically Hispanic clientele. They advertise almost exclusively in Spanish and, unlike standard American tire stores, they sell a variety of brand names and usually offer both new and used products. All *llanteras* in Phoenix are found in the Hispanic core of the city, with two-thirds of them locating in census tracts with a greater than 50 percent Hispanic population. Only one of the eighteen *llanteras* is in a neighborhood that is less than 25 percent Hispanic. There are a few likely explanations for this pattern. First, because tires and rims are only infrequently purchased, it is likely that *llanteras* require a large customer base and thus have historically served the older Hispanic areas. Second, zoning regulations may restrict *llanteras* to the core of Phoenix, where light industry and manufacturing mixes with residential areas.

Business Landscapes As Indicators of Hispanic Populations

The existence of these varied Hispanic business landscapes is testament to Phoenix's large and rapidly growing Latino population. In addition, these

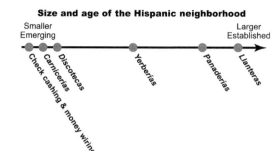

12.5.   Latino business type and Hispanic neighborhood continuum, Phoenix. *Source: Field survey, 2001.*

landscape features serve as indicators of the size, age, and internal heterogeneity of a particular area's Latino population. Figure 12.5 illustrates a continuum of Hispanic settlement, such as occurs in Phoenix.

The left side of the axis represents a more recent, emerging Latino neighborhood while the right side signifies a larger, more established Hispanic neighborhood. Some businesses, like *carnicerías* and check-cashing/money-wiring outlets, are among the first types of establishments to appear in emerging Hispanic neighborhoods. *Discotecas* also tend to be among the first businesses to appear in areas of more recent Latino settlement. *Yerberías* generally do not exist in Hispanic neighborhoods until there is a more substantial threshold of customers. *Panaderías* occur primarily in more established Hispanic communities, while *llanteras* exist almost exclusively in the older, core Latino neighborhoods.

Day labor, in the form of groups of people on street corners or a physical day labor center, is more difficult to place. Many Latinos live in close proximity to day labor pickup sites, but others may arrive from some distance away via bicycle, city bus, or private transportation. Therefore, day labor sites may be a less-specific indicator of the nature of the adjacent Latino neighborhoods.

The Hispanic business landscape can also serve as an indicator of local Latino national or state origin. Although the majority of Phoenix's Hispanics are of Mexican ancestry, other national groups are emerging. Additionally, there is a high degree of internal heterogeneity among the Mexican-heritage population. Second- and third-generation Latinos in Phoenix tend to have ties with the northern Mexican states of Sonora and Sinaloa. More recent immigrants are arriving from states like Guerrero, Michoacán, and Oaxaca in southern Mexico. The commercial landscape often signifies differences in nationality or Mexican state of origin, as exemplified in names of businesses, the use of national flags or colors, and the existence of typically region-specific products (Fig. 12.6).

12.6.   Tienda Centroamericana in Phoenix illustrates how Hispanic immigrant business landscapes use national insignia like maps (of Central America) and national flags (of El Salvador) to attract clients. *Photograph by A. Oberle, 2001.*

CONCLUSION

The Hispanic commercial landscape continues to evolve as Latin American immigration to Phoenix remains steady or even increases. The expansion and diffusion of Latinos into ever more suburban and peripheral locations leads to the emergence of niche markets. Yet some current trends may change over time. Phoenix's predominantly Mexican-ancestry population may be challenged by the growing influx of immigrants from El Salvador, Guatemala, and other Central and South American nations. Furthermore, there is the potential for a guest worker program that might have a significant impact on the city's Hispanic population. Certain groups might be granted immediate immigration amnesty, while others might be unable to shed their illegal status. The effects of this type of legalization program are difficult to foresee, but such a program would undoubtedly alter the fabric of the local Hispanic community. The Latino business landscape can be a key diagnostic of potential changes.

13 | HISPANICS IN THE AMERICAN SOUTH AND THE TRANSFORMATION OF THE POULTRY INDUSTRY

William Kandel and Emilio A. Parrado

Findings from the 2000 Census indicate two important trends affecting the Hispanic population. The first is the extraordinarily high rate of Hispanic population increase outside of urban areas over the past decade, with growth rates exceeding both metropolitan and nonmetropolitan growth rates for all other racial and ethnic groups (Cromartie 1999; Pérez 2001). In addition, for the first time in U.S. history, half of all nonmetropolitan Hispanics currently live outside the five southwestern states of Arizona, California, Colorado, New Mexico, and Texas (Cromartie and Kandel 2002). The diversity of new rural areas raises questions about forces outside of the Southwest that are attracting migrants, the Hispanic population's assimilation patterns into communities unaccustomed to dealing with immigration, and the connection between structural economic change and Hispanic population growth.

The main objective of this chapter is to link changes in the poultry industry with the growth of the Hispanic population in nonmetropolitan counties in nine southeastern states: Alabama, Arkansas, Georgia, Louisiana, Mississippi, North Carolina, South Carolina, Tennessee, and Virginia. We document the restructuring of the poultry industry and spatially correlate poultry production and areas of Hispanic settlement. Next, given the impact of these population changes on local communities, we examine two case studies to elaborate more directly on the implications of Hispanic growth for the culture, organization, and everyday life of two nonmetropolitan counties in Virginia and North Carolina. Finally, we derive implications for further research to address relations between Hispanics and other minority groups.

TABLE 13.1 — NONMETROPOLITAN STATE POPULATIONS RANKED BY HISPANIC POPULATION GROWTH

RANK	STATE	NONMETRO HISPANIC POPULATION			NONMETRO POPULATION			HISPANIC SHARE (%)	
		1990	2000	% CHANGE	1990	2000	% CHANGE	1990	2000
1	North Carolina	16,714	98,846	491	2,252,775	2,612,257	16	1	4
2	Delaware	1,221	6,915	466	113,229	156,638	38	1	4
3	Alabama	5,198	26,155	403	1,330,857	1,453,233	9	0	2
4	South Carolina	5,830	27,853	378	1,064,088	1,205,050	13	1	2
5	Georgia	26,270	124,296	373	2,126,654	2,519,789	18	1	5
6	Tennessee	7,119	32,737	360	1,579,336	1,842,679	17	0	2
7	Arkansas	9,559	36,504	282	1,310,724	1,434,529	9	1	3
8	Virginia	8,136	28,258	247	1,407,096	1,550,447	10	1	2
9	Mississippi	7,774	24,321	213	1,797,542	1,932,670	8	0	1
10	Minnesota	11,283	34,860	209	1,364,205	1,456,119	7	1	2
11	Iowa	11,807	35,611	202	1,576,857	1,600,191	1	1	2
12	Indiana	12,260	36,921	201	1,581,713	1,690,582	7	1	2
13	Kentucky	8,479	24,465	189	1,905,535	2,068,667	9	0	1
14	Nebraska	16,641	44,564	168	791,050	811,425	3	2	5
15	Wisconsin	11,098	28,893	160	1,560,597	1,723,367	10	1	2
16	Missouri	10,822	27,807	157	1,626,202	1,800,410	11	1	2
17	Pennsylvania	11,004	27,403	149	1,798,645	1,889,525	5	1	1

Sources: U.S. Bureau of the Census 1990, 2000.
Note: Shaded columns are the eight southeastern states highlighted in the study.

NEW DESTINATIONS IN NONMETROPOLITAN AMERICA

The degree to which Hispanic residential settlement has expanded outside of traditional migrant-receiving states can be illustrated with 1990 and 2000 Census data. Table 13.1 presents state-level nonmetropolitan population in absolute and percentage terms for the top seventeen states, sorted by Hispanic population growth rate. Eight of the nine southeastern poultry-producing states appear among the ten states with the fastest-growing nonmetropolitan Hispanic populations; the remaining seven include midwestern states with large beef and pork meatpacking industries.

While Hispanics continue to be overwhelmingly located in metropolitan areas, during the 1990s their nonmetropolitan growth of 70.4 percent exceeded their metropolitan growth rate of 60.4 percent (Cromartie and Kandel 2002). By the decade's end, according to Census 2000 data, Hispanics represented approximately 5.5 percent of the nonmetropolitan population, but had accounted for over 25.0 percent of its growth during the decade. Moreover, Hispanic population growth during the 1990s surpassed total population growth in nonmetropolitan areas in every state except Hawaii.

Widespread media attention on Hispanics in new destinations, however, owes more to their geographic concentration. In 2000, over a third of the 3.2 million rural Hispanics lived in just 109 of all 2,288 nonmetropolitan counties (Cromartie and Kandel 2002).

Since the 1990s, a number of ethnographic studies have documented the immigrants' reception in relatively small communities with few foreign-born residents (Griffith 1995; Guthey 2001; Hernández-León and Zúñiga 2000). The growing nonmetropolitan presence of Hispanics can be attributed to several concurrent trends. First, increased enforcement policies by the Immigration and Naturalization Service to reduce undocumented immigration, ironically, have pushed undocumented migrants away from the traditional migrant-receiving states of California, Arizona, and Texas and into southeastern and midwestern states that previously had few Hispanic migrants (Durand, Massey, and Charvet 2000).

Second, several informants and anecdotal accounts describe labor market saturation in the traditional migrant gateway cities of Los Angeles, Houston, and Chicago and suggest that growing numbers of "pioneer migrants" are seeking employment in new parts of the country. Hispanic settlement in nonmetropolitan areas also was facilitated by an economic recession in the early 1990s in the urban Southwest and other U.S. metropolitan centers. In addition to looking for employment opportunities in nonmetropolitan areas, many Hispanic immigrants may seek to escape problems associated with urban settings, such as poor schools, youth gangs, violence, and expensive and crowded housing.

Third, immigrants are also moving to nontraditional areas because of employers' recruiting efforts to sustain the number of workers needed in industries with less-than-desirable jobs (Johnson-Webb 2002). Consequently, the proportion of Hispanics in industries with low wages and harsh working conditions—meat processing, carpet manufacturing, oil refining, and forestry, to name a few—has increased dramatically since the 1990s (Broadway 1994; Engstrom 2001; Gouveia and Stull 1995; Hernández-León and Zúñiga 2000; Díaz McConnell forthcoming; McDaniel 2002). Because the U.S. Department of Labor does not classify these positions as temporary or highly skilled, firms cannot use special immigration provisions, such as the H2A or H2B visas, to obtain foreign workers. Information on recruitment practices consists of mostly qualitative journalistic accounts that, nevertheless, describe a host of practices that firms use to recruit workers (Carlin 1999; Katz 1996a, 1996b; Smothers 1996; Taylor and Stein 1999).

An influx of immigrants and newcomers into rural communities often generates conflicting feelings among local residents. Hispanic population growth in many nonmetropolitan places coincides with revived economic activity and reversals of stagnant or declining demographic patterns of previous decades (Broadway 1994; Brown 1993). Nevertheless, immigrant population growth may challenge the ability of rural communities to meet increased demands for social services, particularly schooling for immigrant children, and often increases poverty rates and income inequality (Reed 2001). While immigrants undoubtedly hold the least-desirable and most poorly paid jobs, their presence may exert downward wage pressure on native-born residents working in other low-skilled industries (Massey, Durand, and Malone 2002). Ethnic diversity is viewed by many Americans as a public good that introduces different cultures, languages, and cuisines to native-born residents and reinforces America's cherished self-image as a nation built on the energy and hopes of immigrants (Lapinski et al. 1997). Yet, popular reports suggest a significant level of social conflict in and municipal response from communities that have experienced influxes of immigrants in a relatively short time (Grey 1995; Guthey 2001; Studstill and Nieto-Studstill 2001). We return to these oppositional perspectives that use qualitative descriptions of poultry-producing communities below.

TRENDS IN POULTRY CONSUMPTION

To see how Hispanic migration to new regions in the southeastern U.S. is related to industrial restructuring, we first consider changes in one of the region's dominant low-skill industries, poultry processing. The poultry industry has been a mainstay in the Southeast for many decades, but since the 1970s, a number of trends have aggregated to influence the demand for labor and, consequently, the settlement patterns of Hispanics. These include (1) increased consumption; (2) increased demand for value-added production; (3) industry consolidation and vertical integration, leading to larger firms; (4) increasing location of production facilities in the Southeast; and (5) the relative attractiveness of meat-processing jobs.

The impetus for changes in the poultry industry began with three consumption trends that strongly influenced the demand for labor. The first

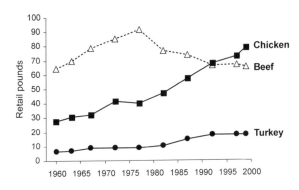

13.1.   Per capita consumption of chicken, turkey, and beef, 1960–1999. *Source: U.S. Department of Agriculture 1960–2000.*

was domestic consumption, which grew as the result of two somewhat contradictory trends. In 1977, when beef consumption far exceeded poultry consumption, widely publicized findings from the Framingham Study explicitly outlined health risks associated with red meat in the diet (Dawber 1980). The report's implications were not lost on the American public, which began to eat less beef and more poultry. Per capita poultry consumption doubled between 1977 and 1999, while beef consumption dropped 30 percent over the same period (Fig. 13.1).

Yet, while the Framingham Study represents a milestone event, increasing consumption of fast food in the United States coincided with the growing demand for convenience food. Growth in fast-food franchises such as Kentucky Fried Chicken and marketing through nontraditional outlets such as McDonald's created an enormous demand for a wide variety of chicken products. Within a little over a decade, per capita consumption of poultry surpassed that of beef for the first time since World War II (U.S. Department of Agriculture [USDA] 1960–2000).

The second consumption trend, growth in poultry exports, paralleled domestic demand. Following domestic consumer demand for further-processed products, poultry firms began supplementing their slaughtering plants with production facilities that cut up chickens and packaged the parts for different segments of the market. Breasts and other white meat met domestic consumption preferences, and dark meat was reserved for the export market. By the mid-1970s, chicken exports had increased significantly, and between 1987 and 2002, they skyrocketed, from 500 million to 6.5 billion pounds (USDA 1960–2000).

The demand for more convenient prepared food generated a precipitous increase in the sale of cut-up poultry and an equally precipitous decline in the sale of whole birds. In 1963, the poultry product mix sold in American supermarkets consisted of 85 percent whole birds and 15 percent cut-up poultry products; by 1997, that proportion was exactly the reverse (Ollinger, MacDonald, and Madison 2000). Consequently, many poultry producers appended "cut-up" operations to their meat-processing plants. The structural shift of value-added production from the retail sector (supermarkets) to the production sector (meat-slaughtering and -processing plants) has had profound consequences for labor demand, and, consequently, for labor supply.

POULTRY INDUSTRY CONCENTRATION AND CONSOLIDATION

Significant increases in both industry concentration and average poultry plant size have accompanied the trend toward increased consumption. Industrial concentration can often be measured using the "four firm concentration ratio," the proportion of total production controlled by the four largest firms (Ollinger, MacDonald, and Madison 2000). For the slaughter of chickens, this ratio more than doubled, from 14 percent to 41 percent, between 1963 and 1992; for turkey slaughter, the ratio increased from 23 percent to 45 percent over the same period. Concentration of poultry-processing firms fluctuated, but it also shows an upward trend during the same period. Data after 1992 are not available, but industry reports suggest that this trend continued throughout the 1990s.

Beginning in the late 1940s, firms began to realize greater scale economies by integrating all facets of operation. Under this mode of production, firms contract out to formerly independent chicken farms and provide the chicks, feed, medicines, veterinary services, and other inputs; contracted growers later return grown birds of consistent size and quality to the plant for slaughter (Bugos 1992). Slaughter operations also became more complex as firms responded to increasingly varied consumer and industry demands by adopting cut-up operations and packaging their products in ready-to-sell containers. By controlling all phases of poultry production, such vertically integrated firms could increase their overall profitability while lowering prices; in real terms, the price of poultry dropped by just over 50 percent between 1960 and 1999 (USDA 1960–2000).

Industry consolidation and production have led to larger plants. To measure the extent of industry consolidation, we use proportion of production from firms with four hundred or more employees, a widely used measure developed by the U.S. Bureau of the Census. Beginning in 1967, the proportion of chicken produced by such large plants tripled; by 1992, they accounted for three-quarters of all poultry slaughter and processing (Ollinger, MacDonald, and Madison 2000).

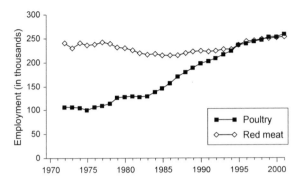

13.2. Employment in poultry and red meat products industry, 1972–2001. *Source: U.S. Department of Labor, 1972–2001* .

Increased consumer demand, growing exports, and industry consolidation trends have combined to expand the demand for labor in the poultry industry. Figure 13.2 presents employment figures in both the poultry industry and the red meat industry for comparison. The above-noted trends in industry consolidation and plant size also occurred to roughly the same extent in the red meat–processing industry (MacDonald et al. 2000). Yet, as Figure 13.2 demonstrates, employment in the red meat industry has not grown at all since 1970. In contrast, employment in the poultry industry has grown by 150 percent during the same period, and today it actually exceeds that of the beef industry (U.S. Department of Labor [DOL] 1972–2001).

GEOGRAPHIC CONTEXT OF POULTRY PRODUCTION

Structural changes in the poultry industry occur in a geographic context. As in most industrial sectors, there is a distinct logic behind the poultry business's economic geography. Poultry can be raised in most areas, and before large firms took over, it was a very competitive industry, because almost anyone could grow chickens almost anywhere. Some locations, however, have certain advantages, and in a competitive market, one seeks advantage by minimizing the most expensive inputs. For poultry, the key inputs are feed and climate. The Southeast, it turns out, has both an ideal climate for raising chickens and access to low-cost grain. Data from the Census of Agriculture show that the Southeast was producing over half of the nation's chicken slaughter products as early as 1963; in recent years, the proportion has increased to roughly two-thirds (USDA 1960–2000).

The expansion and consolidation of the poultry industry in the Southeast has occurred within the context of a simultaneous economic transformation that, in just a few decades, changed the American South from a relatively depressed region to an economically booming destination (Cobb 1982; Griffith 1995). This economic growth began in the 1960s with the active recruitment of manufacturing industries and promotion of the South as a competitive location for firms seeking a low-wage, nonunionized workforce. With the rediscovery of the Sunbelt as a vacation and retirement destination, the tourism and retirement-community industries expanded significantly.

Tourists and retirees embody two populations which economic development officials everywhere hope to attract, because they use relatively few social services and inject much of their disposable income into the local economy. However, they may unbalance local labor markets, because while they create a large demand for service, construction, and other types of workers, they contribute little, if anything, to the local labor supply.

HISPANICS IN THE POULTRY INDUSTRY

Attracting workers to the poultry industry is a growing challenge. Nationwide, wages paid in the industry are significantly higher than the minimum wage. However, at $7.39 an hour as of 1997, they had not changed in real terms in more than thirty years and remained among the lowest for manufacturing and food industry employment (Hetrick 1994; U.S. Department of Commerce [DOC] 1967–1997). The wage data we used do not specify region, but wages in southern states were probably below the average. Unionization rates, never high in the South in general, have remained well below 5 percent in meat-processing industries since the early 1980s, according to the Current Population Survey. Poultry processing, like other meat processing, is a relatively hazardous and unattractive occupation, with harsh working conditions that have been continually exposed as bad in media and scholarly accounts (Bjerklie 1995; Sun and Escobar 1999). Moreover, economic growth that began in the early 1980s and continued for almost two decades created employment options that diminished relative incentives for working in the poultry industry.

Under these circumstances, it is not surprising that the poultry industry in the southeastern states has experienced difficulty finding a sufficient supply of local workers willing to accept their wages and working conditions. Consequently, the industry's expansion and concentration within a geographic region whose economic development was already creating an immense demand for low-skilled workers forced the sector to look elsewhere.

As with other low-skill, low-wage industries, the poultry business began actively recruiting immigrants, most coming from Mexico and Central America. Numerous reports have documented the extreme lengths firms

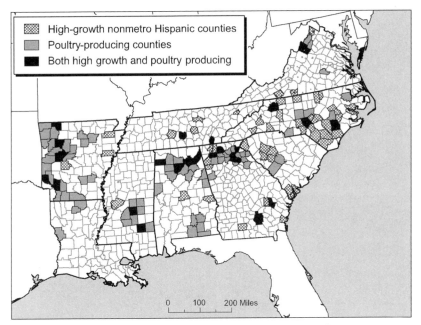

13.3.   Poultry-producing and high-growth Hispanic counties, nine southeastern states, 1990–2000. *Sources: U.S. Department of Agriculture, 1987, 1992, 1997; U.S. Bureau of the Census 1990, 2000.*

have gone to recruit workers for their plants (Barboza 2001). For a region that had low absolute numbers of Hispanics, the size of the poultry-processing workforce has grown significantly.

The results of these recruiting efforts can be seen in Figure 13.3, which maps the confluence of the location of significant poultry production with Hispanic settlement within the nine southeastern states. Areas denoted by light shading represent counties in these states which, according to the U.S. Census of Agriculture, ranked, in 1987, 1992, and 1997, within the top 100 chicken-producing counties in the nation. Areas with crosshatching represent rapid-growth nonmetropolitan Hispanic counties, defined as those in which the Hispanic population grew in absolute and percentage terms by one thousand persons and 150 percent, respectively, between 1990 and 2000. Combining the two patterns yields counties that overlap, shown in solid black. Note that while the rapid Hispanic growth counties are nonmetropolitan, the poultry-growing counties include nonmetropolitan as well as metropolitan counties. Since the Census of Agriculture data refer to where poultry is raised, as opposed to where it is slaughtered and processed, we would expect most of the poultry counties to be

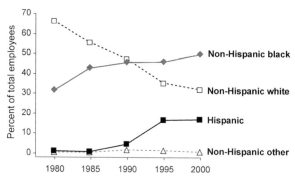

13.4.   Racial and ethnic composition of meat-processing industry employees, nine southeastern states, 1980–2000. *Source: U.S. Department of Commerce, 1963–1997.*

in rural, nonmetropolitan areas. Moreover, because of the economics of poultry transportation, we can reasonably assume that most are close to poultry-processing facilities. Thus, contiguous counties in Figure 13.3 account for a significant number of all counties highlighted.

The proximity of the Hispanic population to poultry-producing regions is unmistakable, and when combined with the qualitative evidence on recruiting practices, it provides a clear picture of the close connection between the poultry industry and Hispanic population growth. Duplin County in North Carolina, for example, has seen its Hispanic population increase by almost seven thousand since the 1990s, owing in no small part to the demand for labor in its Carolina Turkey, Nash Johnson, and Butterball Turkey plants. The Hispanic population in Hall County, Georgia, has grown by twenty-three thousand, not only because of its proximity to Atlanta, but also because of the poultry plants in the town of Gainsville. Marshall County in Alabama employs over three thousand poultry workers, owing to a Tyson Poultry plant in Guntersville, and its Hispanic population has grown by forty-three hundred in the same period.

We have argued that the transformations in this industry correlate with Hispanic population growth in the area. As such, we would expect important changes in the racial and ethnic composition of the labor force working in the poultry industry. However, it is unclear whether Hispanics are replacing or complementing blacks and whites. Figure 13.4 presents changes in the racial and ethnic composition of the labor force in the meat-processing industry between 1980 and 2000, using Current Population Survey (CPS) data (DOC 1963–1997). Meat processing is a broad category that includes the processing of red meat, pork, turkey, and chicken. However, outside of some pork processing in Mississippi, North Carolina, and Virginia, almost all meat processing in the nine southeastern states consists of poultry processing.

Changes in the racial and ethnic composition of the industry are telling of the potential differential effect of migration on racial groups. Whites have dropped from just under 70 percent to just over 30 percent of the workforce. The proportion of blacks has increased from 30 percent to 50 percent, and the proportion of Hispanics has increased from one percent to 17 percent. Figure 13.2 shows that the actual number of workers in the poultry industry nationwide had more than doubled between 1980 and 2001, so the lower percentage of whites does not necessarily indicate that there are fewer whites involved in poultry processing, but it does indicate that there are many more blacks and Hispanics.

Because the CPS tends to undercount Hispanics, these percentages are conservative. To provide some sense of the potential understatement, consider the case of hired farmworkers, another employment group with a high proportion of Hispanics. The National Agricultural Workers Survey, considered the most representative survey of farmworkers, places the Hispanic composition of the agricultural farmworker population at more than double the proportion estimated by the CPS.

The National Agricultural Workers Survey evaluates the degree to which immigrant labor complements or substitutes for domestic workers. Hispanics may be replacing non-Hispanic whites, which, assuming the latter are moving into higher-paying jobs, leaves everyone better off. Non-Hispanic blacks may also be leaving the poultry industry in absolute numbers, but their increasing proportion suggests that immigrants may be competing for the same low-skill jobs.

We now turn to case studies of two poultry-producing counties in the Southeast to illustrate how some of the issues noted above—the rapid incorporation of Hispanics into the American South and the consequent impact on receiving communities—manifest in real places. We consider one county in Virginia and one in North Carolina that typify the economic and demographic patterns that we suggest are occurring throughout the southeastern United States.

ACCOMACK COUNTY, VIRGINIA, AND DUPLIN COUNTY, NORTH CAROLINA

Accomack County, along the eastern shoreline of Virginia, is the northern part of a slender peninsula at the base of the well-known Delmarva

(Delaware-Maryland-Virginia) poultry-producing region. Duplin County, along the southeastern coastal plain of North Carolina, is among the leading turkey-producing counties in the country.

These two nonmetropolitan counties reflect similar population and economic conditions. By 2000, Accomack and Duplin Counties had populations of thirty-eight thousand and forty-nine thousand, respectively, and their 1997 median household incomes of roughly $25,000 and $27,000 were well below the $40,000 and $35,000 averages for Virginia and North Carolina, respectively. Temperate climates in both areas are well suited for raising poultry and growing corn, soybeans, and other feed grains used by the industry. In addition, both counties have long been known for their production of cash crops, including vegetables, fruit, nursery and greenhouse crops, and tobacco. As one drives south from the Maryland border along Virginia's Highway 13 or along I-40 across North Carolina, farmland, food stands, and the occasional tourist billboard interrupt the rural landscape. Few locations have sizable populations or notable geographies beyond one or two traffic lights; according to one Accomack County resident, "There isn't any town here, there are towns."

Poultry Plants

Virginia ranks eighth or ninth in broiler output, and Accomack County produces about 10 percent of that. Two processing plants, the Tyson plant in Temperanceville and the Perdue plant in the town of Accomac, have been in business for over thirty years and together employed roughly twenty-six hundred persons in 2002. Both Tyson and Perdue are among the top four poultry-producing firms in the nation, and their plants are among the largest in the Delmarva region (Delmarva Poultry Industry [DPI] 2002). Temperanceville is not incorporated; since Accomac is the county seat, it is there that most of the poultry regulation and social-service provision occurs.

North Carolina's annual output of forty-one million turkeys ranks second in the nation, and Duplin County produces one-quarter of that. The poultry industry in the county began in the early 1950s and soon became Duplin County's largest industry. In 1986, Carolina Turkeys built the nation's largest turkey-processing plant in the town of Mount Olive. In 2002, the plant employed close to three thousand workers and had become the world's largest turkey-processing facility, with integrated operations that combined diagnostic labs, research farms, breeder farms, hatcheries, growing farms, and feed mills. Additional poultry plants include Nash Johnson & Sons, Butterball Turkey, and House of Raeford, which together employ an additional twenty-two hundred workers.

13.5.   Signs of a nascent Hispanic community in Accomack County, Virginia. *Photograph by W. Kandel, 2002.*

Hispanics

Hispanic population growth in Accomack and Duplin Counties during the 1990s illustrates the dramatic inflow of Latinos into southern communities (Fig. 13.5). In 1990, the census counted 450 and 1,015 Hispanics in Accomack and Duplin Counties, respectively. By 2000, the numbers were 1,680 and 7,426, representing increases of 272 and 633 percent, respectively.

These changes altered the racial and ethnic makeup of both counties as they rapidly moved from a biracial white-black population to a multiethnic population with significant Hispanic representation. As of 2000, the population of Accomack had become 62.0 percent white, 31.0 percent black, and 5.5 percent Hispanic, while that of Duplin County had became 55.0 percent white, 29.0 percent black, and 15.0 percent Hispanic. Disaggregating by national origin shows that most Latinos are Mexicans and represent around 65 percent of the Latino population in both counties. Next in line are Guatemalans, 20 percent of Accomack County's Hispanic population, and Hondurans, 15 percent of the same in Duplin County. Differences in the country of origin of the Latino population reflect the highly structured process guiding migration decisions and the role of work, friends, and family networks in determining the destinations of individual migrants (Massey and Espinosa 1997). For example, informants in Accomack County indicate that a sizable portion of the Guatemalan population actually originates from a single *departamento* (province) of the country.

Moreover, while the census captures permanently settled Hispanics, it often undercounts the large number of seasonal agricultural migrant workers who pass through both counties. These annual migratory streams usually begin in Florida or Texas and continue through Georgia and the Carolinas before stopping in the Delmarva Peninsula. Seasonal workers typically work for farm-labor contractors and accompany them from one location to another. While traveling through these counties, in either direction, some migrants find work in the poultry plants and decide to stay. Since poultry work is year-round, those who switch from agricultural work to poultry processing have a greater likelihood of settling permanently.

An example from Duplin County illustrates the close connection between seasonal and permanent migration. One of our interviewees, currently a high-ranking administrator coordinating housing services for one poultry plant, initiated his migration experience when a relative, a former seasonal farmworker, decided to settle in North Carolina. In the late 1970s, growing employment opportunities in the poultry industry provided seasonal workers a channel for upward mobility. After settling in Duplin County, the relative sent word to the interviewee's family about promising employment opportunities in the United States, triggering our interviewee's first U.S. trip in 1980. Most of his brothers and sisters, using his settlement, family networks, and waves of legalizations in the 1980s, followed by the end of the decade. In 2000, his mother immigrated with his youngest sister. Thus, after twenty-two years of experience in the United States, this Mexican family from the State of Veracruz was reconstituted in North Carolina. Only his father remains in Mexico, despite our interviewee's assurances that life in the United States is not so bad and that the whole family awaits his arrival.

Employment Context

The majority of Hispanic immigrants in Accomack County work in agriculture, not poultry processing, even though the relative size of both industries in the county is roughly the same. In Duplin County, the mix is about equal. Agricultural work typically pays the current minimum wage of $5.15 per hour, although piece-rate pay scales during the harvest season may roughly double this. Poultry plant employment, on the other hand, is year-round work with a starting wage of about $8.00 per hour and includes health and retirement benefits. Any employment progression from agriculture to poultry processing tends to convert residency tenure from temporary to permanent. Some selectivity of legal status occurs; agricultural farmworkers are more likely to be unauthorized than are poultry workers, whose legal documents are more carefully reviewed.

While the processing of poultry is considered year-round work, a significant portion of the workforce cycles through for short periods (Griffith 1995; Horowitz and Miller 1999). Workers may leave because they don't like the work, are using poultry work as stopgap employment between farm-labor jobs, visit family in their home countries, or because they have violated attendance rules. Some also leave to maintain seasonal migration patterns with their undocumented family members. Firms, anticipating that a significant number of hires will leave within months of starting, adjust their wage and benefits structures to reward workers who stay for over six months. According to unofficial estimates and anecdotal reports, turnover rates in poultry plants average from 70 percent annually, with considerable variation by plant. In North Carolina, the high turnover rates permit poultry workers to qualify for programs providing assistance to seasonal workers.

The dynamics of migration and working conditions contribute to the high turnover rate. In addition, crackdowns on undocumented migrants after September 11, 2001, have also affected the stability of poultry employment. There are increasing reports of employees and employers receiving letters from the Social Security Administration notifying them of violations. Employees are notified first, usually because they have used a false or incorrect Social Security number. If the employee does not correct the situation, a letter is sent to the employer, who must notify the employee and terminate employment.

The racial composition of agricultural and poultry workers in Accomack County resembles that found in the nine southeastern states surveyed. Although exact figures do not exist, industry officials estimate the makeup of the poultry-processing workforce nationwide at approximately 50 percent black, 40 percent white, and 10 percent Hispanic. In Duplin County, the Hispanic component in poultry is far greater, approaching 65 percent in one plant.

Within plants, fairly rigid racial and ethnic divisions characterize productive activities, with most whites and some blacks occupying managerial positions and Hispanics confined to manual work in production, packing, mailing, and housekeeping. These divisions have several sources. As one of our informants observed, inability to speak English and low levels of education are central factors in maintaining Hispanics in manual positions. At the same time, what he considered cultural differences also facilitate segregation of activities along racial and ethnic lines.

Labor Market and Demographic Impacts

A central question driving most arguments in favor of or against immigration is the extent to which Hispanic inflows displace or complement local workers. Particularly important is the interaction between Hispanic employment and labor-market outcomes of other minority groups, especially African Americans. While this question well exceeds the scope of this chapter, we contend that labor-market compositional shifts are intertwined with industrial transformations. When such shifts are applied to the poultry industry, we can expect growth in product demand, industrial concentration, and production variability to facilitate demand for Hispanic workers. In this process, Hispanic population inflows do not necessarily imply worker displacement, because all three macrotrends create additional employment.

Some of these expectations are confirmed by our two case studies. Despite very rapid population growth, the unemployment rate declined in Accomack and Duplin Counties, from 9.6 percent to 4.2 percent, and from 8.6 percent to 5.0 percent, respectively, between 1992 and 2000 (DOC 2002). In fact, in 2001, the unemployment rates in both counties were much lower than the nationwide nonmetropolitan average. In addition, when asked why poultry companies were increasingly hiring Hispanic workers, our informants consistently replied that new jobs were opening up and that nobody else wanted them. This is especially true in Duplin County, with its large, new Carolina Turkeys processing plant. In such a context, the expectation of worker displacement may not be reasonable.

Moreover, informants acknowledged the creation of many skilled positions in, for example, administrative, government, or educational employment for which Hispanics do not qualify. Overall, evidence suggests that while industrial transformations in the poultry industry expanded the demand for low-skilled workers and thus attracted Hispanics, the concomitant and multiplicative effect of economic growth and population increase also facilitated upward occupational mobility and better employment for more educated local residents.

In addition to their racial and ethnic impact on the labor market, Hispanic inflows change the demography of Accomack and Duplin Counties in other ways. Two changes are particularly relevant: gender composition and age distribution.

Gender ratios in these counties vary significantly by racial and ethnic group. According to the 2000 Census, the number of men per 100 women in Accomack County is 94 for whites, 85 for blacks, and 166 for Hispanics. In Duplin County, the gender ratio is 95 for whites, 84 for blacks, and 156 for Hispanics. For the United States as a whole, the gender ratio for Hispanics is 105 men per 100 women. Clearly, the two counties are anomalies within the United States, reflecting the predominantly male component of recent immigration there.

In addition, differences in gender ratios highlight a diverging pattern between Hispanics and blacks. The relative undersupply of women in the Hispanic case contradicts their relative oversupply among African Americans. Studies have found that gender ratios have significant importance in marriage patterns, particularly among blacks, making it more difficult for individuals to find partners in contexts of unbalanced gender markets (Lichter, LeClere, and McLaughlin 1991; Lichter et al. 1992). It is unclear how these patterns will affect the marriage behavior of single Hispanic men and women (Oropesa and Lichter 1994; Parrado and Zenteno In press). If Hispanic men try to find partners in the United States, the relative undersupply of Hispanic women may promote interracial marriage. Alternatively, to the extent that marriage is still constrained across racial and ethnic lines, single men may be forced to return to their local communities to find a partner (Parrado 2002). In this scenario, gender imbalances can also affect patterns of return migration. Given their cultural background, forming a union is still a central personal objective among Hispanics, particularly Mexicans. Conversations with immigrants in these communities suggest that gender imbalances and the difficulties in finding a partner, above and beyond economic success, critically affect settlement decisions.

In addition, gender imbalances have an effect on broader sexual behaviors. Immigrant communities are particularly vulnerable to the proliferation of prostitution and other forms of sexually risky behaviors. Use of prostitutes is particularly prevalent among single and married migrants who leave their families behind, which increases the risk of spreading sexually transmitted diseases, including AIDS. In fact, researchers have hypothesized that migration to the United States is a central contributor to the diffusion of the AIDS epidemic in Mexico, even in rural areas (McQuiston and Parrado 2002; Mishra, Conner, and Magaña 1996). Within the guidelines of the Healthy People objectives established by the U.S. Department of Health and Human Services, Latino organizations in Duplin County have begun to address sexually risky behavior by developing training programs and educational campaigns promoting condom use and AIDS prevention.

The other demographic trait with striking community impacts, age distribution, varies similarly across racial and ethnic groups. Figure 13.6 plots

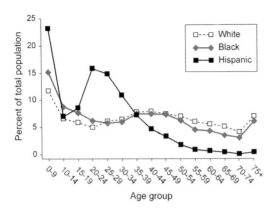

13.6.   Age distribution, by race and ethnicity, Duplin County, North Carolina, 2000. *Source: U.S. Bureau of the Census 2000.*

the percentage of the population in different age groups by race and ethnicity in Duplin County; patterns for Accomack County are very similar. Hispanics represent a much younger population than either blacks or whites. If we look at migration dynamics, the percentage Hispanic peaks very early, zero to nine years old and again at twenty to twenty-four; it declines at older ages. The two peaks reflect the fact that labor migration is initiated in the early twenties, while children migrate early on or are born following their parents' settlement. The age distribution of blacks and whites is more even, with relatively higher proportions above age forty.

The age distribution of the Hispanic population has affected local communities in these counties in two ways. First, the rapid arrival of school-aged children has increased demand for educational facilities and contributed to school overcrowding. In addition, given the lack of knowledge of English among students and their parents, their arrival has suddenly increased the need for English as a second language (ESL) classes as well as interpreters to facilitate parent-teacher communication. The challenges that immigrants pose for public education systems are particularly relevant; some schools in Duplin County have become 50 percent Hispanic within the space of just a few years. Educators in both counties often find that the new arrivals have little educational background or familiarity with the U.S. educational system. Financing is particularly problematic. In Duplin County, for instance, Carolina Turkeys has recognized the tremendous burden that ESL classes pose on school budgets and now provides financial assistance for their provision.

Second, younger populations increase the prevalence of certain risk behaviors, including crime, alcoholism, and motor vehicle accidents. The higher representation of Hispanics in younger groups makes them particularly vulnerable to such problems, and special programs to address these issues might be required. In addition, age can also affect racial and ethnic relations. Research on neighborhood transitions in cities like Chicago shows that resistance to ethnic change stems not only from the different ethnicity of the arriving population but also from its youth (Flippen 2001). Elderly residents, in particular, may feel threatened by the arrival of younger groups, who they sense can disrupt their way of life or increase their vulnerability to crime. Such feelings can fuel anti-immigrant sentiments among native residents.

Community Impacts and Reaction

Signs of a Hispanic influx into Accomack County in the 1990s generally appeared muted, with only an occasional store sign in Spanish to suggest the presence of Hispanics. From the perspective of social-service delivery, however, indications of a Hispanic presence have cropped up in many small ways. The county court now has a certified court interpreter; previously, anyone with some bilingual ability would be asked to volunteer a translation for defendants. The two health clinics in the area now have Spanish-speaking personnel. The local hospital now uses a commercial phone service to automatically translate conversations. Some county schools have begun canvassing other districts for Spanish-speaking teachers. Employees at the Virginia Employment Commission frequently help Hispanic workers find new or better-paying jobs and often provide emergency food aid, a benefit frequently requested by those just arriving. However, other services, such as securing a driver's license or alcohol counseling, still require people to find their own translator or interpreter. At the community level, Hispanics now enjoy soccer matches all day each Sunday, a local weekly radio program in Spanish, a small Spanish-language newspaper, and church services in Spanish.

In Duplin County, where community impacts are more noticeable, several institutions have emerged that specifically attend to the needs of the Hispanic population and facilitate assimilation and incorporation into U.S. society. Latinos Unidos, for example, provides information about health and legal issues, offers ESL classes, and trains community members to serve local communities. County government has also adapted to the growing Latino community. A leadership program offered through a local college to promote entrepreneurship is now being reformatted into Spanish, an effort that has had a measurable impact on the emergence of Hispanic businesses. Small grocery, video, and music stores cater directly to the Hispanic community and can easily be identified when visiting the counties. In addition,

Carolina Turkeys donated two lots to local Hispanic residents on which to construct churches.

Not surprisingly, Hispanic growth is changing the cultural landscape of these communities, from the types of food and consumer goods being sold in stores to the festivities that are celebrated. These changes sometimes occur in conjunction with shifts within the companies that hire Hispanics. For instance, in September 2000, workers from Carolina Turkeys in Duplin County organized an international festival to recognize the growing diversity of the county's Hispanic population. During the successful Semana de la Hispanicidad (Hispanic Heritage Week) in 2001, flags from every Latin American country were posted throughout the company's hallways. Following their lead, black employees decided to celebrate African-American Week in January 2002. In 2002, Carolina Turkeys invited the Mexican consul to give a speech in Duplin County, a widely publicized event that drew over three hundred people, garnered media attention for the Latino population, and created closer links with other groups. Many hope these kinds of initiatives will increase awareness and understanding of the growing diversity of Duplin County's population.

None of the informants we interviewed in Accomack and Duplin Counties suggested that the growth of the Hispanic population had caused concern among community residents, and they offered several reasons for the amenable reception. As part of the Delmarva region, Accomack County has been accustomed for decades to hosting migrants who work in the area's vegetable and grain farms. Moreover, the growth of the Hispanic population here was never as dramatic as it has been in some southeastern towns, such as Siler City, North Carolina, or Dalton, Georgia, where large numbers of Hispanics have recently settled in areas with relatively smaller base populations. In addition, there is increasing recognition of the contribution of the Hispanic population to the local economies. As one informant acknowledged, "We understand that without them, our vegetables wouldn't be picked because we don't have domestic workers that can do the job— or that would want to do the job."

When pressed, however, some of our informants mentioned hearing gripes about job competition between the Hispanic migrant workers and local blacks. Another issue that disturbs local residents in both counties is the trafficking in false driver's licenses, particularly because some of the recipients have little or no driving experience. Hispanic residents, on the other hand, are worried about crime and being targeted for robbery, in particular, because they often carry their money with them or keep their savings in their houses instead of in banks.

Racial and ethnic inequalities in access to housing also create tension. In Accomack County, 82 percent of white households live in owner-occupied housing units, compared with 63 percent of black households, and only 36 percent of Hispanic households. Figures for Duplin County are almost identical. In addition, Hispanics tend to live in overcrowded conditions in both counties, with an average household size of 4.5 persons compared with 2.5 for blacks and whites. Management at Carolina Turkeys in Duplin County and the Tyson and Perdue plants in Accomack County recognize the companies' role in providing adequate rental housing for Hispanic workers and have built homes or purchased house trailers close to their plants.

CONCLUSIONS AND POLICY IMPLICATIONS

In this chapter, we have presented evidence to illustrate how industrial restructuring correlates with changes in labor force composition and, by implication, with patterns of international migration and settlement. If similar trends in industrial development occur in other industries, we can expect them to generate further migration and population change. The visibility of prominent manufacturing firms will require greater attention by policy makers to labor-recruitment practices and the growing number of proposals for changing current immigration policies.

To show how industrial restructuring of the poultry industry plays out at the local level, we presented two case studies of poultry-producing counties in the Southeast, both with similar structural characteristics, but at different phases in their incorporation of Hispanic workers. To the extent that recent local history has been relatively incident free, these vignettes offer some degree of guarded optimism for the incorporation of Hispanic immigrants into the rural South as they create what Haverluk (1998) calls "new communities."

Nevertheless, a central concern of researchers is the degree to which outcomes of industrial development, such as international migration, differentially affect native residents. A sizable literature suggests that the presence of immigrant labor can be significant for wages, benefits, and working conditions (U.S. Department of Labor 1989). Moreover, as the relatively rapid settlement of immigrants in rural communities continues, it may also exacerbate existing patterns of spatial separation and inequality. This may require greater local expenditures on social services and programs that facilitate social integration between new and established residents. Given the geographic proximity of Mexico to the United States, increasing economic integration resulting from the North American Free Trade Agreement, age-specific migration, immigration laws favoring family reunification, and relatively high fertility, Hispanic demographic growth in rural areas will invariably increase. Consequently, many of the issues discussed above will likely continue for the foreseeable future.

HISPANIZATION OF HEREFORD, TEXAS

Terrence W. Haverluk

Hispanization is the process by which a place or person absorbs characteristics of Hispanic/Latino society and culture. Hispanization of a place is illustrated by, but is not limited to, Mexican restaurants, tortilla factories, *panaderías* (bakeries), *taquerías* (taco restaurants); Spanish-language churches, newspapers, television, and radio stations; as well as specialty clothing stores, music stores, and nightclubs. A non-Hispanic person may also absorb Hispanic characteristics, including, but not limited to, the Spanish language; Latin food, dress, music, interior design; and participation in Latin festivals and holidays.

Hispanization is the opposite of assimilation. Assimilation is the process by which a minority culture absorbs characteristics of the dominant society and culture. In the United States, Anglo, not Hispanic/Latino, has long been the dominant culture, and, historically, U.S. immigrants have typically assimilated by the third generation. My Ukrainian American grandparents, for example, spoke Ukrainian in the home, ate Ukrainian food, wore Ukrainian clothes, attended a Ukrainian Orthodox Church, and knew how to make those colorful Easter eggs. I am a third-generation Ukrainian American and do none of the above.

Spanish-language retention rates are a common index of assimilation. In 1990, about 70 percent of all Hispanic/Latino Americans used Spanish in the home (U.S. Bureau of the Census 1990a). Spanish-language retention rates vary geographically. Parts of Texas and New Mexico have retention rates over 90 percent, whereas parts of California and Colorado have less than 30 percent.

Intermarriage is thought to facilitate assimilation and the loss of language. It is generally assumed that marriage between an Anglo and a Hispanic/Latino will result in the assimilation of the Hispanic/Latino into the dominant Anglo society (Crester and Leon 1982; Jiobu 1988; Mittelbach, Moore, and McDaniel 1966; Peach 1980). This assumption must be questioned, however, when an Anglo intermarries into a society dominated by Hispanics/Latinos. Anglos who intermarry in Laredo, Texas—where Hispanics/Latinos constitute 97 percent of the population—are just as likely to Hispanicize as to assimilate.

As a framework for analyzing Hispanization and assimilation, I have identified three types of Hispanic communities: continuous, discontinuous, and new (Haverluk 1998). Continuous communities are those that were founded by Hispanics and maintained Hispanic demographic and political dominance even after they were annexed by the United States. Examples include Laredo, Texas, and Chimayó, New Mexico. Hispanics in continuous communities retain the Spanish language, hold elected office, and occupy managerial positions at greater rates than in other Hispanic communities. Anglos moving to these communities are more likely to Hispanicize.

Discontinuous communities are those that were settled by Hispanics, but that then lost Hispanic demographic and political dominance after annexation. Examples include San Antonio, Texas, and Los Angeles, California. Hispanics in discontinuous communities have lost political authority, maintain lower rates of Spanish-language retention, and occupy fewer managerial positions than in continuous communities. In Texas, however, several discontinuous communities now have Hispanic majorities: El Paso, San Antonio, Carrizo Springs, Corpus Christi, Cotulla, and Crystal City. In these communities, Hispanics often argue that "I didn't cross the line [the border], the line crossed me." In these communities, Hispanics have regained much political power and are capitalizing on their Hispanic roots to facilitate "heritage tourism" (Arreola 2002).

New communities are those that were founded by Anglos. Only later, often after several decades, did Hispanics arrive, usually to address local labor shortages. Hispanics in new communities have lower rates of Spanish-language retention, hold fewer elected offices, and fill fewer managerial positions than in continuous and discontinuous communities. They constitute the classic minority population, which is expected to assimilate into the majority Anglo population (Gómez 2002). And, in fact, assimilation rates are greater in new communities. What happens, however, when a new community becomes majority Hispanic?

According to the 2000 Census, Deaf Smith County, Texas, is 57 percent Hispanic, and the city of Hereford, its county seat, is 61 percent Hispanic. In Hereford, a new community, as in most of Texas, the overwhelming majority of Hispanics are of Mexican ancestry. Although several discontinuous communities are again dominated by Hispanics, it has never happened in a new community. When a new community becomes dominated by Hispanics—by that, I mean Hispanics control the politics, economy, and culture of the city—should it be called a *nuevo* community?

HISPANICS TO HEREFORD, TEXAS

Hereford, a railroad town situated in the Panhandle of Texas, became the county seat in 1909, more than a decade after Deaf Smith County was organized. Deaf Smith County's regional economy followed the typical ranching-to-farming pattern of the Texas High Plains, and by 1907, farming had replaced the open range. Deaf Smith County was too far north to grow cotton; instead, farmers concentrated on cattle feeding and sorghum farming. The 1940 Census enumerated 6,056 persons, the majority of whom were Anglo. In 1948, the population of the county was almost completely native white (Brown 1948: 31, 45).

In the late 1940s, two Idaho farmers—Howard Gault and Ira Loving—moved to the Texas High Plains to grow potatoes. Drawn by the cheap land, other farmers soon followed. These young farmers experimented with onions, lettuce, potatoes, and carrots, which soon became important crops in Deaf Smith County. Labor, however, was hard to find during and after World War II, which limited production (Gault 1974).

In 1951, a California farmer named Williams planted extensive tracts of lettuce in Deaf Smith County. Williams was familiar with the Bracero Program in California and realized that braceros—Hispanics who labored in fields with their arms, *brazos*—who were employed to pick cotton around Lubbock, to the south, could also work vegetables in Hereford. The Bracero Program, Public Law 45, passed in 1942, was an agreement between Mexico and the United States that allowed Mexican laborers to work in this country at a guaranteed wage with assurances of adequate food and housing. Bracero labor remained relatively scarce during WWII and did not take off until 1949, when 107,000 Mexicans were admitted as temporary workers (Grebler, Moore, and Guzmán 1970: 176). Sometime during the late 1950s, shortly after Williams arrived in Texas, braceros began moving north from Mexico to pick lettuce in Deaf Smith County (Fig 14.1).

With bracero labor, vegetable production expanded in the county. Some of the braceros liked the area and the work, received visas, and permanently relocated. The farmers appreciated the reliable labor force and welcomed them. According to Howard Gault (1974), "We never had it so good."

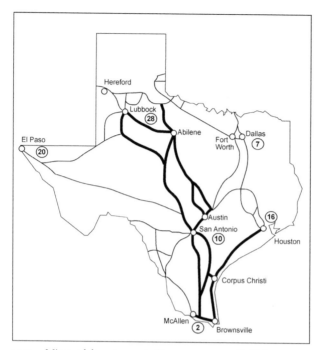

14.1.   Migrant labor streams in Texas, 1943–1944. Bold lines indicates major migratory routes; lighter lines indicate minor routes. Circles with numbers represent incidents of discrimination reported during a four-month period in 1944. *Source: Adapted from Robert C. Eckhardt 1944, Southwest Collection, Texas Tech University, Lubbock.*

The Bracero Program ended in 1964, which meant there were not enough laborers to maintain previous levels of production without mechanization. Farmers had resisted mechanization because it was more expensive than using braceros. After losing their supply of low-wage laborers, however, they mechanized. Even with mechanization, though, farmers needed field crews to maintain the irrigation ditches, work the potato sheds, and maintain the farm. Without braceros, Deaf Smith County's farmers turned to South Texas and Mexican Americans for labor (Gault 1974).

The creation of migration streams between specific source areas in South Texas and Mexico and specific receiving areas in the United States is predicated on the existence of migration networks that include ties of kinship, friendship, and *paisanaje* (regional links), with kinship being the most important. Migration networks provide jobs, food, housing, transportation, and social opportunities for recent migrants. These networks gradually emerge after a few individuals, historically, single males, return to South Texas or Mexico with money and consumer goods and inform kin of the many employment opportunities. Jones (1995) calls this migration "channelization."

Hispanics from South Texas, and Mexicans from Mexico, are often recruited for seasonal, low-paying, dangerous work. After several years of farm labor, and as their English improves and knowledge of the area increases, Hispanics often change jobs. Scheck (1971) found that four-fifths of Hispanic migrants to the High Plains began in agriculture, but that only 7 percent remained in this category. Similar diversification rates have been identified in the meatpacking industry, which is an important employer in Hereford. Figure 14.2 shows the increasing employment diversity of Hereford's Hispanics. In 1970, only 5 percent of them were employed in teaching jobs, yet, in 1990, that number had risen to 25 percent. Similar changes are evident for skilled craftspeople, engineers, firefighters, and police. Once someone enters a professional job, it is unlikely that his or her sons and daughters will work the fields or in meatpacking. Thus, there is a continual need to replenish workers, especially in meatpacking, where turnover rates and injuries are the highest in American manufacturing (Stull and Broadway 1995).

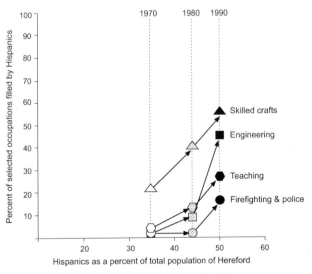

14.2.   Hispanic occupational changes, Hereford, Texas, 1970–1990. *Source: U.S. Bureau of the Census 1970, 1980, 1990b.*

Alex Torres (1977) exemplifies migrant channelization and the process of occupational diversification. Alex's father knew a man in Hereford who ran a potato shed that needed help, so he moved his family of eight to Hereford for the summer and returned to South Texas in the fall. Using the money saved from his summer job, Alex attended a local junior college and earned a two-year degree. When the Texas Employment Commission (TEC) was looking for a bilingual, educated Hispanic to work with migrants in 1965, Alex applied for and was offered the job. He moved to Hereford for a few years, but did not stay. He felt that the TEC would not promote him because, at that time, Anglos considered Hispanics fit only for farm labor. He moved back to South Texas, where educated Hispanics contribute at all levels of society. The low level of discrimination in South Texas reflects the dominance of Hispanics in that region (see Fig. 14.1).

Many young people like Alex moved back and forth between the High Plains and South Texas from the 1960s through the 1990s. When someone like Alex leaves the agricultural labor force for which he was recruited, that labor must be replaced—usually by another Hispanic, often a relative or a friend. These kinship networks are an important component of the economy and labor force of Texas and, increasingly, of migrant labor.

Until the 1970s, the influx of Hispanics into Deaf Smith County was continuous, but small. The enormous growth in the Hispanic population began in 1970, when Hereford Bi-Products built a facility in town, an economic decision with precedence in other regions. Meatpackers began moving to small, rural towns near large herds of cattle in 1960, when Iowa Beef Processors (IBP) opened a plant in Denison, Iowa. IBP streamlined the meatpacking industry by eliminating the need for skilled labor. It turned meatpacking into a factory system. By using unskilled labor for repetitive tasks, IBP lowered labor costs and increased profit margins in an industry accustomed to less than one percent return on investment. Another IBP innovation was boxed beef. Before IBP, meatpacking plants provided supermarkets with cuts of beef that were finished by skilled, unionized butchers. These two innovations—factory production and boxed beef—directly threatened the jobs of unionized butchers and packers.

In 1968, the Amalgamated Meat Cutters union merged with the United Packinghouse Workers to fight IBP's work environment and the downward trend in wages. In 1970, they struck the IBP plant in Dakota City, Nebraska. IBP locked out the strikers and brought in workers from Mexico. IBP fed and housed the Mexicans in the plant and resumed production at about 50 percent. After a protracted eight-month battle, with deaths on both sides, the union lost. IBP got what it wanted—it broke the union and continued to hire lower-wage, unskilled labor (Rodengen 2000).

After 1970, IBP began opening plants where there was not only ready access to livestock, but also ready access to low-wage, pliable Mexican and Hispanic labor: 1973 in Amarillo, Texas; 1976 in Pasco, Washington; and 1980 in Garden City, Kansas. During the late 1980s and the early 1990s, the unusually low unemployment rates in the United States increased IBP's reliance on imported labor. The company worked with the Immigration and Nationalization Service to help maintain a steady supply of legal Latin American immigrants.

There was nothing, however, to stop illegal immigrants from presenting fraudulent documents. Employers are required to check for documentation; they do not have to verify the legality of those documents. This loophole created a large underground network of document providers and increased the number of Hispanics employed in meat, pork, and poultry packing ("I.N.S. Is Looking the Other Way as Illegal Immigrants Fill Jobs" 2002; "Under the Counter, Grocer Provided Workers" 2000; "With Help from INS, U.S. Meatpacker Taps Mexican Work Force" 1998). In 1990, for example, IBP opened a state-of-the-art facility in Lexington, Nebraska. The 1990 Census enumerated 329 Hispanics in Lexington. Ten years later, the 2000 Census enumerated 5,121 Hispanics, 51 percent of the total population.

Other meatpacking companies had to follow the IBP model or go out of business. One of these firms was Hereford Bi-Products. Today, Hereford Bi-Products is the second-largest employer in Hereford (after the school district). Other meatpacking and processing firms established plants in and around Hereford, and by 1998, the industry raised and slaughtered three million cattle annually within a fifty-mile radius and employed 38 percent of Hereford's labor force. In the summer of 2002, large agribusiness firms Archer Daniels Midland and Farmland were planning new facilities near Hereford (Community Fact Sheet 1998).

Meatpacking and processing have notoriously high turnover rates, averaging about 100 percent a year. This is actually advantageous to the industry because, after six months of full-time employment, many companies must provide health care and wage increases (Rodengen 2000). Because of the high turnover rates, the level of occupational diversification in meatpacking is higher than in agriculture. When a recruited migrant leaves the plant, his or her labor must be replaced, thereby creating a constant flow of Hispanic immigrants. Hereford was almost completely Anglo in 1948, but was 61 percent Hispanic in 2000. The Hispanic population continues to grow at a faster rate than the non-Hispanic. Although much of the meatpacking industry relies on immigrants from Mexico, in Hereford, most of the employees are U.S. citizens from South Texas. The many Spanish-speaking South Texans in Hereford brought much of their social and material culture to the High Plains.

HISPANIZATION OF HEREFORD

Since 1950, Hereford's material landscape has changed with its population. Food is one way to gauge the level of Hispanic influence in the everyday construction of place identity. Food is a highly condensed social fact and no longer simply about sustenance (Appadurai 1981). Foods readily available in grocery stores, convenience stores, and restaurants reflect the eating habits of the local population. In 1970, Hispanic foodways were uncommon in Hereford; today, they are integrated into the community.

The Homeland Grocery Store, located on North Highway 385, is the only major grocery store in town. With over 60 percent of Hereford's population Hispanic, Homeland Grocery finds it expeditious to cater to Hispanic tastes. As one enters the store, the first things seen are bilingual Spanish videos and newspapers. The videos are from Mexico. Of the two newspapers, one is from Amarillo, the other from Hereford; the latter claims to serve West Texas, the Oklahoma Panhandle, and eastern New Mexico. As one continues past the videos, there are large drums of dried spices, rice, and beans. Interspersed among the drums are Mexican candles, Mexican juices, Mexican cookies, and Mexican *mole*. Continuing to the bakery, one finds eight kinds of tortillas, made in Moundridge, Kansas; Albuquerque, New Mexico; Los Angeles, California; and Kress, Irving, Fort Worth, Plainview, and Hereford, Texas. There are *dulces* (sweets) made in-house and from Mexico. The produce department has a large selection of fresh chiles, including habanero, serrano, jalapeño, anaheim, hungarian wax, bell, and poblano. Chips and salsa and other Mexican snack items can be found in six different places. One of the salsas is made in nearby Amarillo. The Mexican food section takes up half an aisle and consists mostly of corporate brands. Colorful piñatas hang from the ceiling throughout the store. The checkout counter is replete with Spanish-language magazines and bilingual cashiers.

Driving south on 385 into Hereford, there are more signs of Hispanization—El Tenampa restaurant, Méndez bakery and *panadería*. Finally, driving through downtown, other signs are evident—Maldonado records, music, and furniture; Chiflo records; Méndez barbershop; Copa Cabana (Mexican curios); Toucana Tina (Latin dance club); and the Chávez flea market.

How does this downtown occupancy compare to 1950? Whereas the physical infrastructure of the three-block downtown area remains the same, the businesses have changed dramatically; not one business that existed in 1950 was in business in 2000 (Fig. 14.3). In 2000, 31 percent of all businesses were operated by Hispanics, compelling evidence of increased Hispanic influence since 1950.

For the first forty years, Hispanics in Hereford were treated much like Alex Torres—shut out of the political process and stuck in dead-end jobs. During the 1980s, due to their increasing numbers and higher levels of education, Hispanics began to integrate politically and to enter professional and managerial positions. In 1970, there were no Hispanic firefighters, police officers, or elected officials, and fewer than 10 percent of Hispanics were employed in professional or management positions. In 2000, Hispanics were much more integrated; there was a Hispanic sheriff, school board member, and two city council members. The local radio station, KPAN, provided a daily prime time (6–8 P.M.) show of Tejano music, hosted by Ed Maldonado and Orlando Holguín.

Hispanic integration did not happen easily or voluntarily. Hispanics had to organize and challenge the entrenched Anglo power structure, which, traditionally, had marginalized them. Since Hispanics were generally not included in Anglo organizations, they created their own, in Hereford and elsewhere, including the Hispanic Chamber of Commerce, and Comerciantes Organizados Mexicano Americanos (COMA). Further, in 2000, there were Spanish language newspapers, soccer leagues, and separate fiesta days. The communication engendered by organizing at the business and cultural levels also facilitated organization at the political level.

Political integration, better education, and higher incomes created a Hispanic middle class that started buying land and controlling their means of production. Figure 14.4 reveals that between 1970 and 1990, there was a movement of Hispanics into middle-class jobs. Even with these advances, Hispanics are still underrepresented, given the fact that they constitute 61 percent of the population.

Intermarriage is considered one of the most sensitive indices of assimilation. It is assumed that intermarriage facilitates minority assimilation into the majority population by increasing primary relations between the groups. This, in turn, signals a decline in discriminatory practices and the eventual loss of ethnicity. A decrease in residential segregation may lead to a propinquity effect, further reinforcing intergroup contacts and increasing intermarriage. In traditional assimilation models, residential segregation, intermarriage, and assimilation are linked: as Hispanic residential segregation decreases, intermarriage increases, and so should assimilation. Yet, in

Main Street, 1950

Food	Star Theatre
Dry goods	
Drug store	Newspaper
Shoes	Truck parts
J.C. Penney	
Jewelry	Candy Kitchen
Foxman Shop	
Clothes	Newsstand

Third	*Street*
Haile Drugs	Drugstore
	Bank
Perry	Variety
5-10-25	H. Parts
Cleaners	Firestone
Insurance	Hardware
Vogue Dress	Auto supply
Caves 5-10-25	Furniture

Second	*Street*
Helt Appliance	Insurance
Food	
Hotel	Shoe store
Auto store	
Appliances	Café
Texas Theatre	
Realtor	Café
Gas	Parking

First	*Street*

Main Street, 2000

Maxwell's Gifts	Empty
Alex the Barber	
Empty	
Gaston's Clothing	First
Cellular One	
Radio Shack	Bank
	Southwest
Sun Loans Co.	
Sew 'n Sell	

Third	*Street*
Yiota's Originals	Springer Ins.
Ideal Rental	Hallmark Shop
Pants Cage	Manly Furniture
Range Western Wear	Continental Credit
Chávez Flea Market	Electrical Specialists
Cowan Jewelry	Merle Norman Cosmetics
Anderson Photography	Maldonado Records
Renee's Repeat Boutique	Maldonado Music
	Maldonado Furn.
Toucana Tina	Andersons Formal Wear

Second	*Street*
Villareal Sons Bakery and Barber	Empty
	Empty
Manly Furniture	Copa Cabana
	Méndez Barber
High Plains Fire Extinguishers	Chiflo Records
Stan Frey Sheet Metal	Campos Restaurant
Empty	Empty
	Empty
Pick-up Parts	Parking

First	*Street*

14.3. Downtown Hereford, Texas, 1950 and 2000. Hispanic-owned businesses (highlighted) were not evident in 1950, but exist side-by-side with others today. *Source: Hereford Museum; field survey.*

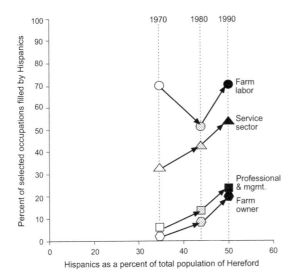

14.4. Hispanic occupational change and middle-class emergence, Hereford, Texas, 1970–1990. *Source: U.S. Bureau of the Census 1970, 1980, 1990b.*

Hereford and many other High Plains cities, Hispanics are now the majority. Are Hispanics in Hereford therefore assimilating?

Because Hereford is too small to analyze at the census tract level, it is difficult to gauge levels of residential segregation. One way to look at Hispanic residential segregation is to look at one family's home purchases over time. The Ramírez family began buying homes in 1953, all on Hereford's south side by the railroad tracks in the Hereford barrio (Fig. 14.5). Over the course of several decades, the family expanded its home purchases away from the south side barrio, and by 1987, family members owned homes all around town, except in the northwest, an upper-income, Anglo neighborhood. The Ramírez family is less segregated today than it was in the 1950s, but some residential segregation still exists.

As residential segregation has decreased in Hereford (if we assume that the Ramírez family is representative of other Hispanic families there), intermarriage has, in fact, increased. Figure 14.6 shows intermarriage data in Hereford for three periods—1949–1957; 1979–1983; and 1997–1999. But how is it possible to know who assimilates when Melchior Romero Silerio marries Donna Sue Ballin?

Perhaps the best way to address this question is by examining Spanish-language retention rates. In 1990, 92 percent of Hereford's Hispanics spoke Spanish in the home and between 9 percent and 13 percent of Hispanics were married to non-Hispanics (Fig. 14.6). It can be assumed, therefore, that at least 5 percent of intermarried Hispanics retained Spanish. If the

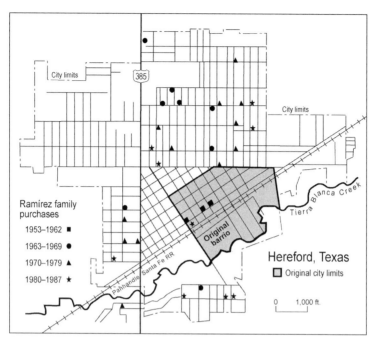

14.5.   Ramírez family real estate purchases, Hereford, Texas, 1953–1987. *Source: Deaf Smith County deed records.*

Hispanic partner continues to speak Spanish in the home, do the children learn Spanish and English? Does the non-Hispanic partner learn Spanish? It could be argued that since Spanish is the dominant language, Anglos may be learning more Spanish. This appears to be the case in Hereford.

I conducted a Spanish-language survey of non-Hispanics in the High Plains in 1990 and found that 76 percent had studied Spanish and more than half of Hereford's non-Hispanic population was able to identify 75 percent of the Spanish-language words in my survey. Without a detailed, longitudinal case study of intermarried couples in Hereford, it is difficult to come to any sort of conclusion, however, except that Hereford's Hispanics speak Spanish in the home at rates similar to those in the South Texas homeland (Arreola 2002). In fact, Hispanics on the High Plains call the area "the Little Valley of the North" because of its historical, cultural, and kinship links to a part of the South Texas homeland.

A MODEL OF HISPANIZATION

Many of the processes identified in Hereford appear throughout the United States, not only on the High Plains. I have found that immigration (entry), organization, occupational diversification, and social and political contesting occur in many new communities.

The first stage of Hispanization, entry, usually occurs when firms or farmers actively recruit Hispanics to address local labor shortages. The special needs of certain economic sectors—demanding physical labor, low wages, and seasonal employment—mean labor requirements cannot be met locally. Agricultural laborers are required in great numbers, but only for a short time. Meatpacking is low paying, dirty, and dangerous, and the new plants are impossible to staff with local labor because they are located in rural areas with small populations. In Hereford, entry began with the Bracero Program; in Lexington, Nebraska, it began with the construction of an IBP plant. Entry also establishes important kinship networks that provide the necessary migrant resources to maintain and reproduce the labor force.

Sometime after entry, Hispanics organize, often by establishing mutual aid societies (*mutualistas*). *Mutualistas* are locally run organizations that pool scarce resources to pay for such basic needs as baptisms, burials, medical assistance, and establishing residency (Valdés 1991: 21). Festivals such as Cinco de Mayo, Diez y Seis de Septiembre (Mexican Independence Day), and *jamaicas* (fairs) also create a nascent organizational structure. These holidays provide an opportunity for hard-working migrants to unwind, ex-

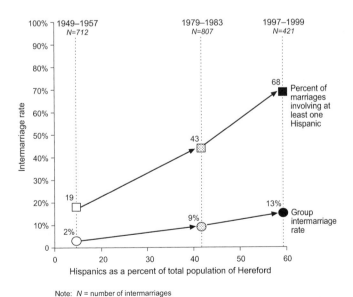

Note: *N* = number of intermarriages

14.6.   Intermarriage rate, Hereford, Texas, 1949–1999. *Source: Deaf Smith County marriage records.*

change information about home, and discuss current problems. Sommers (1991) describes how these celebrations symbolize and reinforce the threatened ethnicity of the Hispanic community, a threat that is common to new communities. Festivals also raise money that is used to support other organizations, such as the church or the educational system.

After Hispanic presence in a new community is established, Hispanics begin to search for and find higher-paying, permanent jobs to diversify their employment. However, low-wage, seasonal jobs must still be filled. Kinship networks come into play, and many jobs are filled by friends or relatives. Occupational diversification, the continual immigration of Hispanics, and higher birth rates among Hispanics mean that the Hispanic population grows at a faster rate than the non-Hispanic.

As the Hispanic population grows and diversifies economically, a Hispanic middle class develops that begins to challenge the Anglo power structure. Foley et al. (1988) describe in detail the Hispanic struggle for political representation in a discontinuous community in Texas. A necessary element of this challenge is the increasing proportion of Hispanics and their successful organization. Hispanics are found to attend city council and school board meetings to assert their need for more services. They establish other organizations, like LULAC (League of United Latin American Citizens) and the G.I. Forum, followed by more radical organizations such as the Raza Unida Party and the Political Association of Spanish-Speaking Organizations. Hispanic-Anglo power relations slowly begin to shift.

In Hereford, a similar pattern emerged. From the 1950s to the 1970s, Hereford Hispanics were deemed suitable only for low-wage labor. As they became more educated, pressed their political agenda, and began occupying professional positions in the community, the Anglo view of them shifted. It is during this period that intermarriage increased in Hereford. Eventually, political struggles may lead to an all-Hispanic school board, and Hispanics could gain control of the town's political infrastructure—a fifth stage of Hispanization called "dominance."

Hereford is a new community where assimilation pressures are greater and where Hispanics have never controlled the political infrastructure. Hereford's Hispanics do not yet possess the demographic, political, and economic power that has been achieved by Hispanics in other towns, but many of the same processes identified above are present in Hereford—entry, organization, occupational diversification, and political and social conflict. Dominance may never occur in Hereford, or any other new community, but if it does, many of the assumptions concerning assimilation, intermarriage, and residential segregation will need to be reassessed.

The landscape of Hereford and its society increasingly reflects the high percentage of Hispanics. Mexican food, Spanish-language newspapers and radio stations; Hispanic politicians, firefighters, police officers; and Hispanic-owned businesses are now common. Unless there is a fundamental shift in the present modes of production and in Hispanic birth rates, Hispanics will constitute 90 percent of Hereford's population by 2030. What will Hereford look like then? Will Anglo flight accelerate? Will Hereford be part of a "High Plains Hispanic Homeland"?

There are now over eleven towns and two counties on the High Plains that are majority Hispanic and many other counties and towns between 45 percent and 49 percent Hispanic. It is possible that we are witnessing the creation of a new Hispanic homeland. The towns of the Texas High Plains, like Hereford, are living laboratories for a number of the contemporary social, economic, demographic, and cultural issues facing Hispanic Americans.

REFERENCES

INTRODUCTION

Allen, James P., and Eugene James Turner. 1988. *We the People: An Atlas of America's Ethnic Diversity.* New York: Macmillan.

———. 1997. *The Ethnic Quilt: Population Diversity in Southern California.* Northridge: Center for Geographical Studies, California State University.

Arreola, Daniel D. 1981. "Fences as Landscape Taste: Tucson's *Barrios.*" *Journal of Cultural Geography* 2 (1): 96-105.

———. 1984. "Mexican American Exterior Murals." *Geographical Review* 74 (4): 409-424.

———. 1987. "The Mexican American Cultural Capital." *Geographical Review* 77 (1): 17-34.

———. 1988. "Mexican American Housescapes." *Geographical Review* 78 (3): 299-315.

———. 1992. "Plaza Towns of South Texas." *Geographical Review* 82 (1): 56-73.

———. 1993a. "Mexico Origins of South Texas Mexican Americans, 1930." *Journal of Historical Geography* 19 (1): 48-63.

———. 1993b. "Plazas of San Diego, Texas: Signatures of Mexican-American Place Identity." *Places: A Quarterly Journal of Environmental Design* 8 (3): 80-87.

———. 1993c. "The Texas-Mexican Homeland." *Journal of Cultural Geography* 13 (2): 61-74.

———. 1995. "Urban Ethnic Landscape Identity." *Geographical Review* 85 (4): 518-534.

———. 2000. "Mexican Americans." In *Ethnicity in Contemporary America: A Geographical Appraisal,* 2nd ed., ed. J. O. McKee, 111-138. Lanham, MD: Rowman and Littlefield.

———. 2001. "La Tierra Tejana: A South Texas Homeland." In *Homelands: A Geography of Culture and Place across America,* ed. R. L. Nostrand and L. E. Estaville, 101-124. Baltimore, MD: Johns Hopkins University Press.

———. 2002. *Tejano South Texas: A Mexican American Cultural Province.* Austin: University of Texas Press.

———, and Terrence W. Haverluk. 1996. "Mexikanische Amerikaner." *Geographische Rundschau* 48 (4): 213-219.

Bailey, Adrian J., and Mark Ellis. 1993. "Going Home: The Migration of Puerto Rican-Born Women from the United States to Puerto Rico." *Professional Geographer* 45 (2): 148-158.

Bailey, Adrian J., et al. 2002. "(Re)producing Salvadoran Transnational Geographies." *Annals of the Association of American Geographers* 92 (1): 125-144.

Berry, Kate A., and Martha L. Henderson, eds. 2002. *Geographical Identities of Ethnic America: Race, Space, and Place.* Reno: University of Nevada Press.

Boswell, Thomas D. 1976. "Residential Patterns of Puerto Ricans in New York City." *Geographical Review* 60 (1): 92–94.

———. 1979. "The Growth and Proportional Redistribution of the Mexican Stock Population in the United States: 1910–1970." *Mississippi Geographer* 6 (Spring): 57–76.

———. 1993. "The Cuban-American Homeland in Miami." *Journal of Cultural Geography* 13 (2): 133–148.

———. 2000. "Cuban Americans." In *Ethnicity in Contemporary America: A Geographical Appraisal*, 2nd ed., ed. J. O. McKee, 139–180. Lanham, MD: Rowman and Littlefield.

———, and Ángel David Cruz-Báez. 2000. "Puerto Ricans Living in the United States." In *Ethnicity in Contemporary America: A Geographical Appraisal*, 2nd ed., ed. J. O. McKee, 181–226. Lanham, MD: Rowman and Littlefield.

———, and James R. Curtis. 1984. *The Cuban-American Experience: Culture, Images, and Perspectives*. Totowa, NJ: Rowman and Allanheld.

Boswell, Thomas D.; Guarione M. Díaz; and Lisandro Pérez. 1982. "Socioeconomic Context of Cuban Americans." *Journal of Cultural Geography* 3 (1): 29–41.

Boswell, Thomas D., and Timothy C. Jones. 1980. "A Regionalization of Mexican Americans in the United States." *Geographical Review* 70 (1):87–98.

Broadbent, Elizabeth. 1941. "Mexican Population in Southwestern United States." *Texas Geographic Magazine* 5 (2): 16–24.

———. [1941] 1972. *The Distribution of Mexican Population in the United States*. San Francisco: A&E Research.

Carlson, Alvar W. 1973. "Seasonal Farm Labor in the San Luis Valley." *Annals of the Association of American Geographers* 63 (2): 97–108.

———. 1982. "A Cartographic Analysis of Latin American Immigrant Groups in the Chicago Metropolitan Area, 1965–76." *Revista Geográfica* 96 (July–Dec.): 91–106.

———. 1990. *The Spanish-American Homeland: Four Centuries in New Mexico's Río Arriba*. Baltimore, MD: Johns Hopkins University Press.

Clark, William. 2001. *Immigration and the Hispanic Middle Class*. Washington, DC: Center for Immigration Studies.

Cravey, Altha J. 1997. "Latino Labor and Poultry Production in Rural North Carolina." *Southeastern Geographer* 37 (2): 295–300.

Curtis, James R. 1980. "Miami's Little Havana: Yard Shrines, Cult Religion, and Landscape." *Journal of Cultural Geography* 1 (1): 1–15.

Dagodag, W. Tim. 1974. "Spatial Control and Public Policies: The Example of Mexican American Housing." *Professional Geographer* 26 (3): 262–269.

———. 1975. "Source Regions and Composition of Illegal Mexican Immigration to California." *International Migration Review* 9 (4): 499–511.

———. 1984. "Illegal Mexican Aliens in Los Angeles: Locational Characteristics." In *Patterns of Undocumented Migration: Mexico and the United States*, ed. R. C. Jones, 199–217. Totowa, NJ: Rowman and Allanheld.

Davis, Mike. 2000. *Magical Urbanism: Latinos Reinvent the US City*. London: Verso.

Flores, William V., and Rina Benmayor, eds. 1997. *Latino Cultural Citizenship: Claiming Identity, Space, and Rights*. Boston: Beacon Press.

Ford, Larry R., and Ernst Griffen. 1981. "Chicano Park: Personalizing an Institutional Landscape." *Landscape* 25 (2): 42–48.

Foulkes, Matt, and K. Bruce Newbold. 2000. "Migration Propensities, Patterns, and the Role of Human Capital: Comparing Mexican, Cuban, and Puerto Rican Interstate Migration, 1985–1990." *Professional Geographer* 52 (1): 133–144.

Godfrey, Brian J. 1985. "Ethnic Identities and Ethnic Enclaves: The Morphogenesis of San Francisco's Hispanic *Barrio*." *Yearbook, Conference of Latin Americanist Geographers* 11: 45–53.

———. 1988. *Neighborhoods in Transition: The Making of San Francisco's Ethnic and Nonconformist Communities*. University of California Publications in Geography 27. Berkeley & Los Angeles: University of California Press.

Gritzner, Charles F. 1974. "Hispano Gristmills in New Mexico." *Annals of the Association of American Geographers* 64 (4): 514–524.

———. 1990. "Log Barns of Hispanic New Mexico." *Journal of Cultural Geography* 10 (2): 21–34.

Gutiérrez, Phillip R. 1984. "The Channelization of Mexican Nationals to the San Luis Valley of Colorado." In *Patterns of Undocumented Migration: Mexico and the United States*, ed. R. C. Jones, 183–198. Totowa, NJ: Rowman and Allanheld.

Harner, John P. 1995. "Continuity amidst Change: Undocumented Mexican Migration to Arizona." *Professional Geographer* 47 (4): 399–411.

———. 2000. "The Mexican Community in Scottsdale, Arizona." In *Yearbook, Conference of Latin Americanist Geographers* 26, ed. D. J. Keeling, 29–46. Austin: University of Texas Press.

Haverluk, Terrence William. 1994. "A Descriptive Model for Understanding the Wider Distribution and Increasing Influence of Hispanics in the American West." Working Paper WP-04. San Antonio: Hispanic Research Center, University of Texas.

———. 1997. "The Changing Geography of U.S. Hispanics, 1850–1990." *Journal of Geography* 96 (May/June): 134–145.

———. 1998. "Hispanic Community Types and Assimilation in Mex-America." *Professional Geographer* 50 (4): 465–480.

Hayden, Dolores. 1995. *The Power of Place: Urban Landscapes as Public History*. Cambridge, MA: MIT Press.

Herzog, Lawrence A. 1986. "Mexican-Americans and the Evolution of the San Diego, California Built Environment." *Critica, a Journal of Critical Essays* 1 (3): 115–134.

Humphrey, Norman D. 1943. "The Migration and Settlement of Detroit Mexicans." *Economic Geography* 19 (4): 358–361.

Johnson, James H.; Karen D. Johnson-Webb; and Walter C. Farrell Jr. 1999. "Newly Emerging Hispanic Communities in the U.S.: A Spatial Analysis of Settlement Patterns, In-migration Fields, and Social Receptivity." In *Immigration and Opportunity: Race, Ethnicity and Employment in the United States*, ed. F. D. Bean and S. Bell-Rose, 263–310. New York: Russell Sage Foundation.

Johnson-Webb, Karen D. 2002. "Employer Recruitment and Hispanic Labor Migration: North Carolina Urban Areas at the End of the Millennium." *Professional Geographer* 54 (3): 406–421.

————, and James H. Johnson. 1996. "North Carolina Communities in Transition: The Hispanic Influx." *North Carolina Geographer* 5: 21–40.

Jokisch, Brad, and Jason Pribilsky. 2002. "The Panic to Leave: Economic Crisis and the 'New Emigration' from Ecuador." *International Migration* 40 (4): 75–99.

Jones, Richard C. 1982. "Channelization of Undocumented Mexican Migrants to the U.S." *Economic Geography* 58 (2): 156–176.

————. 1984. "Changing Patterns of Undocumented Mexican Migration to South Texas." *Social Science Quarterly* 65 (2): 465–481.

————. 1994. "Spatial Origins of San Antonio's Mexican American Population." Report RE-06. San Antonio: Hispanic Research Center, University of Texas.

Jordan, Terry G. 1982. "The 1887 Census of Texas' Hispanic Population." *Aztlán* 12 (2): 271–278.

Kanellos, Nicolás, ed. 1993. *Reference Library of Hispanic America*, 3 vols. Detroit: Gale Publishing.

Kent, Robert B., and Augusto F. Gandia-Ojeda. 1999. "The Puerto Rican Yard-Complex of Lorain, Ohio." In *Yearbook, Conference of Latin Americanist Geographers* 25, ed. C. Caviedes, 45–60. Austin: University of Texas Press.

Leclerc, Gustavo; Michael J. Dear; and J. Dallas Dishman, eds. 2000. *El Nuevo Mundo: The Landscape of Latino Los Angeles*. Photographs by Camilo José Vergara. Los Angeles: Southern California Studies Center, University of Southern California.

Leclerc, Gustavo; Raúl Villa; and Michael J. Dear, eds. 1999. *Urban Latino Cultures: La Vida Latina en L.A.* Thousand Oaks, CA: Sage Publications.

Manger, William F. 2000. "The 'Idealized' Mexican American Housescape." *Material Culture* 32 (1): 1–36.

McGlade, Michael S. 2002. "Mexican Farm Labor Networks and Population Increase in the Pacific Northwest." In *Yearbook, Association of Pacific Coast Geographers* 64, ed. D. Danta, 28–54. Honolulu: University of Hawaii Press.

McHugh, Kevin E. 1989. "Hispanic Migration and Population Redistribution in the United States." *Professional Geographer* 41 (4): 429–439.

————; Inés M. Miyares; and Emily H. Skop. 1997. "The Magnetism of Miami: Segmented Paths in Cuban Migration." *Geographical Review* 87 (4): 504–519.

McKee, Jesse O., ed. [1985] 2000. *Ethnicity in Contemporary America: A Geographical Appraisal*. Lanham, MD: Rowman and Littlefield.

Méndez, Noemi, and Inés M. Miyares. 1997. "Changing Landscapes and Immigration: The 'Mexicanization' of Sunset Park, Brooklyn Migration." In *From the Hudson to the Hamptons: Snapshots of the New York Metropolitan Area*, ed. I. M. Miyares, M. Pavlovskaya, and G. Pope, 102–107. Washington, DC: Association of American Geographers.

Miyares, Inés M., and Kenneth J. Gowen. 1998. "Recreating Borders? The Geography of Latin Americans in New York City." In *Yearbook, Conference of Latin Americanist Geographers* 24, ed. D. J. Keeling and J. Wiley, 31–43. Austin: University of Texas Press.

Moore, Joan, and Raquel Pinderhughes, eds. 1993. *In the Barrios: Latinos and the Underclass Debate*. New York: Russell Sage Foundation.

Mountz, Alison, and Richard A. Wright. 1996. "Daily Life in the Transnational Migrant Community of San Agustín, Oaxaca, and Poughkeepsie, New York." *Diaspora* 5 (3): 403–428.

Noble, Allen G., ed. 1992. *To Build in a New Land: Ethnic Landscapes in North America.* Baltimore, MD: Johns Hopkins University Press.

Nostrand, Richard L. 1970. "The Hispanic-American Borderland: Delimitation of an American Culture Region." *Annals of the Association of American Geographers* 60 (4): 638–661.

———. 1975. "Mexican Americans Circa 1850." *Annals of the Association of American Geographers* 65 (3): 378–390.

———. 1980. "The Hispano Homeland in 1900." *Annals of the Association of American Geographers* 70 (3): 382–396.

———. 1982. "El Cerrito Revisited." *New Mexico Historical Review* 57 (2): 109–122.

———. 1987. "The Century of Hispano Expansion." *New Mexico Historical Review* 62 (4): 361–386.

———. 1992. *The Hispano Homeland.* Norman: University of Oklahoma Press.

———. 1993. "The New Mexico–Centered Hispano Homeland." *Journal of Cultural Geography* 13 (2): 47–60.

———. 2001. "The Highland-Hispano Homeland." In *Homelands: A Geography of Culture and Place across America,* ed. R. L. Nostrand and L. E. Estaville, 155–167. Baltimore, MD: Johns Hopkins University Press.

———, and Lawrence E. Estaville, eds. 2001. *Homelands: A Geography of Culture and Place across America.* Baltimore, MD: Johns Hopkins University Press.

Novak, Robert T. 1956. "Distribution of Puerto Ricans on Manhattan Island." *Geographical Review* 46 (2): 182–186.

Romero, Mary; Pierrette Hondagneu-Sotelo; and Vilma Ortiz, eds. 1997. *Challenging Fronteras: Structuring Latina and Latino Lives in the U.S.: An Anthology of Readings.* New York: Routledge.

Ropka, Gerald W. 1975. *The Evolving Residential Pattern of the Mexican, Puerto Rican and Cuban Populations in the City of Chicago.* Ann Arbor, MI: University Microfilms.

Roseman, Curtis C., and J. Diego Vigil. 1993. "From Broadway to Latinoway." *Places: A Quarterly Journal of Environmental Design* 8 (3): 20–29.

Scheck, Ronald C. 1971. "Mexican-American Migration to Selected Texas Panhandle Urban Places." Discussion Paper No. 20. Columbus: Department of Geography, Ohio State University.

Skop, Emily, and Cecilia Menjívar. 2001. "Phoenix: The Newest Latino Immigrant Gateway?" In *Yearbook, Association of Pacific Coast Geographers* 63, ed. D. Danta, 63–76. Honolulu: University of Hawaii Press.

Smith, Jeffrey S. 1998. "Spanish-American Village Anatomy." *Geographical Review* 88 (3): 440–443.

———. 1999. "Anglo Intrusion on the Old Sangre de Cristo Land Grant." *Professional Geographer* 51 (2): 170–183.

———. 2000. "Los Hermanos Penitentes: An Illustrated Essay." *North American Geographer* 2 (1): 70–84.

———. 2002. "Cultural Landscape Change in a Hispanic Region." In *Geographical Identities of Ethnic America: Race, Space, and Place,* ed. K. A. Berry and M. L. Henderson, 174–200. Reno: University of Nevada Press.

———, et al. 2001. "La Cultura de la Acequia Madre: Cleaning a Community Irrigation Ditch." *North American Geographer* 3 (1): 5–28.

Suárez-Orozco, Marcelo M., and Mariela M. Páez, eds. 2002. *Latinos: Remaking America.* Berkeley & Los Angeles: University of California Press.

Thernstrom, Stephen, ed. 1980. *Harvard Encyclopedia of American Ethnic Groups.* Cambridge: Belknap Press of Harvard University Press.

Tovares, Carlos. 2001. "Urban Redevelopment and the Multicultural Politics of Public Space: The San Antonio, Texas Central Library." *North American Geographer* 3 (1): 63–91.

Usner, Don J. 1995. *Sabino's Map: Life in Chimayó's Old Plaza.* Santa Fe: Museum of New Mexico Press.

Valdez, Avelardo, and Richard C. Jones. 1984. "Geographical Patterns of Undocumented Mexicans and Chicanos in San Antonio, Texas: 1970 and 1980." In *Patterns of Undocumented Migration: Mexico and the United States,* ed. R. C. Jones, 218–235. Totowa, NJ: Rowman and Allanheld.

Veregge, Nina. 1993. "Transformations of Spanish Urban Landscapes in the American Southwest, 1821–1900." *Journal of the Southwest* 35 (4): 371–459.

Villa, Raúl Homero. 2000. *Barrio-Logos: Space and Place in Urban Chicano Literature and Culture.* Austin: University of Texas Press.

Ward, David. 1971. *Cities and Immigrants: A Geography of Change in Nineteenth-Century America.* New York: Oxford University Press.

Zecchi, Kristen Frances. 2002. "Creating Community: Marking Hispanic Identity in Chicago's Barrios." Master's thesis, University of Chicago.

Zelinsky, Wilbur. [1973] 1992. *The Cultural Geography of the United States,* rev. ed. Englewood Cliffs, NJ: Prentice Hall.

CHAPTER 1

Acuña, Rodolfo F. 1996. *Anything but Mexican: Chicanos in Contemporary Los Angeles.* London: Verso.

Allen, James P., and Eugene James Turner. 1988. *We the People: An Atlas of America's Ethnic Diversity.* New York: Macmillan.

———. 1997. *The Ethnic Quilt: Population Diversity in Southern California.* Northridge: Center for Geographical Studies, California State University.

———. 2002. *Changing Faces, Changing Places: Mapping Southern Californians.* Northridge: Center for Geographical Studies, California State University.

Arreola, Daniel D. 1995. "Mexican Texas: A Distinctive Borderland." In *A Geographic Glimpse of Central Texas and the Borderlands: Images and Encounters,* ed. J. F. Petersen and J. A. Tuason, 3–9. Indiana, PA: Pathways in Geography, National Council for Geographic Education.

———. 1997. "Hispanic American Capitals." In *Regional Geography of the United States and Canada,* 2nd ed., ed. T. L. McKnight, 44–46. Upper Saddle River, NJ: Prentice Hall.

———. 2000. "Mexican Americans." In *Ethnicity in Contemporary America: A Geographical Appraisal,* 2nd ed., ed. J. O. McKee, 111–138. Lanham, MD: Rowman and Littlefield.

———, and Terrence W. Haverluk. 1996. "Mexikanische Amerikaner." *Geographische Rundschau* 48 (4): 213–219.

Bachelis, Faren. 1990. *The Central Americans.* New York: Chelsea House Publishers.

Bailey, Adrian J., et al. 2002. "(Re)producing Salvadoran Transnational Geographies." *Annals of the Association of American Geographers* 92 (1): 125–144.

Bean, Frank D., and Marta Tienda. 1987. *The Hispanic Population of the United States*. New York: Russell Sage Foundation.

Boswell, Thomas D. 2000. "Cuban Americans." In *Ethnicity in Contemporary America: A Geographical Appraisal*, 2nd ed., ed. J. O. McKee, 139–180. Lanham, MD: Rowman and Littlefield.

————, and Ángel David Cruz-Báez. 2000. "Puerto Ricans Living in The United States." In *Ethnicity in Contemporary America: A Geographical Appraisal*, 2nd ed., ed. J. O. McKee, 181–226. Lanham, MD: Rowman and Littlefield.

Boswell, Thomas D., and James R. Curtis. 1984. *The Cuban-American Experience: Culture, Images and Perspectives*. Totowa, NJ: Rowman and Allanheld.

Boswell, Thomas D., and Emily Skop. 1995. *Hispanic National Groups in Metropolitan Miami*. Miami: Cuban American National Council.

Brewer, Cynthia A., and Trudy A. Suchan. 2001. *Mapping Census 2000: The Geography of U.S. Diversity*. Redlands, CA: ESRI Press.

Cardoso, Lawrence A. 1980. *Mexican Emigration to the United States, 1897–1931: Socio-Economic Patterns*. Tucson: University of Arizona Press.

Carlson, Alvar W. 1990. *The Spanish-American Homeland: Four Centuries in New Mexico's Río Arriba*. Baltimore, MD: Johns Hopkins University Press.

————. 1997. "A Geographical Analysis of America's Ethnic Radio Programming." *Social Science Journal* 34 (3): 285–295.

"Coming from the Americas: A Profile of the Nation's Foreign-Born Population from Latin America (2000 Update): Census Brief." 2002. *Current Population Survey*. Washington: U.S. Bureau of the Census.

Cullison, Alan. 1991. *The South Americans*. New York: Chelsea House Publishers.

Davis, Mike. 2000. *Magical Urbanism: Latinos Reinvent the US City*. London: Verso.

de la Garza, Rodolfo O., et al. 1992. *Latino Voices: Mexican, Puerto Rican, and Cuban Perspectives on American Politics*. Boulder, CO: Westview Press.

De León, Arnoldo. 1983. *They Called Them Greasers: Anglo Attitudes toward Mexicans in Texas, 1821–1900*. Austin: University of Texas Press.

del Pinal, Jorge, and Audrey Singer. 1997. "Generations of Diversity: Latinos in the United States." *Population Bulletin* 52 (3). Washington, DC: Population Reference Bureau.

Dwyer, Christopher. 1991. *The Dominican Americans*. New York: Chelsea House Publishers.

Fitzpatrick, Joseph P. 1987. *Puerto Rican Americans: The Meaning of Migration to the Mainland*. Englewood Cliffs, NJ: Prentice Hall.

Flores, William V., and Rina Benmayor. 1997. "Constructing Cultural Citizenship." In *Latino Cultural Citizenship: Claiming Identity, Space, and Rights*, ed. W. V. Flores and R. Benmayor, 1–23. Boston: Beacon Press.

Fox, Geoffrey. 1997. *Hispanic Nation: Culture, Politics, and the Construction of Identity*. Tucson: University of Arizona Press.

Gann, L. H., and Peter J. Duignan. 1986. *The Hispanics in the United States: A History*. Boulder, CO: Westview Press.

Georges, Eugenia. 1990. *The Making of a Transnational Community: Migration, De-*

velopment, and Cultural Change in the Dominican Republic. New York: Columbia University Press.

González, David. 1992. "What's the Problem with 'Hispanic'? Just Ask a 'Latino.'" New York Times (Nov. 15): E6.

Granados, Christine. 2000. "Hispanic vs Latino." Hispanic (Dec.): 40–42.

Grasmuck, Sherri, and Patricia Pessar. 1991. Between Two Islands: Dominican International Migration. Berkeley & Los Angeles: University of California Press.

Grebler, Leo; Joan W. Moore; and Ralph C. Guzmán. 1970. The Mexican-American People: The Nation's Second Largest Minority. New York: The Free Press.

Guarnizo, Luis E. 1997. "Los Dominicanyorks: The Making of a Binational Society." In Challenging Fronteras: Structuring Latina and Latino Lives in the U.S.: An Anthology of Readings, ed. M. Romero, P. Hondagneu-Sotelo, and V. Ortiz, 161–174. New York: Routledge.

Guzmán, Betsy. 2001. "The Hispanic Population." Census 2000 Brief. Washington: U.S. Bureau of the Census. http://www.census.gov/prod/2001pubs/C2kbr01-3.pdf

Hamilton, Nora, and Norma Stoltz Chinchilla. 1991. "Central American Migration: A Framework for Analysis." Latin American Research Review 26 (1): 75–110.

———. 2001. Seeking Community in a Global City: Guatemalans and Salvadorans in Los Angeles. Philadelphia: Temple University Press.

Hart, Dianne Walta. 1997. Undocumented in L.A.: An Immigrant's Story. Wilmington, DE: Scholarly Resources.

Haslip-Viera, Gabriel, and Sherrie L. Baver, eds. 1996. Latinos in New York: Communities in Transition. Notre Dame, IN: University of Notre Dame Press.

Haverluk, Terrence W. 1998. "Hispanic Community Types and Assimilation in Mex-America." Professional Geographer 50 (4): 465–480.

Hendricks, Glen. 1974. The Dominican Diaspora: From the Dominican Republic to New York City—Villagers in Transition. New York: Teachers College Press.

Hernández, Ramona, and Silvio Torres-Saillant. 1996. "Dominicans in New York: Men, Women, and Prospects." In Latinos in New York: Communities in Transition, ed. G. Haslip-Viera and S. L. Baver, 30–56. Notre Dame, IN: University of Notre Dame Press.

"Hispanics Now Largest Minority Group." 2003. Arizona Republic (June 19): A2.

Jokisch, Brad D. 1997. "From Labor Circulation to International Migration: The Case of South Ecuador." In Yearbook, Conference of Latin Americanist Geographers 23, ed. D. J. Robinson and C. E. Doenges, 63–75. Austin: University of Texas Press.

———, and Jason Pribilsky. 2002. "The Panic to Leave: Economic Crisis and the 'New Emigration' from Ecuador." International Migration 40 (4): 75–99.

Jones, Richard C. 1989. "Causes of Salvadoran Migration to the United States." Geographical Review 79 (2): 183–194.

Kent, Robert B., and Maura E. Huntz. 1996. "Spanish-Language Newspapers in the United States." Geographical Review 86 (3): 446–456.

Larmer, Brook. 1999. "Latino America." Newsweek (July 12): 48–51.

Lipski, John M. 1993. "Language." In The Hispanic-American Almanac: A Reference Work on Hispanics in the United States, ed. N. Kanellos, 209–227. Detroit: Gale Research.

López, David E.; Eric Popkin; and Edward Telles. 1996. "Central Americans: At the Bottom, Struggling to Get Ahead." In *Ethnic Los Angeles,* ed. R. Waldinger and M. Bozorgmehr, 279–304. New York: Russell Sage Foundation.

McGlade, Michael S. 2002. "Mexican Farm Labor Networks and Population Increase in the Pacific Northwest." In *Yearbook, Association of Pacific Coast Geographers* 64, ed. D. Danta, 28–54. Honolulu: University of Hawaii Press.

McHugh, Kevin E.; Inés M. Miyares; and Emily H. Skop. 1997. "The Magnetism of Miami: Segmented Paths in Cuban Migration." *Geographical Review* 87 (4): 504–519.

McWilliams, Carey. [1948] 1968. *North from Mexico: The Spanish-Speaking People of the United States.* New York: Greenwood Press.

Martínez, Rubén. 2001. *Crossing Over: A Mexican Family on the Migrant Trail.* New York: Metropolitan Books.

Menjívar, Cecilia. 2000. *Fragmented Ties: Salvadoran Immigrant Networks in America.* Berkeley & Los Angeles: University of California Press.

Miyares, Inés M., and Kenneth J. Gowen 1998. "Recreating Borders? The Geography of Latin Americans in New York City." In *Yearbook, Conference of Latin Americanist Geographers* 24, ed. D. J. Keeling and J. Wiley, 31–43. Austin: University of Texas Press.

Monroy, Douglas. 1990. *Thrown among Strangers: The Making of Mexican Culture in Frontier California.* Berkeley & Los Angeles: University of California Press.

Moore, Joan, and Raquel Pinderhughes, eds. 1993. *In the Barrios: Latinos and the Underclass Debate.* New York: Russell Sage Foundation.

National Directory of Latino Elected Officials (NALEO) 2000. *2000 National Directory of Latino Elected Officials.* Los Angeles: National Association of Latino Elected and Appointed Officials.

Nostrand, Richard L. 1970. "The Hispanic-American Borderland: Delimitation of an American Culture Region." *Annals of the Association of American Geographers* 60 (4): 638–661.

———. 1992. *The Hispano Homeland.* Norman: University of Oklahoma Press.

———. 2001. "The Highland-Hispano Homeland." In *Homelands: A Geography of Culture and Place across America,* ed. R. L. Nostrand and L. E. Estaville, 155–167. Baltimore, MD: Johns Hopkins University Press.

Oboler, Suzanne. 1997. " 'So Far from God, So Close to the United States': The Roots of Hispanic Homogenization." In *Challenging Fronteras: Structuring Latina and Latino Lives in the U.S.: An Anthology of Readings,* ed. M. Romero, P. Hondagneu-Sotelo, and V. Ortiz, 31–54. New York: Routledge.

Oleksak, Michael, and Mary Adams Oleksak. 1991. *Béisbol: Latin Americans and the Grand Old Game.* Grand Rapids, MI: Masters Press.

" 'Other Spanish' Led to Census Missteps." 2002. *Arizona Republic* (May 11): A10.

Padilla, Félix M. 1987. *Puerto Rican Chicago.* Notre Dame, IN: University of Notre Dame Press.

Portes, Alejandro, and Alex Stepick. 1993. *City on the Edge: The Transformation of Miami.* Berkeley & Los Angeles: University of California Press.

Reisler, Mark. 1976. *By the Sweat of Their Brow: Mexican Immigrant Labor in the United States, 1900–1940.* Westport, CT: Greenwood Press.

Rodríguez, Richard. 2002. *Brown: The Last Discovery of America.* New York: Viking.

Rosales, F. Arturo. 1999. ¡Pobre Raza!: Violence, Justice, and Mobilization among México Lindo Immigrants, 1900–1936. Austin: University of Texas Press.

Roseman, Curtis C. 2002. "The Changing Ethnic Map of the United States." In Geographical Identities of Ethnic America: Race, Space, and Place, ed. K. A. Berry and M. L. Henderson, 15–37. Reno: University of Nevada Press.

Shorris, Earl. 1992a. "Latino, Sí. Hispanic, No." New York Times (Oct. 28): E3.

———. 1992b. Latinos: A Biography of the People. New York: W. W. Norton.

Silva-Corvalán, C. 1994. Language Contact and Change: Spanish in Los Angeles. New York: Oxford University Press.

Skop, Emily. 1997. "Hispanic or Latino? The Geography of Words." Unpublished manuscript.

Stavans, Ilan. 2001. The Hispanic Condition: The Power of a People. 2nd ed. New York: Rayo.

"Strike Would Hit Dominican Economy Hard." 2002. USA Today (Aug. 29): C1.

Suro, Roberto. 2002. "Counting the 'Other Hispanics': How Many Colombians, Dominicans, Ecuadorians, Guatemalans and Salvadorans Are There in the United States?" Washington, DC: Pew Hispanic Center (May). http://www.pewhispanic.org/site/docs/pdf/other_Hispanics.pdf

———, and Audrey Singer. 2002. "Latino Growth in Metropolitan America: Changing Patterns, New Locations." Washington, DC: Brookings Institution Survey Series (July).

Therrien, Melissa, and Roberto R. Ramírez. 2001. "The Hispanic Population in the United States: Population Characteristics." Current Population Reports. Washington, DC: U.S. Bureau of the Census. http://www.census.gov/prod/2001pubs/p20-535.pdf

U.S. Bureau of the Census. 1990. Census of Population and Housing. Summary Tape Files 1C and 3C. Washington, DC.

———. 2000. 2000 Census. Summary File 1. Washington, DC.

Valdés, M. Isabel, and Marta H. Seoane. 1997. Hispanic Market Handbook: The Definitive Source for Reaching This Lucrative Segment of American Consumers. New York: Gale Research.

Waldinger, Roger, and Mehdi Bozorgmehr, eds. 1996. Ethnic Los Angeles. New York: Russell Sage Foundation.

Zentella, Ana Celia. 2002. "Latin@ Languages and Identities." In Latinos: Remaking America, ed. M. M. Suárez-Orozco and M. M. Páez, 297–315. Berkeley & Los Angeles: University of California Press.

CHAPTER 2

Andrés, Benny J., Jr. 2000. "La Plaza Vieja (Old Town Albuquerque): The Transformation of a Hispano Village, 1880s–1950s." In The Contested Homeland: A Chicano History of New Mexico, ed. E. Gonzales-Berry and D. R. Maciel, 239–268. Albuquerque: University of New Mexico Press.

Arrellano, Anselmo. 1996. "Nuestra Señora de los Dolores de Las Vegas Grandes." In Las Vegas–San Miguel County, New Mexico: The Official Visitor's Guide, ed. L. Flores Fenzi, 4–7. Las Vegas, NM: Las Vegas/San Miguel Conference and Visitor's Bureau.

Arreola, Daniel D. 1992. "Plaza Towns of South Texas." Geographical Review 82 (1): 56–73.

————. 1993. "Plazas of San Diego, Texas: Signatures of Mexican-American Place Identity." *Places: A Quarterly Journal of Environmental Design* 8 (3): 80–87.

Bressi, Todd W. 1993. "Plaza, Parque, Colonia." *Places: A Quarterly Journal of Environmental Design* 8 (3): 91–93.

Campbell, Clay, and Jim Strozier. 1996. "Las Vegas (New Mexico) Community Master Plan." *The Western Planner* 17 (7): 17–19.

Carlson, Alvar W. 1990. *The Spanish-American Homeland: Four Centuries in New Mexico's Río Arriba*. Baltimore, MD: Johns Hopkins University Press.

Citizens' Committee for Historic Preservation (CCHP). 1999. *Historic Las Vegas, New Mexico: Along the Santa Fe Trail* (pamphlet). Las Vegas, NM: Las Vegas/San Miguel County Chamber of Commerce.

Crouch, Dora P.; Daniel J. Garr; and Axel I. Mundigo. 1982. *Spanish City Planning in North America*. Cambridge, MA: MIT Press.

Cullen, Bradley T. 1992. "What Has Happened to the 'City Different'? A Santa Fe Case Study." *Papers and Proceedings of the Applied Geography Conferences* 15 (1): 75–84.

de Borhegyi, Stephan F. 1954. "The Evolution of a Landscape." *Landscape* 4 (2): 24–30.

Fugate, Francis L., and Roberta B. Fugate. 1989. *Roadside History of New Mexico*. Missoula, MT: Mountain Press Publishing.

Garduño, Lorraine E. 2001. Zoning/licensing coordinator, City of Las Vegas, NM, interview, Apr. 3.

Gottschalk, Marcus C. 2000. *Pioneer Merchants of the Las Vegas Plaza*. Las Vegas, NM: M. C. Gottschalk.

Huchmala, John A. 2002. Personal correspondence from property manager, Archdiocese of Santa Fe. March 20.

Jackson, John B. 1952. "Village Types in the Southwest." *Landscape* 2 (2): 14–19.

————. 1988. "Images of the New Mexico Plaza." *El Palacio* 94 (2): 20–30.

Knowlton, Clark S. 1969. "Changing Spanish-American Village of Northern New Mexico." *Sociology and Social Research: An International Journal* 53 (4): 455–474.

Las Vegas Including East Las Vegas and Montezuma, San Miguel County, New Mexico. 1883. New York: Sanborn Map Co.

Las Vegas Including East Las Vegas and Montezuma, San Miguel County, New Mexico. 1898. New York: Sanborn Map Co.

Las Vegas Including East Las Vegas and Montezuma, San Miguel County, New Mexico. 1930. New York: Sanborn Map Co.

Low, Setha M. 2000. *On the Plaza: The Politics of Public Space and Culture*. Austin: University of Texas Press.

Meinig, Donald W. 1971. *Southwest: Three Peoples in Geographical Change, 1600–1970*. New York: Oxford University Press.

Morley, Judy M. 1999. "Albuquerque, New Mexico, or Anywhere, USA?: Historic Preservation and the Construction of Civic Identity." *New Mexico Historical Review* 74 (2): 155–178.

Mulligan, Linda W. 1992. "Santa Fe, New Mexico: Place of Style and Postmodern Transformation." In *Geographical Snapshots of North America*, ed. D. G. Janelle, 313–316. New York: Guilford Press.

Nestor, Sarah. 1988. "Letter from the Editor." *El Palacio* 94 (2): 3.

Nostrand, Richard L. 1992. *The Hispano Homeland*. Norman: University of Oklahoma Press.

Rodríguez, Sylvia. 1998. "Fiesta Time and Plaza Space: Resistance and Accommodation in a Tourist Town." *Journal of American Folklore* 111 (439): 39–56.

Romero, Levi. 2001. "La Nueva Resolana: Norteños Find Respite in New Gathering Places." *New Mexico Magazine* 79 (5): 26–31.

Romero de Herrera, Flora F. 2002. Marquez, New Mexico, native, telephone interview, Feb. 18.

Smith, Jeffrey S. 1998. "Spanish-American Village Anatomy." *Geographical Review* 88 (3): 440–443.

Suisman, Douglas R. 1993. "Plaza Mexicana." *Places: A Quarterly Journal of Environmental Design* 8 (3): 4–19.

Vander Meer, Sharon. 1999. *Las Vegas & San Miguel County: The Official 1999-2000 Tourism and Relocation Guide*. Albuquerque: Legacy Publishing.

———. 2001. Representative of the Las Vegas/San Miguel County, NM, Chamber of Commerce, interview, Apr. 3.

Veregge, Nina. 1997. "Traditional Elements and the New Urbanism: A Regional and Historical Critique." *Traditional Dwellings and Settlements Review* 8 (2): 49–62.

Weigle, Marta, and Kyle Fiore. 1982. *Santa Fe and Taos: The Writer's Era 1916-1941*. Santa Fe, NM: Ancient City Press.

Wilson, Chris. 1994. "Spatial Mestizaje on the Pueblo-Hispanic-Anglo Frontier." *MASS: Journal of the School of Architecture and Planning, University of New Mexico* 10 (1): 40–49.

———. 2001. *Doña Ana Plaza Plan*. Albuquerque: Center for Regional Studies, University of New Mexico.

CHAPTER 3

Abrahamson, Mark. 1996. *Urban Enclaves: Identity and Place in America*. New York: St. Martin's Press.

Adams, John. 2000. Director, Laredo Development Foundation, interview, Dec. 14.

Arreola, Daniel. 2002. *Tejano South Texas: A Mexican American Cultural Province*. Austin: University of Texas Press.

———, and James R. Curtis. 1993. *The Mexican Border Cities: Landscape Anatomy and Place Personality*. Tucson: University of Arizona Press.

Beasley, Eleanor. 1981. "City of Laredo Cultural Resources Survey." Typescript. Laredo, TX: Webb County Heritage Foundation.

Calderón, Roberto. 1993. "Mexican Politics in the American Era, 1846-1900: Laredo, Texas." PhD diss., University of California at Los Angeles.

City of Laredo. *See* Laredo, City of.

Cowley, Jennifer S., and Dana M. Pechacek. 2001. "Real Estate Market Overview: Laredo." College Station: Texas A&M University, Real Estate Center. http://www.recenter.tamu.edu [Accessed June 23, 2002]

Davis, Mike 2000. *Magical Urbanism: Latinos Reinvent the US City*. London: Verso.

De León, José María 2002. Owner of Laredo customs brokerage/freight forwarding business, interview, Mar. 1.

Demographia. 1999. http://www.demographia.com [Accessed May 30, 2002]

Devine, Ella. 1967. "Laredo Electric Railway Company." *Southern Traction Annals* (Apr. 28).

"Eastern Division Research." 1981. Typescript. Laredo, TX: Webb County Heritage Foundation.

Everitt, James H., and D. Lynn Draw. 1993. *Trees, Shrubs and Cacti of South Texas.* Lubbock: Texas Tech University Press.

Giermanski, James R. 1997. "NAFTA and the South Texas Border: Is the Border Fit to Compete?" *Journal of the Southwest* 39 (2): 287–302.

———. 1998. Professor of transportation logistics, Texas A&M International University, interview, Nov. 4.

Guajardo, Luciano. 1981. Typescript of 1980 interview. Laredo, TX: Webb County Heritage Foundation.

Guerra, Joe. 2002. Councilmember, City of Laredo, TX, interview, May 17.

Guide to Laredo Air Force Base. N.d. N.p.

Herrera, Velia. 2002. Administrative assistant, KGNS Television, Laredo, TX, interview, May 17.

Klein, Alan M. 1997. *Baseball on the Border: A Tale of Two Laredos.* Princeton, NJ: Princeton University Press.

Laredo, City of. 1996. *Historic Preservation Plan.*

———. Department of Planning and Zoning. 1998. *1998 Median Household Income by Traffic Analysis Zone (TAZ).*

Laredo Development Foundation (LDF). 2000a. *Los Laredos: Trade Center of the Americas.* Laredo, TX: Laredo Development Foundation.

———. 2000b. "Major Employers." http://www.laredo-ldf.com/lp11.htm [Accessed May 12, 2002]

———. 2001. *Maquiladora Plants in Los Dos Laredos.* Laredo, TX: Laredo Development Foundation.

———. 2002. "Major Employers." http://www.laredo-ldf.com/images/page33 .html [Accessed May 12, 2002]

Love and Duggan Real Estate Consultants and Appraisers. 1989. *Fair Market Value Appraisal Twelve Improved and Unimproved Blocks Located in or Adjacent to the Azteca District of Laredo, Webb County, Texas.* Laredo, TX: Webb County General Services Administration.

Moore, Steven A. 1996. "Critical and Sustainable Regions in Architecture: The Case of Blueprint Demonstration Farm." PhD diss., Texas A&M University.

Myers, Terri. 2000. *Historic Resources Survey of the El Azteca Neighborhood, Laredo, Texas: An Inventory and Survey Report Prepared for the City of Laredo, June 2000.* Austin, TX: Hardy Heck Moore and Myers.

Pacione, Michael. 2001. *Urban Geography: A Global Perspective.* London: Routledge.

The Real Estate Source: Laredo's Catalog of Homes. 2002. Various issues.

Rust, Carol. 1993. "Colonias." *Houston Chronicle,* magazine supplement, Texas (July 25).

Shanks, Ann. 1993. "The Heights." Typescript. Laredo, TX: Webb County Heritage Foundation.

Smith, Amy Erika. 2000. "Challenges and Opportunities for Development of Jobs in the Colonias of Webb County." Unpublished manuscript, Texas A&M University Colonias Program.

Texas Center and Laredo Chamber of Commerce. 2002. *Vision 2002: Economic Outlook Report*. Laredo, TX: Texas A&M International University.

Texas Workforce Commission. 2000. Laredo MSA, http://204.65.3.20/lmi/texasjs/areprofiledata.asp?session=area&geo=4802004080 [Accessed May 12, 2002]

Thompson, Jerry 1986. *Laredo, TX: A Pictorial History*. Norfolk, VA: Donning Co.

U.S. Bureau of the Census. 1992. *Census of Population: 1990*. Washington, DC.

———. 2000. *Census of Population: 2000*. Preliminary data. http://www.census.gov/main/www/cen2000.html.

Valdez, Avelardo 1993. "Persistent Poverty, Crime, and Drugs: U.S.-Mexican Border Region." In *In the Barrios: Latinos and the Underclass. Debate*, ed. J. Moore and R. Pinderhughes, 173–194. New York: Russell Sage Foundation.

Ward, Peter. 1999. *Colonias and Public Policy in Texas and Mexico: Urbanization by Stealth*. Austin: University of Texas Press.

"Warehouses Are Booming in Laredo." 2000. *Wall Street Journal* (Sept. 13).

Wilson, Patricia Ann. 1992. *Exports and Local Development: Mexico's New Maquiladoras*. Austin: University of Texas Press.

Yoder, Michael, and Michael Pisani. Forthcoming. "Overshadowed by International Trade: The Uncertainty of Maquiladoras in Laredo-Nuevo Laredo." In *The Geography of the Maquiladora Industry of the U.S.-Mexico Border*, ed. O. Verkoren. Utrecht, Netherlands: Utrecht University.

CHAPTER 4

Alejandrino, Simon V. 2000. "Gentrification in San Francisco's Mission District: Indicators and Policy Recommendations." Mimeograph. San Francisco: Mission Economic Development Corporation, Summer.

Ancona, George. 1998. *Barrio: José's Neighborhood*. San Diego: Harcourt Brace and Company.

Apartment Association of San Francisco. 2002. Telephone interview, May 10.

Arrieta, R. M. 2001a. "Single Room Occupancy Hotels: Unsafe and Unhealthy." *El Tecolote* (June 3): 16.

———. 2001b. "Single Room Occupancy Hotels: Part 2." *El Tecolote* (July 3): 20.

Bay Area Economics (BAE). 2002. "San Francisco Housing Databook." Mimeograph.

Castells, Manuel. 1983. *The City and the Grassroots: A Cross-Cultural Theory of Urban Social Movements*. Berkeley & Los Angeles: University of California Press.

Collins, Chris. 2002. "Carnaval 2002 King and Queen." *New Mission News* (May 6).

Curtis, Mary. 1999. "New Money Driving Out Working-Class in San Francisco." *Los Angeles Times* (June 21): A1, A16.

Garofoli, Joe. 2002. "Mission Divided." *San Francisco Chronicle* (July 8): A1, A10.

Godfrey, Brian J. 1988. *Neighborhoods in Transition: The Making of San Francisco's Ethnic and Nonconformist Communities*. Berkeley & Los Angeles: University of California Press.

———. 1997. "Urban Development and Redevelopment in San Francisco." *Geographical Review* 87 (3): 310–333.

Helfand, Glen. 2002. "The Mission School: San Francisco's Street Artists Deliver

Their Neighborhood to the Art World." *San Francisco Bay Guardian* (Apr. 10): 31–34.

Kim, Ryan. 2002. "Planners Look Hard at San Francisco's East Flank." *San Francisco Chronicle* (Mar. 30): A13, A16.

KQED. 1994. *Hidden Cities of San Francisco: The Mission.*

Levine, M. Toby. 2000. "Planning Our History and the History of Planning in the Mission." *New Mission News* (Oct. 8).

López, Albertina. 2002. Salvadoran immigrant, interview, San Francisco, May 7.

Metrorent. 2002. Telephone interview, Apr. 15.

Mele, Christopher. 2000. *Selling the Lower East Side: Culture, Real Estate and Resistance in New York City.* Minneapolis: University of Minnesota Press.

Mission Anti-Displacement Coalition. 2002. "The Hidden Costs of the New Economy: A Study of the Northeast Mission Industrial Zone." http://www.uncanny .net/~wetzel/macreport.htm

Nieves, Evelyn. 1999. "In Old Mission District, Changing Grit to Gold." *New York Times* (Jan. 21): A11.

———. 2000. "Mission District Fights Case of Dot-Com Fever." *New York Times on the Web* (Nov. 5). http://www.nytimes.com/2000/1//05/technology.htm

"Open Homes." 2002. *San Francisco Chronicle* (May 5): 22.

Rowen, Angela, and Gabriel Roth. 1998. "The Mission: Lofts and Lattes." *San Francisco Bay Guardian* (Oct. 7): 20.

San Francisco. Department of City Planning. 1994. *Mission District Ten Year Neighborhood Plan, 1994–2004.* City and County of San Francisco.

———. 2002. *Profile of Community Planning Agencies: San Francisco's Eastern Neighborhoods.* San Francisco: Reproduction Bureau and Mail Services.

San Francisco. Residential Rent Stabilization and Arbitration Board. 2001. "Rent Board Statistical Summary." Mimeograph.

San Francisco Association of Realtors. 2002. Computer printout of housing costs.

Solnit, Rebecca. 2000. *Hollow City: The Siege of San Francisco and the Crisis of American Urbanism.* London: Verso.

Sommers, L. K. 1986. "Alegría in the Streets: Latino Cultural Performance in San Francisco." PhD diss., University of Michigan.

Suttles, Gerald D. 1972. *The Social Construction of Communities.* Chicago: University of Chicago Press.

U.S. Bureau of the Census. 1952. *Census of Population: 1950. Census Tract Statistics, San Francisco–Oakland California and Adjacent Area.* Vol. III, Chap. 49. Washington, DC.

———. 1961. *Census of the Population and Housing: 1960. Census Tracts, San Francisco–Oakland, Calif. Standard Metropolitan Statistical Area.* Washington, DC.

———. 1972. *Census of the Population and Housing 1970. Census Tracts, San Francisco–Oakland, Calif. Standard Metropolitan Statistical Area.* Washington, DC.

———. 1981. *1980 Census of the Population and Housing. Census Tracts, San Francisco–Oakland, Calif. Standard Metropolitan Statistical Area.* Washington, DC.

———. 1993. *1990 Census of the Population and Housing, California.* Washington, DC.

———. 2000. *Census 2000.* Summary File 1. Washington, DC. http://factfinder .census.gov

Willliams, Bruce. 2001. "Census Surprise: Diversity Survives." *New Mission News* (Sep. 1): 4.

Zukin, Sharon. 1982. *Loft Living: Culture and Capital in Urban Change.* New Brunswick, NJ: Rutgers University Press.

CHAPTER 5

American Institute of Architects (AIA). 1988. *Adelante San Ysidro.* San Diego: AIA.

Arreola, Daniel D. 1984. "Mexican American Exterior Murals." *Geographical Review* 74 (4): 409–424.

———. 1988. "Mexican American Housescapes." *Geographical Review* 78 (3): 299–315.

———. 1995. "Urban Ethnic Landscape Identity." *Geographical Review* 85 (4): 518–534.

———. 2001. "Curio Consumerism and Kitsch Culture in the Mexican-American Borderland." *Journal of the West* 40 (2): 24–31.

Banham, Reyner. 1971. *Los Angeles: The Architecture of Four Ecologies.* New York: Penguin.

Barrera, Mario, and Marilyn Mumford, 1988. "Chicano Park." Video documentary. New York: Cinema Guild.

Britton, Stephen. 1982. "The Political Economy of Tourism in the Third World." *Annals of Tourism Research* 9: 331–358.

Camarillo, Albert. 1979. *Chicanos in a Changing Society: From Mexican Pueblos to American Barrios in Santa Barbara and Southern California, 1848-1930.* Cambridge: Harvard University Press.

De Kadt, Emanuel, ed. 1979. *Tourism: Passport to Development?* Oxford: Oxford University Press.

de la Garza, Rodolfo, and Claudio Vargas. 1992. "The Mexican Origin Population of the United States As a Political Force in the Borderlands: From Paisanos to Pochos to Potential Allies." In *Changing Boundaries in the Americas,* ed. L. A. Herzog, 89–111. La Jolla: Center for U.S.-Mexican Studies, University of California.

Eckbo, Garrett. 1969. "The Landscape of Tourism." *Landscape* 18: 29–31.

Ford, Larry, and Ernst Griffin. 1981. "Chicano Park: Personalizing an Institutional Landscape." *Landscape* 25: 2–48.

García, Mario. 1981. *Desert Immigrants: The Mexicans of El Paso, 1880-1920.* New Haven, CT: Yale University Press.

Griswold del Castillo, Richard. 1978. *The Los Angeles Barrio, 1850-1890: A Social History.* Berkeley & Los Angeles: University of California Press.

Herzog, Lawrence A. 1990. *Where North Meets South: Cities, Space, and Politics on the U.S.-Mexico Border.* Austin: University of Texas Press.

———. 1999. *From Aztec to High Tech: Architecture and Landscape across the Mexico-United States Border.* Baltimore, MD: Johns Hopkins University Press.

Jenkins, C. L. 1982. "The Effect of Scale in Tourism Projects in Developing Countries." *Annals of Tourism Research* 9: 229–249.

Juárez, Richard. 2002. President, Urban West Consultants, San Diego, CA, field interview, July 25.

Kowinski, William. 1985. *The Malling of America.* New York: Morrow and Co.

O'Connor, Anne Marie. 2002. "Seduction of a Generation." *Los Angeles Times Magazine* (July 28): 10–13, 31–32.

Paz, Octavio. 1961. *The Labyrinth of Solitude*. New York: Grove Press.

Relph, Edward. 1987. *The Modern Urban Landscape*. Baltimore, MD: Johns Hopkins University Press.

Ritzer, George. 1996. *The McDonaldization of Society*. Thousand Oaks, CA: Pine Forge Press.

Romo, Ricardo. 1983. *East Los Angeles: History of a Barrio*. Austin: University of Texas Press.

Sassen, Saskia. 1991. *The Global City*. Princeton, NJ: Princeton University Press.

———. 1998. *Globalization and Its Discontents*. New York: The New Press.

Sheridan, Thomas E. 1986. *Los Tucsonenses: The Mexican Community of Tucson, 1854–1941*. Tucson: University of Arizona Press.

Sklair, Leslie. 1991. *Sociology of the Global System*. Baltimore, MD: Johns Hopkins University Press.

———. 1994. *Assembling for Development*. La Jolla, CA: Center for U.S.-Mexican Studies.

Urry, John. 1990. *The Tourist Gaze*. London: Sage.

Villa, Raúl Homero. 2000. *Barrio-Logos: Space and Place in Urban Chicano Literature and Culture*. Austin: University of Texas Press.

CHAPTER 6

Acuña, Rodolfo F. 1984. *A Community under Siege: A Chronicle of Chicanos East of the Los Angeles River 1945–1975*. Monograph No. 11. Los Angeles: Chicano Studies Research Center Publications, University of California at Los Angeles.

Allen, James P., and Eugene Turner. 1997. *The Ethnic Quilt: Population Diversity in Southern California*. Northridge: Center for Geographical Studies, California State University.

Arreola, Daniel D. 1988. "Mexican American Housescapes." *Geographical Review* 78: (3) 229–315.

———. 2000. "Mexican Americans." In *Ethnicity in Contemporary America: A Geographical Appraisal*, 2nd ed. J. O. McKee, 111–138. Lanham, MD: Rowman and Littlefield.

Bluestone, Barry, and Bennett Harrison. 1982. *The Deindustrialization of America*. New York: Basic Books.

Brodsly, David. 1981. *L.A. Freeway: An Appreciative Essay*. Berkeley & Los Angeles: University of California Press.

Davis, Mike. 1994. "The Empty Quarter." In *Sex, Death and God in L.A.*, ed. D. Reid, 54–71. Berkeley & Los Angeles: University of California Press.

Donahoe, Myrna Cherkoss. 1987. "Workers' Response to Plant Closures: The Cases of Steel and Auto in Southeast Los Angeles, 1935–1986." PhD diss., University of California, Irvine.

Griswold del Castillo, Richard. 1979. *The Los Angeles Barrio, 1850–1890: A Social History*. Berkeley & Los Angeles: University of California Press.

Hise, Greg. 2001. " 'Nature's Workshop': Industry and Urban Expansion in Southern California, 1900–1950." *Journal of Historical Geography* 27: 74–92.

Nelson, Howard J. 1983. *The Los Angeles Metropolis*. Dubuque, IA: Kendall/Hunt Publishing.

Nicolaides, Becky M. 2002. *My Blue Heaven: Life and Politics in the Working-Class Suburbs of Los Angeles, 1920-1965.* Chicago: University of Chicago Press.

Ríos-Bustamante, Antonio, and Pedro Castillo. 1986. *An Illustrated History of Mexican Los Angeles, 1781-1985.* Los Angeles: Chicano Studies Research Center, University of California.

Rocco, Raymond A. 1996. "Latino Los Angeles: Reframing Boundaries/Borders." In *The City: Los Angeles and Urban Theory at the End of the Twentieth Century,* ed. A. J. Scott and E. W. Soja, 365-389. Berkeley & Los Angeles: University of California Press.

Romo, Ricardo. 1983. *East Los Angeles: History of a Barrio.* Austin: University of Texas Press.

Sánchez, George J. 1993. *Becoming Mexican American: Ethnicity, Culture, and Identity in Chicano Los Angeles, 1900-1945.* New York: Oxford University Press.

Sassen, Saskia. 1988. *The Mobility of Labor and Capital: A Study in International Investment and Labor Flow.* New York: Cambridge University Press.

Scott, Allen J. 1998. *Regions and the World Economy: The Coming Shape of Global Production, Competition, and Political Order.* Oxford: Oxford University Press.

Soja, Edward W. 1989. *Postmodern Geographies: The Reassertion of Space in Critical Social Theory.* London: Verso.

———. 2000. *Postmetropolis: Critical Studies of Cities and Regions.* Oxford: Blackwell Publishers.

U.S. Bureau of the Census. 2000. *Census of Population.* Summary Tape File 1. Washington, DC.

Villa, Raúl Homero. 2000. *Barrio-Logos: Space and Place in Urban Chicano Literature and Culture.* Austin: University of Texas Press.

CHAPTER 7

Aponte Parés, Luis. 1997. "Casitas, Place and Culture: Appropriating Place in Puerto Rican Barrios." *Places: A Quarterly Journal of Environmental Design* 11 (1): 53-61.

Arreola, Daniel D. 1988. "Mexican American Housescapes." *Geographical Review* 78 (3): 299-315.

———. 1992. "Plaza Towns of South Texas." *Geographical Review* 82 (1): 56-73.

———. 2002. *Tejano South Texas: A Mexican American Cultural Province.* Austin: University of Texas Press.

———, and James R. Curtis. 1993. *The Mexican Border Cities: Landscape Anatomy and Place Personality.* Tucson: University of Arizona Press.

Coutin, Susan Bibler. 2000. *Legalizing Moves: Salvadoran Immigrants' Struggle for U.S. Residency.* Ann Arbor: University of Michigan Press.

Ford, Larry R. 1995. "Continuity and Change in the American City." *Geographical Review* 85 (4): 554-568.

Haslip-Viera, Gabriel. 1996. "The Evolution of the Latino Community in New York City: Early Nineteenth Century to the Present." In *Latinos in New York: Communities in Transition,* ed. G. Haslip-Viera and S. L. Baver, 3-29. Notre Dame, IN: University of Notre Dame Press.

Herbstein, Judith. 1983. "The Politicization of Puerto Rican Ethnicity in New York: 1955-1975." *Ethnic Groups* 5 (1-2): 31-54.

Hernández, Ramona, and Silvio Torres-Saillant. 1996. "Dominicans in New York:

Men, Women, and Prospects." In *Latinos in New York: Communities in Transition*, ed. G. Haslip-Viera and S. L. Baver, 30-56. Notre Dame, IN: University of Notre Dame Press.

Jackson, Kenneth T. 1995. *The Encyclopedia of New York City*. New Haven, CT: Yale University Press.

Kraly, Ellen P., and Inés M. Miyares. 2001. "Immigration to New York: Policy, Population and Pattern." In *New Immigrants in New York*, ed. N. Foner, 33-80. New York: Columbia University Press.

"Latino Culture Wars." 2002. *New York Times* (Feb. 24): 21.

Mahler, Sarah J. 1995. *Salvadorans in Suburbia: Symbiosis and Conflict*. Boston: Allyn and Bacon.

Méndez, Noemi, and Inés M. Miyares. 2001. "Changing Landscapes and Immigration: The 'Mexicanization' of Sunset Park, Brooklyn Migration." In *From the Hudson to the Hamptons: Snapshots of the New York Metropolitan Area*, ed. I. M. Miyares, M. Pavlovskaya, and G. A. Pope, 102-107. Washington, DC: Association of American Geographers.

Miyares, Inés M. 2001. "Jackson Heights, Queens: From Exclusionary Covenants to Ethnic Hyperdiversity." Paper presented to the Annual Meeting of the Association of American Geographers, Feb. 27-Mar. 3, New York.

———, and Kenneth S. Gowen. 1998. "Recreating Boundaries: The Geography of Latin American Immigrants to New York City." *Yearbook, Conference of Latin Americanist Geographers* 24, ed. D. J. Keeling and J. Wiley, 31-43. Austin: University of Texas Press.

New York City Department of City Planning. 1992. *The Newest New Yorkers: A Statistical Portrait*. New York.

———. 1996. *The Newest New Yorkers: 1990-1994*. New York.

———. 1999. *The Newest New Yorkers: 1995-1996*. New York.

Nostrand, Richard L. 1987. "The Spanish Borderlands." In *North America: The Historical Geography of a Changing Continent*, ed. R. D. Mitchell and P. A. Groves, 48-64. Totowa, NJ: Rowman and Littlefield.

Ortiz, Vilma. 1986. "Changes in the Characteristics of Puerto Rican Migrants from 1955 to 1980." *International Migration Review* 20 (3): 612-628.

Sánchez Korrol, Virginia E. 1983. *From Colonia to Community: The History of Puerto Ricans in New York City, 1917-1948*. Westport, CT: Greenwood Press.

Smith, Jeffrey S. 1999. "Anglo Intrusion on the Old Sangre de Cristo Land Grant." *Professional Geographer* 51 (2): 170-183.

Smith, Robert C. 1996. "Mexicans in New York: Memberships and Incorporation in a New Immigrant Community." In *Latinos in New York: Communities in Transition*, ed. G. Haslip-Viera and S. L. Baver, 57-103. Notre Dame, IN: University of Notre Dame Press.

U.S. Bureau of the Census. 2002a. *1990 Census of Population and Housing*. Summary Tape File 3A. Washington, DC. http://factfinder.census.gov/servlet/BasicFacts Servlet

———. 2002b. *2000 Census of Population and Housing*. Summary Tape File 1. Washington, DC. http://factfinder.census.gov/servlet/BasicFactsServlet

Valenzuela, Abel, Jr. 2000. "Day Laborers as Entrepreneurs?" *Journal of Ethnic and Migration Studies* 27 (2): 335-352.

Wright, Richard A., et al. 2000. "Legal Status, Gender, and the Division of Labor among Salvadorans in Northern New Jersey." *International Journal of Population Geography* 6 (4): 273–286.

CHAPTER 8

Armstrong, Gary, and Richard Giulianotti. 1997. *Entering the Field: New Perspectives on World Football.* Oxford: Berg.
Bale, John. 1989. *Sports Geography.* London: E. & F. N. Spon.
———. 1991. *The Brawn Drain: Foreign Student-Athletes in American Universities.* Urbana: University of Illinois Press.
———. 1994. *Landscapes of Modern Sport.* Leicester: Leicester University Press.
———. 2001. *Sport, Space and the City.* London: Blackburn Press.
———, and Joseph Maguire. 1994. *The Global Sports Arena: Athletic Talent Migration in an Interdependent World.* Portland, OR: Frank Cass.
Cronin, Mike, and David Mayall. 1998. *Sporting Nationalisms: Identity, Ethnicity, Immigration and Assimilation.* London: Frank Cass.
Díaz, Kevin. 2000. "La Vida Fútbol." *Washington City Paper* (July 28–Aug. 3).
Dyck, Noel. 2000. *Games, Sports and Cultures.* Oxford: Berg.
Eichberg, Henning, et al. 1998. *Body Cultures: Essays on Sport, Space and Identity.* London: Routledge.
Escobar, Gabriel. 1998a. "Overflowing Ballfields Force Order on Futbol; Suburbia Juggles Demands for Playing Space." *Washington Post* (Nov. 29).
———. 1998b. "The Other Pro Soccer: In Area's Latino Leagues, Part of the Game Is Profit, and the Best Players Are Paid." *Washington Post* (Nov. 29).
Fox, Geoffrey. 1996. *Hispanic Nation: Culture, Politics, and the Constructing of Identity.* New York: Carol.
Galeano, Eduardo. 1998. *Soccer in Sun and Shadow.* London: Verso.
Goff, Steven. 2001. "Arena Not Feeling Very Much at Home." *Washington Post* (Sept. 3): D1.
Goldring, Luin. 1998. "The Power of Status in Transnational Social Fields." In *Transnationalism from Below,* ed. M. P. Smith and L. E. Guarnizo, 165–195. New Brunswick, NJ: Transaction Publishers.
Lamb, Courtney. 2001. "Latino Immigration to Metropolitan Washington: The Effects of *Ligas de Fútbol* on Maintaining Ethnic Communities." Master's thesis, George Washington University.
Luna, Ronald. 2000. "Transforming *Espacios Culturales* into Cultural Spaces: A Study of How Fútbol/Soccer Has Become a Cultural Symbol of National Identity for Latinos in the Washington, DC Metropolitan Area." Master's thesis, University of Maryland, College Park.
Massey, Douglas. 1998. "The Social Organization of Mexican Migration to the United States." In *The Immigration Reader: America in a Multidisciplinary Perspective,* ed. D. Jacobson, 200–214. Cambridge, MA: Blackwell Publishers.
———; Jorge Durand; and Nolan J. Malone. 2002. *Beyond Smoke and Mirrors: Mexican Immigration in an Era of Economic Integration.* New York: Russell Sage.
Menjívar, Cecilia. 2000. *Fragmented Ties: Salvadoran Immigrant Networks in America.* Berkeley & Los Angeles: University of California Press.
Newman, Kristin E., and Marta Tienda. 1994. "The Settlement and Secondary Mi-

gration Patterns of Legalized Immigrants: Insight from Administrative Records." In *Immigration and Ethnicity*, ed. B. Edmonston and J. S. Passel, 187–226. Washington, DC: Urban Institute Press.

Price, Marie. 2000. "Placing the Transnational Migrant: The Sociospatial Networks of Bolivians in Washington." Paper presented to the Latin American Studies Association, Mar. 18, Miami, Florida.

Raitz, Karl, ed. 1995. *The Theater of Sport*. Baltimore, MD: Johns Hopkins University Press.

Rosaldo, Renato, and William Flores. 1997. "Identity, Conflict and Evolving Latino Communities: Cultural Citizenship in San Jose, California." *Latino Cultural Citizenship: Claiming Identity, Space and Rights,* ed. W. Flores and R. Benmayor, 57–96. Boston: Beacon Press.

Singer, Audrey, and Amelia Brown. 2001. "Immigration to the Washington, DC, Metropolitan Area." In *Encyclopedia of American Immigration*, ed. J. Ciment, 974–982. Armonk, NY: M. E. Sharpe.

Singer, Audrey, et al. 2001. "The World in a Zip Code: Greater Washington, DC as a New Region of Immigration." Washington, DC: Brookings Institution Survey Series (Apr.).

Soja, Edward. 1996. *Thirdspace: Journeys to Los Angeles and Other Real-and-Imagined Places*. Malden, MA: Blackwell.

Suro, Roberto. 1998. *Strangers among Us: How Latino Immigration Is Transforming America*. New York: Alfred A. Knopf.

———, and Audrey Singer. 2002. "Latino Growth in Metropolitan America: Changing Patterns, New Locations." Washington, DC: Brookings Institution Survey Series (July).

Thomas, Jim. 2001. "Fútbol a Way of Life for Valley Latinos." *Arizona Republic* (Dec. 15).

U.S. Bureau of the Census. 2000. *Census of Population*. Washington, DC.

U.S. Immigration and Naturalization Service. 1999. *Annual Report: Legal Immigration, Fiscal Year 1998*. Washington, DC.

———. 1990–1998. Annual Immigrant Files. Unpublished.

Waldinger, Roger. 2001. *Strangers at the Gate: New Immigrants in Urban America*. Berkeley & Los Angeles: University of California Press.

Wilbon, Michael. 2000. "In Crowded Field, MLS Adjusts Goals." *Washington Post* (Mar. 25): D1.

CHAPTER 9

Arreola, Daniel D. 1981. "Fences As Landscape Taste: Tucson's *Barrios*." *Journal of Cultural Geography* 2 (1): 96–105.

———. 1988. "Mexican American Housescapes." *Geographical Review* 78 (3): 299–315.

Benedict, Albert. 1998. "Religious Diversity in the Latin American Community: An Analysis of Three Urban Neighborhoods in Cleveland, OH." Paper Presented to the Annual Meeting of the Association of American Geographers, Boston.

Bonutti, Karl, and George Prpic. 1977. *Selected Ethnic Communities of Cleveland: A Socio-Economic Study*. Cleveland, OH: Cleveland Ethnic Heritage Studies, Cleveland State University.

Curtis, James R. 1980. "Miami's Little Havana: Yard Shrines, Cult Religion, and Landscape." *Journal of Cultural Geography* 1 (1):1–15.

Jopling, Carol F. 1988. *Puerto Rican Houses in Sociohistorical Perspective.* Knoxville: University of Tennessee Press.

Kent, Robert B., and Augusto F. Gandia-Ojeda. 1999. "The Puerto Rican Residential Landscape of Lorain, Ohio." *Yearbook, Conference of Latin Americanist Geographers* 25, ed. C. Caviedes, 45–60. Austin: University of Texas Press.

Long, Karen R. 1997. "Answer to a Prayer: New Hispanic Church Closer to Being a Reality." *Cleveland Plain Dealer* (May 17): 4E, 5E.

Meléndez, Michele M. 1997. "Cleveland's Heritage: Puerto Ricans." *Cleveland Plain Dealer* (May 3): 6B.

Miggins, Edward, ed. 1984. *A Guide to Studying Neighborhoods and Resources in Cleveland.* Cleveland, OH: Cleveland Ethnic Heritage Studies, Cleveland State University.

Pap, Michael. 1973. "Ethnic Communities of Cleveland." Typescript. University Heights, OH: John Carroll University.

Rapoport, Amos. 1982. *The Meaning of the Built Environment: A Nonverbal Communication Approach.* London: Sage Publications.

Santana, Rosa María. 1999. "Mexican Immigration Here Dates to World War I Era." *Cleveland Plain Dealer* (Oct. 17): 15A.

U.S. Bureau of the Census. 1990. *Census of Population.* Summary Tape File 1. Washington, DC.

————. 2000. *Census of Population.* Summary Tape File 1. Washington, DC.

Zentos, Nicholas J. 1987. "Hispanic Community." In *Encyclopedia of Cleveland History,* ed. D. D. Van Tassel and J. J. Grabowski, 508–509. Bloomington: Indiana University Press.

CHAPTER 10

Burns, John F. 1957. *Olathe "The City Beautiful" Centennial "Arrows to Atoms" 1857–1957.* Olathe, KS: Olathe Centennial.

Calderón, Roberto R. 2000. "All Over the Map: *La Onda Tejana* and the Making of Selena." In *Chicano Renaissance: Contemporary Cultural Trends,* ed. D. R. Maciel, I. D. Ortiz, and M. Herrera-Sobek, 1–47. Tucson: University of Arizona Press.

Callon, Linda. 2002. Director, Westside Community Action Network, Kansas City, MO, personal communication, Feb. 22.

Cardona, Joe. 2002. "Hispanic Workers Not an INS Focus, Deputy Director Asserts." *KC Hispanic News* (Mar. 21–Apr. 6): 5.

Chávez, Gene T. 2001. "Hispanics in the Kansas City Metropolitan Area." http://www.pei.edu/Riverweb/diversity/mexa.html [Accessed July 1, 2002]

Coalition of Hispanic Organizations. 2001. *Newsletter* (Dec. 1).

————. 2002. *Minutes* (May 3).

Danneberg, Tim. 2002. Communications director, City of Olathe, KS, personal communication, Mar. 1.

Driever, Steven L. 1996. "Midwest." In *The Latino Encyclopedia,* ed. R. Chabran and R. Chabran, 1019–1021. New York: Marshal Cavendish.

Estrada, Anthony. 2002. Price Chopper grocery manager, Roeland Park, KS, personal communication, Mar. 15.

García, Juan R. 1996. *Mexicans in the Midwest, 1900-1932.* Tucson: University of Arizona Press.

González, Juan. 2000. *Harvest of Empire: A History of Latinos in America.* New York: Viking.

Greater Kansas City Map. 1998. Skokie, IL: Rand McNally.

Guadalupe Centers, Inc. 2001. "History." http://guadalupecenters.org/History.htm

Guzmán, Betsy. 2001. *La población hispana.* Washington, DC: U.S. Bureau of the Census.

Harlow, Summer. 2002. "Dominican Pride Fills Stadium." *Kansas City Star* (June 26): A-1, A-8.

"Hispanic Newcomers Should Show Proper Social Conduct." 2002. *Dos Mundos* (Feb. 7-13): 2.

Kansas City on Parade: The Meat Packing Industry. 1950. Kansas City, MO: Kansas City Chamber of Commerce.

Laird, Judith Fincher. 1975. "Argentine, Kansas: The Evolution of a Mexican-American Community, 1905-1940." PhD diss., University of Kansas.

Lambert, Edie R. 2002. "Overland Park McDonald's Workers Protest, Allege Ethnically Motivated Harassment." *Dos Mundos* (Jan. 31-Feb. 6): 1-2.

Lewis, Melinda K. 2001. "*Así es la Vida:* An Analysis of the Demographic, Economic, Social, and Political Realities of Latino Immigrants in Kansas City." Typescript.

López, David A. 2000. "Attitudes of Selected Latino Oldtimers toward Newcomers: A Photo Elicitation Study." *Great Plains Research* 10 (2): 253-274.

Mayer, Barbara. 2002. "Guillermo Gomez Stops at Nothing on His Road to Education." *KC Hispanic News* (Apr. 4-17): 5.

Mendoza, Valerie Marie. 1997. "The Creation of a Mexican Immigrant Community in Kansas City, 1890-1930." PhD diss., University of California, Berkeley.

Mid-America Regional Council (MARC). 2001. *Metro Outlook: Measuring the Progress of Metropolitan Kansas City.* Kansas City, MO: MARC.

Montgomery, Rick, and Shirl Kasper. 1999. *Kansas City: An American Story.* Kansas City, MO: Kansas City Star Books.

Moore, Michael. 2001. *Stupid White Men . . . and Other Sorry Excuses for the State of the Nation.* New York: Regan Books.

Murguia, Raul. 2002. Director, Family Center, Johnson County, KS, personal communication, Mar. 8.

1914 Map of Greater Kansas City. 1913. Kansas City, MO: Berry Map Co.

Olathe Planning Commission. 1990. *The Olathe Demographic and Development Report.* Olathe, Kansas.

Ortiz, Isidro D. 1996. "Chicana/o Organizational Politics and Strategies in the Era of Retrenchment." In *Chicanas/Chicanos at the Crossroads: Social, Economic, and Political Change,* ed. D. R. Maciel and I. D. Ortiz, 108-129. Tucson: University of Arizona Press.

Ramero Brown, Sylvia. 2002. Hispanic Alliance Ministry of the Center of Grace Methodist Church, Olathe, KS, personal communication, Mar. 1.

Ramírez, Vickie. 2002. "It's a Quiet 5th Anniversary for Kansas City Hispanic News." *KC Hispanic News* (Jan. 22-Feb. 6): 8.

Ruiz, Art. 2002. Executive director of Economic Development, Belton, MO, personal communication, Feb. 28.

Sánchez, Mary. 2002a. "Immigrant Labor Under Scrutiny: Latino Group Meets with KC Officials of McDonald's." *Kansas City Star* (Mar. 6): C-1, C-2.

———. 2002b. "Useful Programs for Latino Children." *Kansas City Star* (Apr. 30): B7.

Sendorff, Jeff. 2002. Director, ECI Development, Inc., Kansas City, KS, personal communication, Mar. 13.

Serl, Emma; Alice Lanterman; and Virginia Sheaff. 1944. *The Story of Kansas City: Early Kansas City.* Vol. 1. Kansas City, MO: Board of Education.

Talwar, Jennifer Parker. 2002. *Fast Food, Fast Track: Immigrants, Big Business, and the American Dream.* Boulder, CO: Westview Press.

U.S. Bureau of the Census. 2000a. Quick Table DP-1: "Profile of General Demographic Characteristics; Geographic Area: Kansas City, MO—KS MSA." Washington, DC. http://factfinder.census.gov/servlet/QTTable?_ts=75981436305

———. 2000b. Quick Table P9: "Hispanic or Latino by Type: 2000." Summary File 1. Washington, DC. http://factfinder.census.gov/servlet/QTTable?_ts=75981708931

Valdés, Donicio Nodín. 2000. *Barrios Norteños: St. Paul and Midwestern Mexican Communities in the Twentieth Century.* Austin: University of Texas Press.

CHAPTER 11

Arreola, Daniel. 2000. "Mexican Americans." In *Ethnicity in Contemporary America: A Geographical Appraisal,* ed. J. O. McKee, 111–138. Lanham, MD: Rowman and Littlefield.

Chilango, Joe. 1994. "The Palm Springs of Washington." *Landscape* 32 (4): 35–41.

City of Reno. 1998. Business permit data base. Unpublished.

Davis, Mike. 2000. *Magical Urbanism: Latinos Reinvent the US City.* London: Verso.

Harries, Keith D. 1971. "Ethnic Variations in Los Angeles Business Patterns." *Annals of the Association of American Geographers* 61 (4): 736–743.

Haverluk, Terrence W. 1998. "Hispanic Community Types and Assimilation in Mex-America." *Professional Geographer* 50 (4): 465–480.

Martínez, Oscar J. 2001. *Mexican-Origin People in the United States: A Topical History.* Tucson: University of Arizona Press.

Miranda, M. L. 1997. *A History of Hispanics in Southern Nevada.* Reno: University of Nevada Press.

Price, John A. 1972. "Reno, Nevada: The City as a Unit of Study." *Urban Anthropology* 1 (1): 14–28.

Reno City Directory, Washoe County, Nev. 1957. Los Angeles: R. L Polk.

Reno City Directory, Washoe County, NV. 2000. Los Angeles: R. L. Polk.

Rodríguez, Thomas. 1984. *A Profile of Hispanics in Nevada: An Agenda for Action.* Las Vegas, NV: Latin Chamber of Commerce.

Shepperson, Wilbur S. 1970. *Restless Strangers: Nevada's Immigrants and Their Interpreters.* Reno: University of Nevada Press.

Shim, Soyeon, and Mary Ann Eastlick. 1998. "Characteristics of Hispanic Female Business Owners: An Exploratory Study." *Journal of Small Business Management* 36 (3): 17–34.

U.S. Bureau of the Census. 1997. *1997 Economic Census, Minority and Women-*

Owned Businesses, Reno, Nevada. Washington, DC. http://www.census.gov
/epcd/mwb97/metro/M6720.html

———. 1990. *Census of Population and Housing.* Summary Tape File 1. Washington,
DC.

———. 2000. *Census of Population and Housing.* Summary Tape File 1. Washington,
DC.

———. 2002. *Minority-owned Businesses: 1997.* Census Brief (Jan.). Washington,
DC.

U.S. Department of Commerce. 2001. "U.S. Businesses Owned by Hispanics Top
1 Million; California, Texas, Florida Lead States." News Release. Census Bureau Reports (Mar. 22). Washington, DC.

CHAPTER 12

Arreola, Daniel D. 1988. "Mexican American Housescapes." *Geographical Review*
78 (3): 299–315.

Arreola, Daniel, et al. 2002. "Geographical Differentiation of Latino Immigrant
Populations in Phoenix." Abstract, *Yearbook, Association of Pacific Coast Geographers* 64, ed. D. Danta, 182. Honolulu: University of Hawaii Press.

Caskey, John. 1994. *Fringe Banking: Check-Cashing Outlets, Pawnshops, and the
Poor.* New York: Russell Sage Foundation.

Castles, Stephen, and Mark Miller. 1998. *The Age of Migration: International Population Movements in the Modern World.* New York: Guilford Press.

City of Phoenix Planning Department. 1992. *A Plan for Nuestro Barrio.* Phoenix, AZ.

Díaz, Elvira. 2002a. "Migrants Accuse Phoenix of Putting Off Labor Center." *Arizona Republic* (Mar. 27).

———. 2002b. "Day Laborer Center Pushed: Valley Communities Search for Ways
to Resolve Conflicts." *Arizona Republic* (Apr. 26).

Dimas, Pete. 1999. *Progress and a Mexican American Community's Struggle for Existence: Phoenix's Golden Gate Barrio.* New York: Pete Lang.

Durand, Jorge; Emilio Parrado; and Douglas Massey. 1996. "Migradollars and Development: A Reconsideration of the Mexican Case." *International Migration
Review* 30: 423–444.

Kurtz, Karen, et al. 2000. *Final Report: Mesa Day Labor Task Force.* Mesa, AZ:
City of Mesa.

Luckingham, Bradford. 1994. *Minorities in Phoenix: A Profile of Mexican American, Chinese American, and African American Communities, 1860–1992.* Tucson:
University of Arizona Press.

Meinig, Donald W. 1971. *Southwest: Three Peoples in Geographical Change, 1600–
1970.* New York: Oxford University Press.

MoneyGram Website. 2000. http://www.moneygram.com [Accessed July 7, 2003]

Qwest Communications International. 2000. *Qwest Yellow Pages, Phoenix Metropolitan Area.* Englewood, CO.

Skop, Emily, and Cecilia Menjívar. 2001. "Phoenix: The Newest Latino Immigrant Gateway?" *Yearbook of the Association of Pacific Coast Geographers* 63,
ed. D. Danta, 63–76. Honolulu: University of Hawaii Press.

U.S. Bureau of the Census. 1990. *Census of Population.* Summary Tape File 1. Washington, DC.

————. 2000. *Census of Population*. Summary Tape File 1. Washington, DC.

Valenzuela, Abel. 2001. "Controlling Day Labor: Government, Community, and Worker Responses." In *California Public Policy Options 2001*, ed. D. J. B. Mitchell and P. Nomura, 41–61. Los Angeles: UCLA Anderson Business Forecast and School of Public Policy and Social Research.

Western Union Website. 2000. http://www.westernunion.com/info/selectcountry .asp [Accessed July 7, 2003]

CHAPTER 13

Barboza, David. 2001. "Meatpackers' Profits Hinge on Pool of Immigrant Labor." *New York Times* (Dec. 21).

Bjerklie, Steve. 1995. "On the Horns of a Dilemma: The U.S. Meat and Poultry Industry." In *Any Way You Cut It: Meat Processing and Small-Town America*, ed. D. D. Stull, M. J. Broadway, and D. Griffith, 41–60. Lawrence: University Press of Kansas.

Broadway, Michael J. 1994. "Hogtowns and Rural Development." *Rural Development Perspectives* 9: 40–46.

Brown, Dennis. 1993. "Changes in the Red Meat and Poultry Industries: Their Effect on Nonmetropolitan Employment." *Agricultural Economic Report 665*. Washington, DC: Economic Research Service, U.S. Department of Agriculture.

Bugos, G. E. 1992. "Intellectual Property Protection in the American Chicken-Breeding Industry." *Business History Review* 66: 127–168.

Carlin, Michael. 1999. "Even Tougher on Farm Labor?" *Raleigh News and Observer* (July 28).

Cobb, James C. 1982. *The Selling of the South: The Southern Crusade for Industrial Development, 1936–1990*. Baton Rouge: Louisiana State University Press.

Cromartie, John. 1999. "Race and Ethnicity in Rural Areas." *Rural Conditions and Trends* 9 (2): 9–19.

————, and William Kandel. 2002. "Did Residential Segregation in Rural America Increase with Recent Hispanic Population Growth?" Poster presented to the Meetings of the Population Association of America, Atlanta, GA, May 8–11.

Dawber, Thomas. 1980. *The Framingham Study*. Cambridge, MA: Harvard University Press.

Delmarva Poultry Industry, Inc. (DPI) 2002. http://www.dpichicken.org/

Díaz McConnell, Eileen E. Forthcoming. "Latinos in the Rural Midwest: Historical Context and Contemporary Challenges." In *Apple Pie and Enchiladas: Latino Newcomers and the Changing Dynamics of the Rural Midwest*, ed. J. Chapa, A. Millard, and R. Saenz. Austin: University of Texas Press.

Durand, Jorge; Douglas S. Massey; and Fernando Charvet. 2000. "The Changing Geography of Mexican Immigration to the United States: 1910–1996." *Social Science Quarterly* 81: 1–16.

Engstrom, James. 2001. "Industry and Immigration in Dalton, Georgia." In *Latino Workers in the Contemporary South*, ed. A. Murphy, C. Blanchard, and J. A. Hill, 44–56. Athens: University of Georgia Press.

Flippen, Chenoa. 2001. "Neighborhood Transition and Social Organization: The White to Hispanic Case." *Social Problems* 48 (3): 299–321.

Gouveia, Lourdes, and Donald D. Stull. 1995. "Dances with Cows: Beefpacking's Impact on Garden City, Kansas, and Lexington, Nebraska." In *Any Way You*

Cut It: Meat Processing and Small-Town America, ed. D. D. Stull, M. J. Broadway, and D. Griffith, 85–108. Lawrence: University Press of Kansas.

Grey, Mark A. 1995. "Pork, Poultry, and Newcomers in Storm Lake, Iowa." In *Any Way You Cut It: Meat Processing and Small-Town America*, ed. D. D. Stull, M. J. Broadway, and D. Griffith, 109–128. Lawrence: University Press of Kansas.

Griffith, David. 1995. "Hay Trabajo: Poultry Processing, Rural Industrialization, and the Latinization of Low-Wage Labor." In *Any Way You Cut It: Meat Processing and Small-Town America*, ed. D. D. Stull, M. J. Broadway, and D. Griffith, 129–152. Lawrence: University Press of Kansas.

Guthey, Greig. 2001. "Mexican Places in Southern Spaces: Globalization, Work and Daily Life in and around the North Georgia Poultry Industry." In *Latino Workers in the Contemporary South*, ed. A. Murphy, C. Blanchard, and J. A. Hill, 57–67. Athens: University of Georgia Press.

Haverluk, Terrence W. 1998. "Hispanic Community Types and Assimilation in Mex-America." *Professional Geographer* 50 (4): 465–480.

Hernández-León, Rubén, and Víctor Zúñiga. 2000. " 'Making Carpet by the Mile': The Emergence of a Mexican Immigrant Community in an Industrial Region of the U.S. Historic South." *Social Science Quarterly* 81: 49–66.

Hetrick, Ron L. 1994. "Why Did Employment Expand in Poultry Processing Plants?" *Monthly Labor Review* (June): 31–34.

Horowitz, Roger, and Mark J. Miller. 1999. "Immigrants in the Delmarva Poultry Processing Industry: The Changing Face of Georgetown, Delaware and Environs." Occasional Paper No. 37, Julián Samora Research Institute, Michigan State University.

Johnson-Webb, Karen D. 2002. "Employer Recruitment and Hispanic Labor Migration: North Carolina Urban Areas at the End of the Millennium." *Professional Geographer* 54 (3): 406–421.

Katz, Jesse. 1996a. "The Chicken Trail: How Migrant Latino Workers Put Food on America's Table." *Los Angeles Times* (Nov. 10).

———. 1996b. "Poultry Industry Imports Labor to Do Its Dirty Work." *Los Angeles Times* (Dec. 8).

Lapinski, John S., et al. 1997. "Trends: Immigrants and Immigration." *Public Opinion Quarterly* 61: 356–383.

Lichter, Daniel T.; F. B. LeClere; and D. K. McLaughlin. 1991. "Local Marriage Market and the Marital Behavior of Black and White Women." *American Journal of Sociology* 96: 843–867.

Lichter, Daniel T., et al. 1992. "Race and the Retreat from Marriage: A Shortage of Marriageable Men?" *American Sociological Review* 57 (6): 781–799.

MacDonald, James, et al. 2000. "Consolidation in U.S. Meatpacking." *Agricultural Economic Report* 322–785. Washington, DC: Economic Research Service, U.S. Department of Agriculture.

Massey, Douglas S.; Jorge Durand; and Nolan Malone. 2002. *Beyond Smoke and Mirrors: Mexican Immigration in an Era of Economic Integration.* New York: Russell Sage.

Massey, Douglas S., and Kristin E. Espinosa. 1997. "What's Driving Mexico-U.S. Migration? A Theoretical, Empirical, and Policy Analysis." *American Journal of Sociology* 102 (4): 939–999.

McDaniel, Josh M. 2002. "Immigrants and Forest Industries in Alabama: Social

Networks and Pioneer Settlements." Paper presented to the Immigration and America's Changing Ethnic Landscapes Conference, Athens, GA, Apr. 12–14.

McQuiston, Chris, and Emilio A. Parrado. 2002. "Migration and HIV Risks among Mexicans: Evidence from Participatory Action Research." Unpublished manuscript.

Mishra, Shiraz I.; Ross F. Conner; and J. Raúl Magaña, eds. 1996. *AIDS Crossing Borders*. Boulder, CO: Westview Press.

Ollinger, Michael; James MacDonald; and Milton Madison. 2000. *Structural Change in U.S. Chicken and Turkey Slaughter*. Agricultural Economic Report 787. Washington, DC: Economic Research Service, U.S. Department of Agriculture.

Oropesa, R. S., and D. Lichter. 1994. "Marriage Markets and the Paradox of Mexican American Nuptiality." *Journal of Marriage and the Family* 56: 889–908.

Parrado, Emilio A. 2002. "International Migration and Men's Marriage in Mexico." Unpublished manuscript.

———, and René Zenteno. In press. "Gender Differences in Union Formation in Mexico: Evidence from Marital Search Models." *Journal of Marriage and Family*.

Pérez, Laura. 2001. "The Changing Geography of Latinos: Evidence from Census 2000." Paper presented to the American Sociological Association Meetings, Anaheim, CA.

Reed, Deborah. 2001. "Immigration and Males' Earnings Inequality in the Regions of the United States." *Demography* 38: 363–373.

Smothers, Ronald. 1996. "Unions Head South to Woo Poultry Workers." *New York Times* (Jan. 30).

Studstill, John D., and Laura Nieto-Studstill. 2001. "Hospitality and Hostility: Latin Immigrants in Southern Georgia." In *Latino Workers in the Contemporary South*, ed. A. Murphy, C. Blanchard, and J. A. Hill, 68–81. Athens: University of Georgia Press.

Sun, Lena H., and Gabriel Escobar. 1999. "On Chicken's Front Line." *Washington Post* (Nov. 28–Dec. 1).

Taylor, Marisa, and Steve Stein. 1999. "Network Helps Recruit Immigrants for U.S. Job Market." *Fort Worth Star-Telegram* (July 4).

U.S. Bureau of the Census. 1990. *Census of Population*. Summary Tape File 3. Washington, DC.

———. 2000. *Census of Population*. Summary Tape File 1. Washington, DC.

U.S. Department of Agriculture. Economic Research Service (USDA.ERS). *Poultry Yearbook*, 1960–2000, various issues. Washington, DC.

U.S. Department of Commerce (DOC). 1963–1997. *Current Population Survey*. Earnings Supplement, various years. Washington, DC.

———. 1967–1997. *Census of Manufactures*. Industry Series, various years. Washington, DC.

———. 2002. *Local Area Unemployment Statistics*. Washington, DC. http://www.bls.gov/lau

U.S. Department of Labor (DOL). 1972–2001. *Occupational Employment Statistics*. Washington, DC.

———. Bureau of International Labor Affairs. 1989. *The Effects of Immigration on the U.S. Economy and Labor Market*. Washington, DC.

CHAPTER 14

Arreola, Daniel D. 2002. *Tejano South Texas: A Mexican American Cultural Province.* Austin: University of Texas Press.

Appadurai, A. 1981. "Gastro Politics in Hindu South Asia." *American Ethnologist* 8: 494–511.

Brown, Clois T. 1948. "The History of Deaf Smith County, Texas." Master's thesis, West Texas State College.

Community Fact Sheet. 1998. Hereford, TX: Hereford Economic Development Corporation.

Crester, Gary A., and Joseph J. Leon. 1982. *Intermarriage in the United States.* New York: Haworth Press.

Foley, Douglas E., et al. 1988. *From Peones to Politicos: Ethnic Relations in a South Texas Town, 1900-1977.* Austin: Center for Mexican American Studies, University of Texas.

Gault, Howard. 1974. *Oral History.* Interviewed by Jeff Townsend, June 6. Lubbock: Southwest Collection, Texas Tech University.

Grebler, Leo; Joan Moore; and Ralph Guzmán. 1970. *The Mexican-American People, the Nation's Second Largest Minority.* New York: Free Press.

Haverluk, Terrence W. 1998. "Hispanic Community Types and Assimilation in Mex-America." *Professional Geographer* 50 (4): 465–480.

"I.N.S. Is Looking the Other Way As Illegal Immigrants Fill Jobs." 2002. *New York Times* (Mar. 9): 1.

Jiobu, Robert. 1988. *Ethnicity and Assimilation.* Albany: State University of New York Press.

Jones, Richard C. 1995. *Ambivalent Journey: U.S. Migration and Economic Mobility in North-Central Mexico.* Tucson: University of Arizona Press.

Mittelbach, Frank G.; Joan W. Moore; and Ronald McDaniel. 1966. *Intermarriage of Mexican-Americans.* Advance Report 6, Mexican American Study Project. Los Angeles: Graduate School of Business Administration, University of California at Los Angeles.

Peach, Ceri. 1980. "Ethnic Segregation and Intermarriage." *Annals of the Association of American Geographers* 70 (3): 371–381.

Rodengen, Jeffrey L. 2000. *The Legend of IBP.* Fort Lauderdale, FL: Write Stuff Enterprises.

Scheck, Ronald C. 1971. "Mexican-American Migration to Selected Texas Panhandle Urban Places." Discussion Paper No. 20. Columbus: Department of Geography, Ohio State University.

Sommers, Laurie K. 1991. "Inventing Latinismo: The Creation of Hispanic Panethnicity in the United States." *Journal of American Folklore* 104 (80): 33–53.

Stull, Donald D., and Michael J. Broadway. 1995. "Killing Them Softly: Work in Meatpacking Plants and What It Does to Workers." In *Any Way You Cut It: Meat Processing and Small-Town America,* ed. D. D. Stull, M. J. Broadway, and D. Griffith, 61–84. Lawrence: University Press of Kansas.

Torres, Alex. 1977. *Oral History.* Interviewed by Jeff Townsend, May 29. Lubbock: Southwest Collection, Texas Tech University.

"Under the Counter, Grocer Provided Workers." 1998. *New York Times* (Jan. 14): 1.

U.S. Bureau of the Census. 1970. *Occupation, Earnings, and Industry of Persons of Spanish Language or Spanish Surname.* Table 115. Washington, DC.

———. 1980. *Occupation of Workers and Employed Persons by Race and Spanish Origin for Places.* Table 164. Washington, DC.

———. 1990a. *American Fact Finder.* Summary Tape File 3, Language Spoken at Home. Washington, DC.

———. 1990b. *Occupation of Employed Persons by Race and Hispanic Origin.* Table 185. Washington, DC.

Valdés, Dennis N. 1991. *Al Norte: Agricultural Workers in the Great Lakes Region, 1917–1970.* Austin: University of Texas Press.

"With Help from INS, U.S. Meatpacker Taps Mexican Work Force." 1998. *Wall Street Journal* (Oct. 15): 1.

CONTRIBUTORS

DANIEL D. ARREOLA received the PhD in geography from the University of California at Los Angeles. He was born and reared in Santa Monica, California, and has lived and taught in three of the four American states that line the U.S.-Mexico border. He has published extensively in scholarly journals and books on topics relating to the cultural geography of the Mexican American borderlands. He is coauthor of *The Mexican Border Cities: Landscape Anatomy and Place Personality* (Tucson: University of Arizona Press, 1993) and author of *Tejano South Texas: A Mexican American Cultural Province* (Austin: University of Texas Press, 2002). Arreola serves on the editorial boards of three leading geography journals and an international cross-cultural architecture journal, and he is a contributing editor to the Hispanic Division of the Library of Congress. He is a past president of the Association of Pacific Coast Geographers and is currently a professor in the Department of Geography and an affiliate faculty member of the Center for Latin American Studies and the Hispanic Research Center at Arizona State University.

ALBERT BENEDICT earned a BA in psychology from the University of Wisconsin, Whitewater, and an MA in geography from the University of Akron. Benedict first became interested in the migration and settlement patterns of Hispanics while growing up in Wisconsin, where he observed Mexican American communities in many rural towns. In graduate school, he developed an interest in the cultural landscape of the Puerto Rican community on Cleveland's Near Westside. Currently, Benedict works at the Center for Neighborhood Technology in Chicago, where he has helped identify and support housing and economic concerns within the Hispanic community. He is coauthoring a book chapter on transit-oriented development and has contributed his Geographic Information Systems and cartography skills to a variety of projects and informal publications. Benedict lives in Chicago.

KATE A. BERRY received the PhD in geography from the University of Colorado, Boulder, and is currently an associate professor of geography at the University of Nevada, Reno. She was reared in Southern California, not far from the border that divides the United States and Mexico, and she has long been interested in Latin America. Her research includes water policy in the western United States, Native American tribal issues, and geographic perspectives on race and ethnicity. She edited a volume of the *Natural Resources Journal* (2000) entitled "Water Issues in the U.S. Mexico Borderlands" and is coeditor of *Geographical Identities of Ethnic America: Race, Space, and Place* (Reno: University of Nevada Press, 2002).

JAMES R. CURTIS holds the PhD in geography from the University of California at Los Angeles. His doctoral dissertation was on the Mexican American barrio of Alviso, California. He has contributed more than seventy-five articles, book chapters, and reviews to the professional literature. He is coauthor of *The Cuban-*

American Experience: Culture, Images, and Perspectives (Totowa, NJ: Rowman & Allanheld, 1984) and *The Mexican Border Cities: Landscape Anatomy and Place Personality* (Tucson: University of Arizona Press, 1993). He also is author of the novel *Shangó* (Houston, TX: Arte Público Press, 1996) and a forthcoming novel titled *Cross the Border*. He is a professor of geography and urban studies at California State University, Long Beach.

STEVEN L. DRIEVER received his PhD in geography from the University of Georgia, where he specialized in the study of Latin America. He has published many articles in geography and interdisciplinary journals, authored the *Spanish/English Dictionary of Human and Physical Geography* (Westport, CT: Greenwood Press, 1994), coedited the *Conference of Latin Americanist Geographers (CLAG) Yearbook* (Austin: University of Texas Press, 1996), and coedited, with F. J. Ayala-Carcedo and L. Mallada, *La futura revolución y otros escritos regeneracionistas* (Madrid: Biblioteca Nueva, 1998). He currently serves on the Advisory Board of *Kawsmouth, a Journal of Regional History* and as the U.S. correspondent for *Bibliographie Géographique Internationale*. Formerly, he served on the Board of Directors of CLAG and the Editorial Advisory Board of *National Forum: The Phi Kappa Phi Journal*. He has been a visiting professor at the Universidad Veracruzana in Jalapa, Mexico (1988–1989) and a Fulbright senior researcher with the Instituto Tecnológico Geominero in Madrid, Spain (1996). He is a professor of geography in the Department of Geosciences, a participating faculty member of the Department of Architecture, Urban Planning and Design, and a member of The Center for the City's Faculty Council on Urban Affairs at the University of Missouri–Kansas City.

BRIAN J. GODFREY received his MA and PhD from the University of California at Berkeley, with an emphasis in cultural, historical, and urban geography. Godfrey was born in Honolulu, Hawaii, and grew up in Southern California. He graduated with a bachelor's degree in history from Pomona College. His scholarship generally concerns cities of the Americas, especially global city-regions, community and neighborhood change, urban redevelopment, and sustainable development. He has carried out research in both the United States and Latin America, including extensive fieldwork in Brazil and the Amazon Basin. Godfrey is the author of *Neighborhoods in Transition: The Making of San Francisco's Ethnic and Nonconformist Communities* (Berkeley & Los Angeles: University of California Press, 1988) and *Brazil Brasil* (New York: American Geographical Society, 1999) and the coauthor of *Rainforest Cities: Urbanization, Development, and Globalization of the Brazilian Amazon* (New York: Columbia University Press, 1997). He is a professor at Vassar College, where he teaches urban and regional geography, Latin American studies, and urban studies. Godfrey has served on the editorial board of the *Geographical Review* and as a councilor for the American Geographical Society.

TERRENCE W. HAVERLUK is an associate professor of geography at the U.S. Air Force Academy. He received his PhD from the University of Minnesota, where he began his studies of Hispanic Americans. He has published articles and book chapters concerning immigration, assimilation, acculturation, and Hispanization. Professor Haverluk is married to Julie and has two lovely daughters, Elena, age 5, and Claire, age 3. He also raises chickens.

LAWRENCE A. HERZOG received his PhD in geography from Syracuse University. He is a professor in the Graduate Program in City Planning, School of Public Administration and Urban Studies at San Diego State University. Herzog specializes in urban/environmental design and planning, with an emphasis on public space, community planning, downtown redevelopment, and comparative urbanization on the Mexico–United States border and in Latin America. His work has been published extensively both in academic outlets and popular media. His published books include *From Aztec to High Tech: Architecture and Landscape across the Mexico–United States Border* (Baltimore, MD: Johns Hopkins University Press, 1999) and *Where North Meets South: Cities, Space, and Politics on the U.S.-Mexico Border* (Austin: University of Texas Press, 1990). He has served as a Fulbright Scholar in Peru and as an urban/regional planning consultant to the U.S. Agency for International Development (in Peru and Bolivia), the U.S. Embassy (Mexico City), the American Institute of Architects, the Environmental Protection Agency, and the California Department of Transportation.

WILLIAM KANDEL received his PhD in sociology from the University of Chicago and conducted postdoctoral research at Pennsylvania State University. His doctoral research examined impacts of international migration on children growing up in migrant-sending communities in Mexico and included eighteen months of fieldwork in Zacatecas, Mexico, and California. He is currently a sociologist with the Rural Economy Branch of the Economic Research Service, U.S. Department of Agriculture, where he conducts research on rural demography, especially minority and immigrant populations. His recent research concerns the study of racial and ethnic segregation in nonmetropolitan counties and the social and economic impacts of rapid structural change in rural America.

ROBERT B. KENT is department chair and professor of geography and planning at the University of Akron. He earned a BA and MA from the University of California, Davis, and a PhD from Syracuse University. Latin America and Latin Americans have been a compelling interest from an early age, when his family lived in Southern California, ten miles from the U.S.-Mexico border. Kent's research and publications have focused broadly on the human geography of Latin America, especially the Andes and Central America, and on the evolving geography of Latin Americans in the United States. He worked for three years as an urban and regional planner in Peru for the United States Agency for International Development (USAID) and has served as a consultant for USAID in Bolivia and Pakistan. He spent a year as a visiting scholar and lecturer at the Universitat Jaume I in Castellón, Spain, and has been a Fulbright Scholar at the Universidad Nacional de San Juan in Argentina and at the Universidad Pedagógica Nacional in Honduras. Kent is past chair of the Conference of Latin Americanist Geographers and formerly a councilor and the treasurer of the Association of American Geographers. He lives in Akron, Ohio, with his wife, Marialena, and their two children, Robert and Anika.

RENÉE LA PERRIÈRE DE GUTIÉRREZ holds graduate degrees in music history, librarianship, and archives management. She is currently a graduate student in public administration at Texas A&M International University. She was born and reared in Denver, Colorado, and lived in California, New Mexico, and Tamaulipas,

Mexico, prior to settling in Laredo, Texas. Her present research interests include the historical geography of Barrio Azteca, the historic neighborhood in which she resides.

INÉS M. MIYARES received her PhD in geography from Arizona State University. She was born in Havana, Cuba, and her family was resettled as refugees in Buffalo, New York. This led to a lifelong interest in the experience of immigrants and refugees. She lived in California's San Joaquin Valley for thirteen years, an area that received a large number of Southeast Asian refugees during the 1980s. She is author of *The Hmong Refugee Experience in the United States: Crossing the River* (New York: Garland, 1998) and of numerous articles and book chapters about the Hmong, Cubans, former Soviets, Salvadorans, and the Latino communities of New York City. Miyares has taught at Hunter College-CUNY in New York City since 1994, offering undergraduate and graduate courses in the geography of Latin America, population geography, and international migration and ethnicity. She coordinates a study-abroad program in Peru and Hawaii and works with several programs to train kindergarten through twelfth grade teachers to teach geography more effectively. She is also a multicultural adviser on a middle-school textbook, *World Geography* (Evanston, IL: McDougal Littell, 2003).

ALEX OBERLE is a PhD candidate in geography at Arizona State University. His present research concerns the cultural and social geography of Latino Americans. He is completing his dissertation, a study that seeks to understand the geography of Latino business enterprise in metropolitan Phoenix. His other research interests include geographic aspects of health and geographical education. Oberle is a native of the greater Southwest, where he enjoys the opportunity to teach and conduct research.

EMILIO PARRADO is from Buenos Aires, Argentina. He received the PhD in sociology from the University of Chicago. He subsequently served as project manager of the Mexican Migration Project at the University of Pennsylvania and is currently an assistant professor of sociology at Duke University. His area of specialization is social demography, with particular emphasis on international migration, family and fertility behavior, and health. Parrado has published extensively about Mexican migration to the United States, in particular, the effect of Mexican migrant remittances on household economy and community development in Mexico.

MARIE PRICE is an associate professor of geography and international affairs at the George Washington University, where she has taught since 1990. A native of California, she earned her BA in geography from the University of California at Berkeley and the MA and PhD in geography from Syracuse University. A Latin American specialist, Price has conducted research in Belize, Mexico, Venezuela, Colombia, Cuba, and Bolivia. From 1999 to 2001, she was the director of the Latin American Studies Program at George Washington University. Her Latin American research has explored migration, natural resource use, environmental conservation, and the impacts of globalization and transnationalism. She is currently researching the rise of Latino immigration to metropolitan Washington through the Washington Immigration Project, an interdisciplinary group of scholars based in Washington, DC. Price is a past president of the Mid-Atlantic Division of the Association of American

Geographers and a councilor of the American Geographical Society. In addition to publications in scholarly journals and book chapters, she is a coauthor of *Diversity amid Globalization: World Regions, Environment, Development* (Upper Saddle River, NJ: Prentice Hall, 2003). She lives in Arlington, Virginia, with her husband and two sons.

JEFFREY S. SMITH was born and reared in Denver, Colorado. He earned his PhD in geography from Arizona State University and is currently assistant professor of geography at Kansas State University. His research concerns rural and urban landscapes and place attachment among culture groups in the American Southwest and Mexico. His work has appeared in multiple books and scholarly journals, including *Geographical Review* and *Professional Geographer*. Smith serves on the Board of Directors of the American Ethnic Studies program at Kansas State University as well as the editorial board of *North American Geographer*. He has been recognized with five teaching awards.

COURTNEY WHITWORTH was born in Sacramento, California. She received a BA in geography from the University of Arizona in 1998 and an MA in geography from the George Washington University in 2001. She works at the U.S. Department of State. She lives with her husband in northern Virginia and continues to be a soccer fan.

MICHAEL S. YODER received the PhD in geography from Louisiana State University. He was born in Marietta, Georgia, reared in Houston, Texas, and has lived in Laredo, Texas, since 1995. His scholarly publications encompass journal articles and book chapters on topics that include agriculture and society in Central America and Mexico, suburban growth in northeastern Mexico, the economic geography of the U.S.-Mexico border, industrial geography of northeastern Mexico, and social housing in Mexico. His current research interests include globalization and its impact on midsized cities of Latin America. He has been appointed by Laredo's City Council to serve on several boards related to land use planning and the environment. He currently is associate professor of geography at Texas A&M International University in Laredo, where he was named scholar of the year in the College of Arts and Humanities in 2000.

INDEX

Afro-Caribbean Latinos, 155
age profiles, 17
ancestry: European, 86; Hispanic, 21; Hispano, 22; Mexican, 7; national origin, 1, 153, 155; Spanish, 30
assimilation, 277–278, 285, 290

barrio, 7–10, 62, 68–69, 72–73, 75, 104, 109, 116, 118; barriers in the, 109–112, **111 fig. 5.1, 112 fig. 5.2**; barrioization, 8, 103–106, 108, 124; barriology, 8, 103–106, 108, 113; connecting the, 123–124; El Azteca in Laredo, 63–65; El Barrio in New York City, 153, 156, 163, 165; formation, 8, 130–133; in Hereford, Texas, 287, **288 fig. 14.5**; identity, 117–118, 124; inner city, 62; in Kansas City, **210 fig. 10.1**, 216, 233; Logan in San Diego, 103, **111 fig. 5.1**; Mission District in San Francisco, 79, 82–86, **87 table 4.3**, 90–92, **90 fig. 4.4**, 98, 102; neighborhoods in Laredo, **58 fig. 3.1**, Tucson, 239; in Phoenix, 241; redevelopment, 105, 109, 122; Santo Niño in Laredo, 65–66; in Southeast Los Angeles, 137–141; in Southwestern cities, 105; Spanish Harlem, 153, 156, 165; superbarrioization, 132; tourism impact on, 117–118; typology, 126, 130, **131 fig. 6.3**
bodega. See businesses
Bolivian, 1, 9, 12; patron saint, 183, **184 fig. 8.4**; soccer leagues and towns, 181–183
botánica. See businesses
Bracero Program, 279–280
businesses: *bodega,* **198 fig. 9.3**; *botánica,* 161, 192, 197; *carnecerías,* 247, 251; in Cleveland, 187, 192, 195, 197–198; *discotecas,* 247, 251; in Hereford, Texas, 284–285, **286 fig. 14.3**, 291; in Kansas City, 212, 216, 218–219; in Laredo, 61, **69 fig. 3.4**; in Las Vegas, New Mexico, 45–48, **47 table 2.1**; Latino, 10; *llanteras,* 252; *mercado,* 89; names as indicators of nationality, 253; in New York City, **147 fig. 7.1**, 152, 158, **159 fig. 7.3**, 160–161, **162 fig. 7.4, 163 fig. 7.5, 164 figs. 7.6, 7.7**; in North Carolina, 273; *panaderías,* 252, 277, 284; in Phoenix, 250–252, **253 fig. 12.5**; in Reno, 227, 229, **230 table 11.2**, 231–232, **233 fig. 11.3, 234 table 11.1**, 235 **table 11.2, 236 fig. 11.4**; in San Diego, 119; in San Francisco, 86, 89; in Southeast Los Angeles, **140 fig. 6.4**; *taquerías,* 229, 237, 277; in Virginia, **267 fig. 13.5**; *yerberías,* 252

cargas (packages shipped overseas), 159
carnes asadas, 8, 71–72
carnicería. See businesses
casa de cambio (money-exchange house), 162
casitas (Puerto Rican symbolic houses), 146
celebrations. *See* festivals
Central American: in cities, 32–33; Honduran, 30, 93, 155, 267; immigrants recruited for poultry industry, 262; immigration to San Francisco, 85, 88, 93–94; in Kansas City, 211; median age, 18; in Nevada, 225; in New York City, 148, 152, 158, boroughs, **154 table 7.1**; Nica-